MW00633762

Photo: Craig Mackintosh

SUSTAINABLE [R]EVOLUTION

PERMACULTURE *in* ECOVILLAGES, URBAN FARMS, *and* COMMUNITIES WORLDWIDE

JULIANA BIRNBAUM & LOUIS FOX

Published by
North Atlantic Books
P.O. Box 12327
Berkeley, California 94712

Art direction and book design by Erika Rand

Front cover photographs by Louis Fox and courtesy of the Green School, Ubud, Bali. Back cover photographs by Lorna Li; the Findhorn Foundation; courtesy of O.U.R. Village; Louis Fox; Satprem, courtesy of Auroville Earth Institute; Robert Cork; Francesco Vicenzi; and Kartikey Shiva

Printed in the United States of America

Sustainable Revolution: Permaculture in Ecovillages, Urban Farms, and Communities Worldwide is sponsored by the Society for the Study of Native Arts and Sciences, a nonprofit educational corporation whose goals are to develop an educational and cross-cultural perspective linking various scientific, social, and artistic fields; to nurture a holistic view of arts, sciences, humanities, and healing; and to publish and distribute literature on the relationship of mind, body, and nature.

North Atlantic Books' publications are available through most bookstores. For further information, visit our website at www.northatlanticbooks.com or call 800-733-3000.

Library of Congress Cataloging-in-Publication Data
Birnbaum, Juliana, 1974- Sustainable revolution : permaculture in ecovillages, urban farms, and communities worldwide / Juliana Birnbaum and Louis Fox.
p. cm.
Permaculture in ecovillages, urban farms, and communities worldwide
Includes bibliographical references and index.
ISBN 978-1-58394-648-0
1. Permaculture—Case studies. 2. Crops and climate—Case studies. I. Fox, Louis, 1974- II. Title. III. Title: Permaculture in ecovillages, urban farms, and communities worldwide.
S494.5.P47F69 2014
631.5'8—dc23 2013023680

1 2 3 4 5 6 7 8 9 Versa 19 18 17 16 15 14

Printed on recycled paper

This book is dedicated to our daughters, Lîla and Serenne. May they—and their generation—have the hope, wisdom, strength, and love needed to face the challenges they've inherited and to bring regeneration and healing to our world.

Photo: Sean Gold

Photo: Erika Rand

"One silk thread is strong,
but many woven together
are stronger."
—Malagasy proverb,
Madagascar

Contents

01 Introduction to Regenerative Design through Permaculture

02 Tropical/Equatorial Climates: Forest and Savanna Zones

03 Arid Climates: Desert and Steppe Zones

04 Temperate/Subtropical Climates: Humid and Highland Zones

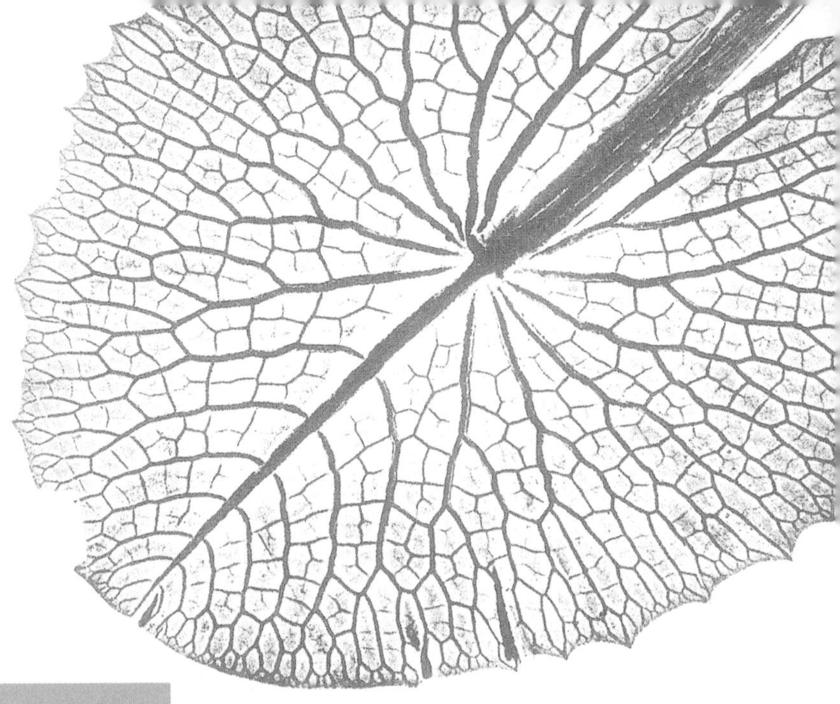

05 Temperate/Subtropical Climates: Mediterranean and Maritime Zones

06 Snow Climates: Continental and Taiga Zones

Foreword

Photo: Jenny Pickerill

The beauty of this book—indeed, the blessing of permaculture—is that it responds so elegantly to impermanence. If one sails out to sea in a small boat, it's good to know the timeworn principles that guide behavior, navigation, and safety. Imagine that we are all in that small boat, sailing into an unknown future, because we truly are. Just as the ocean teaches sailors, the earth teaches its denizens. The lessons are grounded in the realization that nature is the antithesis of everything static, that unceasing change defines life. Over the ages, the dynamics of life have been passed on in language, songs, stories, and practices, what Stewart Brand calls "local science." These principles are now distilled into a body of knowledge that has spread around the world: permaculture. This book is about how permaculture is pollinating the creation of farms, cities, and communities—the crafting of a new earth.

We are leaving a period of history in which cultures have been able to maintain a measure of stability for many centuries. That resiliency has been eroded by an industrial system based on force. Without gainsaying the benefits of modernity, it is glaringly true that its price has been exorbitant to people, places, and the future. The technologies of the internal combustion engine, synthetic chemistry, agribusiness, industrial forestry, driftnet fishing, nuclear power, modern education, allopathic medicine, and finance all have at their root a type of molecular or systemic violence toward living systems—taking, overtaking, exploitation, toxicity, concentration of power, eradication, deracination, and explosions (a four-cylinder engine creates four thousand explosions per minute at 2,000 rpm, and its emissions double-glaze the planet). It is a long list. It is ours; it is the world we were born to. It is the world that brought us wonders and a world that poses the greatest peril ever encountered in the history of humankind.

In the multivariant, dynamic, and infinitely complex system called *life*, which approach will survive? Force or flow? Resistance or harmony? Hoarding or sharing? I wish the answers were obvious, but apparently they are not . . . as yet. What we see in Juliana and Louis' articulate book—a work that documents their pilgrimage to some of the most imaginative and healing communities on earth—are templates for the future that will become increasingly evident and important. If you have a disease, you turn to those who know the cure. We have developed a type of "progress" that is more a disease than a boon. If we are to heal, it is to those who have created a new form of progress that we will turn for counsel, learning, and connection. We are so human. When darkness falls, we seek light.

What you hold in your hands *is* light, understanding, and insight. The question I pondered after reading this book is simple, how will each reader change who he or she is? What will readers do after reading Louis and Juliana's work? It makes me smile, because it is impossible not to want to rethink, reimagine, and renew our purpose after hearing about those who deeply understand the plight we are in, those who have chosen to mimic nature's exquisite nutrient and energetic pathways in their existing or newfound communities.

The farmers and craftspeople you meet herein are not mere artisans, not simply yeowoman and yeoman horticulturists, builders, or organizers generously giving their vastly underpaid labor to these ideas. They are, in fact, the vanguard of a movement that is reclaiming our land, our place, and our culture. How we let our communities, our finances—our very future—end up in the hands of General Foods, General Motors, and General Electric I will leave to cultural historians to decide. But we now know that if we are to take back ownership and responsibility for the biological integrity of our only home and its numberless, interdependent life-forms, we have to take back our bodies and minds from those who would use them to accumulate financial capital. We have to return the gift of life—our existence, for which we are so grateful—to those who create *biological* capital. We must turn away from those who steal the future and move toward those who heal the future. We must offer our trust to those who, in Adrienne Rich's words, treasure the "enormity of the simplest things"; to those who hold a universe of humility and humus in safekeeping for a world that has lost its sight. We must offer our trust to people who understand that without our farms and deep-rooted relationships with each other, without our exquisite connection to dandelions and thistle honey, to our watersheds and soils, we will live in a world with "no memory, no faithfulness, no purpose for the future, nor honor to the past."

Paul Hawken
Cascade watershed, New Moon, June 2013

Photo: Craig Mackintosh

PART 01

An Introduction to Regenerative Design through Permaculture

Revolutionary change does not come as one cataclysmic moment (beware of such moments!) but as an endless succession of surprises, moving zigzag toward a more decent society. We don't have to engage in grand, heroic actions to participate in the process of change. Small acts, when multiplied by millions of people, can quietly become a power no government can suppress, a power that can transform the world. . . . If we remember those times and places—and there are so many—where people have behaved magnificently, this gives us the energy to act, and at least the possibility of sending this spinning top of a world in a different direction. . . . The future is an infinite succession of presents, and to live now as we think human beings should live, in defiance of all that is bad around us, is itself a marvelous victory.

—*Howard Zinn*[1]

Introduction

by Juliana Birnbaum

Photo: Ammar Keylani

An ecological design revolution is here, and I pray it has arrived in time. *Ecology* can be defined as the totality or pattern of relations between organisms and their environment. If human culture is to sustain itself and thrive, we must consider our place in the larger pattern. The permaculture design approach considers the interwoven whole of our connections with each other, as well as our broader relationship with the natural world.

My mother was born in 1946, when the population of the globe was two billion. That spring, Albert Einstein wrote a piece for the *New York Times,* stating, "a new type of thinking is essential if mankind is to survive and move toward higher levels."[2] He went on to expand this argument in an interview: "Often in evolutionary processes a species must adapt to new conditions in order to survive. . . . Today we must abandon competition and secure cooperation."[3]

Einstein's comments were in the context of a world emerging from the Second World War and newly possessed of nuclear power. I am reading his words today, in 2013, now a mother myself in a world of over seven billion people. Radioactive waste continues polluting the Pacific after the Fukushima nuclear disaster, and I am finding deeper shades of urgency. The portentous-feeling 2012 was the hottest year ever recorded in the continental United States. That year also had the second most extreme weather on record, with widespread droughts; raging forest fires; and a destructive hurricane season, including Sandy, which hit New York (where my coauthor Louis Fox and I both grew up) and the surrounding area, wreaking destruction and death.[4] The year dawned with the international protests of the Occupy movement and the building revolutionary wave of the Arab Spring, and it closed to the clamor of demonstrations and strikes in Greece and Spain.

Economic instability, climate change, environmental degradation. The limits of a global system based on unlimited growth are becoming painfully exposed, telling us that clearly that we must adapt—we must

Photo courtesy of NASA

fundamentally shift our relationships with each other and the earth. While tapping into fossil fuels has allowed for an explosion in human numbers and technology, the current system was developed for a very different world than the one we now face. We are, as an increasingly global culture, starting to recognize the need for change, even to *demand* change on a systems level.

Permaculture is a design approach founded on the patterns and relationships of nature and the ethics of sustainable societies. Based on indigenous knowledge from cultures throughout history, it is geared toward transitioning communities to a new paradigm. Brock Dolman, who cofounded an ecovillage near my home on the Northern California coast (see OAEC, page 242), likes to paraphrase permaculture's co-originator, Bill Mollison, calling the approach "the cutting edge of a ten-thousand-year-old technology." The paradox of his words reflects the concept of the sustainable revolution catalogued in this book, where cultural pioneers are adapting for the future with a connection to ancient principles. We are being called forth to evolve, but moving forward in a healthy direction means a return to the ethics that sustained healthy cultures of the past.

This evolutionary and revolutionary change is not an abstract idea; it is happening right now on every continent, in cities, in suburbs, and in isolated villages. It is taking form as a blossoming network of sites developed with the intertwined goals of meeting community needs and stewarding thriving ecosystems.

Sustainable [R]evolution documents the growing international sustainability movement, using the permaculture framework as a lens to identify locally based projects (and networks) that are **cultivating beneficial relationships between humans and the natural world.** Beyond developing systems that are simply sustainable, permaculture holds the promise of regenerating communities and landscapes and even mitigating global warming. The book details the culture of permaculture on five continents and catalogues its successful design solutions at urban farms, indigenous villages, and suburban cohousing communities.

The profiles featured here include educational projects from Japan to South Africa; ecovillages from Los Angeles to Sri Lanka; and regenerative design solutions from China to Australia to Belize. These projects empower local people with techniques that provide sustainable sources of food, water, and energy, while conserving and restoring ecologies and strengthening communities. The book's sections are divided by climate zone, grouping sites with comparable ecologies and design strategies together into **five distinct parts: Tropical Forest/Savannah, Arid, Subtropical Humid/Highlands, Temperate, and Snow.**

Permaculture has many layers. Today, the word is used to describe the design approach, the international social movement and its local applications, the general philosophy and worldview, and the bundle of practices associated with it.[5] Its roots, as a theory of *permanent agriculture,* are traced to Australians Bill

Photo: Jason Taylor

"ACT WITHOUT DOING; WORK WITHOUT EFFORT. THINK OF THE SMALL AS LARGE AND THE FEW AS MANY. CONFRONT THE DIFFICULT WHILE IT IS STILL EASY; ACCOMPLISH THE GREAT TASK BY A SERIES OF SMALL ACTS." —TAO TE CHING

Mollison and David Holmgren. They developed the concept while studying perennial farming practices that are modeled on nature's patterns, inventing the term *permaculture* in the 1970s. The framework is based on three simple ethics (page 15) and design principles that can guide decision making by the individual, the community, or the nation (page 18). It has grown to incorporate the larger philosophy of a more *permanent* or enduring broader *culture*, embracing a systems-based approach to designing beneficial relationships. Holmgren addresses the paradox of the impermanence within the concept of permanence and the way that, beneath all of the change in nature, there are steady states characterized by cycles:

While it is important to integrate this understanding of impermanence and continuous change into our daily consciousness, the apparent illusion of stability, permanence and sustainability is resolved by recognising the scale-dependent nature of change. In any particular system, the small-scale, fast, short-lived changes of the elements actually contribute to higher-order system stability. We live and design in a historical context of turnover and change in systems at multiple larger scales, and this generates a new illusion of endless change with no possibility of stability or sustainability. A contextual and systemic sense of the dynamic balance between stability and change contributes to design that is evolutionary rather than random.[6]

In this book, Louis and I (along with a small, dedicated army of contributors) have collected profiles of sixty sites that demonstrate a wide variety of permaculture design approaches. While not every site featured here identifies specifically with Mollison and Holmgren's permaculture with a capital *P*, all are aligned with its principles and ethics and are case studies in the budding international culture of sustainability.

At the time of this writing, hundreds of thousands of people worldwide have completed permaculture design courses, and the network continues to expand on the original ideas through thousands of related trainings, publications, garden projects, and internet forums. There are projects in at least seventy-five countries around the world, and during the period we were doing the research for and writing this book, the number of those projects grew exponentially. The approach is being used to design new sites, both urban and rural. It is being applied by individuals and communities in existing towns and cities on every scale. Permaculture design initiatives have achieved inspiring results, restoring degraded landscapes, reversing desertification, and creating self-sustaining food systems. It includes hundreds of strategies that together begin to mitigate climate change, some directly drawing carbon out of the atmosphere through healthy soil-building cycles, no-plow farming methods, and tree planting.

THE ESSENTIAL ROLE OF CULTURAL PIONEERS

Considering that consumerism is such a powerful force and that the majority of resources and wealth are still overwhelmingly being used to stimulate it, how realistic is it to think that the pattern can shift? James Davison Hunter's analysis of how cultures change is instructive. As Hunter, the director of the Institute for Advanced Studies in Culture at the University of Virginia, explains, cultural change can best be understood not through the Great Man approach (whereby heroic individuals redirect the course of history) but through the Great Network approach. "The key actor in history is not individual genius but rather the network."[7]

When networks come together, they can change history. But not always. Change depends on "overlapping networks of leaders" of similar orientation and with complementary resources (cultural clout, money, political power, or other assets) acting "in common purpose." Networks can spread many ideas: consumption patterns, habits, political views, or even a new cultural paradigm.

But as Hunter notes, as culture is driven by institutions, success will depend on pulling ideas of sustainability into the center of these institutions, not allowing them to remain on the periphery. This means that, as individuals internalize new norms and values, they need to actively spread these ideas along their networks. They need to bring these ideas directly to the center of leading human institutions—spreading them through all available vehicles—so that others adopt them and use their own leadership capacities to spread them even further. Like brand agents, who now volunteer to surreptitiously promote the newest consumer product, individuals who recognize the dangerous ecological and social disruptions arising from unsustainable consumerism need to mobilize their networks to help spread a new paradigm.

These networks, tapping whatever resources they have—financial, cultural, political, or familial—will play essential roles in pioneering a new cultural orientation. And if all these networks of pioneers fail? As scientist James Lovelock notes, "Civilization in its present form hasn't got long."[8]

Consumerism—due to its ecological impossibility—cannot continue much longer. The more seeds sown by cultural pioneers now, the higher the probability that the political, social, and cultural vacuum created by the decline of consumerism will be filled with ideas of sustainability instead of humanistic ideologies.

Excerpted with permission from Erik Assadourian, "The Rise and Fall of Consumer Cultures" in ***State of the World 2010: Transforming Cultures from Consumerism to Sustainability****, the Worldwatch Institute, Washington DC.*

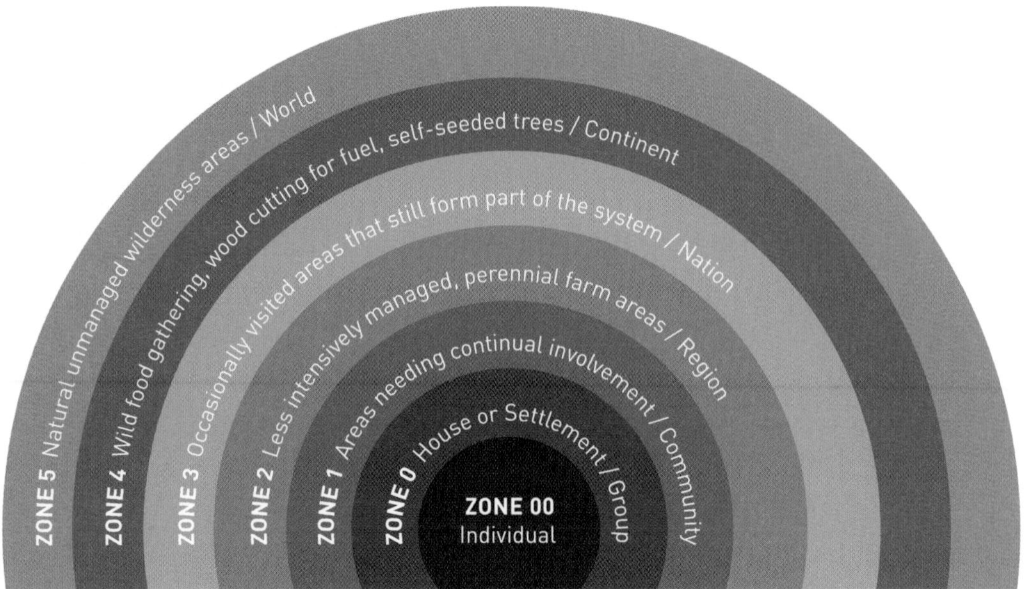

Zone 00—From Personal to Cultural Transformation

Permaculturists design in zones that radiate outward from the individual in concentric circles. The approach, when applied to a landscape, incorporates its human-use patterns, its animals and plants, and the broader ecosystem. *Zone 1* in a homestead is the area closest to the home, where one might plant kitchen herbs; *zone 5* is minimally touched wildlife areas. *Zone 0* is the home in this framework.

Zones can also be applied to the idea of individual and collective action. In this scheme, *zone 00* is the heart and mind of the individual, where we cultivate our inner landscape. Besides representing the physical center of activity in a permaculture design scheme, the term *zone 0* has been used to describe the broader dimension of the human relationships in a community or system. The reality is that in many of the sites we visited, community members had a similar refrain: building soil or more sustainable structures to live in is the simple part. The challenge is in the human relationship element of the system—the invisible structures.

Ain't that the truth? The inner zones of this book reflect my own personal, somewhat obsessive, sometimes rocky seven-year journey into positive future scenarios. But I didn't do it alone; I wouldn't have had the courage. The conception of the book is closely connected to that of our daughter Lîla Naomi in 2006. Back then, Louis and I were an idealistic young duo who had just moved in together in Berkeley, California, unaware that we were about to become parents.

Louis had cofounded Free Range Studios, a progressive, values-driven communications firm, in his mid-twenties. He had designed hundreds of campaigns and short films on environmental and social issues—some that were met with great success and discussed in the mainstream media, such as *The Meatrix*, his online animation about factory farming, which was seen by more than twenty million people. Despite the small victories, it felt like real change might never come. George W. Bush was reelected in 2004, and the majority of Americans still didn't believe climate change was real. Louis started to become frustrated with the approach of "putting out fires," and was looking for a broader, more systems-level approach to solutions.

The news that we were having a baby forced us to ask difficult questions and to intensify our search for answers. Was bringing a new person into such a chaotic, unjust, and destructive world the right thing to do? What about overpopulation and the fact that, raised in American culture, this child would be poised to consume five times as many resources as someone in the global south?

During the fourth month of my pregnancy, we spent a week at Plum Village, a Buddhist retreat center in the south of France founded by Thich Nhat Hanh, a Vietnamese monk and peace activist. Hanh coined the term "engaged Buddhism," and his teachings stress integrating one's inner work with labors to improve the world. He teaches that *sangha*, "sacred community," is at the heart of human evolution. A truly integrated community itself may be the highest form of consciousness.

Photo: Geoff Livingston (Creative Commons)

"IT IS POSSIBLE THAT THE NEXT BUDDHA WILL NOT TAKE THE FORM OF AN INDIVIDUAL. THE NEXT BUDDHA MAY TAKE THE FORM OF A COMMUNITY, A COMMUNITY PRACTICING UNDERSTANDING AND LOVING KINDNESS, A COMMUNITY PRACTICING MINDFUL LIVING. AND THE PRACTICE CAN BE CARRIED OUT AS A GROUP, AS A CITY, AS A NATION." —THICH NHAT HANH[9]

Plum Villagers are organized into family groups who eat, work, meditate, and share experiences together. In our week there, many in our group spoke about the alienation of living in modern society, the lack of mindfulness about how our daily acts affect each other, the earth, and its legion life-forms. For a short time, we took on the beautiful challenge of being together—deep listening, withholding judgment, collaborating—as a spiritual practice. It was at Plum Village that my daughter first made her presence obvious, with a few fluttery kicks. With that tiny sensation I began to grok the immensity of the path set before us. I felt a new determination, as a mother, to seek spaces of hope and resistance in the context of a profoundly broken world. As we left the retreat, Louis and I felt that we had been given the seeds of that hope. We resonated with Hanh's vision of the next stage of human evolution, with sustainable community at its center. And so we were inspired to begin our research into eco-social movements, where that kind of bottom-up, participatory redesign is thriving.

We found that permaculture philosophy wove together many of the community-based sites we began to study. The approach also helped us to organize our research into the specific domains of action needed to develop a more sustainable culture. We completed an urban permaculture design course with gifted teachers Starhawk (see p. 88) and Kevin Bayuk, which took us to gardens blossoming within the urban-industrial neighborhood of San Francisco's Hunter's Point. With baby in backpack, we trekked into the Alps to explore the intricately adorned cave-temples at Damanhur Ecovillage (p. 299), into the desert to visit "green" kibbutzim in Israel (p. 98), and became members of a collective permaculture farm forming in Costa Rica (p. 47). Each site we visited led us to dozens more. When we discovered how broad and diverse the

Photo: Louis Fox

PATCHES OF GREEN SPARED BY FLOWING LAVA ARE KNOWN AS *KIPUKAS*, "PLACES OF REGENERATION." THE KA'ALA CENTER IS A CULTURAL *KIPUKA*, WITH A MISSION TO RECONNECT HAWAIIAN CHILDREN WITH TRADITIONAL ECOLOGICAL KNOWLEDGE THAT HAS NEARLY BEEN WIPED OUT.

permaculture movement was, we realized that we needed a global network of researchers to do it justice.

Our pursuit led us to reach out to and collaborate with an incredible corps of photojournalists, bloggers, and activists around the world who are also passionate about documenting the regenerative design movement. We include the projects of both of permaculture's co-originators, Bill Mollison and David Holmgren, the Permaculture Research Institute (p. 160) and Melliodora (p. 279). Holmgren's iteration of permaculture ethics and principles and his articulation of the movement's "domains of action" inform the structure of each profile (see p. 24 for his Permaculture Flower diagram and more on the organization of the book).

Permaculture as a Revolutionary Act

Among the first places we visited in our research, the Ka'ala Center on the Hawaiian island of Oahu was started in 1978 in the form of organized youth action for water rights (see p. 84). Today it welcomes over four thousand youth each year to take part in what founder Eric Enos called the "revolutionary act" of reconnecting native Hawaiian children to traditional (and permacultural) practices of aquaculture, taro cultivation, and natural building. Kina Mahi, an organizer at the center, described it as a *kipuka*, a place of regeneration:

When Pele, the goddess of the volcano, unleashes, she goes down the mountain with her lava trails and everything in her way is destroyed. The fingers of lava often go around little spots of green, and they remain. That's what a kipuka is. A couple of years ago, our State legislature passed a resolution where they coined the term "cultural kipuka." Our people and culture have been bulldozed by a lot of different things. . . . The disconnection of people from land has been the destructive course it has gone. But we have pockets of hope and regeneration like this. Our vision is that someday there will be a kipuka in every community.

Photo courtesy of Green Beat

PERMACULTURE CAN BE A LIFELINE FOR INDIGENOUS COMMUNITIES WHO HAVE BEEN EXPELLED FROM THEIR ANCESTRAL LAND AND ARE FORCED TO MIGRATE TO CITIES FOR LOW-PAID LABOR OR TO FIND A WAY TO BECOME SELF-RELIANT IN A NEW AREA, SUCH AS THE BATWA COMMUNITY OF THE DEMOCRATIC REPUBLIC OF THE CONGO, PICTURED HERE.

The broader cultural re-evolution we need has already started, but must be expanded. It is made up of a multiplicity of these *kipuka*, a global and grassroots web of people working for social and environmental change. Author and activist Paul Hawken (see foreword) describes this network as "the largest movement on earth, a movement that has no name, leader, or location, and that has gone largely ignored by politicians and the media. Like nature itself, it is organizing from the bottom up, in every city, town, and culture, and is emerging to be an extraordinary and creative expression of people's needs worldwide."[10]

Indigenous Permaculture is an organization with intertribal leadership and both native and nonnative members. Its goal is to "share information, build relationships and establish a local, organic food source for residents, inspired by indigenous peoples' understanding of how to live in place."[11] Director Guillermo Vasquez speaks of permaculture as a new form of activism and a healing process, describing the movement as not just indigenous but universal—and educational rather than political.

Vasquez describes his vision of permaculture as a universal philosophy that builds bridges between contemporary and native cultures through "indigenous science." It can strengthen alliances among native groups through its network for knowledge sharing and as a common term for the environmental ethic shared by aboriginal cultures worldwide. "Permaculture is a way of cultural resistance," he says. "Perhaps the way I plant trees or grow food for my family is the way to create a real green revolution and make change."

Cultures throughout the world and throughout history that developed stable, sustainable relationships with nature did so through observation—a primary principle in permaculture. This is the indigenous science Vasquez speaks of: a thousand practices based on a deep integration with the local ecology and an awareness of natural patterns and relationships. Bill Mollison worked with aboriginal people in his native Tasmania and worldwide, and credits them with inspiring his work. "I believe that unless we adopt

Photo: Craig Mackintosh

MODERNIZATION? IN PLACES LIKE THE CITY OF LEH IN LADAKH, INDIA, MODERN NOTIONS OF "PROGRESS" ARE BEING RECONSIDERED.

sophisticated aboriginal belief systems and learn respect for all life, then we lose our own," he wrote in the seminal *Permaculture: A Designers' Manual.*

Beyond Perma-Colonialism

Indigenous Permaculture offers its trainings on a pay-what-you-can basis, open to anyone willing to take the information back home and put it to use. Through networking with a variety of native communities worldwide, the aim is to train a cadre of local permaculturists who can share skills with their neighbors.

"If you bring people from the outside the community, they may not accept a 'permaculture teacher.' People may come and take plants, intellectual property, and they never give back," Vasquez says. "This has gone on for too many years. Indigenous people need to decide their own destiny." Permaculture teacher Robyn Francis agrees, having trained thousands of students from different parts of the world (see p. 165 for a profile of the neighborhood she designed). She discusses teaching with an awareness of histories of imperialism and traditional knowledge appropriation. When she taught a permaculture course in Indonesia in 1999, there was concern among participants about whether "it was just another kind of colonialism—an Australian concept taught by an Australian teacher."

"The risk is greatest when the teacher sees permaculture as a kind of formula. . . . When this happens then—yes—it's a new perma-colonialism," Francis admits. "What I see as being the most valuable thing about permaculture, and the greatest challenge for a permaculture teacher to teach, is the process of lateral thinking and questioning, of developing the art of analytical observation."[12]

Histories of imposed assimilation into industrial economies have alienated native people from their traditional cultures across the globe, creating poverty and environmental destruction. The irony of "teaching" permaculture to people who traditionally lived its principles is not lost on Vasquez, who points out that when he teaches, he doesn't always use the term. "We don't talk about it as *permaculture* in the indigenous community because we are talking about a way of life. . . . They practice it, and it works, that's it."

I had the opportunity to witness for myself this harmonious integration of principles and culture when I volunteered at a village school in Nepal in 1999. The experience led me to question mainstream notions of progress and development (for more on this theme, see the profile on Ladakh, p. 123). I decided to study cultural anthropology at a radical graduate school in San Francisco that focused on *decolonizing* it.* This approach recognizes the imperialist perspective that spawned anthropology and questions the hierarchy

* I received a master's degree in 2004 in social and cultural anthropology from the California Institute of Integral Studies.

Photo: Filiz Telek

"WHAT DISTINGUISHES PERMACULTURE IS THE THINKING PROCESS OF THE PRINCIPLES THAT LEADS YOU TO THE DECISIONS THAT YOU MAKE. IT'S NOT SO MUCH ABOUT THE DECISIONS THAT YOU MAKE, BUT RATHER IT'S ABOUT THE RATIONALE BEHIND THEM. THE PERMACULTURE PRINCIPLES ARE BRILLIANT . . . WORKING WITH AN AWARENESS OF PATTERNS IN NATURE AS A DESIGN TOOL. WHAT WE ARE PROMOTING IN PERMACULTURE IN TERMS OF METHODS AND STRATEGIES IS BASICALLY THE OPPOSITE OF WHAT IS BEING DONE, IN CONVENTIONAL DEVELOPMENT PRACTICES TODAY."—PENNY LIVINGSTON STARK, REGENERATIVE DESIGN INSTITUTE, BOLINAS, CALIFORNIA

that gives value to rational, scientific knowledge over indigenous and intuitive knowledge. The focus is on recognizing the continuing effects of colonialism and shifting the discipline toward cross-cultural advocacy for indigenous social and environmental justice.

"Postcolonial" anthropology introduced me to the concept of cultural hegemony: the domination of the global imagination by an ideology that describes the social, political, and economic status quo as inevitable and beneficial for everyone (rather than chiefly for those whom the Occupy movement dubbed "the 1 percent").

Mollison calls permaculture a positivist philosophy, one that focuses on what we want and can do, rather than what we want others to change. Permaculture is revolutionary in that it gives people concrete tools to take power back, to become more reliant on local community resources, and to heal relationships. It is based on the assumption that the dominant global system is not inevitable, doesn't benefit the majority of people, and is, in fact, leading us to the brink of environmental collapse. I came to believe that this design approach can be a catalyst for resistance and transformation within communities seeking alternatives to the globalized economy. The word *permaculture* usually brings up images of rural life, but it can equally be applied by individuals and groups at the center of the industrialized world, shifting the system from within the heart of the inner city (see Los Angeles Eco-Village, p. 226).

Photo: ©iStockphoto.com/goldhafen

FRACTALS AND OTHER NATURALLY OCCURRING PATTERNS POINT THE WAY FOR PERMACULTURE DESIGNERS.

A Language Based in Nature's Patterns

The word *culture* comes from the concept of cultivation or improvement and evolved from *cultura animi,* a term invented by the Roman writer Cicero in the century before Christ, using an agricultural metaphor to describe the cultivation of the soul. A culture can be seen as the shared worldview, system of knowledge, and symbols of a people, demonstrating the way a society has evolved to meet its basic needs. The choices they make form a set of cultural practices and develop into a unique identity and relationship with their environment and each other.

A culture also shares a common language. The language of permaculture is the universal language of nature's patterns. These patterns are the interconnections that, in their perfection, help us see ourselves as part of an intricate and interdependent web. Mollison writes, "an understanding . . . of the underlying patterns that link all phenomena creates a powerful abstract tool for designers."[13] Dr. Joanne Tippett, a pioneer in community participation for ecological planning, uses the phrase "a pattern language of sustainability" to describe a language that "could be used to design places on many levels of scale, from a window box to a town . . . built up from observing patterns in nature and in chaos theory."[14]

This book provides a view into the budding culture and pattern language of sustainability around the globe. A catalog of sites speaking this language is offered here, but it represents only a handful of the hundreds of thousands of permaculture-related projects out there. While our research didn't lead us to the next Buddha in the form of an ideal community, in the places featured here I glimpse some of the pieces of the puzzle. Fit together, they start to form the new way of thinking Einstein described.

Photo courtesy of the Green School

BALI'S GREEN SCHOOL SHOWCASES ORGANIC, BIOINTENSIVE GROWING METHODS THAT FOCUS ON MAXIMUM YIELDS FROM A MINIMUM AREA OF LAND, WHILE ALSO IMPROVING THE SOIL.

Einstein and his circle of nuclear physicists used science to probe matter and watched it become energy, waves, dancing particle strings. He realized that every "thing" he observed was changed by his presence, that everything in the universe is connected to everything else. Shamans have witnessed the same truth throughout time, using indigenous technologies. "The shift we need to make is to see the world not as a bunch of separate things but as a web of relationships. . . ." Starhawk writes. "We are parts of whole, interdependent, interconnected. True abundance, true happiness, is found in relationship. When we seek to apply this understanding, one set of guidelines can be found in the system of ecological design called permaculture."[15] The focus of regenerative design is not on each separate element but on the relationships created among those elements by the way they are placed together; the whole being greater than the sum of its parts.

Fractals and Synergy

A fractal is a geometric pattern, often found in nature, that is repeated (either exactly or with slight variations) at ever-smaller scales to produce irregular shapes and structures. That is, if you were to zoom in on a part of the fractal, you would see the same pattern as the whole repeated to infinity.

Each profile in this book depicts what permaculturists call a "node," or center of human activity. Each node can be seen as an information fractal, featuring patterns that encode a great deal of knowledge and observation. Like the fractal structures that form the blueprints of our universe, the emerging whole may be made up of a pattern that is repeated ad infinitum, in larger and smaller scales, each slightly unique and locally adapted. Permaculturists focus on fractal patterns because their distinctive structures allow a deep interlock between systems, increasing the "edge effect" (see inset p. 206). The edge—where two elements meet—is key to regenerative design, because of the expanded possibility for cycling of materials and information, allowing for more *synergy*. With synergy, mutually beneficial relationships between elements of a system create a result greater than the sum of their individual effects.

Photo: Brad Farmer

LOUIS AND JULIANA WITH THEIR DAUGHTERS, LÎLA AND SERENNE, AT TACOTAL, THE ECOVILLAGE THEY COFOUNDED IN COSTA RICA.

"The edge is seen as increasing possibilities for creativity, as it is the zone of merging, change and new ideas," writes Tippett. "Permaculture design could be seen to be acting at the edge of chaos, at the edge of a change between systems. Information is echoed throughout the system. It is implicit in each of our actions. Small changes can act as the trigger element to restructure a system."[16]

Regenerative design strategies must move from the margins to the center and become the mainstream approach to community development—for the sake of those to come. Our daughters were born in 2006 and 2009, in a generation yet to be labeled. For them, Louis and I continue to dream that change will come through a global design re-evolution, not a bloody revolution. This book collects a tiny handful of efforts among a multitude. Together they offer a vision of healing and renewal for the earth and her seven—soon to be nine—billion people. It is our hope that the small brave acts of the many, collected together, can create the synergy we desperately need for a cultural shift. May it be enough to send "this spinning top of a world" in a vital new direction.

Juliana Birnbaum. San Geronimo Valley, West Marin, California. April 2013

THE ETHICS OF PERMACULTURE

The process of providing for people's needs within ecological limits requires a cultural revolution. Inevitably, such a revolution is fraught with many confusions, risks, and inefficiencies, and we appear to have little time to achieve it. In this context, the idea of a simple set of principles that have universal application is attractive. These principles can be divided into ethics and design principles.

Ethics act as constraints on survival instincts and other personal and social constructs of self-interest that tend to drive human behavior in any society. They are a more inclusive view of who and what constitutes "us" and a longer-term understanding of good and bad outcomes.

The greater the power of human civilization (due to energy availability), and the greater the concentration and scale of power within society, the more critical ethics become in ensuring long-term cultural and even biological survival. This ecologically functional view of ethics makes them central in the development of a culture for energy descent. Like design principles, the ethics were not explicitly listed in early permaculture literature. Since the development of the Permaculture Design course, ethics have generally been covered by three broad maxims:

- Care for the earth (husband soil, forests, and water)
- Care for people (look after self, kin, and community)
- Fair share (set limits to consumption and reproduction, and redistribute surplus)

These are distilled from research into community ethics, as adopted by older religious cultures and modern cooperatives. The second and third ethic can be seen as derived from the first.

These maxims have been taught and used as simple and relatively unquestioned ethical foundations for permaculture design within the movement and within the wider "global nation" of like-minded people. More broadly, they can be seen as common to all traditional "cultures of place" that have connected people to land and nature throughout history, with the notable exception of modern industrial societies.

This focus in permaculture on learning from indigenous, tribal, and cultures of place is based on the evidence that these cultures have existed in relative balance with their environment and survived for longer than any of our more recent experiments in civilization. Of course, in our attempt to live an ethical life, we should not ignore the teachings of the great spiritual and philosophical traditions of literate civilizations or the great thinkers of the scientific enlightenment and current times. But in the long transition to a sustainable, low-energy culture, we need to consider—and attempt to understand—a broader canvas of values and concepts than those delivered to us by recent cultural history.

David Holmgren. ***The Essence of Permaculture****, electronic edition (Hepburn Springs, Australia: Melliodora, 2013), 6–7. www.holmgren.com.au*

The Principles of Permaculture

by Rachel Kaplan

One of the most important things about permaculture is that it is founded on a series of principles that can be applied to any circumstance—agriculture, urban design, or the art of living. The core of the principles is the working relationships and connections between all things. The focus is on small-scale, energy- and labor-efficient, intensive systems that use biological resources instead of fossil fuels. Designs stress ecological connections and closed loops of energy and materials. A key to efficient design is observation and the replication of natural ecosystems.

In a city, permaculture makes much use of the synergy of human energies and works to create generative connections between people. Pioneering permaculturists Bill Mollison and David Holmgren each articulated underlying principles for permaculture; Holmgren's are outlined here. The titles and connected aphorisms are Holmgren's; the descriptions are my own understanding of the principles. Although humorously stated, the principles provide simple yet profound guidance for people interested in changing their actions and their lives with an eye toward regeneration. When you begin to embody these principles in all the different aspects of your life, you can begin to step toward sustainability at a whole new level.

1. Observe and Interact (Beauty Is in the Eye of the Beholder). Observing nature makes it possible to design made-to-fit solutions. An example is the gardener who allows a season to pass before planting her garden, taking the time to observe the arc of the sun and the moon, the direction of the wind, the flow of water, and the impact of neighbors on her garden. While our timing is urgent, it is more urgent to make intelligent choices within the limits of the ecological system than it is to move fast, as these more grounded choices have a better chance of sustaining life through difficult and abundant times. Within the problem lies the solution; observing and interacting slows down the action enough to allow us to meet a problem on its own terms and gives rise to outside-the-box thinking.

2. Catch and Store Energy (Make Hay While the Sun Shines). Develop systems that collect resources at times of peak abundance for use in times of need. A solar array catches and stores the sun's energy for later use. A composting toilet, rather than flushing our excrement into the sea, composts it and turns it into fertilizer for our garden. Contemplative practices (like yoga and meditation) catch personal energetic resources and store them up for another time.

3. Obtain a Yield (You Can't Work on an Empty Stomach). Good work yields rewards. A garden is an excellent example: we till the soil, sow the seeds, pull the weeds, manage the pests, and harvest the food. The yield is good food, good work, beauty, and a sense of knowledge and relaxation in the environment. Children gain skills and knowledge in the garden for later production of their own food. We also see practical yield in our relationships. When we build communities in which we rely upon one another to help

raise the children, the food, and the management of resources, the yield is in dynamic, interdependent relationships that can sustain us throughout life and up to our deaths.

4. Apply Self-Regulation and Accept Feedback (The Sins of the Parents Are Visited on the Children unto the Seventh Generation). This is an important principle that encourages us to modify behaviors that do not work and to enhance behaviors that support the functioning of the system. When you get feedback that something you're doing isn't working, don't spin off into defensiveness—look at the feedback and integrate it to make your actions more effective. This reflects the maturation of consciousness from adolescence to adulthood: our actions have consequences. The homeostasis of the earth as a single, self-regulating system is the best example of this kind of self-regulation and feedback.

5. Use and Value Renewable Resources and Services (Let Nature Take Its Course). Access the resources of nature to reduce excessive consumption and dependence on nonrenewable resources. Solar power, wind power, and intellectual power are all examples of renewable resources.

6. Produce No Waste (Waste Not Want Not). Nature produces no waste—everything is food for someone. In permaculture, we value and make use of all available resources. Nature's best example of this principle is the earthworm, which lives by consuming plant "wastes" and converting them into valuable soil. A compost pile is the garden's best example.

7. Design from Patterns to Details (Can't See the Woods for the Trees). The patterns in society and nature can form the backbone of our designs. Details arise from patterns. Consider the spider web—each one designed to serve a specific function, yet each is each unique to its location. The human body is another example of this principle—we're all built on the same model but have individual differences stemming from our experience, family life, and culture. With design solutions, as with people, one size does not fit all.

8. Integrate Rather than Segregate (Many Hands Make Light Work). Don't leave anyone behind. Put elements in the right place, and relationships of support will arise between them. In human communities, segregation hurts everyone, but it most often places the burden on the least powerful member of the equation. Cohousing communities show how much can be accomplished when more people participate and how much richer our human gardens are when populated by different kinds of people. The segregation of cities, on the other hand, reflects a poverty of design and the waste of human resource and potential.

Another crucial concept embedded in this principle is that of ***stacking functions***—every element in a design doing more than one thing at a time. A chicken provides eggs, meat, and feathers while she turns our kitchen scraps into nitrogen-rich fertilizer for our gardens. The chicken is popular because she does so many things at once. Some plants have stacking functions as well, offering pollination opportunities and providing food, medicine, and beauty. Built structures can have multiple functions—greenhouses along the south side of a home access and store passive-solar energy, and they are a place to both grow food and share meals. Stacking functions is an important concept at times when—like now—there simply is no more time to waste.

9. Use Small and Slow Solutions (Slow and Steady Wins the Race). Small and slow systems are easier to maintain than big ones, make better use of local resources, and produce more sustainable outcomes. The snail is nature's exemplar of this principle. Slow and steady, carrying its home wherever it goes, the snail is amazingly versatile and adaptable in a wide range of environments and—as any gardener can tell you—a remarkably powerful creature.

10. Use and Value Diversity (Don't Put All Your Eggs in One Basket). Diversity provides insurance from the vagaries of nature and everyday life, reduces vulnerability and utilizes the unique nature of its environment, and maintains and evolves culture and horticulture. Different foods and crops arise in different regions as an expression of cultural, aesthetic, spiritual, and sentimental needs. This diversity brings quality and texture to living and shapes the way people come to understand themselves.

An aligned concept is that *each function is supported by many elements,* which is a fancy way of talking about planned redundancy. Different plants that have the same function provide security for one another. If any one of them fails, we still have access to the benefits of the other plants serving that function. Nature employs planned redundancy all the time; the designs of our gardens and our cities should do the same.

11. Use Edges and Value the Marginal (Don't Think You Are on the Right Track Just Because It's a Well-beaten Path). The interface between diverse elements is where the most interesting events take place. These are often the most valuable, diverse, and productive elements in a system. "Marginal" subcultures are often the places where the most inventive, ingenious, and creative innovations take place. The long fight for food and environmental justice in impoverished communities of color—which predates the current urban homesteading movement by decades—is an example of this principle.

12. Creatively Use and Respond to Change (Vision Is Not Seeing Things as They Are, but as They Will Be). Change is inevitable; we can have a positive impact on it by carefully observing and intervening at the right time. Evolutionary change impacts stability. While we need to create durable and natural living situations, paradoxically, the durability we need depends on our capacity to be flexible and to change. This idea is reflected in science and spirituality. Within the center of stillness is a vast, unending motion. We must learn to ride the rapids of change in our little paper canoes—together.

---

*Excerpted with permission from Rachel Kaplan with K. Ruby Blume, **Urban Homesteading: Heirloom Skills for Sustainable Living**, (New York, Skyhorse Publishing 2011). Photo credits for collage on page 16 appear on pages 162, 164, 265, 234, and 67 except for photos of men with map by IPEC, seedlings by Jacob Goldberg, girl and bamboo bridge courtesy of the Green School, sunflowers by O-Farm, and meditating woman by Mahatma Brinton.*

Referencing This Book by Site Location

The Climate Zones

Sustainable Revolution can be used as a catalog, reference tool, and guide to the culture of regenerative design around the world. It features profiles of sixty sites in thirty countries, marked on the map on the following pages. Rather than group the sites by continent or geopolitical boundaries, we chose to group them by climate zone, (as broadly classified by Wladimir Köppen): tropical, arid, subtropical/temperate, and snow. There are no sites profiled in the sparsely populated polar climate. Because the subtropical/temperate zone is the most densely populated, we split it into two parts, using Köppen's subzones: humid/highland and Mediterranean/maritime.

Climates, microclimates, and a strong sense of the unique qualities of each bioregion are central to permaculture design. Observation is the first step; permaculturists allow for at least a year of careful reflection on the natural web of relationships within a landscape before developing it. The movement of the sun, the shifting flow of water, the seasonal changes, the network of plant and animal life present on the site—taking note of these elemental patterns allows the designer to become more integrated into the whole before taking action.

It is our hope that the book's structure will call attention to specific techniques appropriate to their particular ecosystem and climate zone (i.e., earth building in the desert, banana circle plantings in the tropics) and encourage the sharing of ideas and resources between sites with corresponding environments.

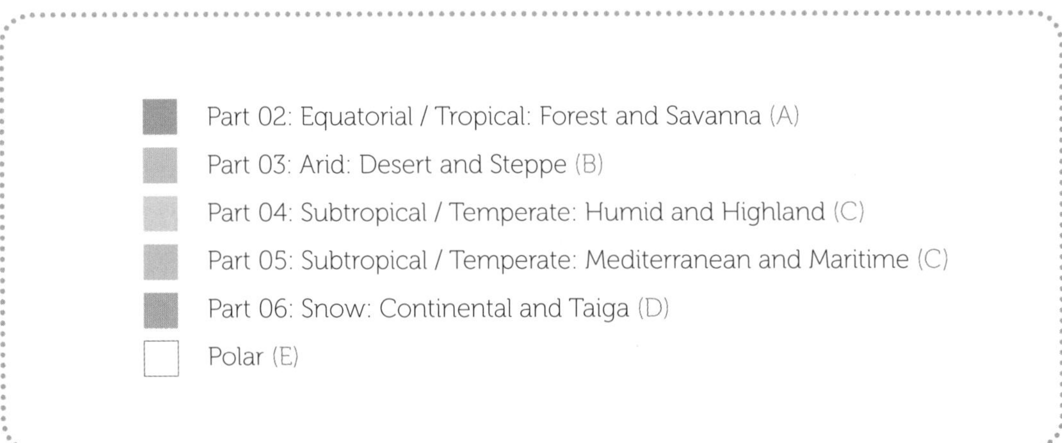

CLASSIFYING THE EARTH'S ECOSYSTEMS

In 1884, Russian-German climatologist and botanist Wladimir Köppen (1846–1940) developed a climate zone classification system that has become one of the world's most recognized and detailed. In the Köppen system, five broad zones are further divided into thirty-one subzones based on temperature and precipitation.

To classify the earth's varied ecosystems into zones by similarity is not a straightforward task. Scientists haven't reached consensus on any one way of defining the planet's diverse bioregions. Some classify areas into ecozones by the plants and animals they contain and those species' evolutionary history. Another system categorizes regions by biome, areas of geographical, biological, and climactic similarity, though a biome may go by many different local names (e.g., grassland may be called *prairie, savanna,* or *pampa*).

Because of this complexity, we chose to use climate alone to classify the profiles, though the Köppen system we used is based on the notion that native vegetation is key to the expression of climate. There is still plenty of room to argue about such things as whether a site has a Mediterranean or maritime (variously called *oceanic* or *marine west coast*) climate, which may feature characteristics of a temperate rainforest or a scrubby chaparral).

While the Köppen system doesn't take into account such things as temperature extremes, average cloud cover, number of days with sunshine or wind, it's a good representation of the general climate regions of the planet. The borders between regions do not represent instantaneous shifts in climate but merely indicate the transitional areas between zones, where climate, and especially weather– can fluctuate.

SOLHEIMAR, ICELAND
FINDHORN, UK
TRANSITION NORWICH, UK
TINKER'S BUBBLE, UK
TAMERA, PORTUGAL
O.U.R. ECOVILLAGE, CANADA
BULLOCK'S HOMESTEAD, WASH.
GROWING POWER, WISCONSIN
ECOVILLAGE AT ITHACA, NEW YORK
OEAC, CALIF.
PEOPLE'S GROCERY, CALIF.
LAMA FOUNDATION, NEW MEXICO
L.A. ECOVILLAGE, CALIF.
EARTHSHIPS, NEW MEXICO
THE FARM, TENNESSEE
HOA'AINA AND KA'ALA, HAWAII
LA'AKEA, HAWAII
HUEHUECOYOTL, MEXICO
FANJ, CUBA
MMRF, BELIZE
IJATZ, GUATEMALA
QACHUU ALOOM, GUATEMALA
BONA FIDE, NICARAGUA
PUNTA MONA, COSTA RICA
ATLANTIDA, COLOMBIA
YORENKA ATAME, BRAZIL
OPA SALVADOR, BRAZIL
IPEC, BRAZIL
ACHE GUAYAKI, PARAGUAY
Tropic of Capricorn

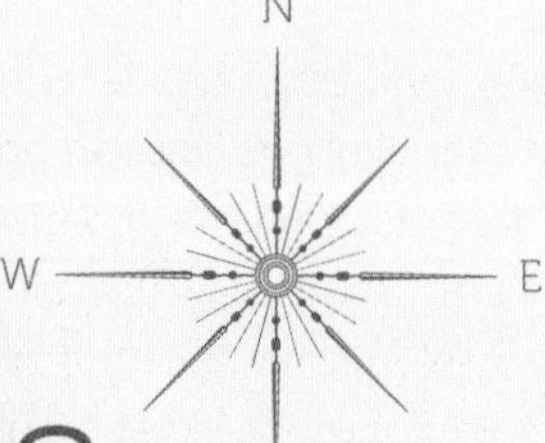

Climate Zones

This broad-perspective map of the planet's climate zones as defined by Köppen can't show the many shades of variation and the microsystems that exist due to elevation and proximity to bodies of water. It is meant to provide a general overview of the major categories of climate and the basic distribution of these zones across the continents of the Earth as they appear in the early 21st century.

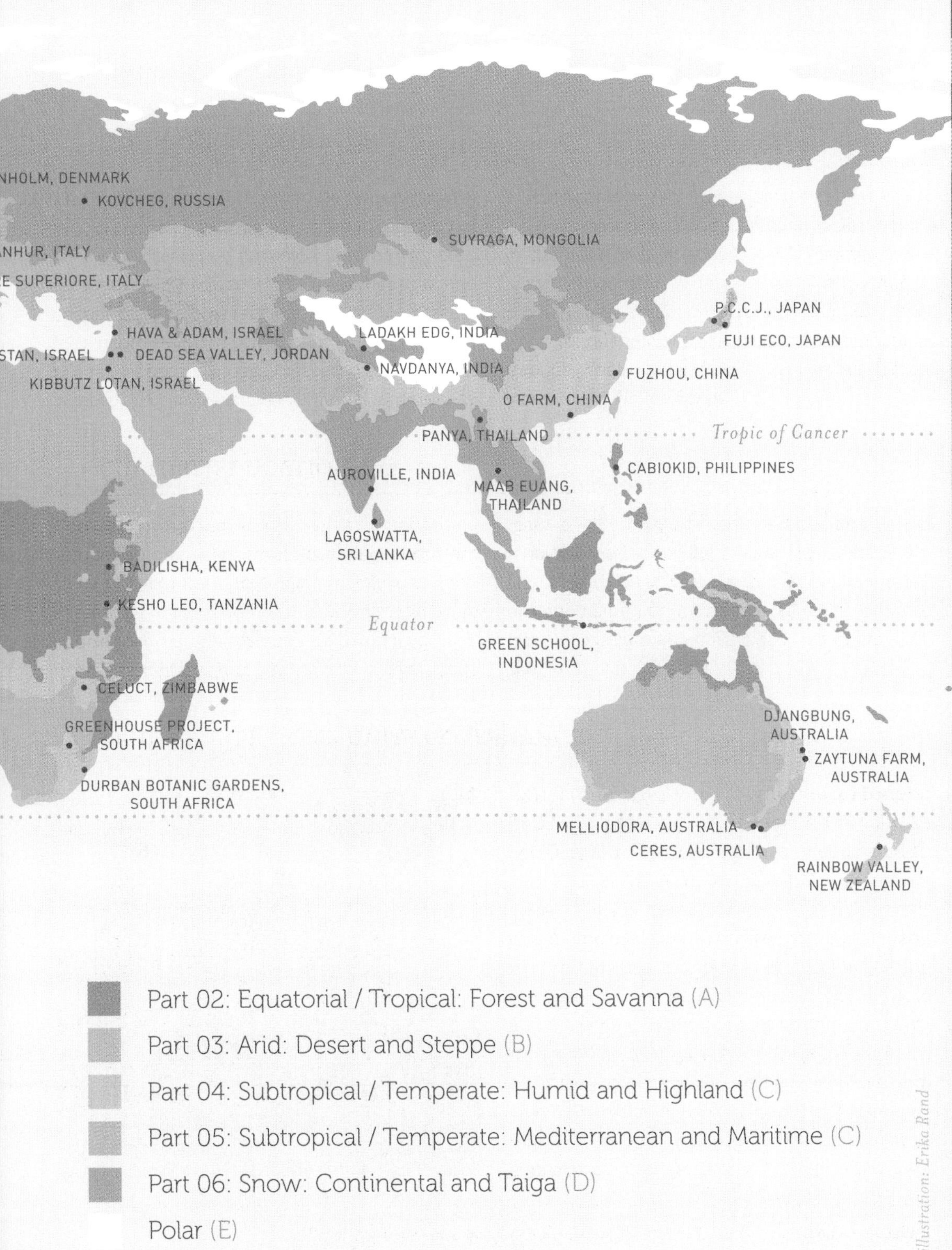
ANHOLM, DENMARK
KOVCHEG, RUSSIA
ANHUR, ITALY
RE SUPERIORE, ITALY
SUYRAGA, MONGOLIA
HAVA & ADAM, ISRAEL
USTAN, ISRAEL
DEAD SEA VALLEY, JORDAN
KIBBUTZ LOTAN, ISRAEL
LADAKH EDG, INDIA
NAVDANYA, INDIA
P.C.C.J., JAPAN
FUJI ECO, JAPAN
FUZHOU, CHINA
O FARM, CHINA
PANYA, THAILAND
Tropic of Cancer
AUROVILLE, INDIA
MAAB EUANG, THAILAND
CABIOKID, PHILIPPINES
LAGOSWATTA, SRI LANKA
BADILISHA, KENYA
KESHO LEO, TANZANIA
Equator
GREEN SCHOOL, INDONESIA
CELUCT, ZIMBABWE
GREENHOUSE PROJECT, SOUTH AFRICA
DURBAN BOTANIC GARDENS, SOUTH AFRICA
DJANGBUNG, AUSTRALIA
ZAYTUNA FARM, AUSTRALIA
MELLIODORA, AUSTRALIA
CERES, AUSTRALIA
RAINBOW VALLEY, NEW ZEALAND
Part 02: Equatorial / Tropical: Forest and Savanna (A)
Part 03: Arid: Desert and Steppe (B)
Part 04: Subtropical / Temperate: Humid and Highland (C)
Part 05: Subtropical / Temperate: Mediterranean and Maritime (C)
Part 06: Snow: Continental and Taiga (D)
Polar (E)
Map illustration: Erika Rand

Referencing This Book by Domains of Action

The Permacultural Flower Diagram

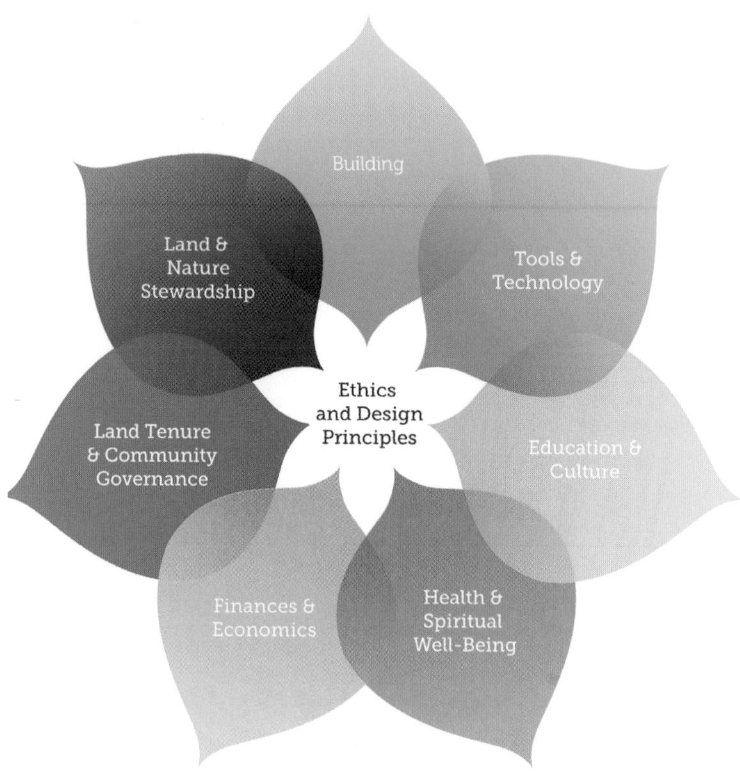

Permaculture is not the landscape or even the skills of organic gardening, sustainable farming, energy efficient building, or ecovillage development as such, but it can be used to design, establish, manage, and improve these and all other efforts made by individuals, households, and communities toward a sustainable future. The Permaculture Design System Flower shows the key domains that require transformation to create a sustainable culture. Historically, permaculture has focused on land and nature stewardship as both a source for and an application of ethical and design principles. Those principles are now being applied to other domains dealing with physical and energetic resources, as well as human organization (often called invisible structures in permaculture teaching). The spiral evolutionary path, beginning with ethics and principles, suggests knitting together of these domains, initially at the personal and the local level, and then proceeding to the collective and global level. —**David Holmgren**

Many of the profiles, as well as the accompanying articles, use headings from the Permaculture Flower diagram, developed by David Holmgren, which delineates seven major "domains of action" necessary for the development of a sustainable culture. The longer-format profiles of the projects in this book include information organized under relevant permaculture domains (e.g.Building or Education/Culture). Articles accompanying the profiles go into more depth about a connected issue or strategy, such as passive solar design or local currencies. These articles can be referenced by the related domain heading and are labeled by Permaculture Flower Diagram icons.

Listed below, and categorized by the "domains of action," are some examples of specific fields, design systems, and solutions that have been associated with this wider view of permaculture:

Land and Nature Stewardship Bio-intensive gardening • Forest gardening • Seed saving • Organic agriculture • Biodynamics • Keyline water harvesting • Wholistic rangeland management • Natural sequence farming • Integrated aquaculture • Wild harvesting and hunting **Building** Passive solar design • Natural construction materials • Water harvesting and waste reuse • Biotechture • Earth-sheltered construction • Natural disaster resistant construction • Owner building • Pattern Language **Tools and technology** Reuse and creative recycling • Bicycles and electric bikes • Efficient and low pollution wood stoves • Wood gasification • Bio-char from forest wastes • Micro-hydro and small scale wind • Grid-tied renewable power generation • Transition engineering **Education and culture** Home schooling • Waldorf education • Participatory arts and music • Social ecology • Action learning • Transition culture **Health and spiritual well-being** Home birth and breast-feeding • Complementary and holistic medicine • Spirit of place, indigenous cultural revival • Yoga, Tai Chi and other body/mind/spirit disciplines • Dying with dignity **Finances and economics** Farmers markets and community supported agriculture (CSA) • Tradable energy quotas • Life cycle analysis and energy accounting • Local and regional currencies • Carpooling, ride sharing, and car share • Ethical investment and fair trade • WWOOFing and similar networks **Land Tenure and community governance** Cooperatives and body corporates • Cohousing and ecovillages • Open space technology • Consensus decision making • Native title and traditional use rights

PART 02

Tropical/Equatorial Climates: Forest and Savanna Zones

Tropical climates lie within five to ten degrees north or south of the equator and include evergreen and seasonal rainforests, semievergreen forests, and monsoon deciduous forests, as well as tropical savanna/grassland ecosystems. The Köppen system calls these climates *equatorial* and identifies them by the first letter A on the climate map (pp. 22–23). Tropical zones are expanding in both hemispheres due to climate change.

In equatorial climates, day and night are each approximately twelve hours, with little variation throughout the year. The temperature averages 68°F–77°F (20°C–25°C) and also shows little change during the year. A characteristic of these climates, according to Köppen, is that the average temperatures of the three warmest and three coldest months do not differ by more than 5 degrees.

Tropical savannas typically have a distinct dry season and less precipitation than tropical forests. They exist mainly on either side of the two desert belts that circle the earth, and plant life is mainly grasses with small plants and widely spaced trees. These ecosystems cover large areas on most continents and support some of the earth's most iconic and endangered wildlife, such as giraffes and lions.

It is estimated that 50 to 70 percent of the world's tropical forests have been destroyed. Tropical rainforests are the most biodiverse regions on earth, holding approximately half of the planet's animal and plant species. While rainforests are more publicly recognized as being endangered, there is evidence that savanna ecosystems face an equal, if not greater threat.[1] Increased human use and warming temperatures are accelerating the spread of invasive species in tropical savannas.

Photo: Andy Isaacson

INTEGRATE RATHER THAN SEGREGATE: THE OLD AND THE NEW BLEND HERE. WHILE BENKI PIYÃKO CONTINUES THE VIBRANT TRADITIONS OF HIS CULTURE, HE ALSO STRESSES THAT MODERN COMMUNICATION AND COMPUTER LITERACY ARE VALUABLE TO THEIR SURVIVAL.

Yorenka Ãtame Center

Marechal Thaumaturgo, Acre, Brazil

Photo: Eliane Fernandes Ferreira

THE YORENKA ÃTAME CENTER PROMOTES THE EMPOWERMENT OF LOCAL PEOPLE THROUGH ECONOMICALLY AND ECOLOGICALLY SUSTAINABLE AGROFORESTRY STRATEGIES. ITS GOAL IS TO CREATE A NEW MODEL OF SUSTAINABLE DEVELOPMENT FOR THE AMAZON REGION.

The concept of the Yorenka Ãtame Center (Forest Wisdom School) came through Ashaninka tribal leaders' realization that it is not enough to protect their indigenous land; it is also essential to spread ethics and techniques for sustainable living to local people. The center was founded in 2007 near the town of Marechal Thaumaturgo, about three hours away from the Ashaninka territory by boat, along the Juruá river. The successful establishment of the center is especially significant considering that tribespeople were not welcome in the town in the 1980s and 1990s, when many nonindigenous inhabitants rejected the official demarcation of the Ashaninka territory.

Under the coordination of the Ashaninka leader Benki Piyãko, the center offers classes on permaculture-related topics, such as traditional polyculture gardening, reforestation, native-seed collection and cultivation, and beekeeping. While the Ashaninka live mainly on their own products, the inhabitants of the town of Marechal Thaumaturgo largely depend on goods produced outside the region. The center is an excellent example of the crossover between indigenous science and permaculture.

The Ashaninka are one of the largest native groups in South America. Tribal members on the Brazilian side of the border number only around 1,200, but there are close to 100,000 on the Peruvian side. The Brazilian community lives on a reservation, created in 1992 in modern state of Acre, deep in the interior of the Amazon rainforest; they continue to be accessible only by air or boat. The remote location of the tribe has played a part in its sporadic contact with devastating forces of colonization.

The Ashaninka reservation represents a small piece of their ancestral territory. In the mid-eighteenth century, an uprising expelled the Spanish soldiers and Franciscan missionaries who had arrived with the first wave of colonization. Then, after warding off invasion for over a century, many Ashaninka were enslaved in the brutal regime of coffee and rubber plantations. It is estimated that a staggering 80 percent of the tribe was decimated from disease and extreme exploitation during the rubber boom of 1839–1913.

In the face of this incomprehensible loss, the Ashaninka in Brazil and Peru have battled to maintain their cultural identity, protect their forest home, and preserve their language and livelihood. The state of Acre is home to a large number of tribes that live in voluntary isolation, likely choosing to resist contact as a result of their disastrous encounters with outsiders in the past.

OVER 250 YEARS SINCE THE FIRST MAJOR UPRISING OF THE ASHANINKA EXPELLED SPANISH SOLDIERS AND FRANCISCAN MISSIONARIES, THE TRIBE CONTINUES THE BATTLE TO MAINTAIN THEIR CULTURAL IDENTITY, PROTECT THEIR FOREST HOME, AND PRESERVE THEIR LANGUAGE.

In the 1980s, the Ashaninka of the Amônia River, a community of about five hundred people, became active participants in the movement for indigenous self-determination and the Aliança dos Povos da Floresta (Alliance of the Forest People). The alliance involved the famous activist Chico Mendes (who was later assassinated by a rancher) and other ecologists and indigenous leaders.

The people of the region have been battling an influx of illegal loggers of the mahogany and other protected hardwood trees on their territory for years. Over the past decade, there have also been issues with illegal hunting and fishing, coca plantations, and murders of native people in the area. "A major pre-occupation used to be the demarcation of the territory," says Escrawen Sompre of the Model Program for Indigenous People, one of the groups working with the Ashaninka in Peru to find strategies to combat illegal activity on their land. "Next is the protection of the territory once marked. . . . Without a cultural force, it will be difficult to achieve."

Within the context of these tensions, the successes of the Forest Wisdom School are even more remarkable. The center was initiated by the leaders of the Ashaninka community in order to educate nonindigenous people in the region about traditional ways of living sustainably in the Amazon.

Photo: Ellane Fernandes Ferreira

IN A VIVARIUM FOR BREEDING TURTLES, BENKI PIYÃKO HOLDS THE FUTURE. A TRADITIONAL FOOD SOURCE, TURTLES ARE ENDANGERED DUE TO MODERN HUMAN INTERFERENCE IN THE REGION. THE ASHANINKA ARE LEADING A WIDESPREAD ACTION AMONG INDIGENOUS GROUPS TO REGENERATE THE TURTLE POPULATION.

LAND/NATURE STEWARDSHIP

Polyculture and Reforestation: The Ashaninka and a number of other Amazonian peoples employ design strategies that take into consideration the use patterns of both human and nonhuman inhabitants of a landscape, similar to permaculture zones (see p. 6). Their forest gardens, traditionally maintained by women, include a number of semidomesticated, transplanted food plants. Gardens often include a polyculture of species such as palm, beans, bananas, yucca, rice, and peanuts. A project undertaken with the climate change group Neutralize has resulted in the planting of thousands of trees in deforested areas of the region.

CULTURE/EDUCATION

Experiential Learning: The Yorenka Ãtame Center is mainly staffed by a group of nonindigenous local people who are very well acquainted with the environmental problems of the region. They call themselves warriors of the forest. They welcome visiting students and talk to them about the importance of protecting nature, reducing and recycling waste, and the benefits of planting polyculture orchards of native fruit and nut trees. Participants learn valuable food-security skills, from beekeeping to regenerating local animal populations, such as turtles. Indigenous people in the region have relied on turtles and their eggs as an essential part of their diet for as long as collective memory serves.[2]

BUILDING

Integrating Design and Cosmology: The Yorenka Ãtame Center includes a greenhouse, a lake for turtle breeding, a vivarium for tortoise breeding, classrooms, hiking trails, an area for beehives, a reforested area, two houses constructed with traditional natural building techniques, a kitchen, dormitory rooms, and an artisanal craft workshop. The Ashaninka applied their cosmological vision to the design of the center, building the classrooms and cafe in the shape of a crescent moon. A star, representing the sun, is engraved on the ground in the middle of the campus, a meeting point and a place for interaction.

PRODUCE NO WASTE: SHARE THE SURPLUS HAS ALWAYS BEEN CENTRAL TO THE SMOOTH FUNCTIONING OF ASHANINKA SOCIETY. THEIR ANCESTRAL WORLDVIEW, KAMETSA ASAIKI, "THE GOOD LIFE," TEACHES THAT THE SHARING OF FOOD IS KEY TO CREATING A BALANCED ASHANINKA PERSON AND CULTURE.

HEALTH/SPIRITUAL WELL-BEING

Kametsa Asaiki: The Good Life: The Ashaninka today speak of defending their right to *kametsa asaiki,* which has been translated as "the good life." The phrase captures a central piece of traditional Ashaninka culture: an approach to life that leads to balance and happiness and is echoed in the permaculture ethics of earth care, people care, and sharing the surplus.[3]

COMMUNITY GOVERNANCE

Building Alliances: The Ashaninka have been active in seeking communication and negotiation with the Brazilian government, as well as national and international environmental organizations. There are alliances with the local and state government of Acre and with Brazilian NGOs. Organizations such as the Comissão Pró-Índio do Acre (CPI-AC) hold political meetings between indigenous and nonindigenous representatives of the state of Acre. Piyãko also coordinates a youth program with residents of the region and an exchange with native communities in the upper Juruá Region.

"People tell me that I am demonstrating the future of Brazil," Piyãko says. "But I think that the future is already here, the way is clear. We just need people who are going to act, who are going to do what needs to be done for the forest, who are going to work. That's what is lacking."

Reporting contributed by Eliane Fernandes and Juliana Birnbaum. Photos contributed by Lorna Li, unless otherwise noted.

Ecocentro IPEC

Pirenópolis, Goiás, Brazil

THE *CERRADO*—THE DRY HIGHLANDS WEST OF BRASÍLIA. THE CLUSTER OF BUILDINGS IN THE LOWER LEFT IS ECOCENTRO.

The Permaculture and Ecovillage Institute of the Cerrado (*Instituto de Permacultura e Ecovilas do Cerrado*—IPEC) is working to establish a model for sustainable living in the tropical savanna of central Brazil. This unique ecosystem, known as the *cerrado,* has been recognized as the most biodiverse tropical grassland/woodland in the world and is estimated to sustain over ten thousand plant species.

Started in 1999, a fundamental premise of IPEC is that a healthy ecovillage is born from a hub of sustainable economic activity. In this case, the work of the institute has enabled an ecovillage to flourish from the principles of permaculture, principles that are at the root of all major decisions and developments within the community. Outreach, including design consultancy and aid services to projects in Haiti, Portugal, and Australia, is done through the Ecocentro Institute, the working hub of the larger ecovillage.

IPEC has grown from twelve people to a community of about 190, including sixteen temporary residents at the training center. It is integrated within the local economy of the broader rural village, and has received numerous awards for architecture, education, and the development of the concept of Social Technologies—solutions not subject to patent or copyright. The water systems of the Ecocentro and the toilets, which transform waste into a resource, are open technologies, certified by the Bank of Brazil Foundation, with the aim of spreading the knowledge in areas of social need. The Ecocentro has built hundreds of these systems as part of its outreach program in other regions of Brazil, Africa, and Portugal.

THE ECOCENTRO BEGAN AS PRIMARILY AN EDUCATIONAL CENTER, OFFERING COURSES IN PERMACULTURE DESIGN AND NATURAL CONSTRUCTION. IT HAS BECOME A WELL-REGARDED SOURCE OF KNOWLEDGE ABOUT SUSTAINABLE DESIGN THROUGHOUT BRAZIL.

BUILDING

New and Old Technologies: All buildings in the Ecocentro and the community are made of natural materials, demonstrating earth construction techniques, including adobe, rammed earth, earth bag, straw bale, and several adapted technologies, to make best use of local materials and traditional knowledge (see inset on earth-based architecture, p. 102). It has held a number of educational events on building technologies and architecture in Brazilian architectural colleges.

All toilets in the community have to be built in accordance with water conservation standards. While most are dry composting toilets, some water toilets exist connected to biological treatment units. Wastewater and animal manure are collected, treated, and used in gravity irrigation to agroforestry plots. A biogas plant treats animal manure and provides energy and biofertilizers to agriculture. The work done at IPEC in sanitation technology has gone beyond supplying the needs of the community—the consultancy teams have built hundreds of composting toilets across Brazil and abroad.

LAND/NATURE STEWARDSHIP

Food and Water Sources: Ecocentro IPEC has pioneered the development of permaculture systems involving agroforestry and animal husbandry. As the center receives thousands of visitors a year, the site-grown food is not always sufficient to meet demand, but a cooperative system with the neighboring farmers brings in a large portion of the remaining food from the local area.

IPEC supplies all of its own water on-site and has achieved a closed-loop system: recycling of 100 percent of all gray water. Water security is a major concern in an ecosystem that is dry for most of the year. The site has an integrated water catchment system with established swales and retention basins using gravity flow to reach 90 percent of the land. More than 132,000 gallons (500,000 liters) of drinking water can be stored in on-site tanks.

FINANCES/ECONOMICS

Social Enterprise: From the start, the Ecocentro has been a hub for social entrepreneurship, and its founders have been awarded international prizes for the sustainable economic activity initiated at the community. A visitors' center receives thousands yearly, and several cottage industries are running within the community. The consultancy department provides architectural services and project management to large organizations and local governments; it has been recognized for excellence in sustainable design. The economic matrix of the project includes an NGO (nongovernmental organization) and several small businesses, integrated with an informal cooperative of service providers. This model of "economic ecosystem" is evolving toward a full proposal on local economic transition in nonmetropolitan regions that will be presented to regional governments.

STACKING FUNCTIONS: A DRY COMPOSTING TOILET ON THE TOP FLOOR AND A BLOCK OF SHOWERS ON THE GROUND FLOOR. WATER IS SOLAR HEATED AND ELEVATED TO STORAGE BY THERMOSIPHON, FOR GRAVITY FLOW ON DEMAND; WASTEWATER IS TREATED IN A REED POND. A STOVEPIPE DRAWS HOT AIR UP THROUGH THE DRY COMPOST BEDS, WHICH ARE HEATED PASSIVELY INSIDE THE ENCLOSURE.

CULTURE/EDUCATION

Expertise in Sustainable Design: The Ecocentro began as an educational center; it offers a variety of courses and has a continuous program for national and international volunteers. It is recognized in the national media for its expertise in sustainable design, and it produces a range of publications and reference materials, which are used for national policy development in education. More than two hundred thousand schools in Brazil use these materials in their programs.

Reporting and photos contributed by André Soares.

The Organization of Permaculture and Art

Salvador, Bahia, Brazil

OPA'S CIRCO ÁGUA VIVA BRINGS SUSTAINABILITY CONCEPTS TO INNER-CITY COMMUNITIES THROUGH CIRCUS TRAINING AND PERFORMANCES.

The Organization of Permaculture and Art (OPA) blends permaculture principles with circus and performing arts, bringing cutting-edge sustainability education to Salvador, in the Brazilian state of Bahia, and the surrounding area. Founded in 2004, OPA's mission is to use the arts as a vehicle to educate people about permaculture and to empower communities to live more sustainably. They have transformed an old colonial house in the heart of Salvador into an urban permaculture center, implementing rainwater catchment and gray-water treatment systems, composting systems, food production, and natural building techniques. The center quickly became an eco-cultural hub in the city, offering performances that include puppetry, aerial acrobatics, miming, fire dancing, stilt walking, clowning, and storytelling.

More recently, OPA's activities have focused on the development of a rural permaculture center in the small, beachside town of Diogo, 56 miles (90 kilometers) north of Salvador. The site features low-tech solutions for sustainable living, including natural building, composting toilets, gray-water treatment, and agroforestry areas. Students and visitors from around the world come to the Diogo EcoCenter, where they can explore sustainability concepts in a hands-on environment.[4]

OPA's "Pedagogy of Potential" program, inspired by the popular education techniques of Paulo Freire and Augusto Boal, is designed to inspire environmental consciousness and artistic exploration. One branch of the education program, Circo Água Viva, works in inner-city communities. "The idea here is taking OPA to the neighborhoods of Brazil, in order to teach circus and permaculture," writes Isabela Coelho, cofounder. "[We're] educating future leaders in their communities, because we believe permaculture and art will play a really important role in the near future of cities of the world."[5]

OPA also partners with a local surf school, Amigos de Jóia, to host camps that combine ecology and permaculture with surfing. Participants, dubbed "eco-surfistas," make the connection between the health of nature, the ocean, the beaches, and the sustainability of human culture.

Reporting and photos contributed by Común Tierra Project.

Project Bona Fide

Ometepe Island, Nicaragua

A 43-acre (17-hectare) farm nestled on the side of the Maderas volcano, Project Bona Fide addresses regeneration, both cultural and agricultural. Its main goal is to improve local and regional food security through research, training, and community participation. Its founder, Michael Judd, first came to Nicaragua from the United States to study local avocados and mangos and to see if natural farming techniques could make them abundant year-round. Established in 2001, Project Bona Fide now has over thirty varieties of each of these crops and at least 120 other species of fruit and nut trees, making it one of the most biodiverse collections in Central America.

A thirty-minute walk from the town of Balgüe, the Bona Fide site was formerly pastures and plantain monoculture (the chief export of Ometepe Island). The farm is now a sea of green, boasting an array of living systems, from herb gardens, plant collections, and cultivated fields to food forests, fruit- and nut-tree orchards, and significant plantings of coffee and cacao. Strategies include active and passive regeneration; seed experimentation to gauge varieties are best adapted for local conditions; interplanting

Photo: Maryellen C. Hearn

THE MADERAS VOLCANO IN BONA FIDE'S VISTA.

fruits and legumes to minimize watering; and the cultivation of bamboo as windbreak, food source, and building material. The community is moving toward establishing base calories from trees rather than grains. Project Bona Fide grows the majority of its food (around 80 percent) and buys the rest from local producers.

"People will see that transition from monoculture, which dominates the island, to a stack system that is grown organically," codirector Christopher Shanks explains.

Dedicated areas, like the zone 1 gardens, mixed plant collections, and the forest garden allows Project Bona Fide to show what plants and trees grow well in this climate and how plant systems can function together. In the mango orchard, jackfruit forest, coffee plantation, and the sorghum field, a number of companion planting trials are in progress. Shanks explains that they are hoping "to see what kind of synergies or non-synergies are created. Large areas of this farm are experimental—we don't know what they are going to boil down to."

"Certain things we thought we were introducing, we were actually reintroducing," Shanks says. "They were here before the Spaniards and they simple fell out of favor. What we found, because they are local, and in some cases native, is that certain plants perform really well." An example of this is yellow sapote, or *canistel*. Originally from the Campeche peninsula in Mexico, it is now finding favor with people's tastes and grows well on the farm.

Bona Fide offers fifteen-day permaculture design courses and has an apprenticeship program. The apprenticeships are several months long and focus on experiential learning and research. The program is being adjusted to sustain itself by placing apprentices in an instructive role; the apprentices will coordinate educational programs that will fund their stay. The farm also invites apprentices, interns, and volunteers to stay and work-trade. Locals serve as mentors and share their knowledge.

Volunteers work alongside local employees in the gardens and fields and help with the preparation of breakfast and lunch. They cook for themselves in the evenings, experimenting with a wealth of recipes concocted and committed to paper by previous visitors.

Bona Fide also has programs to help the local community. Cafe Infantil, a children's nutritional program, addresses food security directly by helping three- to six-year-olds get the vitamins and minerals that

BONA FIDE'S ESCUELA DE CAMPO PROGRAM GIVES LOCALS THE OPPORTUNITY TO BECOME EDUCATIONAL MENTORS. IN AN AGE BLINDED BY THE LATEST BIOTECHNOLOGY, RECOGNIZING THE EXPERTISE OF THE COUNTRY FOLK IS PERMACULTURE'S **VALUE THE MARGINAL** PRINCIPLE IN ACTION.

school-age children often lack. The program helps seventy children, providing a breakfast of milk, eggs, and fruit and educating them about dental hygiene. A cadre of concerned mothers has run the program since July 2005; as of 2013, it is financially independent.

Another program, the Proyecto Mano Amiga Community Center, is within walking distance of the farm. The center began as a library and has grown to offer affordable classes in math, English, Spanish, environmental studies, art, and computer skills. Proyecto Mano Amiga is fully organized and operated by locals.

Shanks considers himself both a student and teacher and says the farm's role in "adding to the pallet of food sovereignty and food security" has been the "question I have been dancing with for a decade and testing here on this farm what is possible. That is my primary drive."

Reporting contributed by Maryellen Hearn and Phil Moore. Photos by Phil Moore and Lauren Simpson unless otherwise noted.

Atlantida Ecovillage

Cajibío, Cauca, Colombia

Photo: Gustavo Rojas

Atlantida was founded in 2003 by a group of biologists inspired by their experience in the Rainbow Peace Caravan (see p. 173) in the year 2000. Three years later they settled on 123 acres (50 hectares) in a rural, mountainous area of the Colombian Andes. The site is 4,100 feet (1,750 meters) above sea level and has a tropical climate. Since the region is currently in the midst of intense conflicts between guerrillas and the Colombian government, an important part of the community's work is maintaining a peaceful and sacred space within the chaos around them. In this spirit, they named the ecovillage Atlantida, and call it "an Altar for Life." Today the site is a model for the growing ecovillage and permaculture movement in Colombia and hosts conferences to strengthen the network throughout the Americas.

COMMUNITY GOVERNANCE

Organizing Community: Atlantida has about thirty-five members, with some residents living in private homes and others sharing housing in a large hexagonal house. Everyone shares meals daily, which they consider a very important part of the communal routine. They make decisions by consensus, and they are exploring ideas based in sociocracy/holacracy and deep democracy, such as informed, consent-based decision processes and organizing leadership in patterns that mimic nature.

LAND/NATURE STEWARDSHIP

Growing Food, Catching Water: The community grows some of its principal foods—corn, yucca, plantain, and banana—and raises cows for milk and cheese. A small, clean creek passes through the land, from which they pump water. Rainwater is harvested and filtered for drinking.

TOOLS/TECHNOLOGY

Making Bricks out of Waste: The recycling process onsite must be as complete as possible, since there is no municipal garbage disposal. The principle of closed-loop cycles is also an integral piece of the community's philosophy. Some strategies in use are dry composting toilets and "mini fillers," plastic bottles transformed into building materials. Bottles are filled with waste packaging, which is compacted to make plastic "bricks," then used as filler for earth-based walls.

CULTURE/EDUCATION

Workshops and Ceremonies: Throughout the year, Atlantida opens its gates for workshops and ceremonies, including Dances of Universal Peace, an annual women's gathering, vision quests, and sacred plant ceremonies. They offer apartments or campsites for visitors. Hosting the Iberoamerican Ecovillage Gathering in 2012 prompted the construction of a large indigenous-style gathering space called a *maloka,* which can seat five hundred people.

HEALTH/SPIRITUAL WELL-BEING

A Hybrid Spirituality: Atlantida is known for its strong spiritual practices. The community integrates North American Red Road practices such as *temazcales* (traditional sweat lodges of Mesoamerica constructed of volcanic rock), which they use in cleansing and rebirthing ceremonies for body and soul. Sacred songs can be heard during the nights, and the *Apus* (spiritual protectors of the mountains) are invoked in the prayers. The elements, the wildlife and subtle beings of the forest environment, the animals, and the community of humans are all respected and honored for their presence and role in the web of life.

Reporting contributed by Rosa Elena Blanco and the Común Tierra Project.

THE ECOVILLAGE MOVEMENT IN COLOMBIA

The story of permaculture in Colombia is closely related to the history of ecovillages and the environmental movement there. One of the first permaculture events in Colombia took place among activities organized in 2001 by the Rainbow Peace Caravan (see article p. 173). In 2002 and 2006 workshops on permaculture design as a tool for sustainability took place in El Retoño (a natural reserve one and half hours from Bogotá). These first workshops showed examples of regenerative design from all around the world and from local Colombian initiatives, such as the eco-farm La Pequeña Granja de Mama Lulu. In 2007, urban permaculture workshops were run in Bogotá, in which participants took on the task of creating urban permaculture gardens, as part of a city literacy program for adults.

Representatives of indigenous communities, such as the Aruhacos and Cofannes, have shown interest in permaculture, integrating its strategies with their traditional knowledge of ecological, sociocultural, economic, and spiritual design. Permaculture is understood in Colombia as a name for nature-based ecological design for land management, and the use of the term is wide and evolving.

RENACE Colombia was founded in 2000 to strengthen the network of mutual support between ecovillages in Colombia and the Americas. Since 2006, it has been organizing an annual gathering of sustainable and alternative communities, the "Call of the Mountain." RENACE has developed a number of relationship-building strategies for members. For example, an ecovillage resident who visits another ecovillage is received as a member, with special privileges and rates. They also created standardized policies that concern volunteers and visitors in different member communities. This allows a volunteer at one ecovillage to have the same work-trade agreement in any ecovillage in Colombia, making it easier for travelers to join the movement and participate in different projects. A complementary currency, the Mountain, functions as an alternative to the Colombian Peso and circulates among members during meetings and events.

Together with the Ecovillage Network of Spain, RENACE has also created the "Ecovillage Incubator," a workshop where people forming a new project can consult with members of community projects who have long-term experience.

Reporting contributed by Melina Angel and the Común Tierra Project.

Punta Mona Center

El Caribe Sur, Costa Rica

Photo: Ana Jaramillo

EVEN WITH ITS REMOTE LOCATION, PUNTA MONA HAS BECOME ONE OF COSTA RICA'S BEST-KNOWN ORGANIC FARMS.

Punta Mona (Monkey Point), established in 1997, is a family-owned, off-the-grid environmental education center, botanical collection, permaculture farm, and eco-lodge dedicated to sustainable ways of living. Accessible only by boat or hike, its mission is to provide an alternative to destructive land-use practices taking place throughout Costa Rica and the world by growing food organically and designing according to permaculture principles. Its 85 acres (34 hectares) feature an open-air kitchen, structures built from local wood (harvested from fallen trees), and hundreds of heirloom species of tropical fruits, vegetables, herbs, and medicinal plants, as well as bamboo and timber.

Punta Mona was a small Afro-Caribbean coastal community, home to about sixty families, until the early

COMMUNAL PRACTICES OFTEN EMERGE OUT OF NECESSITY IN REMOTE LOCATIONS, WHERE RESOURCES ARE LIMITED. GROUP MEALS AT PUNTA MONA ARE A SIGNATURE PART OF ITS CULTURE.

1970s, when it was decided that the road would not be extended to the village. At that point, a large portion of the population moved to neighboring towns in search of work. A decade later, Punta Mona's only inhabitant was an elderly fisherman named Blas Martinez, better known as Padi, who fished and farmed the land, collecting rainwater to drink and reading by kerosene lantern.

In 1995 Stephen Brooks, a college student from Miami, Florida, who had studied and lived in Costa Rica for several years, began bringing groups of North American teenagers to Costa Rica to teach them sustainable solutions and indigenous values. In search of a beach for camping with a group, he sought help from a local guide, who brought him to Punta Mona and introduced him to Padi, who was harvesting pigeon peas in a garden next to his small wooden house. The two quickly developed a close rapport, and over the next several years Stephen would be a constant visitor and companion, camping in the elder's front yard.

In 1997 Stephen arranged to purchase 30 acres (13 hectares) of land adjacent to Padi's. There was a house on the property, over fifty years old, and a second, small house in back. It was completely off the grid and much of the property was overgrown.

His epiphany about the need for sustainable living had come years earlier in Costa Rica, when he witnessed a playground of indigenous children being "dusted" by a plane spraying a nearby industrial banana plantation. "I knew that if people really understood what was going on, that they would want to change, to do something about it," he says.

His intention was to create a center for sustainable living and education that was off the grid and dedicated to growing an abundance of tropical foods organically. Costa Ricans (locally known as *ticos*) have started to move away from eating the diverse fruits and vegetables that were formerly common in their diet, many of which have unique health benefits. Without that healthy, traditional diet, *ticos* are beginning to suffer more and more from diabetes, heart disease, and other maladies connected to the modern industrial diet.[6]

"There were no food stores here, no electricity, no municipal water; we had no choice but to live sustainably as possible," Brooks explains. "I didn't take a permaculture course until a few years later. Permaculture was just life here. What I love about permaculture is that it doesn't really say, 'do this, this, and this and you will succeed.' It gives you the philosophy that will help you make decisions that make sense. . . . Living out here, we had to figure these things out, where to get our water, how to grow food."

LAND/NATURE STEWARDSHIP

Food and Water: Even with only about 20 percent of the land in production, the Punta Mona Center is often able to supply about 90 percent of its food needs. When Brooks purchased the land it was mainly grassy lawn, with just a few fruit trees. "Depending on who is here and their dietary needs, the variety of foods cooked on the farm will change," Brooks says. "We could probably grow all of our own food if we gave up grains and temperate climate foods like garlic, cabbage, onion and carrots and ate only fruits and vegetables." Brooks is known for his culinary skills and often designs the menu for visiting groups; such as a recent one including mainly food harvested on-site: salads with nutty katuk greens and a mandarin-lime dressing, yucca, pumpkin with crushed peppercorns, turmeric, and ginger, and fresh juices with star fruit and cashew. He has appeared as host on several Costa Rican and American cooking shows and hosted a series called *Edible Adventures* for the Travel Channel in 2006.

In the years since the center was established, the unique climate of the Caribbean coast has helped a veritable food forest to thrive, with several "stories" of plantings, including a number of trees that grow vegetables—*ackee, pejibaye,* heart of palm. Brooks enthusiastically leads tours of the site. He loves to pick an exotic fruit, slice it open, and urge people to try it, "Taste this! Is it not the best thing ever?" Or, thrusting a crushed leaf under the noses of his audience, "Just smell this!"

THIS BIKE-POWERED LAUNDRY MACHINE **STACKS FUNCTIONS** NICELY: GET CLOTHES CLEAN AND GET A LITTLE EXERCISE AT THE SAME TIME.

The site's beachfront location allows residents to easily fish by kayak just off shore. There is a flock of fifty chickens and a handful of ducks, which supply the center with eggs. There is also an extensive system of *chinampas,* traditional Mesoamerican floating gardens (see p. 48).

"Being in Costa Rica, a relatively progressive country, environmentally speaking, we still have to be aware that the banana plantations are still happening the way they always have, so it's hard to say things have really changed that much," Brooks observes. "There are, though, many organic initiatives in various communities to produce organic food and regain local control over the diet."

Rainwater is captured from building rooftops and goes through a slow sand filter and then a UV filter before being used for drinking. Another rainwater catchment system is located on a hill, which creates water pressure, and is augmented by a well with a pump for periods of high demand.

TOOLS/TECHNOLOGIES

Energy and Waste Cycles: Costa Rica has a fairly comprehensive municipal recycling program, which accepts plastics, metals, glass, and other materials in comingled loads. To remove recycled materials

Photo courtesy of Punta Mona

STEPHEN BROOKS AND SARAH WU OPERATE THE CENTER AS A TRIPLE BOTTOM LINE (PEOPLE/PLANET/PROFIT) BUSINESS.

from Punta Mona, however, they must load them onto a boat to Puerto Viejo and then drive them to the recycling depot, thirty-five minutes north; trash also has to leave the farm via boat. "At times we have to weigh the effect of sending the trash to someone else's backyard or burying it in our backyard," Brooks says. "We also will burn certain materials based on how 'clean' they will burn, such as scrap wood, cardboard, paper, and other organic materials."

For human waste, the center uses composting toilets that create humanure. "In the rainforest, the topsoil is very shallow and in our greenhouse and gardens we needed more soil," Brooks explains. "Here in the tropics, the heat and humidity assists the breakdown of the 'humanure,' and in four to six months the human waste turns to rich compost."

The center manages its gray water from the sinks and showers by sending it through a simple coral filtration system located under water runoff pipes, and using biodegradable cleaning products. A system of photovoltaic panels and deep cell acid batteries powers the site. Methane biogas (see p. 139) from the septic system has been used for the stove, along with natural gas, and the chefs cook on fire as often as possible, especially for foods that require a longer cook time, such as beans, soups, or rice.

FINANCES/ECONOMICS

The Triple Bottom Line (people,planet, profit): Brooks and Sarah Wu, his wife, are dedicated to the principle of "fair share," providing a platform for educators to utilize the center as a teaching site and encouraging staff to find creative ways to augment their income through participating at the local farmer's market, hosting groups, or running day tours. "We want to serve as a sustainable model for business, where people and the planet can thrive," says Wu.

Recognizing the need to support local farmers, in 2005, Brooks cofounded Kopali Organics, a company that sources and develops sustainable, organic products from small farms and small farm cooperatives around the world. The products are distributed through Whole Foods Market and other health food stores in the United States.

CULTURE/EDUCATION

Eco-Missionaries: Punta Mona has changed throughout the years, from accepting a constant stream of volunteers to hosting mainly long-term internship programs and two or more permaculture courses per year. It hosts numerous student groups, from elementary through university level; yoga teacher trainings; women's retreats; and herbal medicine workshops. It also organizes events at the annual Envision festival, a music and cultural event designed along permaculture principles. A future goal is to create an *ecoversidad* that offers a full spectrum of university-level courses.

LAND TENURE/COMMUNITY GOVERNANCE

Photo courtesy of Tacotal

Experimenting with Ownership Models: In 2006, Brooks envisioned and cofounded La EcoVilla, a design-build company dedicated to permaculture-based development. The first project is a 46-acre (18-hectare) planned community featuring renewable energy, a methane digester and on-site organic food sources. It is located on the Machuca River, between the capital city of San Jose and the central Pacific coast. Its neighboring community, Tacotal (of which this book's authors are a part), is a collectively owned permaculture farm with both foreign and Costa Rican residents, which makes decisions by "consensus minus one" at its annual members' meeting.

Reporting contributed by Juliana Birnbaum. Photos by Louis Fox, unless otherwise noted.

"WE ALWAYS DIG IN THE DRIEST OF TIMES, AND IMMEDIATELY AFTER DESIGNING AND DIGGING . . . PLANT IT OUT." —STEPHEN BROOKS

LAND / NATURE STEWARDSHIP

CHINAMPAS

Chinampa agriculture has been described as "a self-contained and self-sustaining system that has operated for centuries as one of the most intensive and productive ever devised by man."[7] A *chinampa* is an agricultural field "island" constructed in shallow lakes, traditionally shaped in a long rectangle, like a typical garden bed. Together these islands form a network of "floating" gardens on a body of fresh water. *Chinampas* are often associated with the Aztecs, who developed an intensive agroecological system using this model, which can still be found in Xochimilco, Mexico.

For centuries before the Aztecs, the lowland Mayans had been designing and constructing *chinampas,* later occupied and further developed by the Aztecs. This unique Mesoamerican agricultural system exemplifies sustainable food production through its ability to maintain continuous, long-term productivity utilizing local resources.

The term *chinampa* is thought to have come from the Nahuatl words *chinamitl* and *pan,* meaning "upon a reed basket"—a phrase that describes the key characteristics of these gardens, which are constructed by "piling bed-clay and mud from the lakes, aquatic plants, dry-crop silage, manure and silted muck upon one another in precise layers, between paralleled reed fences anchored in the lake bottom."[8]

The construction process typically begins with *chinamperos* using a long pole to find an appropriate base in the wetland. The *chinamperos* marks the dimensions of the bed with reeds stuck into the ground and then smothers those reeds with mud excavated from around the base, creating canals surrounding the *chinampa* for canoe access. Next, they make thick mats of water lily and tule reeds, layered with mud, to create a nutrient-rich compost pile. They secure the sides of these garden beds with posts interwoven with reeds or branches. Finally, they plant willow trees around the edges to provide structural support and to create a favorable microclimate. Water flows through the porous structure of these garden beds, which are self-irrigated through capillary action.[9]

Soil fertility is renewed by scooping up material from the bottom of the lake and canals onto the *chinampa.* Aquatic plants, cultivated in waterways to be used as fertilizer, and are piled onto the bed along with the mud. Planted willows contribute to fertility as foliage falls on the garden, creating nutrient-rich mulch. The leaves that fall into the water feed the aquatic life, and the nutrients from aquatic animals and decomposing leaves return to the lake bottom, only to be scraped back onto the *chinampa.* The willow trees produce a microclimate by functioning as a windbreak and creating an air pocket with higher temperatures and humidity, greatly reducing frost damage.

Another key feature of the design is the establishment of seedling germination beds and nurseries, created at the edges of the *chinampa* by forming low terraces. These terraces are perpetually humid and layered with nutrient-rich mud scooped from the bottom of the canal or lake—an ideal environment for seedlings. To make them, *chinamperos* spread a thick layer of mud over a bed of waterweeds, allow the mud to dry, and then cut it small rectangular blocks. They plant a seed or cutting in a small hole in each block, and then transplant the blocks in the designated low terrace of the *chinampa.*[10] This is a great example of "relative location," as plants are propagated where they will be transplanted and harvested, with little energy wasted for transport.

In this ancient design, a number of permaculture principles are at play: the extensive utilization of on-site biological resources, complete nutrient cycles, maximization of edges, relative location (within the water source the garden needs), elements having multiple functions (reeds, willows), energy-efficient planning (irrigation through capillary action). *Chinampas* are highly productive and ecologically elegant, especially when compared to fossil fuel–intensive practices of modern agriculture, with heavy chemical inputs (fertilizers, pesticides) transported from faraway factories. There is much that we can learn today about sustainable food production from this ancient Mesoamerican agroecological system, which sustained enormous populations.[11]

Reporting contributed by Kai Sawyer. Photos courtesy of Punta Mona.

Maya Mountain Research Farm

Near San Pedro Columbia, Toledo, Belize

CACAO IS HEARTY AND DOESN'T REQUIRE FERTILIZER OR OTHER AGROCHEMICAL INPUTS. EVERY TIME AN OLD TREE FALLS OVER, A NEW STEM SPROUTS FROM THE STUMP. BEYOND ITS HEALTH AND NUTRITIONAL QUALITIES, CACAO IS THE KEYSTONE PLANT OF MMRF'S HEALTHY ECOSYSTEM. AFTER REMOVING THE SEEDS, MMRF USES THE EMPTY PODS AS A BIOCHAR FUEL.

Maya Mountain Research Farm (MMRF) is located near a large Kekchi Maya settlement on the Columbia Branch of the Rio Grande, southern Belize's largest river. The river's source is a massive spring that bursts from the ground a short distance from the MMRF, part of a vast underground river system that drains the adjacent Columbia River Forest Reserve. This reserve, a pristine 100,000-acre (40,500-hectare) broadleaf tropical forest replete with howler monkeys, jaguars, monarch butterflies, and birds of paradise, rises up the slopes of the Maya Mountains to the Belize-Guatemala border.

Christopher Nesbitt decided to buy a 70-acre (28-hectare) piece of land on the river in 1988. He was

"WHAT WOULD BE HERE IF WE WEREN'T HERE? THE RAINFOREST BECAME THE MODEL TO ASPIRE TO."—CHRISTOPHER NESBITT

fresh out of Antioch College in Ohio and had taken a job in Belize. The land had been used for conventional cattle ranching and citrus orchards.

For the past two decades Nesbitt has worked in different facets of organic farming, training locals, Peace Corps volunteers, government agriculture researchers, and international students. He has managed to successfully regenerate the soil at what has now become MMRF, his off-the-grid training and research center. Today, the farm is largely self-reliant and a nonprofit research site that trains students and uses permaculture techniques to cultivate a surplus of produce that is donated to local food banks. MMRF also hosts a popular permaculture design course taught by such experts as Albert Bates, Toby Hemenway, Penny Livingston Stark, Larry Santoyo, and Andrew Goodheart Brown.

One area of MMRF's research is in vanilla beans. After years of gathering specimens they established a gene bank of 250 indigenous vanilla vines and began keeping growth records on them. In Belize, as in other parts of the world, wild vanilla bean varieties have been decimated, and untold genotypes lost. With its low population density, however, the Toledo District still has many remnant indigenous vines. MMRF has identified twenty-seven distinct cultivars in the region so far, including a self-pollinating variety. The farm is demonstrating how vanilla and cacao can be grown most profitably in the way that the ancient Maya did, as part of an agroforestry polyculture. The hillside landscape is a tree-based agricultural system that resembles the structure, complexity, and interconnectivity of a natural ecosystem, providing ecological services such as erosion control, air purification, soil and water retention, and wildlife habitat.

For the rest of the plant species at MMRF, Nesbitt divides his new seedlings into three categories, depending on when they can be harvested. The short-term crops are the annuals like corn and beans—or the pineapple, squash, and melons planted between the corn contours—along with perennials that yield crops quickly, like nopal cactus, yam, purslane, basil, amaranth, and gourds. The intermediate crops are perennials like avocado, golden plum, *zapote,* almond, allspice, bamboo palms, breadfruit, coconut, coffee, cocoyam, banana, citrus, mango, cacao, papaya, tea tree, euphorbia, *noni,* raspberries, gooseberry, *chaya,* and ginger. They will yield sweet fruits, jams, wines, basket-fiber, soaps, beverages and medicines after

MISS GUADELUPE, A MAYAN WOMAN FROM SAN PEDRO COLUMBIA VILLAGE MAKES MASA.

a few years of fast growth. The long-term crops are Malabar chestnut, sea chestnut, *samwood, moringa,* mahogany, cedar, teak, and other slow-growing trees that will close the overstory (and, as Nesbitt observes, could be sustainably harvested to put his children through college, if they want to go). Animal systems include ducks, chickens, and pigs. Among Nesbitt's future goals is the use of the manure to make methane for his kitchen. He's also constructing a tank aquaponic system.

An important feature of the tropical landscape design is the creation of soil. In equatorial latitudes, much of the nutrient value of soils is carried in the standing plants, and the process of returning soil elements through decomposition into to next year's crops is very fast. On most farms, soil is lost through overexposure, erosion, and short swidden cycles (the traditional, shifting method of rotational agriculture and burning, whose cycles have been shortened by population pressure to as few as three years). Many farmers struggle to supplant those losses by increasing fertilizer applications, at untold cost—both to farm profits and the soil. Nesbitt says the damage agrochemicals cause "is sneaky, as it means thousands of years of agroecological knowledge have been discarded because we have cheap oil. We're in danger of losing this knowledge."

Many of the MMRF's neighbors in the Toledo District have been miseducated in government-run agricultural schools subsidized by seed and chemical companies. They see tree and farm crops working in opposition—you can do one or the other, but not both. Through the work with the cacao and vanilla cooperatives, MMRF is helping to change that way of thinking. Nesbitt explains how visiting local farmers, "walk around and 'get it'—especially the younger ones. Their visual literacy is so much better. That's how we'll get people to grow trees."

A permaculture design course in 1991 "changed everything" for Nesbitt. "I knew enough to know I didn't know enough to do anything without spinning my tires." He looked to the rainforest as a model. He put swales across his hillsides and added a number of ground-hugging plants and vines to keep the soils shaded and protected from erosion. For him, cacao was the keystone plant in the system. He realized there was a good reason that the Maya placed a high social value on it, beyond its health and nutritional qualities. Its scientific name, *Theobroma,* means "food of the gods." Cacao trees do not require fertilizer and are only rarely attacked by blights, fungi, and viruses in small holdings. Moreover, when an old cacao tree falls over, its stump throws out a new main stem—so many trees in Belize that are now in production are original stock—centuries old.

For more than two thousand years, the Maya of Central American practiced *milpa*-style swidden agriculture, something that has gotten a bad name ("slash-and-burn"). Practiced correctly, it was actually a very effective and productive way to farm in the tropics while building soil and sequestering carbon. A *milpa* starts with clearing a forest plot, but leaving some nitrogen fixers, timber trees, or other valued species. The Maya, like the Amazonian creators of the *terra preta* soils and the Aborigines of Australia, fired the remaining brush, which had the added benefit of depositing char, nutrient-rich ash, and curing firewood and construction-grade trees. The short-term annuals fill much of the opened space for the first two to four years, while the farmers set in place and mulch the seedlings of plantains, avocados, fruits, and fiber plants; cacao and leguminous trees and bushes sprout from their stumps. Over the next five to eight years, the canopy closes, and the farmers stop planting annuals and start training vanilla and interspersing coffee, ginger, allspice, and other understory plants. Cattle and poultry forage between the emergent trees.

Photo: Phil Moore/Lauren Simpson

PRODUCE NO WASTE: MAKING VINEGAR IS A GREAT WAY TO TURN SOME PERISHABLE FRUIT, LIKE PINEAPPLES AND BANANAS, INTO A VALUE-ADDED PRODUCT WITH A LONG SHELF LIFE.

The managed forest stage was typically fifteen years, but could be double that time in a *milpa* of particularly fruitful serendipity. Then the farmers cleared the land and renewed the cycle. In sharp contrast to the traditional technique, today's farmers employ a modified *milpa,* burning corn and rice fields yearly, focusing on the highest-paying crops to the exclusion of nitrogen-fixers and wildlife habitat, and planting into steep terrain without swales or terracing. It is this kind of farming practice that nearly erased the Maya Mountain Research Farm from the map in 2008. A neighbor's uncontrolled fire burned 300 to 400 acres. Of the 70 acres of MMRF, a little over 50 were completely burned, leaving only ash. The fire spared most of MMRF's cultivated areas, but destroyed the forest and thousands of young timber trees that had been planted. With the canopy opened and the native habitat destroyed, wildlife such as jaguar, brocket deer, peccary, and ocelots have been forced to migrate.

Restoration after the fire is ongoing. MMRF planted a mix of other plants within the cornfields, including timber species, leguminous species, fruit trees, and biomass accumulators. In the areas adjacent to the buildings, they planted pioneer species like banana, vetiver grass, pigeon pea, corn, and a mixture of timber trees. On the hills, they planted thousands of linear feet of vetiver rows along the contour to control erosion, along with fruit trees and pineapples were between the rows.

While the Maya Mountain Research Farm has faced challenges since its inception, it stands today as an example of the best practices in tropical agroforestry—"ecoagriculture" in United Nations parlance—and permaculture. "The energy returned on energy invested is off the charts," reports Nesbitt.

Reporting and photos contributed by Albert Bates, unless otherwise noted.

Antonio Núñez Jiménez Foundation

Havana and throughout Cuba

AFTER TAKING A FANJ PERMACULTURE COURSE, SANCHEZ, A RETIRED ARMY OFFICER, CONVERTED THIS VACANT LOT INTO A HIGHLY PRODUCTIVE GARDEN, COMPLETE WITH A DRY COMPOSTING TOILET, SEVERAL SMALL AQUACULTURE PONDS, CHICKENS, DIVERSE FOOD CROPS, AND A GRAY-WATER SYSTEM. HIS PASSION SPREAD, HELPING TO TURN THE NEIGHBORHOOD OF SEVILLANO INTO A PERMACULTURE HOTSPOT.

Known affectionately throughout Cuba as "La Fundación," this organization bears the name of Antonio Núñez Jiménez, the extraordinary Cuban revolutionary, geographer, anthropologist, agricultural reformer, and writer. Perhaps best known for his epic journey from the heart of the Amazon all the way to Cuba in a dugout canoe, Núñez Jiménez left a legacy of works expressing his vision, in which nature becomes an integral part of human identity, and human civilization is conceived and constructed in harmony with its surroundings. Just a few years before his death, in 1997, he declared that permaculture could

POST-CARBON PIONEERS? WITHIN A SPAN OF EIGHTEEN MONTHS, CUBA LOST 66 PERCENT OF ITS FOOD IMPORTS, 90 PERCENT OF ITS FOSSIL-FUEL AND AGROCHEMICAL IMPORTS, AND 80 PERCENT OF ITS MACHINERY IMPORTS FROM THE COLLAPSING SOVIET UNION. PERHAPS A BLESSING IN DISGUISE, THE EMERGENCY PUSHED THE COUNTRY TO RE-LOCALIZE AND FIND ALTERNATIVES—SOMETHING WE MAY ALL NEED TO DO SOON.

be a key force in the development of a "culture of nature" in Cuba.

The Antonio Núñez Jiménez Foundation for Nature and Humanity (FANJ) is a strong advocate for environmental education, geo-historical research, and the protection of Cuba's cultural and ecological diversity. Through its sustainable development programs in local communities, FANJ is part of a vibrant permaculture movement in the country, a response to the tremendous challenges faced by its people over the past two decades.

Cuba's quest for a re-localized and sustainable food system began in earnest with the collapse of the Soviet Union in the late 1980s. The country's food supply went into a dangerous free fall, bringing Cubans to the brink. Somehow the country needed to produce far more of its own food with far fewer outside inputs, or it would face widespread starvation and the end of its political and economic sovereignty.

Drawing on a very well educated and resourceful population, Cuba's response to the crisis was a wide-ranging package of land-reform measures and agroecological farming methods that significantly altered the country's agricultural landscape within a few short years. Some of the key initial features of this transformation were the establishment of large numbers of family farms and cooperatives, strategies to increase biodiversity and soil fertility, the revival of the use of animal traction, and widespread composting operations, including vermicomposting.

In an effort to ramp up food production in close proximity to where the majority of the population lived, in the early 1990s the Cuban state mandated commercialized urban organic agriculture, called *organoponico*, in towns and cities throughout the country. While all of this urban food production is—by law—organic, the majority of Cuba's urban agriculture continues to reflect the dominant agricultural paradigm: monoculture in long straight rows with little biodiversity and high inputs.

Permaculture has evolved in Cuba within the context of the wider agroecological movement and is in constant dialogue with the many initiatives for organic farming, urban agriculture, and food security throughout the country. While the initial stimulus for permaculture in Cuba was certainly the food crisis, the movement has broadened its focus to integrate many of the other key permaculture domains, such as water, energy, housing, appropriate technology, arts and culture, and community governance.

CULTURE/EDUCATION

Campesino to Campesino: When Australian volunteer permaculture teachers came to Cuba in the mid 1990s, the leaders of the Antonio Núñez Jiménez Foundation for Nature and Humanity (FANJ) were eager to add new techniques to their toolkit. FANJ had a long history of environmental conservation and sustainable community development, and they were searching for ways to respond to the crisis Cuba faced with a vision of ecological living that could engage communities and provide the concrete tools to help people meet their basic needs during the crisis and beyond.

In a few short years, FANJ began offering permaculture design courses (PDCs) to people across the country and created an infrastructure that could nurture this new movement: the *campesino* to *campesino* model, in which farmers and urban agriculturalists receive their training, and they, in turn, share their knowledge with their communities and peers. Thus the permaculture movement in Cuba has been deeply imbedded into communities and social movements, thereby avoiding the somewhat fragmented and isolated approaches that characterize the movement in some other parts of the world.

FANJ was also careful to ensure that the permaculture they taught reflected the geographical and social context of Cuba, eventually resulting in the publication of the Cuban permaculture manual, *Permacultura Criolla,* in 2006. By some estimates, over five hundred Cubans have now taken PDCs, and FANJ has held several national and international permaculture convergences including the International Permaculture Convergence in November of 2013.

Prior to the crisis, the majority of Cuba's urban population (67 percent) had very little involvement with food production at any level. As in many other parts of the world, agriculture in Cuba was seen to be the work of slaves, the uneducated, and the uncultured. The food emergency deeply altered that attitude and began to reconnect large numbers of urban people to food production. FANJ's initial efforts were aimed at empowering urbanites to produce food for themselves and their families in yards, patios, vacant lots, and on rooftops.

LAND/NATURE STEWARDSHIP

Protecting a Cave Ecology: In 2008, when the Cuban state announced plans for a massive housing project on the edge of the city of Matanzas to accommodate a growing workforce for a new thermoelectric plant, most Cubans praised the idea. After all, housing was in short supply, and most people in the country supported any initiative to boost the country's marginal power grid. There were opposing voices, however, as the proposed building site was directly above one of Cuba's most extensive and unique cave systems—many miles of caverns, galleries, and tunnels resplendent with some of the most unique stalagmites, stalactites, columns, crystals, and other rare formations in the world.

FANJ, the organization most intimately involved in the exploration, protection, and conservation of Cuba's rich diversity of caves, lobbied hard to press the state to reverse its plans. Indeed, the cave ecology had already suffered significant degradation from deforestation and an extensive, industrial-scale poultry operation, which had collapsed at the beginning of the 1990s. The lobbying efforts succeeded, and the state changed course and granted 27 acres (11 hectares) of land to FANJ to protect the cave. Locals and project leaders underwent an intensive permaculture training and visioning process in 2009, culminating in the development of a comprehensive design and implementation strategy for the site and the community. The project vision articulated three primary objectives: protecting the cave ecology by undertaking extensive reforestation work; generating additional food, water, housing, income, and other resources for the twenty-eight families living in the area; and creating a living permaculture model and resource center for the Matanzas province and beyond.

Within two years, the project had reforested about half of the land, with primarily native tropical species in the most ecologically sensitive areas. They started edible forest garden in another section. The design focuses on fast-growing, hardy fruit- and nut-bearing species; wind break species; timber species; animal fodder species; and medicinal species—many of which are already providing yields for community members. They established intensive vegetable gardens in places where some existing mature trees offer protection from the intense sun and winds. And in the sites of the former chicken barns, they planted roots and tubers, which benefited from a couple decades of accumulated manure. They integrated small livestock, such as rabbits and chickens, into the site for their manure and other harvestable products.

Slowly this land is being transformed from an informal dumping ground (many truckloads of rubble and garbage have been repurposed into useful structures) into a beautiful oasis. A community center provides a hub for the community and for visitors, and its buildings—including a traditional *caney* (a round, open-walled structure with a thatched roof), guest dormitory, cooking area with solar cookers, a small library, and ponds with tilapia aquaculture—all demonstrate natural building techniques. Delegations of cavers and permaculturists from throughout Cuba and beyond are camping at the site and contributing to its ongoing evolution.

Transforming Agriculture Growing up on his family's 17-acre (7-hectare) farm near Sancti Spiritus, Jose Casimiro wasted no time in moving to the city as soon as he was old enough to leave home. For fifteen years he worked as a traffic cop and fully embedded himself in the urban lifestyle that he desired. But something was always missing. City life grew tiresome, and Jose found himself longing for the country once again. Yet he dreaded the drudgery of working the cane and tobacco fields that he labored in as a youth. Casimiro attended a PDC and emerged with a heart and mind full of

JOSE CASIMIRO AND HIS FAMILY WALKED AWAY FROM CHEMICALS AND MONOCULTURE CASH CROPS; THEY TRANSFORMED THEIR FARM INTO A BIOLOGICALLY RICH, ECONOMICALLY VIABLE PERMACULTURE SYSTEM.

THE INDIO HATUEY RESEARCH STATION IN MATANZAS FOCUSES ON INNOVATING NEW AGROECOLOGICAL METHODS AS PART OF THE STATE-SPONSORED URBAN AGRICULTURE PROGRAM.

new possibilities. He knew the only way he could return to the land was to transform the family farm into a biologically rich, beautiful, and economically viable permaculture system.

He began by swearing off of chemical farming and by refusing to grow any more cane or tobacco than he and his family could use. Along with his wife, Maricela, and their three adolescent children, they placed their emphasis on subsistence—providing for as many of their own needs as possible, and sharing or selling any surpluses. Calling in favors from friends and contacts, they used excavators and front-end loaders to create several swales and a large pond that would secure their water needs throughout the dry winter months. They installed a ram pump (powered by the flow of the stream) to move water from the lagoon to ponds at higher ground, which would supply gravity-fed irrigation systems.

In time, the Casimiro family introduced cows, pigs, goats, rabbits, chickens, and turkeys to the land, carefully working out rotational grazing patterns. They planted hundreds of fruit, timber, and shade trees, along with living fences throughout the property. Recently they have incorporated bees, windmills, and a biogas digester, and their range of perennial and annual food crops is constantly increasing. Two of their three children—now grown and with kids of their own—have chosen to stay on the farm; their 17-acre farm is comfortably supporting an extended family of nine people. Seen from the distance, the Casimiro farm is a green oasis surrounded by barren, deforested hills.

While Cuba continues to struggle with many external and internal challenges to the reconstruction of its food system, it offers the world a powerful example of the widespread transition toward ecological, low-energy food production that will be required in the coming decades. FANJ's work demonstrates the important contribution that permaculture can play in this transition, in partnership with other, allied movements. While the acute food crisis in Cuba has passed, the permaculture movement continues to grow, with new teachers, leaders, projects, and expressions continuing to emerge. Not only has permaculture been a powerful tool for confronting a serious crisis, it appears to share a deep resonance with Cuba's beautiful and passionate revolutionary spirit.

Reporting and photos contributed by Ron Berezan.

Badilisha EcoVillage Trust

Kaswanga, Rusinga Island, Kenya

TENDING THEIR OWN FUTURE—THANKS TO BADILISHA'S "ONE CHILD, ONE TREE" PROJECT, KASWANGA PRIMARY SCHOOL'S STUDENTS PLANT ONE TREE A YEAR UNTIL THEY GRADUATE. THESE CHILDREN WILL LIVE IN A DESERT IF THE TREND OF DEFORESTATION IS NOT REVERSED.

On the small island of Rusinga, nestled between green rolling hills and the vast shores of Lake Victoria, lies the village of Kaswanga. Evans Owuor Odula was born and raised here, and founded the Badilisha project in 2008, with the vision of creating a permaculture-based response to challenges in his community. The beauty of the landscape and warmth of the people aside, Rusinga is considered one of the poorest districts in Kenya and all of sub-Saharan Africa. Traditionally, the population relied on farming, mainly corn and millet, and fishing for tilapia and other species. But in this post-colonial era, fisheries in the region are collapsing, deforestation, and poor farming practices have created erosion and depleted soils, and the

EVANS OWUOR ODULA.

"EVANS HAS A VISION, AND THAT VISION IS TRANS-FORMATION."

island suffers from food insecurity. Kaswanga also faces high rates of malnutrition, illness, and disease (including HIV/AIDS).

"Evans has a vision, and that vision is transformation," says Elin Lindhagen, director of the Permaculture Research Institute in Kenya. "He loves Rusinga Island and knows that it is a beautiful island, though now plagued by such harsh deforestation [that] it is turning into a desert."

The EcoVillage Trust targets the nutritional needs of orphans and children with HIV, who especially benefit from a healthy diet. The goal is for produce from the permaculture farm to supplement the program, now sponsoring sixty vulnerable children in the community.

The 2-acre (0.75-hectare) learning center includes a solar-powered office and library where locals can charge their cell phones for free. The demonstration farm includes a plant nursery, mandala and herb gardens, experimental food forest, banana circles, compost heaps, and an indigenous forest zone. Chickens, quail, and rabbits are integrated into the farm as "animal tractors," keeping the soil healthy and providing valuable manure.

Other facilities include a kitchen with solar cookers, on-site guest huts, composting toilets, a meditation center, and a conference hall. Rainwater harvested from roofs is the main source of water for the center most of the year. During the dry season a motor-driven pump brings water from nearby Lake Victoria; the project hopes to convert to a wind-powered pump in the future.

Badilisha promotes informal education, sharing information and knowledge with all those interested in permaculture and community development. Its programs include local and international permaculture workshops and training, "voluntourism," orphan support, school food programs, beach sanitation programs, and reforestation campaigns.

Reporting contributed by Rachel Rosenbluth, Rebecca Rottapel, and Sam Appel. Photos courtesy of Badilisha Ecovillage Trust.

Kesho Leo Children's Village

Arusha, Tanzania

COMMUNITY COMPOST MAKING ALLOWS CHILDREN TO PARTAKE IN MEANINGFUL CHORES WITH ADULTS, PROVIDES PRACTICAL EDUCATION OPPORTUNITIES, AND STRENGTHENS CONNECTION BETWEEN THE GENERATIONS.

Kesho Leo is a sustainably designed shelter for vulnerable women, children, and orphans located near Arusha, a city of one million on the southern slopes of the volcano Mount Meru. This region of north-east Tanzania includes Mount Kilimanjaro, Africa's highest point, and is considered tropical savanna, with a wet-dry climate. Just outside the city, a group of families make their home at Kesho Leo, a project founded

DUCKS HELP TO AERATE THE WATER DURING THEIR DAILY ACTIVITIES AND ASSIST TO CYCLE NUTRIENTS AROUND THE FARM. AND NUTRIENT RICH SEDIMENTS CAN BE REMOVED FROM THE PONDS TO PLACED BACK ON THE GARDENS.

COWS, GOATS, AND PIGS PROVIDE STABILITY THROUGH DIVERSITY AND PRODUCE MEAT AND DAIRY PRODUCTS, AS WELL AS MANURE, USED BOTH AS ORGANIC FERTILIZER AND TO MAKE BIOGAS. SECONDARY BENEFITS INCLUDE EDUCATION, EMPLOYMENT OPPORTUNITIES, AND INCOME. ALL KESHO LEO SYSTEMS AIM TO STACK FUNCTIONS.

POSSIBLY THE MOST ICONIC APPLICATION OF PERMACULTURE THINKING, SWALES WEAVE THEIR WAY THROUGH WHAT WILL BECOME KESHO LEO'S FOOD FOREST. SWALES ARE USED TO CONTROL WATER AND ORGANIC MATTER, MAXIMIZE INFILTRATION, AND PROVIDE ENVIRONMENTS FOR PLANTS.

through an Australian organization called FoodWaterShelter (FWS). The "children's village" was built with the combined efforts of local people and a skeleton volunteer team of outsiders, and has been internationally recognized for its innovations in sustainable building and project design.

The Kesho Leo project uses permaculture systems to provide food, water, and energy to its residents. It also works within the "invisible structures" of permaculture, providing access to family and social support, education, health, and—very importantly—community. The support of vulnerable and orphaned children is based on the establishment of a home environment headed by a Tanzanian mama. Basic necessities such as water, sanitation, and power are provided through rainwater harvesting, innovative composting toilet systems, and photovoltaic set-ups. Three separate farms—each with an individual aim and all undergoing continued development—provide food, manage organic waste, and provide income. The project can provide facilities for up to sixteen women and eighty children. The site is part of a fast-growing network of projects in Tanzania that aim to bring permaculture design solutions to the challenges of this region.

Tanzania has a large number of orphans, with the majority related to the HIV epidemic, which has taken its toll on every part of society here.[12] The concept for Kesho Leo began in Australia in 2005. A group of five passionate women founded FWS after they each had returned from extended volunteer experiences in Tanzania. After initial fundraising and permaculture design planning, construction began in 2007. A team-building effort between volunteers and local farmers saw the residents move into Kesho Leo in 2009. While supporting its residents and creating ongoing employment opportunities for the community, they have continued to develop education, health, social welfare programs, and permaculture projects. These have grown to include everything from daily kindergarten to permaculture design certificate (PDC) courses.

☼ LAND/NATURE STEWARDSHIP

Increasing Food Production: The homes are supported by three small farms that have been designed to include cyclic, closed systems. Each farm aims to integrate locally used organic practices with appropriate innovations and limited introduction of new techniques.

The first farm developed through the Kesho Leo project is approximately 1 acre (less than half a hectare) in size and includes traditional shelters for livestock such as goats, cows, and pigs. The animals' manure serves the farm in several ways, including producing biogas for cooking, fertilizing the gardens, and finally providing nutrients for phytoplankton and algae in the ponds to feed tilapia. These ponds are the final stages in preventing many of the normal farm losses and allow nutrients, soil, and water to be recaptured and returned to where they are needed. Not only does this farm manage water, nutrients, and soil in a cyclic system, but it provides a variety of produce for the Kesho Leo residents and educational opportunities for the nearby community and visitors.

Another, smaller farm at Kesho Leo aims to break the cycle of sanitation-related disease by treating waste safely and locally through the management and utilization of gray water and humanure in a food forest and a chicken run. A third farm associated with Kesho Leo uses biointensive techniques to produce organic vegetables sold for profit in Arusha, while supporting the secondary aim of developing a local market for organic vegetables.

The systems implemented at Kesho Leo strive

PEOPLE CARE: NURTURING HUMAN BEINGS IS CORE TO PERMACULTURE. WITH OVER TWO MILLION ORPHANS IN TANZANIA, KESHO LEO CHILDREN'S VILLAGE HELPS MEET A GREAT NEED. ITS SUCCESS IS INSPIRING THE REGION AND SHIFTING THE PLIGHT OF SOCIETY'S MOST VULNERABLE MEMBERS.

to sustainably increase production of the land while decreasing the impact on the environment and rebuilding the local soils. As this goal is met, so are the food needs of the residents. At the same time, income-generating activities connected to the site will support ongoing community projects.

CULTURE/EDUCATION

A Broad Spectrum: Kesho Leo's model for educating its children includes time spent learning in mixed-age classrooms, sharing nutritious meals, learning and playing outdoors in the garden, and studying in the library. Community and adult education programs have encompassed a broad spectrum of offerings, from HIV awareness to making compost, and now include international and Kiswahili permaculture design courses.

TOOLS/TECHNOLOGY

Closed-Loop Cycles: To meet the ongoing challenge of sanitation, FWS has developed an innovative system of composting toilets that is both affordable and suitable for use within both local households and communal sanitation systems. Made from repurposed, locally available 52-gallon (200-liter) plastic drums, batch-type composting toilets provide an efficient system that requires no water and produces a disease-free organic fertilizer for use in the Kesho Leo food forests.

The Kesho Leo rainwater collection systems supply all the clean-water needs of residents, staff, and animals. The expansive roofs harvest rainwater, which is then stored in a series of underground tanks constructed with recycled tires and totaling 65,000 gallons (245,000 liters) in volume. Systems such as rainwater catchment and drip irrigation have not been widely utilized in the area before, but implementing these techniques successfully is a ripple effect in the wider community.

Also on the roof, an array of photovoltaic panels generates all of the electricity needed at the site. The project experiments with other locally developed, appropriate technologies, such a bicycle-mounted corn sheller and a grain silo made from a damaged water tank.

FINANCES/ECONOMICS

Toward Self-Sufficiency: Kesho Leo was developed with outside funding from small fundraisers, supportive donors, and grants. But a priority from day one has been to build the income-generating capabilities and self-sufficiency of the shelter. Many of the income-generating projects leverage off the core permaculture principle of developing systems with multiple benefits. For example, Kesho Leo has a beekeeping operation that produces honey and also ensures the pollination of crops in the area, which boosts crop yields. The established organic vegetable farm generates income by selling produce at the weekly market and to local hotels, while other business activities—such as growing mushrooms and raising poultry—create high-value outputs with low-cost inputs.

METHANE GAS PRODUCED BY THE ANAEROBIC DECOMPOSITION OF MANURE IN THE BIODIGESTER IS USED FOR COOKING FUEL. THE MANURE ITSELF CAN THEN BE COMPOSTED, APPLIED DIRECTLY TO THE FARM THROUGH SWALES, OR DIRECTED INTO THE FISH PONDS, WHERE IT PROMOTES ALGAL GROWTH THAT, IN TURN, FEEDS THE TILAPIA.

BUILDING

Local and International Participation: The architectural award-winning main buildings include the clinic and manager's residence; the classrooms, kitchen, storerooms, and dining area; and the accommodation building—all connected by a central walkway. The design uses the slope of the land to its advantage, by incorporating lower-level storage rooms (reused shipping containers) and a wash area, where laundry, showers, and composting toilets are located. Sustainably harvested timber was the main construction material.

A number of passive-solar technologies were implemented (see p. 110 for more on this):

Raising buildings off the ground to enable passive cooling during the hot seasons and to keep out of the mud during the wet season.

THANKS TO **PROTRACTED OBSERVATION** OF THE SITE, THE MAIN BUILDINGS WERE ORIENTED FOR MAXIMUM PASSIVE HEATING AND COOLING. THEY ALSO HAVE A UNIQUE ROOF DESIGN WITH HORIZONTAL CHIMNEY STRUCTURES THAT USE CONVECTION TO PASSIVELY COOL THE BUILDING. AS THE ROOF SURFACE HEATS, WARM AIR RISES UP THROUGH THE CEILING AND DRAWS COOLER AIR FROM UNDERNEATH THE RAISED BUILDING.

Direct sun on the roof drives convection currents through ceiling ventilations, draws cooler air up through the building and dispels hotter air.

Maximizing the length of the north-facing facades, combined with the correct amount of roof overhang, captures the lower sun angles in the cooler months to enable passive heating—while offering protection from the higher sun angles in the hotter months.

Minimizing the lengths of the east- and west-facing facades, which receive the hot morning and afternoon sun, to help keep buildings cooler.

Designing long, narrow single-rooms especially for sleeping—to promote natural flow cross-ventilation.

One of the greatest strengths of the project is that it was members of the local community who built the site, along with a small team of dedicated volunteers. The participation of the local community not only resulted in creation of jobs and training opportunities but also gave those involved a sense of connection, pride, and ownership.

Reporting and photos contributed by Robert Cork. Photos by the volunteers of FoodWaterShelter.

The Panya Project

Mae Taeng, Chiang Mai, Thailand

ABOVE AND OPPOSITE PAGE: A CLUSTER OF SMALL HUTS SERVES AS THE LIVING QUARTERS FOR THE LONG-TERM RESIDENTS, BUILT WITH A VARIETY OF EARTH-BUILDING TECHNIQUES AND ON-SITE MATERIALS, MAINLY ADOBE, COB, OR WATTLE AND DAUB.

Situated in the lush low hills of northern Thailand, the Panya site is 10 acres (4 hectares) tucked between the conventional rice/soy/corn farms of a local village and the wild expanse of a second-growth national forest. The area experiences both a tropical wet and dry climate. The project is an education center that teaches sustainable living, focusing on permaculture principles and their application in various realms, including ecology, society, and spirituality.

In 2002, Christian Shearer, the founder of the project, was approaching the close of his college years and facing the reality of the conventional options laid out before him. He decided an alternative approach and wrote up a creative proposal, called the Baan Thai Project, inviting friends and family to join him in purchasing land in Thailand. He suggested that the project could do nothing but bring their lives to more

"Make hay while the sun shines."
—Thai proverb

fully reflect their integral goals—or far more so than their current lives did. Eleven individuals contributed the seed money that funded the purchase of the land and the construction of the first building, as well as the first permaculture course, taught by Geoff Lawton (for more on Lawton's work, see pp. 94 and 160).

LAND TENURE/COMMUNITY GOVERNANCE

Decision Making: The Panya Project is a volunteer-run education center dependent on the participation of short- and long-term visitors from abroad. There is one Thai family that anchors the project and has been living the property since its start: Kae Sodtamna and her daughter, Ping, who was born on the land. Sodtamna was part of a neighboring sustainability project, Pun Pun, and brought her experience and education from there to help run Panya.

The short-term volunteers join for at least one week. They pay a fee for their stay in exchange for hands-on learning, taking part in permaculture courses, and learning valuable tools to share with their communities. The long-term interns, who join the project through an application process, are committed to a minimum stay of six months at the project.

There are various tiers of decision making: Shearer and the other owners hold the final say on major choices about the site, but the residents and volunteers guide a lot of the decision making through an altered consensus process in which each member has the opportunity to share his or her voice to help direct the movement of the community.

"PERMACULTURE IS A PART OF A MUCH HEALTHIER, MORE ENJOYABLE AND FULFILLING LIFESTYLE THAT COULD BE MADE AVAILABLE TO ALL PEOPLE ON THIS PLANET. . . . WHEN WE SHIFT FROM BEING PRIMARILY A CONSUMER INTO LIVING A LIFE OF BEING PRIMARILY A PRODUCER, THERE ARE WONDERFUL BENEFITS TO THE INDIVIDUAL— AND WE REDUCE NEGATIVE IMPACTS ON SOCIETY AND THE PLANET."

—CHRISTIAN SHEARER

THE SALA, A LARGE CENTRAL BUILDING, SERVES AS AN AREA FOR DINING, TEACHING, COOKING, DANCING, AND OTHER ACTIVITIES.

RAINWATER, CAPTURED IN SEVEN LARGE TANKS DURING THE WET SEASON, PROVIDES AMPLE DRINKING WATER FOR THE COMMUNITY YEAR-ROUND. AS PERMACULTURE THINKING ENCOURAGES REDUNDANT SYSTEMS, THERE ARE ALSO FOUR SWALES, TWO PONDS, AND A SHALLOW WELL, THE WATER FROM WHICH CAN BE PUMPED UP THE HILL FOR GRAVITY FEED.

LAND/NATURE SVSHIP

Food Production and Water Systems: Each year, the community produces more and more of the food they consume, although the high numbers of visitors to the site dictates that over half of their food is sourced from outside. In purchasing outside food, they have a priority of supporting organic farms and local tribal markets.

The food forest on-site has forty varieties of tropical fruit in a multilayered, polyculture landscape that mimics natural systems. In addition to this, there are about forty rows of vegetable gardens irrigated by a drip system, with a focus on companion planting, to take advantage of the mutually beneficial relationships between the plants. A rainwater-catchment system provides drinking water year round.

CULTURE/EDUCATION

Cross-Pollination: The Panya Project primarily hosts courses in permaculture design, natural building, community living, ecovillage design, nonviolent communication, and clowning. Community members are always encouraged to participate in the courses or sit in on any particular lesson or activity. The many travelers who come through the site allow for cross-pollination of ideas and connections to other ecovillages and permaculture communities.

TOOLS/TECHNOLOGY

Powering Down and Recycling Waste: The lighting system in the main building is solar powered, and the project hopes to provide solar power to the rest of the site as well. At the moment, most of the electrical power of the site is sourced from the grid, and energy efficiency is the main goal. Residents observe that the entire site uses less energy than the average house in the developed world. The main demand for energy on-site is the use of power tools for building projects.

The community largely uses a shared transportation system. There is a local bus that arrives at the village each morning that runs to Chiang Mai, the local city. They also use a motorcycle and sidecar for market runs and a pickup truck for large purchases.

Panya uses dry composting toilets that take a year to fully break down waste, which they use to fertilize the trees. The community reuses many recyclables in creative ways on-site and sends what is left to a conventional recycling center. What cannot be recycled or reused they take to the local landfill, which serves as a prominent reminder to be mindful of what is brought onto the site, as it may have to be taken back off as waste.

Reporting contributed by Amelia Heron. Photos by Jenny Pickerill unless otherwise noted.

Maab Euang Learning Center

Chonburi, Thailand

RESILIENCE BRILLIANCE—THE CATASTROPHIC FLOODS THAT PARALYZED THAILAND IN 2011 INSPIRED THE DESIGN AND CONSTRUCTION OF THE MAAB EUANG'S "FLOATING GARDEN," MADE FROM EMPTY PLASTIC DRUMS AND BAMBOO, WHICH WILL SIMPLY RISE WITH FLOOD WATERS, ALLOWING UNINTERRUPTED FOOD PRODUCTION.

Dr. Wiwat Salayakamtorm started the Maab Euang Learning Center, an eco-farm in Chonburi province, Thailand, in order to "develop practical solutions to environmental and socio-economic crises of modern times." He founded the center in 2001, after he quit his job as a royal servant, in order to put into practice the Thai king's philosophy of sufficiency economy. He adopted 16 acres (6.5 hectares) of his brother's land and transformed the depleted, hardpan soil into a productive edible forest and garden, incorporating several rice paddies and aquaculture farms. He has studied permaculture and the natural farming practiced by Masanobu Fukuoka, as evidenced throughout the property (see p. 326 for more on Fukuoka's natural farming techniques).

The sufficiency economy philosophy stresses the importance of the middle path and the need to balance forces of globalization with the needs of local resilience. *Sufficiency* here means moderation and resistance to internal and external shocks, such as disease, economic instability, and natural disasters. It is an approach designed to cope with rapidly changing natural and sociocultural environments.

The motto of the eco-farm, "learning by doing," is put into practice through nine learning stations: (1) rice production; (2) household product construction; (3) biodiesel production; (4) charcoal; (5) soil management; (6) forest gardening; (7) natural health care; (8) water management; and (9) natural building. Workshops, internships, and visits are paid for with donations, consistent with the king's teaching, "the more you give, the more you receive."

Today, over eighty other Agri-Nature Learning Centers have been established throughout Thailand, serving as hubs to teach sufficiency economy–based living to farmers, government, businesses, and the general public. All centers also serve as survival shelters in case of crisis. These Buddhist-influenced eco-farms are a living example of permaculture in practice, even though they don't specifically use the term.

Reporting and photograph contributed by Kai Sawyer.

THE PROJECT WAS STARTED ON FARMLAND WHERE CONVENTIONAL MONOCROPPING HAD BEEN COMMON PRACTICE. IT HAS TRANSFORMED THE SITE INTO AN OASIS WITH DIVERSIFIED ORGANIC AGRICULTURAL, AQUACULTURE, AND FOREST AREAS.

Cabiokid Project

Cabiao, Nueva Ecija, Luzon, Philippines

The Cabiokid Project was started in 2001 on an 11-acre (4.5-hectare) rice field by an engineer, an agronomist, and a product developer—each frustrated with modern farming techniques and their negative impacts on communities. Located 55 miles (90 kilometers) north of Manila, the project is a model permaculture development site and one of the leading sustainability organizations in Southeast Asia. Its name combines the name of its location, Cabiao, with the prefix *bio-* and *bukid*, "field," in Filipino.

In its first decade, the site nearly tripled in size, with residents creating diversified agricultural, forest, and aquaculture areas. The fifteen permanent residents are a mixed group of local people. In addition, there are people from other parts of the Philippines, who mainly come to learn from Cabiokid. According to two of the founders, Bert Peeters and Estrelito Santos, many of their visitors have studied at the site and returned to their home regions to apply regenerative-design techniques in their own ecosystems.

LAND/NATURE STEWARDSHIP

LOCALLY HARVESTED *KAMANSI* IS OFTEN COOKED WITH COCONUT MILK TO MAKE A DELICIOUS TRADITIONAL STEW.

Self-Sufficient Food Systems: Cabiokid is able to feed its residents and visitors primarily from the community's own supply of fruit, vegetables, grains, and animal products, with some supplemental food coming from very local sources. They cultivate rice and sell the surplus to the local community and in Manila. They raise poultry and native pigs for meat and eggs. Four fish species are cultivated in the aquaculture ponds, and the orchards produce bountiful fruits at varying times of the year. The forested parts of the land, minimally managed and known in permaculture as zone 4, provide residents with root crops, fruits, spices, and other wild-harvested foods (for more on zones, see p. 6).

The project was started on land that had been a monoculture farm, though it had the benefit of being well-irrigated rice land. Pioneer residents implemented permaculture-based landscape design and soil-building techniques. They used the soil gathered from digging the aquaculture ponds to create the vegetable gardens (zones 1 and 2), a reforestation area, and an orchard. Despite the changes at the farm, they still cultivate rice, but using a chemical-free organic system that involves planting seedlings instead of sowing grains of rice.

TOOLS/TECHNOLOGY

Closing the Loop in Waste Cycles: Located in an area without an effective waste-management system, Cabiokid has created a system of waste processing and recycling that is becoming a local model. Residents are committed to being as close to zero waste as possible, and accept segregated wastes from nearby communities, which they process as building materials, recyclables, or compost. The community's plastic wastes are mainly reused in construction projects. They reuse plastics as material to elevate floors, which they then surface with fired clay tiles; they have used plastics under boardwalks and pathways to stabilize and compact the soil. At the same time, the resident community is making a conscious effort to minimize solid waste in the broader community. One initiative has been the reintroduction of handmade woven bags in regional markets, to minimize plastic waste.

Although still connected to the grid, the community is moving toward more renewable energy sources, and there is currently a 1-kilowatt solar and wind-turbine system. They aim to expand these, but the initial investment in these technologies has been prohibitively high, so the community is working to bring down electricity consumption as a general rule. They are also exploring passive-solar construction techniques and the potential to eventually feed energy back to the local grid.

LAND TENURE/COMMUNITY GOVERNANCE

The Local Community: Cabiokid has become an integral part of the surrounding community, known as *barangay* (local district) Santa Rita. When they were first building the project, they provided housing for those working at the site, and some of those workers stayed on as members. Later, the founders opened up to new members, allowing them to build homes and become residents. Cabiokid is a nonprofit organization run by people living and working at the site, and they own the land collectively. Interested individuals go through a process of work-study on the site and have the opportunity to become a resident of the community by applying for use of an existing house on-site or by building a new home.

Photo: Nars Gumangon

THROUGHOUT THE PHILIPPINES' CENTRAL VISAYAS REGION, CABIOKID TRAINS PEOPLE TO MOBILIZE PUBLIC OPINION AND PUSH LOCAL POLITICIANS TO ADOPT THE PERMACULTURE FRAMEWORK ON A BROADER SCALE IN ORDER TO FIGHT CLIMATE CHANGE. THEY HAVE SUCCESSFULLY CONVINCED LOCAL COMMUNITIES AND POLICYMAKERS TO IMPLEMENT STRATEGIES SUCH AS COMPOSTING TOILETS, RAINWATER COLLECTORS, AND THE USE OF BAMBOO AS A BUILDING MATERIAL.

Key members of the community are actively working with international donors on permaculture projects being implemented in other parts of the Philippines. They have a running collaboration with the municipalities of Cabiao, in Nueva Ecija, and Tiwi, in Albay, and they work with local and indigenous communities in the island provinces of Palawan and Mindanao (see accompanying piece by Victoria Tauli-Corpuz, a native Igorot activist from the Cordillera region of the Philippines, on indigenous resistance to globalization).

FINANCES/ECONOMICS

Creating Green Livelihoods: As the site grew from a monoculture rice field into a diversified and lush permaculture site, Cabiokid generated a whole host of livelihood potentials. The project aimed to involve community members and local people in developing the entrepreneurial opportunities that became possible on site. A women's cooperative was established in the *barangay*, which helps women to work in or with Cabiokid on green livelihood opportunities. As a result, locals are earning incomes growing vegetables in Cabiokid's garden, beekeeping, making shoes, soap and bamboo bikes, bottling fruit juices and a number of other activities. The goal is to create alternatives to the necessity of migrating to work in the city, where families are uprooted and ultimately need more cash to support unsustainable urban lifestyles. The community also receives income from members doing outside consultancies, freelance work and maintaining jobs with other agencies.

BUILDING

Photo: Nars Gumangan

Regenerative Design: The houses built on-site have been designed according to permaculture principles and incorporate features such as composting toilets, rainwater collectors, and gray-water systems feeding personal zone 1 gardens. Cabiokid includes a farmhouse, a classroom, an office, a workshop, and a guesthouse with a terrace and garden, as well as the main communal house with a kitchen. Tent cabins and bamboo cabins dot the site and are used by students, workers, and guests. There is a food-processing center, fuelled by renewable energy and constructed out of bamboo. It is located near the renewable-energy powerhouse, and surrounded by the gardens and animals that supply the ingredients for the food being processed. Roofs are natural plant materials harvested from *nipa* (mangrove swamp palms), *cogon* (tropical dryland grasses) and *anahaw* (Philippine fan palm) Most incorporate skylights to allow for passive-solar gain, and rainwater-collecting systems are standard in all resident houses and communal structures.

CULTURE/EDUCATION

The Needs of Local People: Cabiokid tailors its permaculture courses to the needs of local residents and the demands of the local ecosystem and resources. Along with the basic and advanced permaculture courses, they offer short courses on bamboo construction and the System of Rice Production (SRI), which uses local seed, organic compost, and cultivates microorganisms as an alternative bio-spray for farming.

The courses bring together international students with the local cohorts. They overcome language barriers with patience and occasional translation into English or Tagalog. By blending the groups, the Cabiokid learning environment becomes richer and allows people to learn from and interact with each other.

Reporting contributed by Nicollette Constante. Photos by Bert Peeters, unless otherwise noted.

LAND TENURE / COMMUNITY GOVERNANCE

TAULI–CORPUZ ON INDIGENOUS PEOPLES' RIGHT TO REMAIN SEPARATE AND DISTINCT

Photo courtesy of IISD/Earth Negotiations Bulletin

I spent my childhood in my ancestral hometown of Besao, among the Igorot peoples of the Philippines. It was a world barely touched by industrialism. There was no electricity; the only motor vehicles we saw were the two buses that arrived in the late afternoon from the only city in our region. We raised our own food—rice, vegetables, taro, chickens, and pigs.

Igorots possess a highly sophisticated knowledge of agriculture. Many communities produce ten or more traditional rice varieties and our rice terraces, found high up in the mountains, feature complex irrigation systems, testifying to Igorot expertise in hydraulics and engineering.

Wet rice production for domestic use still remains the main preoccupation of most Igorots who live in traditional villages. The agricultural cycle revolves around the phases of rice production, from seedbed preparation to harvesting. During planting and harvesting, we practiced *ug-ugbo,* a traditional form of mutual labor exchange.

The more I see the decline of Western civilization and the role science and technology play in the decline, the more I am convinced that the wisdom and knowledge of indigenous peoples can help lead humanity forward. The continuing survival of humanity will largely depend on how diverse cultural and biological systems coexist and flourish.

For indigenous peoples, keeping our territorial or ancestral lands is the most important thing. This is what determines our identity. This is where our ancestors walked and where they learned everything they left to us. Our land is where we forge our relations with Mother Earth and create social bonds with each other. It is no wonder, then, that rapidly increasing so-called ethnic conflicts in the world are really pitting indigenous peoples, asserting our rights over our territories, against the global institutions that want to *separate* us from our land. Globalization policies and activities play a huge part in inflaming these conflicts by erasing borders and erasing identities that are inextricably linked to our rights as indigenous peoples.

Indigenous peoples are being pressured to permit conversion of our economic systems into the capitalist framework of high production and profitability, which are not primary values that we share. If we go along, it means losing control over our

Photo: Craig Mackintosh

territories, knowledge, and resources. Why should we allow foreign or national mining corporations to lease our lands for seventy-five years when we know fully well that what will be left for us will be polluted and devastated lands and the disappearance of waters? Why should we be forced to share our knowledge of seeds, medicinal plants, and resource management with corporations who claim ownership, simply because they can wave a patent in our faces? What will the world gain if our diverse and sustainable ways of living are destroyed so we can fit into the cogs and wheels of the globalized capitalist world?

Six Crucial Steps Forward

Our ancestors told us that land is sacred, that animals and plants are our relatives, and that it is our duty to ensure that they are defended for the next generations. Our resistance to these efforts to homogenize us must be supported—our right to self-determination and our right to be allowed to remain different and diverse. Legal instruments that conflict with our indigenous values, cosmologies, lifestyles, and customary laws should not be imposed on us from any outside body. These are not decisions for the World Trade Organization or the International Monetary Fund or the World Bank. We fight for the right to defend ourselves and to maintain our continued existence as indigenous peoples on our own ancestral lands.

What are the challenges and strategies we should pursue to ensure that our indigenous ways of thinking and doing will not be obliterated? What policy recommendations are being proposed? Here are six important standards and policies we should push for:

First, it should be recognized that our role in promoting truly sustainable development lies in our ability to continue practicing our indigenous systems of production. We demand that governments and financial institutions allow our economic, cultural, and sociopolitical systems to coexist with other systems. They should not force us to be assimilated into the mainstream if it means the destruction of our diverse worldviews, diverse ways of producing and consuming, diverse cultures, and diverse governance systems.

Second, it is urgent that the roots of the unrest in indigenous people's territories be addressed by governments and the international community. Threats to the existence of indigenous peoples are very serious, especially those whose populations have been reduced to the mere hundreds (the U'wa in Colombia, the Batwa in Burundi and Rwanda, the Shor peoples in Siberia, among others). If the United Nations is not able to play its role in building peace, other mechanisms should be built to address conflict situations.

Third, institutions that claim that they are promoting sustainable development should be informed about what indigenous people want. There is a need to sensitize those involved in development and environmental work on indigenous people's vision and practices.

Fourth, case studies, reviews, and assessments of how mainstream development has destroyed or distorted indigenous models of sustainable development should be undertaken. If such were done, the results could be widely disseminated. Assessments of policy guidelines on indigenous peoples made by the World Bank, other regional banks, United Nations bodies, the European Union, and others, both in terms of substance and how those could be implemented, should also be undertaken. There have been initial efforts made in this direction, but they do not ensure the direct participation of indigenous peoples themselves and are in need of expansion.

Fifth, efforts should be expanded to ensure that our issues and concerns be addressed in a holistic manner. We have recently had some successes on this point in international agencies. For example, for many years we urged the United Nations to set up a Permanent Forum on Indigenous Peoples, because we were frustrated that our issues were always being addressed in a fragmented manner. It was unworkable. We were tired of being told that we could discuss our rights as peoples only in the Commission on Human Rights. We were forced to present our attempts at preserving our peoples and nations in reductionist arguments about environment or biodiversity. We sought a mechanism within the United Nations that would be at a higher level within the hierarchy, thus allowing us to address the environment, economic and social development, health, culture, and human rights as one comprehensive issue, consistent with our own views. Finally, the United Nations agreed to establish the Permanent Forum on Indigenous Peoples, with indigenous peoples sitting as equal partners in all discussions.

Sixth, the assertion of indigenous peoples of our right to self-determination and our rights to "free, prior, and informed consent" to all development plans affecting us should be recognized and promoted, not only by the governments and the United Nations, but also by society at large.

Indigenous peoples have come a long way in asserting our identities and rights. However, there is still much to be done. There are still indigenous peoples in many parts of the world who are in danger of extinction. This would mean the loss of the diverse knowledge and cultures that they embody. Actions from civil society are as crucial as those from governments and international institutions. Indigenous peoples have shown, time and again, the viability and sustainability of their economic, sociocultural, political, and knowledge systems. Whatever is lost is a loss for the entire world, not for indigenous peoples alone.

Green School

Ubud, Bali, Indonesia

The emerald green Ayung River valley outside of Ubud, Bali, seems an appropriate home for Green School, the world's first school designed and built explicitly on permaculture principles. Open-air bamboo classrooms are surrounded by organic gardens, rice paddies, and fruit trees, and the curriculum is geared toward preparing children to be leaders of a sustainable future.

The school's founders, John and Cynthia Hardy, have lived in Bali for over twenty-five years, and their commitment to the environment began with the business they started in the 1980s, John Hardy Jewelry. The company, focusing on traditional Balinese techniques, incorporates a number of green practices and programs, and today the brand is sold internationally at major stores. In 2006, the Hardys decided to use some of the returns they had made on their enterprise to give back to Bali and develop a school guided by ecological values.

CULTURE/EDUCATION

Connecting to the Natural World: With about 120 students from preschool through grade eight, the Green School aims to provide an education that wraps the traditional academic disciplines in a rich layer of experiential, environmental, and eco-entrepreneurial learning "We have an academic curriculum to make sure kids get the 'nuts and bolts,' but it's wrapped in a green studies program that gives the students the chance to plant gardens, build structures, and make solar ovens," says Ben Macrory, head of communications at the school.

And while traditional subjects like math, language arts, social studies, science, and the arts still remain the focus, the school also offers courses in eco-entrepreneurial subjects, such as chocolate production, organic farming, and new methods of sustainable building with bamboo. Eighty percent of the students are international; 20 percent are local Balinese children and attend for free. A major goal of the school is to create a truly integrated international school, one that models cross-cultural cooperation and sharing. "In many private international schools, they dress up once a year in traditional garb, but the only local kids who can attend are from the elite, and there are big walls," Macrory observes. "We really wanted to break that model, so we have a good security team but no walls, and the local communities have full access to the campus. It seems to be working well."

LAND/NATURE STEWARDSHIP

Biointensive Techniques: The site showcases biointensive growing methods, with soil-preparation practices that create growing beds with more surface area to maximize the effect of nature's life

"KIDS HERE GET TO STEP OUTSIDE THE CLASSROOM AND APPLY THEORY TO PRACTICE, CONNECTING TO THE NATURAL WORLD AND CREATING AUTHENTIC MOTIVATIONS FOR LEARNING."
—BEN MACRORY, HEAD OF COMMUNICATIONS

processes. Double-dug beds, with soil loosened to a depth of 24 inches (61 centimeters), aerate the soil, facilitate root growth, and improve water retention. They use compost to maintain the health and vigor of the soil. Biointensive techniques for growing food in small spaces fit into the permaculture design framework but include specific techniques developed by John Jeavons, an American author, researcher, and teacher of these methods.

Biointensive methods encourage closely spacing plants to protect soil microorganisms, reduce water loss, and maximize yields. Companion planting facilitates the optimal use of nutrients, light, and water, encourages beneficial insects, and creates a vibrant mini-ecosystem within the garden. The use of open-pollinated seeds helps to preserve genetic diversity and enables gardeners to develop their own acclimatized cultivars. All of the components of this system must be used together for optimum effect and to avoid depleting the soil.

BUILDING

Taking Bamboo to a New Level: The twenty-five structures of the Green School include eight standalone classrooms, offices, the "Heart of School," a gym, a coliseum, and a green-studies house. All are built primarily from local, natural, and renewable materials, primarily bamboo. All are open air and designed to allow for natural light and ventilation. The Hardys had a lofty vision for the physical environment of the school, which they wanted to soar and inspire, but with a minimal environmental impact. PT Bambu, the company they founded to design, build, and furnish the school, is located across the street. They set up a community bamboo program, which distributed fifty thousand seedlings to the local community free of charge and will buy back the mature bamboo after four years.

There is a basic composting toilet system, with two toilets in every bathroom—one for liquids, one for solids. The liquids go into the ground through a gray-water cycle, adding nitrates to the soil. Solids go into a bucket and is composted in a separate system.

TOOLS/TECHNOLOGY

Redundant Energy Systems: Energy to power the school comes from photovoltaic panels, supplemented by the grid. They are also developing a micro-hydropower system using vortex technology. The river on-site has sufficient volume, but not a lot of vertical head, so instead of building a dam, the Green School constructed a 81-foot (25-meter) tunnel that diverts river water into a large stone cylinder. Gravity and centrifugal force creates a very strong whirlpool—a vortex—that spins a turbine to create power.

Reporting contributed by Juliana Birnbaum. Photos courtesy of the Green School.

THESE ANCIENT HAWAIIAN IRRIGATION SYSTEMS, RESPECTFULLY BORROWED WATER, DIVERTED IT THROUGH A CASCADING PATTERN OF KALO (TARO) PONDS, AND ULTIMATELY RETURNED THE WATER TO ITS ORIGINAL STREAM WHERE IT COULD FINISH ITS JOURNEY TO THE SEA.

Ka'ala and Hoa'Aina

Wai'anae, Oahu, Hawaii, U.S.A.

These two centers, founded in the late 1970s, are located close to each other in Wai'anae on the Hawaiian island of Oahu and are intertwined in their goals and origins. Both serve a large number of local indigenous youth, revitalizing the students' relationship to their native culture and its sustainable practices. Ka'ala Farm, located on 97 acres (39 hectares), receives over four thousand visitors a year, mainly school children. It aims to "reclaim and preserve the living culture of the *Po'e Kahiko* (people of old) in order to strengthen the kinship relationships between the land and all forms of life, necessary to sustain the ecological balance on these vulnerable islands." Hoa'Aina is a spiritually based community program rooted in a strong relationship to the land and a dedication to establishing peace through education, equitable economic development, and social justice.

The Wai'anae area of Oahu has one of the largest native populations in the Hawaiian archipelago and was once a thriving, self-sufficient community—the "*poi* bowl," or breadbasket, of the region. Today it's nearly impossible to find any food that's locally grown, and poverty and health problems are rampant.

HAO'AINA'S FOUNDER, GIGI COCQUIO, SUBSCRIBES TO AN OLD HAWAIIAN PROVERB THAT REFLECTS THE WISDOM OF THE PRINCIPLE **INTEGRATE RATHER THAN SEGREGATE**: "A'OHE HANA NUI KE ALU 'IA" (NO TASK IS TOO BIG WHEN DONE TOGETHER BY ALL).

As both Kina Mahi, an organizer at the Ka'ala Center, and Gigi Cocquio, the founder of Hoa'Aina, pointed out, in traditional Hawaiian society, arrivals were always marked with a welcoming chant. When one arrived at a place, one would honor it by offering a chant that described and celebrated its natural features. Both programs incorporate this practice into their work with young people. "We have the kids sing to us, when they arrive, about their *ahupua'a,*" Mahi says. "The *ahupua'a* is the name for an area, like a micro-ecoregion—it could be a watershed or a community sharing resources."

Ka'ala teaches traditional canoe and home construction skills and has restored precontact *kalo* (taro root) pondfields. Founder Eric Enos sees this as a revolutionary act, essential to the survival of his people, since according to the *Kumulipo,* the creation chant, *kalo* is the elder brother of the Hawaiian people.

When Ka'ala's founders discovered ancient rock walls on the site, they went to local archives and saw a 1906 map that showed the area had been used for *kalo* cultivation. The organization has taken on the Board of Water Supply to ensure that their stream can continue to run, arguing that the stream itself has an inherent right to exist, as an ancestor.

"The idea was to move back to these uses that once were able to provide food to our community," Mahi explains. "There used to be five streams that came down from this mountain. The sugar industry took the water first, then a lot was diverted to pineapples. Now, they're planting housing and shopping malls, and the streams do not reach the sea because of the development."

Gigi Cocquio came to Oahu from Italy as a priest and founded Hoa'Aina in 1979 on a piece of church property next to an elementary school. Most of the buildings on the site have been built over the years by the children. "We'll never be able to tear them down because of all the nails," Cocquio jokes.

Today, six hundred students learn how to take care of the land. They plant fields of corn, beans, lettuce, green onions, *wonbok,* bok choy, peanuts, taro, and culinary and medicinal herbs. They learn how native Hawaiians have used different plants and trees for specific purposes. The children harvest what they have planted and when they take the vegetables home, they learn about how to cook and enjoy them. "That, to me, is organic," says Cocquio.

Reporting contributed by Juliana Birnbaum. Photos by Louis Fox.

La'akea Permaculture Community

Pahoa, Puna, Big Island, Hawaii, U.S.A.

LA'AKEA'S TWO GREENHOUSES PROVIDE OVER HALF OF THE COMMUNITY'S FOOD. **OBTAIN A YIELD** IS AN ESSENTIAL PERMACULTURE PRINCIPLE—ONE SO OBVIOUS THAT IT CAN BE FORGOTTEN. THE DESIGNER'S SYSTEM MUST RETURN TRULY USEFUL REWARDS TO HELP SUSTAIN THE DESIGNER. IT'S PART OF "CLOSING THE LOOP"—YOU CAN'T WORK ON AN EMPTY STOMACH.

La'akea was founded in 2005 on 23 acres (9 hectares) that had already been a permaculture demonstration center, giving the founders a good head start on creating a more self-reliant food system, one of their major goals. The community is 4 miles south of Pahoa, Hawaii, on the humid, eastern edge of the Big Island, in the Puna region, where permaculture design is being implemented through a web of initiatives, including ecovillages, retreat sanctuaries, and schools.

The residents include teachers, administrators, gardeners, carpenters, healers, and counselors, who collectively own the land. "We embrace sustainability in our relationships and in our interactions with the Earth, and attempt to produce most of our food on the land," writes founding member Dona Willoughby in *Communities*.[13] Willoughby resides at La'akea along with her daughter, Aniko, and grandson, Kai'ea.

The farm faces south to maximize solar exposure, and the irrigation system works with the contours of the land. They designed the irrigation system also to be a simple, working with the natural topography of the land and the laws of physics. Strategically placed catchment tanks collect rainwater, and gravity pulls the water through pipes to wherever it is needed.

The water supplies the farm's two greenhouses, spilling over with vegetables and greens arranged around keyhole-shaped paths, a classic permaculture design which maximizes available growing space and allows access to the plants.

THE COMMUNITY PLACES A SPECIAL EMPHASIS ON SUSTAINABLE RELATIONSHIPS BETWEEN MEMBERS, PRACTICING NONVIOLENT COMMUNICATION, A TECHNIQUE DEVELOPED BY PSYCHOLOGIST MARSHALL ROSENBERG TO HELP GROUPS RESOLVE CONFLICTS PEACEFULLY.

Animals incorporated into the agriculture system at La'akea have included chickens, geese, wild pigs, and sheep. Beyond the zone 1 gardens and greenhouses, the landscape has the appearance of a naturally evolved woodland ecosystem, though it is actually the result of intelligent planning—permaculture-style. "Figs, mango, peach palm, *awa,* jackfruit, *longen, callandria,* and a multitude of other flora appear to dot the landscape in nature's usual whimsical fashion, yet most were thoughtfully chosen and placed together to form balanced symbiotic units," reads an article about the former La'akea Permaculture Gardens in the local journal *Ka'u Landing.* "This method is referred to in permaculture as 'stacking.' Stacking is another way that farming takes its cue from nature, where plants with beneficial relationships to one another with often grow together in a community."[14]

La'akea has ties to the Network for New Culture, which focuses on healthy community relationships through emotional communication (rooted in the ZEGG and Tamera Ecovillages in Europe—for more on this, see p. 219.). At one point the ecovillage experienced a steep learning curve in this regard, when one of the founding members decided to leave, based on irreconcilable differences with the others.

Over half the food consumed at La'akea comes from the land. Biko, a founding member, explains, "It's harder to get people to change their eating habits than to grow food. There are hundreds of kinds of edible plants here. We recently did a month of eating exclusively Hawaiian food, mostly from the land, and adapted to what is here."

The ecovillages hosts permaculture courses and long-term internships. "We make important, long term decisions (capital improvements, new members, changes to existing agreements) by consensus of community members. We delegate more detail-oriented decisions to individuals or small committees. We value personal empowerment, trust, and accountability in our decision-making process. A key concept of consensus is that members know and communicate their individual truth and desires, while holding the well-being of the community above their personal preferences," Willoughby says.

Reporting contributed by Juliana Birnbaum. Photos by Louis Fox.

CULTURE / EDUCATION

STARHAWK ON SOCIAL PERMACULTURE

Photo: Bert Meijer

Patrick Whitefield calls permaculture "the art of designing beneficial relationships." Most permaculturists are expert at understanding the relationships between landforms and water harvesting or between soil microorganisms and plant health. But when it comes to our human relationships, we often founder. Nurturing the vegetables in the garden is a lot easier than nurturing our connections to the people who decide where to plant the vegetables and who will water them. Meeting the needs of chickens or goats is far easier than meeting the needs of your fellow farmers. Many permaculture groups, like many intentional communities, start up with the highest ideals, only to come apart in painful discord and strife.

Diana Leafe Christian, who studied successful ecovillages and intentional communities, found that "no matter how visionary and inspired the founders, only about one out of ten new communities actually get built. The other ninety percent seemed to go nowhere, occasionally because of lack of money or not finding the right land, but most often because of conflict."[15]

Our human relationships are our biggest constraining factor in the work of transforming society. So is there a way to do them better?

I've been working in collaborative and collective groups of many sorts for more than four decades now, and this question has always been in the forefront of my mind. I've been through many painful learning experiences of my own and have observed many groups struggle with conflict. I've founded one organization, Reclaiming, an extended network focused on earth-based spirituality, that is now more than thirty years old. I've worked in hundreds of other groups and facilitated thousands of meetings. I teach permaculture courses called Earth Activist Trainings, which include group dynamics and decision making along with a grounding in spirit and a focus on organizing. Over the last few years I've taught a number of social permaculture courses, several in collaboration with Bill Aal and the late Margo Adair of Tools for Change. I've compiled much of my own learning into a book: ***The Empowerment Manual: A Guide for Collaborative Groups.***

My practice of permaculture informs my approach to group social design and conflict, and my understanding of group dynamics informs my practice of permaculture. Permaculture principles can be translated into guidelines and approaches that will help us to work together more effectively and joyfully, as we strive to change the world. Here are a few of my Social Permaculture Principles:

1. Abundance springs from relationships:

True abundance, whether measured in garden produce or ecstatic experiences, has little to do with how much stuff we have but rather how rich we are in relationships. So—cherish your relationships. Value them. Give them time and attention. Nurture and maintain them. When conflict arises, don't simply discard people, but learn the skills and tools to work things through. Nurture your relationship to yourself and spirit as well. As you face your own shadows and develop your strengths, your relationships with others will be enriched and deepened.

2. Recognize and work with patterns:

Permaculture teaches us to look for patterns in nature and apply that knowledge to our designs. We can also look for social patterns. Hierarchy is a pattern we're all familiar with, but when we try to work collaboratively, outside of a command and control structure, we encounter different challenges. Recognizing them can help us structure our groups more effectively. Collaborative structures differ from hierarchies in many ways:

Communication is more complex: In a hierarchy, we generally know to whom we report and where we are on the chain of command. A collaborative group, however, is more like a web, with many possible pathways for any message to follow to get from person A to person B. People get left out of the loop, often unintentionally, because the loop becomes a knot or a snarl. In a well-run top-down structure, we know who is responsible for carrying out decisions. In a circular structure, we may make a decision, but each person in the circle may assume someone else is going to carry it out.

So, pay rigorous attention to communication. Whenever a decision is made, ask, "Who else needs to know about this?" "Who will inform them?" "How will the rest of us know this is done?" When a plan is made, ask "Who will be responsible for making sure this is carried out?" Doing so can forestall much conflict and hurt feelings.

Mom isn't there to make the kids behave: In a hierarchy, generally someone at the top can say, "Okay, you two stop fighting and make up." In a collaborative group, there's no mom, no dad, but we carry over our family patterns and expect that someone, somehow, can step in and sort things out for us. When they don't, groups often fall apart, because they have no way to move conflict out of the system or resolve it.

Build in conflict-resolution systems, mediation, and clear agreements. Develop skills in conflict transformation, and devote group time and resources to training in communication and mediation. Conflict will always arise in groups. Just as you put an overflow valve on a pond to handle the hundred-year storm, be sure to design an "overflow" for group conflict so that it doesn't erode trust and enthusiasm or burst the dam and flood the production fields.

3. Feed what you want to grow:

Industrial agriculture works on the principle: "Kill the pests!" If bugs attack a field, nuke them with chemicals! Organic farmers know that attacking pests with powerful toxins only breeds resistance. Instead, we create healthy soil that provides what our plants need to repel pests. We plant flowers that attract beneficial insects that keep the chompers in check. We look at insect damage as information—it tells us something is out of balance.

Photo: Nigel Dickinson

In our social relations, too often we revert to "Kill the pests!" Instead of attacking the people whose behavior offends us or trying to drive them out of the group, we can look at conflict as information. Something in the group is out of balance. Somehow we've created a habitat that allows destructive behavior to thrive. How do we give a competitive edge to the behaviors that we want?

We can clear the air by creating a group culture of direct engagement. When we learn to embrace conflict, to openly argue for our ideas or values without resorting to personal attack, we create an atmosphere that discourages malicious gossip and scapegoating and encourages respect.

4. Value diversity:

In nature, diversity gives an ecosystem resilience. In groups, a diversity of opinion, ages, ethnic and class backgrounds, and experiences can broaden our perspective and let us see multiple facets of an issue. If we want a diverse group, we must make the extra effort to bring people in who represent that diversity and to do it in a meaningful way, not as tokens—early in our process, so that a wide range of people help form the group and participate in the creative aspects of the project. We can build alliances with diverse communities not just by inviting them to support our work but by sharing information and resources, educating ourselves about their history and current struggles, and showing up in support of their issues.

5. Develop respect, kindness, and trust:

Trust is built in many ways: by creating opportunities to share something of our lives and feelings, by encouraging people to argue passionately for their ideas and positions while still respecting their opponents' right to differ, by meeting responsibilities and building a track record of dependability, and by sharing risks together.

Kindness, respect, compassion, and encouragement are the compost tea of relationships—they feed all the beneficial impulses. When we respect one another's ideas, think well of one another's motives, and support one another's visions, we create a high-energy atmosphere in which creativity is able to flourish.

These five principles are merely a sketch of how we might begin to look at our human groups as ecologies. Social permaculture is an emerging discipline, and the study of human behavior, in groups and outside of them, is a lifelong pursuit. But as we become more skillful at nurturing our human relations, we will become more effective in every aspect of our work. At this crucial time for the earth, we need the power of creative, effective, loving, and joyful groups to move us forward. When we can be as skillful in our human interactions as we are in our garden designs, we'll become an invincible force of healing for our communities and our earth.

Starhawk. Excerpted with permission from "Social Permaculture," Communities Magazine, Winter 2011

PART 03

Arid Climates: Desert and Steppe Zones

The Köppen system defines arid climates as those in which annual precipitation is less than evaporation and there are no permanent rivers. Arid and semiarid climates are classified with the first letter B on the Köppen climate map (see p. 22). Desert ecosystems are characterized by low rainfall—on average less than 10 inches (25 centimeters) annually.

Hot deserts are often located on the west coast of continents, between twenty and thirty degrees latitude. Some of the world's driest deserts are right on the coast, including Baja California in North America, the western Sahara in northern Africa, the Atacama in South America, and the Namib in southern Africa.

The semiarid steppe climate, also called a "cold desert," is found in the middle of continents and in the "rain shadow" of high mountains—places where mountains block moist air from oceans or tropical climates from reaching the steppe, leaving not enough precipitation for trees to grow, except by rivers. Plants adapt to these drought conditions by staying small and growing extensive root systems. Animals often burrow into the ground to stay cool or warm and to find protection on the open plains of the steppe.

The temperature varies greatly between summer and winter in this climate zone. Summer temperatures on the steppe aren't much different from the tropical savanna, but in the winter, there are no clouds to keep heat from escaping into the upper atmosphere, and the land gets colder and colder. Winter temperatures that dip to 40°F (40°C) below freezing are not uncommon.

The mean annual temperatures and precipitation determine the difference between steppes and dry deserts. With a bit less rain, the steppe could become an arid desert; more rain, and it would be classified a prairie. Deserts currently cover about one-fifth of the earth's land surface, but climate change is causing increased desertification across the globe.

Photo: Erika Rand

Dead Sea Valley Permaculture Project

Al Jawfa Region, Jordan

LOCAL CHILDREN ENJOY A LITTLE SHADE. PERHAPS IN THEIR LIFETIMES THEY WILL SEE THE FERTILE CRESCENT BECOME GREEN ONCE AGAIN.

The Permaculture Research Institute (PRI) has tackled two demonstration sites in Jordan's Dead Sea Valley—the lowest place on earth, as well as one of the hottest and driest, with temperatures up to 122°F (50°C) in the summer. While this was once part of the Fertile Crescent, deforestation, rapid urbanization, soil erosion, inappropriate land use and cultivation practices, climate change, and drought have all contributed to increasing desertification.[1]

Geoff Lawton—a student of Bill Mollison—and his wife, Jordanian-born Nadia Abu Yahia Lawton, lead the Dead Sea Valley Permaculture Project (for more on PRI and Mollison, see p. 160). They first reported the results in 2009 in an internet video called "Greening the Desert," showing the transformation that occurred within a few short years on 10 acres (4 hectares) of arid land when a system of rain-harvesting swales

THOUGH MUCH SMALLER THAN THE ORIGINAL GREENING THE DESERT SITE, THE "SEQUEL" SITE ENJOYS A MORE PRACTICAL LOCATION IN TOWN. IT IS A TEACHING/DEMONSTRATION CENTER, AND ITS LOCATION DEMONSTRATES THE LOGIC OF THE PERMACULTURE ZONE SYSTEM: ONE CHOOSES A DESIGN ELEMENT'S PLACEMENT BY CONSIDERING THE OPTIMAL PROXIMITY TO THOSE WHO WILL BE INTERACTING WITH IT.

were developed. The video went viral and has inspired many with the potential it shows for permaculture techniques to reverse desertification.

For another site, affectionately known as the "sequel," which is less than 1 acre (0.4 hectare), the Lawtons determined to work within the boundaries of a village, where locals could closely monitor the site's successes, and this time they are working toward financial sustainability. Though the original site lost funding for its maintenance, its design continues to allow the regeneration of the soil, plants, and wildlife there. The agricultural department at the national university has studied the site, which could potentially result in a wider application of its techniques.

The Tenth International Permaculture Conference (IPC10) in Amman, Jordan, shared situation-appropriate solutions to Jordan's low rainfall and ultrahigh evaporation rate and the Dead Sea Valley projects are PRI Jordan's practical attempt to apply them. If sites across the region were to implement permaculture revitalization techniques in concert, the net improvement in soil rehydration and the resulting restoration of regional rainfall patterns could be immense.

The Fertile Crescent refers to an ancient area of rich soil and major rivers stretching in an arc from the Nile to the Tigris and Euphrates. It stretched through Israel, Lebanon, Jordan, Syria, and Iraq. In 2001 images from NASA satellites showed scientists at the U.N. Environment Program (UNEP) showed that the formerly marshy region had almost completely dried up, leaving only a small fringe on the Iraq-Iran border. The researchers concluded that the damage was a result of extensive damming and heavy draining of the river basin in the previous two decades. An indigenous group known as Marsh Arabs—who trace their culture to ancient Sumerians and Babylonians—continue to be displaced by the loss of the marshlands. Coastal fisheries in the northern Persian Gulf, which depend on the marshlands for spawning grounds, have experienced a sharp decline, as have the populations of mammals and migratory birds in the region. The Tigris and the Euphrates are among the most intensively dammed rivers in the world, fragmented by more than thirty large dams, whose combined storage capacity is several times greater than the volume of both rivers.

THE MANURE FROM RABBITS, DUCKS, AND PIGEONS SHOULD HELP THE SITE DEVELOP MORE RAPIDLY.

NOW THAT THE PROJECT HAS THE BEGINNINGS OF A SHADE-PROVIDING OVERSTORY, THEY HAVE INTRODUCED ANIMAL SYSTEMS. PIGEONS ARE A KEYSTONE SPECIES FOR FERTILE DESERT SYSTEMS.

The dams have substantially reduced the water available to downstream ecosystems and eliminated the floodwaters that once nourished the marshlands. Even the last patch of the once vast marshlands is at risk, scientists warn, as its water supply is impounded by new dams and diverted for irrigation. To save the remaining marsh, the UNEP called for action to reassess the role of the area's water engineering works and modify them as necessary.[2]

"Ancient irrigation systems have collapsed, underground water sources have run dry and hundreds of villages have been abandoned as farmlands turn to cracked desert and grazing animals die off. Sandstorms have become far more common, and vast tent cities of dispossessed farmers and their families have risen up around the larger towns and cities of Syria and Iraq," reported the *New York Times* in 2010.[3]

The collapse of farmlands in the region, exacerbated by several years of drought, has become a dire economic challenge and a rising security concern for the governments of the once-fertile crescent.

LAND/NATURE STEWARDSHIP

Catching Every Drop of Rainwater: Geoff Lawton describes the beginning of the project in his "Greening the Desert" video. "This is as hard as it gets! This is hyper-arid . . . almost dead flat, completely salted landscape . . . the lowest place on earth, a few kilometers from the Dead Sea. . . . We've hardly got any rainfall, we've got temperatures in August that go over [122°F (50°C)]. Everybody's farming under plastic strips; everybody's spray, spray, spray; everybody's putting synthetic fertilizer on, overgrazing goats, just like maggots eating the flesh off the bones of the country. . . . So we designed up a system that would catch every drop of rainwater that fell on it."

At the heart of the design is a swale system of water channels that allow millions of gallons of water to be caught during the winter months and to soak back into the earth, creating an underground reservoir for the hot summer months. After collecting excess and scrapped organic matter from neighboring farms, the team was able to mulch the site, and they installed a micro-irrigation system and planted nitrogen-fixing tree species. The trees help rehabilitate the soil, prevent excess evaporation from the wind, and provide shade for successor species. Within four months of planting at the first "Greening the Desert" location, fig trees were over three feet high and already bearing fruit. They planted other species to create a food forest, including date palm, pomegranate, guava, mulberry, and citrus.

The smaller, newer Dead Sea Valley site—the "sequel"—was mainly rock, which they collected to create a terraced mainframe design for better water retention. The next stage was to create an environment in which edible plants could survive, which necessitated planting hardy desert pioneers that could multitask. Some were leguminous and nitrogen fixing. These amazing plants love being planted into dead soils, where they do everything they can to make themselves redundant. They contribute to a process of soil regeneration that ultimately leads to their giving way to other plants. They turn lifeless minerals below the ground into mulchable, compostable material that can nurture the soil and its biological processes back into life. Unlike soil depletion, however, this regeneration cannot happen overnight. It takes time, patience, and experimentation. Hastening the process takes human ingenuity and energy—the former needing to harmonize with the laws of nature in order to make wise use of the latter.

CULTURE/EDUCATION

Educating the Agriculture Experts: The project held the first permaculture design course in October 2009 and by the following year, it had hosted programs in site management and teacher training for local instructors, with mentorship from the original Permaculture Research Institute in Australia. This has led to the establishment of a Jordan branch of the institute, helping to ensure that the knowledge and benefits of permaculture are being disseminated to the local communities.

Bringing together local and international students, the project offers educational courses and practical demonstrations on energy-efficient, culturally appropriate housing with natural cooling systems; solar hot water; biological wastewater-treatment systems; and diverse, interactive systems of plants, animals, and trees for local food production and processing.

The project has become of interest to the agriculture department of the national university, and studies have been done that show the salinity of the soil has dramatically dropped. "The soil has come alive, and the fungi net that's underneath the mulch is putting off a waxy substance that is repelling the salt away from the area," Lawton explains. "The decomposition is locking the salt up, and [while] the salt is not gone, it's become inert and insoluble. So we could re-green the Middle East; we could re-green any desert. And we could de-salt it at the same time."

Reporting and photos contributed by Craig Mackintosh.

Kibbutz Lotan Community

Arava Valley, Israel

MIKE KAPLIN HELPED TO FOUND LOTAN'S CENTER FOR CREATIVE ECOLOGY, WHICH OFFERS A "GREEN APPRENTICESHIP" PROGRAM THAT TEACHES PERMACULTURE, NATURAL BUILDING, AND SUSTAINABLE TECHNOLOGIES.

The Arava Desert—*arava* (or *arabah*) means "dry, desolate" in Hebrew—is a sparsely populated, arid landscape, part of the larger Jordan Rift Valley (the same broader region that the Dead Sea Valley Permaculture Project is in, but on the other side of the border). It extends to the Dead Sea and covers most of the border between Israel and Jordan.

Israel is home to hundreds of *kibbutzim,* collective settlements that are part of a broad movement bringing together elements of socialism and Zionism. Today, some of these communities have gone beyond social innovation and have integrated principles of environmental sustainability into their vision. Kibbutz Lotan is one of the best-known "Green Kibbutzim." The Arava is not an easy region to make sustainable, with extreme climactic and soil conditions that make farming a challenge. Lotan's Center for Creative

Ecology has become a leader in the environmental movement in Israel, focusing on recycling, green-construction techniques, and permaculture.

Established in 1983, Lotan is home to approximately sixty adults, from at least nine different countries, and sixty children, all living on 143 acres (57 hectares). These kibbutzniks are striving for a modern interpretation of the Jewish concept of *tikkun olam*—repairing and transforming the world—through ecological design strategies.

Historically, kibbutzim have mainly been based on agriculture, but this is starting to change. Some are gaining popularity in the twenty-first century by shifting from their ideological and agricultural roots toward industry, tourism, environmentalism, and varying degrees of privatization. The move toward privatization came out of a debt crisis in the 1980s, which nearly wiped out many kibbutzim, and around the year 2000 over half were in financial trouble. Today that number is down to about 5 percent, and with their reputation for a high quality of life, more young people are choosing to stay on the kibbutz, and newcomers from the city are eager to move in. Today, Israel's 270 kibbutzim have a population of over 120,000.

Lotan, formed by a mix of American immigrants and native Israelis affiliated with Israel's arm of the Reform movement, considered privatization after the debt crisis, but has remained a cooperative kibbutz. It is one of a number of groups in the Arava Valley that identify ecological sustainability as core to their purpose. One of these, Neot Smadar, is known for its artistic focus; another, Samar, is home to the SunEnergy project, whose photovoltaic panels power the community and feed energy back to the grid. Another of Lotan's neighbors, Kibbutz Ketura, is powered by the first photovoltaic field (5 megawatts) in Israel and is home to the Arava Institute for Environmental Studies.

BUILDING

The Eco-Campus: The desert environment has lent itself to a focus on alternative building techniques, and Lotan is gaining a reputation as a

LOTAN'S CENTER FOR CREATIVE ECOLOGY FEATURES AN ECO-CAMPUS COMPOSED OF TEN "DOME-ATORIES," MADE OF STRAW BALES AND EARTHEN PLASTER, BUILT ON GEODESIC FRAMES BY PAST COURSE PARTICIPANTS AND ECO-VOLUNTEERS.

THE ARAVA DESERT IS NOT AN EASY PLACE TO BE "GREEN," YET KIBBUTZ LOTAN STRIVES TO INTEGRATE THE PRINCIPLES OF REGENERATIVE DESIGN IN ITS COMMUNAL AND ECONOMIC ENDEAVORS.

USE AND VALUE DIVERSITY—LOTAN'S CROSS-CULTURAL NATURAL BUILDING COURSES BRING TOGETHER ADOLESCENT ISRAELI JEWS AND ARABS. THEY ARE AS MUCH ABOUT BUILDING PEACE AS BUILDING SHELTER.

leader in earth-construction research and practice. The Center for Creative Ecology features an Eco-Campus that includes solar ovens and hot-water collectors, photovoltaic panels, waterless sanitation systems, gray-water treatment, vermicomposting, and LED pathway lighting. In cold months, the buildings are passively heated by sunlight entering the southern windows—the heat is stored in the walls and floors and heats the rooms at night, with no need for additional mechanical heating. Selective window placement for ventilation cools the buildings in the evenings during the hot seasons.

"The mud bricks are the way our forefathers and mothers built in Egypt—and this is our take on what was written in the Bible," says Dr. Michael Livni, a kibbutz member and ecological activist. Research at the center has focused on building sustainably in the desert with straw and mud, and on finding the ideal recipes for various construction methods through combining local, natural materials (see inset below on earth-based architecture).

"We have sand here, so we need the clay, which we are reusing from a byproduct of well drilling in the area," Livni explains. "Other groups bring their earth from different parts of Israel, and we teach them how to analyze it in order to enable them to know how much sand, straw, or clay needs to be added to make earth plaster in their locality."

TOOLS/TECHNOLOGY

Creative Recycling: The kibbutz separates food scraps from other forms of waste to make compost. It sorts other forms of recyclable materials (paper, cardboard, glass, plastic bottles, containers) at its collection center—built with the help of Israel's Ministry for the Environment—for processing at Lotan's Center for Creative Ecology. Many of the recyclables find their way into alternative building projects.

FINANCES/ECONOMICS

Collective Responsibility: Lotan's truly cooperative economy allows for members to contribute differing amounts of money to the community—based on their salary—but all benefit equally from kibbutz living, which provides for most of their needs. They consider themselves collectively responsible for their livelihoods and share resources, as an expression of their "belief in communal action."[4] The kibbutz as a whole receives income mostly from its dairy sales (the only local source in the region), its date groves, and its ecotourism program, which includes workshops in organic gardening and renewable energy. Other tourist-related income areas are a bird-watching center, a guesthouse, and an ecological park.

"The traditional model of kibbutz still suits us," reports kibbutz member Daphna Abel. "We find lots of positive things from being a cooperative community. It is something that helps us invest in our social relations. It's the glue that safeguards our community."

Communal living reduces costs for individual households and to the environment. "The fact that we have a collective dining room (bulk shopping and cooking significantly reduce packaging and energy consumption) and share just a few cars for the whole community, these have a carbon-saving aspect," Livni says. "Living collectively is one way of reducing consumption."

CULTURE/EDUCATION

Building Peace: Kibbutz member Mike Kaplin is most excited about the peace-building potential of the projects Lotan hosts that bring together Israelis, Palestinians, Jordanians, and Bedouins. The community works with Project Bustan and the Middle Eastern branch of Friends of the Earth to host natural building and youth conferences (see p. 103 for more on Project Bustan).

"Since we're so far away from everything, people can be together without the charge of being in a contested area. We are more neutral ground," Kaplin observes. "The most special moments are when the kids describe what they have gotten from the course. One of the most moving is when they describe coming to see the students working with them not as Jewish or Arab, but as people."

"Today's youth are hard to penetrate, to connect to nature—they can be a tough crowd," he continues. "Touching the mud, using their hands, and doing what they're often forbidden to do—get dirty—can help connect them both to nature and to each other. Sometimes we take them out at night to the sand dunes, which surround us here, where you can see the incredible stars, more stars than some of them have ever seen before, living in or near cities. We try to sow the seed of transformation."

Reporting contributed by Juliana Birnbaum. Photos by Louis Fox.

EARTH-BASED ARCHITECTURE

Photo: Louis Fox

Earth building is probably as ancient as humanity. Mud can be made into blocks, packed between forms, or molded by hand, and its flexibility and availability continues to make it one of the most popular building techniques in the world. ***Adobe,*** a word that passed from Arabic to Spanish to English, is the term for blocks of earth, sometimes strengthened with straw, which are dried in the sun and stacked into walls. An earth-based plaster is usually used to protect the walls and roof. Adobe is approved by building codes and ubiquitous in the United States Southwest and is thriving throughout the world. ***Superadobe,*** developed by Iranian architect Nader Khalili, uses long, snakelike sandbags to form a beehive-shaped compressive structure that employs arches, domes, and vaults in its structures. This method creates strong buildings that are better equipped to withstand earthquakes. Kiln-baked earthen blocks—basically the everyday brick—are durable and practical in a wider range of climates.

Rammed earth, another variation on earth building, involves a mixture of earth—with proper proportions of sand, gravel, and clay—being compressed in an externally supported frame or mold. Walls or blocks can be built with this technique, which uses traditionally uses lime as a stabilizer.

In England, a construction technique called ***cob*** involves a mix of mud, clay, manure, and straw, which is spread around a frame and air dried. ***Wattle-and-daub,*** a variation of cob that uses a network of woven sticks as a frame, was used to make the Tudor-style buildings of Medieval Europe. Cob is gaining popularity as a green-building technique, even in places where it wasn't historically used. It is inexpensive, surprisingly durable, and its walls, by responding to humidity, help deter the growth of mold and maintain good interior air quality.

Straw-bale construction began in the early twentieth century in the midwestern United States, when machine-baled straw was commonly available and other materials were not. Straw-bale building typically consists of stacking the bales on a raised footing or foundation, with a moisture barrier between the bales and the foundation. Bale walls are often bound together with bamboo, rebar, or wire mesh and then stuccoed or plastered. Straw-bale buildings can have a structural frame of other materials, with bales simply serving as insulation or infill, or the bale walls themselves can be load bearing, providing the structural support for the building.

Juliana Birnbaum.

Project Bustan

Negev Region, Israel

INTEGRATE RATHER THAN SEGREGATE. THE FIRST JEWISH-ARAB PERMACULTURE COURSE ORGANIZED BY BUSTAN, IN 2008. BUSTAN BELIEVES THAT THE PEOPLES OF THIS LAND ARE INTERTWINED AND MOST PRODUCTIVE IN FELLOWSHIP WITH ONE ANOTHER.

In both Hebrew and Arabic, *bustan* refers to a biodiverse, productive orchard, symbolic of the mission behind Project Bustan, an innovative project that mainly works in the harsh Negev desert of southern Israel. Founded in the early 1990s by Devorah Brous, a Jewish woman, and directed by Bedouin activist Ra'ed Al Mickawi, Bustan is part of a larger movement in Israel that links environmental issues and social justice. It hosts cross-cultural permaculture courses and educational programs that highlight the value of traditional Bedouin techniques for sustainable self-reliance. Its goal is to promote genuine convergence around Jewish and Arab interests and the necessity of sharing land, water, and energy.

"A *bustan* is sustainable due to its diversity: one plant is a natural insecticide for another, another acts as a trellis for a vine, another preserves water in its roots and sustains neighboring plants," reads the project's vision statement. "Conversely, in a monoculture, plants are weak and must be doused with harmful chemicals to protect themselves from parasite and weed invasion. Bustan believes that the peoples of this land are intertwined and survive most productively in fellowship with one another."

The Negev is home to approximately 180,000 Bedouins, who were traditionally nomadic, herding sheep and surviving sustainably in one of the driest deserts on the planet. Today, the Bedouin have been forced to settle in villages that are often unrecognized by Israel and on the least-desirable pieces of land, close to industry. The Negev region is home to Israel's nuclear reactor, twenty-two agrochemical and petrochemical factories, an oil terminal, closed military zones, a munitions plant, multiple quarries, a toxic-waste incinerator, cell-phone towers, a power plant, several airports, a prison, and two open sewage rivers. Predictably, the region suffers from the highest infant mortality and unemployment rates in the country.

In the forty-five unrecognized villages where approximately half the Bedouin reside, people live in conditions vastly inferior to other Israeli citizens. Unable to build permanent structures, they usually have no running water, sewage service, or electricity. The roads are inferior and access to healthcare and education is severely limited. There is also a constant threat that the Israeli government will demolish their homes. The unrecognized villages have organized themselves into the Regional Council of Unrecognized Villages (RCUV) to fight together for recognition and equal services.

One of the Bustan organization's first major projects was to organize five hundred Jewish and Bedouin volunteers to build a solar-powered medical clinic in the unrecognized village of Wadi el Na'am. In 2005, they transformed a school dump in another unrecognized settlement into a water-conserving orchard, as a means to teach the children about local ecology and sustainability. In 2008, Bustan organized the first Jewish-Arab permaculture course, held at the Hava & Adam Eco-Educational Farm, and a group of Bedouins and Israeli and American Jews studied the principles and techniques together (see p. 222 for more on Hava & Adam). Since then, they have held similar courses several times a year. They are holding their latest courses at Eco Khan, a sustainability center being constructed in the Bedouin village of Qasr-a-Sir, where participants can be immersed in Bedouin culture and can learn directly about traditional approaches to life in the Negev.

"We challenge the forced displacement of rural culture, fully aware of the cultural sensitivities around 'resuscitating traditional wisdom' and 'preserving indigenous knowledge,' " the organization's mission statement explains. "Jews and Arabs can both teach and learn from the ways the original inhabitants of Israel/Palestine answered food, energy, shelter and water needs using the most readily accessible materials. There is a need to garner the best of traditional wisdom and merge it with the benefits of renewable technologies."

The "PermaNegev" course Bustan is teaching at Qasr-a-Sir's Eco Khan brings participants to live and work within a Bedouin village for five months; it teaches the Arabic language and Middle East studies along with permaculture. The Eco Khan is part of a larger village project that aims to restore a structure that was once a small fortress along an ancient trade route. The project both connects the Bedouin community with its heritage and is creating new, sustainable livelihoods. As part of the course, students are helping to construct the center, following permaculture principles; in future courses, students will design other projects together with local people. Bustan returns the income from the courses to Eco Khan to help further community education and microbusiness initiatives.

Photo: Alice Gray

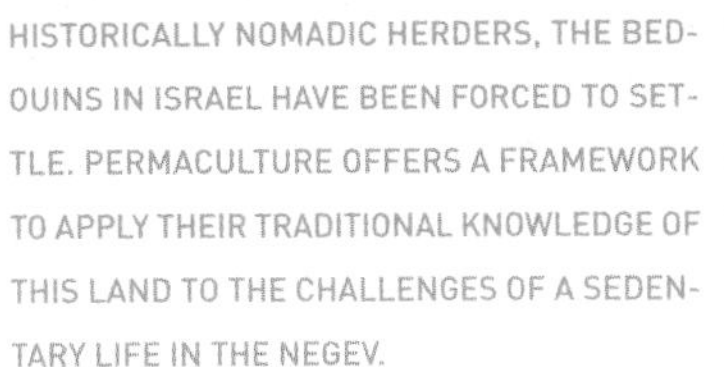

HISTORICALLY NOMADIC HERDERS, THE BEDOUINS IN ISRAEL HAVE BEEN FORCED TO SETTLE. PERMACULTURE OFFERS A FRAMEWORK TO APPLY THEIR TRADITIONAL KNOWLEDGE OF THIS LAND TO THE CHALLENGES OF A SEDENTARY LIFE IN THE NEGEV.

"WE HOPE THAT FROM THIS GROUP, BEDOUIN-LED SUSTAINABILITY PROJECTS WILL START TO SPREAD."—DOR HAVKIN, ISRAELI PERMACULTURE TEACHER FOR BUSTAN

"THE CLOSEST THINGS IN THE WORLD TO THE PRINCIPLES OF PERMACULTURE I'M LEARNING IN THIS COURSE ARE THE PRINCIPLES OF TRADITIONAL BEDOUIN CULTURE."—HALED ELOUBRA, BEDOUIN COMMUNITY LEADER AND ARCHITECT

Haled Eloubra, a Bedouin community leader and architect who participated in the first course, said he was planning to build a "green kindergarten" when he finished the permaculture course. He focused on what he felt was most needed in the Bedouin settlements—educational facilities—and realized kindergarten would be the best place to start. "I wanted to build using natural materials and realized that building [with mud] made the most sense. . . . In a community without power, it makes sense to build with mud, whose natural insulating qualities helps keep buildings cool in summer and warm in winter. The building will be solar powered, the water will be collected rainwater and there will be a gray-water system—it will be an efficient, ecological building."

"Most of the participants are engineers and architects. They are educated people who already know the communities and are respected within them. We are fostering self-sufficient leadership within the community," said Dor Havkin, an Israeli permaculture teacher at the first Bustan-run course.

There was no doubt in Eloubra's mind that this approach offers real answers to the environmental challenges faced by his Bedouin community and the planet as a whole. "The solution for the world's problems today and the diseases within it is to move in the direction of permaculture," he asserted.

Reporting contributed by Alice Gray and Juliana Birnbaum.
Photos contributed by Louis Fox, unless otherwise noted.

Photo: Ron Guillen (Creative Commons)

Greater World Earthship Community

Taos, New Mexico, U.S.A.

EFFICIENT USE OF WATER. GRAY WATER FROM THE KITCHEN SINK IS FILTERED AND IRRIGATES RAISED BEDS. ONCE FILTERED AGAIN, THE WATER WILL FLUSH THE HOME'S TOILET, AND THEN IT WILL GO INTO A BLACK-WATER TREATMENT PLANTER OUTDOORS.

In the sagebrush desert surrounding the Rio Grande gorge outside of Taos, New Mexico, lies a community of homes that are built with recycled materials and earth, are completely solar and wind powered, and are equipped with water catchment and recycling systems. The Greater World Earthship Community was the first of three subdivisions of these homes in the region, which now cover a total of 1,338 acres (541 hectares). Earthships have multiplied exponentially over the past decade, with projects in countries across the globe, including a Waldorf school in Sierra Leone, housing projects in earthquake-ravaged Haiti (providing an efficient way of recycling rubble), and demonstration homes in a number of diverse climate zones.

Earthships demonstrate the permaculture principles of storing energy, using renewable resources, and reducing waste. Accepting feedback and adapting to change have also been a major part of the development of this pioneering approach to architecture and community development. As the Earthships are built in more diverse locations each year, builders must continually adapt the design, integrating it with local conditions.

The innovative design of the Earthship is the brainchild of maverick architect Mike Reynolds. He began to develop the structures in the 1970s, and today they have been built in nearly every state in the United States and in a number of countries around the world. Although the Taos area typically receives only 7–12 inches (18–30 centimeters) of rainfall a year, the unique water system, which catches water and then recycles it from shower to greenhouse to toilet, allows some residents to collect all the water needed for home use from rainfall. Reynolds's vision was to create an easy-to-build, sustainable home design that would use and reuse materials accessible worldwide and generate its own utilities. Residents are also able to grow food in the greenhouses integrated into the home design and to treat waste on-site.

RECYCLED GLASS BOTTLES PROVIDE LOW-COST STRUCTURAL MATERIALS WHILE CREATING UNIQUE LUMINESCENT WALLS.

The experimental nature of this type of building has had its challenges. The Greater World community is limited by being a conventional subdivision, with residents united solely by their interest in this particular architecture. Some have expressed disappointment in the lack of cohesion within the community, as few opportunities exist for group interaction, "It is more of a collection of individual homesteads with shared qualities, rather than an intentional community," says one resident. "We don't gather for activities or share much more than our interest in more self-sufficient living." In this way, however, this limitation of the subdivision is also a benefit, as it makes it more accessible to mainstream American culture, allowing residents to buy into a more sustainable lifestyle without dealing with the challenges of communal ecovillage living.

Another setback came when the design collided with conventional building codes restricing some of the innovations Reynolds developed. Progress has been made in changing the building codes, but it has been a slow process. "People can live in carbon-zero homes right now," Reynolds said in a 2012 interview on the Discovery Channel's *Planet Green*. "The technology is here. Allowing it to happen is the problem. Our rules and regulations won't let us do it, [they] are about things that aren't pertinent any more—stick frame houses that you pump heat into, endless of amounts of energy and water—wasteful methods of living. Those days are over due to climate change, population explosion, and dwindling resources."[5]

BUILDING

Interior Climate and Water Systems: Earthships are arranged in horseshoe-shaped modules that face south. The rammed-earth tires are made on-site, and each weighs about 300 pounds (136 kilos),

AN EARTHSHIP OWNER MAINTAINS A WATER CATCHMENT GULLY ON HER ROOF. THE HOME IS DESIGNED TO CATCH AND STORE ENOUGH WATER FROM RAIN AND SNOW TO MEET THE NEEDS OF ITS RESIDENTS.

with excellent load-bearing capacity and resistance to fire. The interior walls are often made of recycled cans, concrete, adobe, or stucco.

One of the most remarkable aspects of an Earthship is its naturally stable interior climate. The properties of thermal mass and passive-solar gain allow most to be free of conventional heating and cooling systems. For Earthships in cooler climates, extra insulation is added on the outside of tire walls. The southern wall (or northern in the southern hemisphere) is nonstructural and made of glass that is angled to be perpendicular to the light from the winter sun, allowing for maximum exposure in the winter and lesser exposure in the summer. In colder climates, insulated shading is used over the windows to reduce heat loss.

An Earthship harvests water on its roof from rain or snow. The water flows through a silt strainer into a cistern, which is positioned to gravity feed a pump and filter panel that makes the water suitable for drinking. After being used in sinks and showers, the gray water passes through a filter/digester and into a deep, rubber-lined botanical cell, or indoor greenhouse. This living machine passes the water through gravel and plant roots, which add oxygen to the water and remove nitrogen. Water from the low end of the botanical cell then flows through a peat moss filter and collects in a reservoir. This reclaimed water then passes once more through a charcoal filter and is used to flush conventional toilets. Once used in the toilet, the water, now black water, flows into the "incubator," a solar-enhanced septic tank, and finally to an outdoor landscaping botanical cell.

TOOLS/TECHNOLOGY

Energy: An Earthship collects its own energy, usually from a prepackaged system using solar and wind power and stores it in batteries. A Power Organizing Module inverts it for AC use.

CULTURE/EDUCATION

Training Earthship Warriors: The Earthship Biotecture Academy offers a two-month training course in Earthship design principles and philosophy. The program consists of sixty-two hours of classroom study, two months of fieldwork, and an independent study.

Reporting by Juliana Birnbaum. Photos by Louis Fox.

PASSIVE-SOLAR ARCHITECTURE

Passive-solar building design uses windows, walls, and floors to collect heat from the sun in winter and repel heat in summer. As a result, it minimizes the need for other energy sources, such as fossil fuels, to maintain a comfortable interior climate. The design approach is closely aligned with permaculture, involving careful consideration of the local conditions so as to strategically use elements such as insulation, window placement and glazing type, thermal mass, and shading. Passive-solar construction makes the most of southern exposure, using properly oriented windows and facades, and typically has thick, well-insulated walls.

Direct solar gain uses the positioning of windows, shutters, and skylights to control the amount of direct sun reaching the interior spaces, so it warms the air and surfaces within the building. In the past, design using direct solar gain has been hindered by the challenge of finding reasonably priced, transparent materials whose insulation value is comparable to standard wall insulation. This is changing with the development of super-insulated windows and the creation of "passive house" architectural standards, first in Germany and now in other parts of the world. In cold climates, a passive house can use as much as 90 percent less energy to heat as a conventional house. The approach is also being used in hot climates, where passive cooling designs slow the transfer of heat to the interior and remove heat from a building through well-designed ventilation systems.

Based on the same materials and design principles as direct solar gain, an indirect gain system places the thermal mass (such as a brick wall) between a window and the space to be heated. The sun's light passes through a window and heats the wall. The heat collects in the narrow space between the window and the wall, rises, and spills into the room through vents at the top of the wall, pulling cold air into the space through vents at the bottom of the wall. Thus the system circulates warm and cold air via convection. Even after the sun has set, the wall will continue to radiate heat. In hot weather, the window can be shaded to prevent sunlight from hitting the wall, and what heat the thermal mass of the wall does absorb is trapped in the wall, keeping the room temperature cooler.

Many traditional cultures designed structures in a way that demonstrates their understanding of passive-solar principles. Pueblo housing structures built in the pre-Columbian era used the rising heat from the south side of the building to heat work and sleep areas in winter. Insulating materials blocked excessive solar gain in summer, and storage areas on the north side of the structures were ventilated and cooler in all seasons.[6]

Juliana Birnbaum.

Lama Foundation

Questa, New Mexico, U.S.A.

AFTER A WILDFIRE NEARLY DESTROYED THE ENTIRE SITE, LAMA RESPONDED IN PERMACULTURE FASHION BY **CREATIVELY USING THE CHANGE**. THEY TOOK THE OPPORTUNITY TO MINDFULLY REASSESS AND REBUILD WITH A PERMACULTURE EYE.

Of all the spiritual teachers the Lama Foundation has had since its establishment in 1967, many residents say that the greatest is the land itself. High in the southern Rocky Mountains in New Mexico, at 8,600 feet (2,621 meters), the 110-acre (44.5-hectare) Lama Foundation site provides a sweeping view, taking in the Rio Grande desert valley and the snowcapped peaks of southern Colorado. Its overlapping desert and alpine ecosystems include ponderosa pine, blue spruce, juniper, and oak trees. The trees are making a comeback after a 1996 fire that turned the old-growth forest into a sea of ash.

Lama began as a spiritual center, not an ecovillage or permaculture school. Ram Dass wrote *Be Here Now* at the site, a seminal spiritual guide for the hippie counterculture. The center was initially powered entirely by propane, and many of the buildings were not insulated, though natural building methods were

Photo: Louis Fox

MIRACULOUSLY UNTOUCHED BY THE 1996 WILDFIRE, THE COMMUNITY'S ICONIC DOME INSPIRED RESIDENTS TO STAY AND REBUILD AFTER THE DISASTER.

used. Permaculturists first surveyed Lama in 1988—"the same year that Bill Mollison published his Designer's Manual," resident Austin Babcock points out. They made some recommendations that led the community to incorporate permaculture values into their decisions about the site. They made a number of changes, including clustering of the buildings and developing gray-water systems. Eight years later, the 1996 fire spared only the bare central infrastructure, including the main Dome and the kitchen, but destroyed almost all the outlying housing and other buildings.

"Despite initial grief that swept through the community, the slate was cleaned, and people could start over," members report. "This also meant that all invested had the great opportunity and responsibility to really assess how to rebuild (and rethink) in a mindful, ecological and sustainable way. With so many lives touched by the event of the fire, resources and talented people started pouring in to help."[7] Much of the Lama site slopes to the south and west, which is favorable for solar power collection and passive-solar building design, but before the fire, Lama did not tap as much solar power, due to the tree coverage. "Up until the fire, we were more isolationist. Since then we've tried to be integrated further into the community and bioregion," says resident Kathy Lyons. Today Lama has evolved into a magnet for permaculture and natural building practice and education, as well as a retreat center and intentional community. There are sixty to one hundred residents during the summer, and ten to twenty-five in the off-season.

HEALTH/SPIRITUAL WELL-BEING

An Eclectic Spiritual Community: Lama Mountain is sacred to the Native Americans of Taos Pueblo, and a trail on the site is part of an old indigenous trading route that stretched from Peru up to the Great Plains. When the community established the site, they consulted Pueblo elders about the settlement's design and intention. Founded by Barbara and Stephen Durkee, it was one of almost thirty communes established in the region in the back-to-the-land movement of the 1960s. By 1973, the vast majority of the communes had closed, but the Lama Foundation was able to continue. Some speculate it was because it had more structure and discipline than most others—demonstrated by its prohibition of drugs and alcohol.

Ram Dass was a friend of the founders, and he stayed at the Lama Foundation as a guest when he returned to America from India. During his visit, he presented the Durkees with a manuscript he had written, entitled *From Bindu to Ojas*. The community's residents edited, illustrated, and laid out the text, and they retitled it *Be Here Now*. Ultimately it became a huge commercial hit. Dass and other spiritual leaders continued to visit and teach at Lama, including Samuel L. Lewis, also known as "Sufi Sam." Lewis was buried there after his death in 1971, and his tomb continues to be a sacred site on the land.

The Lama Foundation embraces an eclectic approach to spiritual discovery rather than adhering to one discipline. It has strong ties to Native American teachings through Taos Pueblo, and also incorporates elements of the Hanuman Temple, Sufi Ruhaniat, the Dervish Healing Order, the Church of Conscious Harmony, St. Benedict's Monastery, and other religious heritages.

STACKING FUNCTIONS IS A PERMACULTURE IDEAL. AT LAMA THE PRACTICE OF BUILDING SHELTERS SERVES BOTH ITS PRIMARY PURPOSE AND IS A SPIRITUAL PRACTICE FOR MANY.

CULTURE/EDUCATION

Build Here Now: Lama offers public programs during the summer, hosting conferences, inviting spiritual teachers, and having members teach. During summer retreat season, the center hosts concerts, dances, and visual arts projects. Lama is unique in the way that it has started "invisible" structures that people have been able to transplant and develop elsewhere. The first Build Here Now natural building convergence was held in 1998 and was one of the pilot programs of its kind. Lama has "grown teachers," Babcock says, and today there are hundreds of similar programs in existence.

BUILDING

A Variety of Techniques: After Build Here Now started, which combined a wide variety of natural construction and permaculture topics with Lama Foundation projects, the community created new buildings to fit in with a larger community plan. They created three zones: residential, agricultural, and hermitage. They designed the new buildings to be true four-season dwellings, using solar gain, straw-bale construction and efficient wood stoves to keep them toasty on freezing nights.

LAMA IS RESEARCHING WHAT GARDEN PLANTS WORK BEST IN THEIR SHORT GROWING SEASON AND IS WORKING TOWARD GREATER SELF-SUFFICIENCY IN FOOD, BUT GROWING ENOUGH FOOD ON-SITE IS CHALLENGING.

Over the years, different visitors and residents have experimented with a variety of methods and styles—particularly hybrid approaches, which use a combination of different methods, such as straw bale alongside adobe blocks or stone walls. The use of straw bale in the north-facing walls (where its greater insulation keeps the place warm) and adobe in a south-facing wall (because it allows a building to heat up more quickly than straw).

The nearby Pueblo constructions in Taos inspired the community to use adobe, and many local indigenous Americans came to the site in the early years to teach the newcomers how to build with earth. The adobe prayer room near the main Dome is particularly interesting: with a very small entrance and a sunken circle to sit inside, it is completely peaceful. Many of the houses are also deliberately small, making them cheaper to build and easy to heat, such as the vaults, designed by Shay Salomon, which are straw bale and have aluminum shingle roofs that hang over to the ground on each side. The communal setting itself also encourages the building of small individual houses and the collective use of large common space. There are communal bathrooms and a shared kitchen, a library, a music room, a winter meeting room, and an outdoor sheltered eating area.

Building here is a collective process and a spiritual practice—as one resident says, they "build with clay, mud, and love." Some buildings, like the stone hermitage, have been built in silence, and others, such as the two vaults, were built just by women. In fact, Lama has hosted several women-only building workshops, with the intention of creating a safe space in which women could experiment with building and expand their confidence without the presence of men.

Photo: Louis Fox

RESPONSIBILITIES FOR HOUSEKEEPING, MAINTENANCE, AND KITCHEN ARE DELEGATED THROUGH GUARDIANSHIPS, WHICH ARE DECIDED AMONG RESIDENTS.

TOOLS/TECHNOLOGY

Sharing resources: The community members make use of shared tools, art studios and workshop space, and Lama has a thriving cottage industry of prayer flags and other sustainable crafts.

An onsite landfill allows residents to monitor how much trash they are creating. Composting outhouses are in place, both pit-vault style and ones with removable barrels. The community uses the humanure to fertilize flowers.

LAND TENURE/ COMMUNITY GOVERNANCE

A Far-Flung Tribe: The Lama Foundation owns the site's land, thus the residents do not own their homes, though they may have the possibility of designing or building them. Most residences house one family or small group; retreat participants primarily camp. Residents get a small stipend from the foundation, and some work outside the community to supplement their income.

The community uses consensus model to make business decisions; residents report this can be challenging, but they are committed to giving each member respect and consideration. "There is lots of rotation, and there is always space for new folks to come in with new ideas and new interests. It's possible to come back again and again, each time with a deeper commitment," Babcock observes. "Lama is like a far-flung tribe that comes together and separates again over the years."

Reporting contributed by Juliana Birnbaum and Jenny Pickerill. Photos by Jenny Pickerill, unless otherwise noted.

Suvraga Aguyt Cooperative

Tosontsengel, Mongolia

Try gardening here: ancient beach sand for soil, an extremely short growing season, little access to water, and winters 40°F below freezing (40°C). Some cooperatives have to water tens of acres by hand. Beyond all of that, the locals don't even like to eat vegetables—they've never had the luxury of choosing to be vegetarian. But that may need to shift, as the temperature does. Researchers believe that climate change is affecting Mongolia more than almost anywhere else on the planet, forcing a traditionally nomadic, pastoralist culture to find a new way to live.

The high, semiarid, grassland ecosystem of Outer Mongolia is part of the enormous Eurasian Steppe, which stretches from Romania to Siberia and has historically connected Europe with China and the Middle East. Suvraga Aguyt Vegetable Growing Cooperative, established in 2010, is a permaculture demonstration and education site. That year, it hosted Mongolia's first-ever permaculture design course, taught by Rick Coleman, who, in his eighteen-plus years of teaching permaculture, has worked on every continent (except Antarctica), in some of the harshest conditions, and with some of the most impoverished people in the world.

"I believe that permaculture has a major role to play on the world stage," says Coleman. "As a design system, permaculture has so much potential to positively impact on aid and development projects around the globe. Not only does it address issues of depleting soil, water, and energy, it also creates empowered communities, who can become more self reliant, less dependent upon aid, and more able to direct what aid they do receive into positive capacity-building projects."

Mongolia was once the center of history's largest land-based empire, founded by Genghis Khan in 1206, which stretched from the eastern shores of the Mediterranean Sea to the western shores of the Pacific Ocean. The Mongolia of today is one of the most sparsely populated areas on the planet, with a population of around three million people spread across almost 580,000 square miles (1.5 million square kilometers) of steppe—a land with neither enough rainfall nor enough fertility to support much of a forest ecosystem.

Over thousands of years, Mongolian culture has adapted to the land in a way that has, in turn, reshaped the landscape. The nomads' herds nibbled away at the edges of the conifer forests, which at one time would have covered the endless hills, until the trees at last retreated to the few precarious holds that remain today, mostly along the more steeply eroded gullies, where animals cannot easily graze.

This is the delicate balance of the steppe: any manure left by the roaming herds that are not harvested by humans for winter fuel provides just enough fertility for hardy grasses to grow. Herd animals are the perfect energy store for the long, cold winters—one has a better chance of keeping a herd alive long enough to feed a family than of growing enough vegetables in the short-lived growing season to last all winter. Families find a sheltered place to hunker down and stay warm through the cold season, then move on to (literally) greener pastures during the warmer months for their herds to reproduce, rear their young, and fatten up enough to survive next year's winter freeze.

MONGOLIANS HAVE A DEEP KNOWLEDGE OF ANIMAL HUSBANDRY, AS LIVESTOCK ARE A PART OF EVERYDAY TRADITIONAL LIFE FROM AN EARLY AGE

Photo: Rick Colman

PRECIPITATION IS SCARCE AND UNPREDICTABLE, A CLIMATIC CONDITION THAT HELPED TO GENERATE BOTH THE STEPPES AND THE HERDING LIFESTYLE THEY HAVE SUSTAINED IN MONGOLIA. HERE A FAMILY ENCAMPMENT, INCLUDING A **YURT**, WEATHERS A SUMMER SQUALL.

These grazing patterns—thousands of years old—are no longer viable, however, due to changing weather patterns, with one study showing a temperature increase of about 3.85°F (2.14°C) since the 1940s, enough to trigger noticeable seasonal changes.[8] The most serious change is, paradoxically, the higher incidence of extreme cold, a counterintuitive result of global warming, which can trigger complex shifts in the broader climate system and, while warming the poles, create high-pressure cycles that bring colder air to Eurasia. Entire herds are freezing to death in their winter shelters, and sometimes the family watching over the herds freezes to death right alongside them. Like all cultures, this one must find a way to adapt in order to survive.

"Mongolians have almost zero crop-growing experience," says Tileuybek "Bek" Ye, the project's native-born food security director, as he gnaws on the bones of a traditional meal of meat, organ meat, and meat broth—the remains of the carcass of a slaughtered sheep. "In the 1930s, during the Socialist era, the Soviet Union started developing state farms to grow hay to feed their livestock but before that, Mongolians had no need to learn how to grow vegetables. Even in the 1980s (by which time the Soviets had begun to grow potatoes, wheat, and other food crops), it was mostly Chinese workers farming the land."

After seventy years of state-run enterprise and subsidy, the Soviet Union collapsed in 1989. Mongols began unsteadily adapting to the new pressures of a free-market democracy, until three back-to-back *dzud* (extreme freezes) wiped out over eleven million head of livestock between 1999 and 2002. Half of the country's population fled to the capital, Ulaanbaatar, in search of a better life after their herds perished, with the inevitable result of leaving too few people spread out too far in rural areas to provide enough food to feed everyone. Mongolia now imports most of its food from China and Russia and is scrambling to find solutions for achieving food security.

There exists, however, a vast well of knowledge about animal husbandry and appropriate traditional building techniques, which the Suvraga Aguyt project taps into. Mongolian herders could be said to be the original organic animal farmers. Some co-op members still graze their family's herds on the pastureland surrounding the *soum* (village), while growing potatoes, radishes, carrots, cabbages, tomatoes, and cucumbers on-site to supplement their primarily meat-based diet. As yields increase, the collective will have a surplus crop to barter or sell—and they will be able to offer the community a much higher quality product than the sometimes moldy, half-rotten, imported produce that passes for vegetables on the store shelves of the *soum*.

WHEN ORGANIC MATTER IS SCARCE, STONE MULCH CAN BE USED, AS IT IS AROUND THIS SEA BUCKTHORN TREE IN THE SUVRAGA AGUYT VEGETABLE GROWING COOPERATIVE.

CULTURE/EDUCATION

Systems for Changing Needs: Coleman's 2010 permaculture course began with Coleman and his students traveling the countryside two weeks with Bek, who served as guide, translator, and assistant instructor while the team visited the other half-dozen or so vegetable-growing cooperatives in the area. The team observed the sites and surrounding landscape and talked with cooperative leaders in order to understand the conditions, challenges, and best practices that each group had developed.

The team designed and held a short course at each site to address each group's immediate concerns, creating practical solutions that could be implemented immediately. Each cooperative then sent their leaders and key members to the customized two-week permaculture design course held at Suvraga Aguyt.

"Permaculture is not about passive-solar greenhouses or water-management systems," Coleman reflects. "These are techniques applied to solve specific problems. It is about design-systems thinking. If we can introduce this methodology, we leave behind an empowered group able to design their own solutions. Permaculture is information and imagination-intensive, lending itself to be followed up even from a distance, by email or internet. If we design well enough, we create spare time and energy. When communities have those, they then have the ability to adapt quickly."

BUILDING

Yurts, Greenhouses, and Water: At Suvraga Aguyt, six *gers* (a.k.a. yurts—see inset) provide on-site housing, and other buildings include four passive-solar greenhouses, a tool shed, and an indoor-outdoor communal kitchen and dining room. The abandoned shells of ten concrete buildings are awaiting adaptive reuse for a variety of purposes, as time and budget permit.

A well currently provides water. Suvraga Aguyt is designing and implementing water-catchment systems to capture runoff from adjacent roadways, and there's a plan to implement more rain catchment from roofed areas on the site. The sanitation system is under development also. Utilizing humanure is not yet culturally acceptable, although rural communities are becoming aware of the need to develop alternative sewage systems to prevent contamination of their water table. Suvraga Aguyt may be the first cooperative in the area to develop an acceptable compromise solution: a "pit-and-plant" design. A shallow pit is designated as a toilet, and a temporary outhouse structure built above it. When the pit is almost full, it is filled in with soil and a fruit tree is planted, and the next pit is dug.

LAND TENURE/COMMUNITY GOVERNANCE

Spreading the Word: Suvraga Aguyt maintains contact with local government to communicate successful design solutions and initiatives that enhance the community's food security. The project also distributes to village residents, who must walk through the demonstration site to collect it, giving them a chance to absorb new strategies. Suvraga Aguyt freely shares information with villagers interested in growing their own vegetables, as well as with family compounds around the community, allowing a gradual transfer of knowledge to the wider village to take place.

TOOLS/TECHNOLOGY

Energy: A small-scale hydroelectric plant provides electricity for the entire *soum* (which has about ten thousand residents) during summer months. During winter, the lake and rivers freeze, and the community relies upon individual household solar panels for their electricity.

LAND/NATURE STEWARDSHIP

Food Security Co-op members' herd animals provide the staple diet for most families, supplemented by what is grown on-site and stored through the winter. During the lean spring months, when there are no crops to harvest, families depend on herd animals and produce imported from China and Russia, often in poor condition.

They are redesigning the animal shelters from a permaculture perspective, moving toward more aerodynamic, yurt-like shapes, and insulating them with animal furs and fleeces not high quality enough for human use, which were previously thrown away. They're heating the shelters biologically by building hot compost heaps inside them. The Suvraga Aguyt compound has a number of abandoned Soviet-era buildings, which they are turning into passive-solar greenhouses (for more on passive solar, see p. 110). The design takes advantage of the significant thermal mass provided by the thick concrete walls soaking up the warmth of the sun, which they trap with double- and triple-insulated layers of glass and plastic sheeting, converting the abundant daylight into heat and storing this energy to be radiated back out during the night. There are cold frames for seedlings inside these greenhouses, further extending the short growing season in a place where every additional growing day is critical.

The co-op is saving seeds from the hardiest plants among the crops, and within a few growing seasons, Mongolia will be well on its way toward developing its own crop varieties, better adapted to the short growing season and harsh conditions. There are no heirloom varieties here. The growing cooperatives of Zavkhan province are currently developing the region's seed bank.

Nitrogen-fixing species growing wild in the fields were identified for use as green manures in broadacre production that is occurring in remote areas. Gas-powered water pumps were previously considered high-valued assets, but viewed from a permaculture perspective, they are inefficient and wasteful liabilities. They have been replaced by hydraulic ram pumps that harness the energy of a flowing river to move water. Planting guilds are being designed and tested to increase resilience, resistance to pests, and overall yields, while suitable native species of tree and shrub have been identified to be planted as windbreaks, living fences, and for future coppicing.

COLD FRAMES DUG INTO THE GROUND AT BUSBUNT COOPERATIVE. BUILDING COLD FRAMES WITHIN THE GREENHOUSE PROVIDES ADDITIONAL PROTECTION AND FURTHER EXTENDS THE GROWING SEASON.

"Designing a replicable permaculture system builds from existing strengths and cultural knowledge, and prepares for the extremes," says Coleman. "Especially when working in aid, we design first for Survival, then Subsistence, then Self-Sufficiency, and then Abundance of Harvest—when crops can be bartered or given away. Finally, we can move on to commercial production. . . . As change is forced upon the world at an unwelcome rate, it will be crucial to have successful models on the ground. Through implementing permaculture, aided communities of today have the potential to become the models for sustainable practices of tomorrow."

Reporting and photos contributed by Matthew Lynch, unless otherwise noted.

THE YURT

The ger, better known in the West as the yurt, is a traditional round housing structure used for thousands of years to survive the extreme climate of the Mongolian steppe. The dwelling is a living example of an appropriate and replicable design, which was forged by environmental conditions and the lifestyle that evolved to adapt to these extremes. Imagine attempting to devise a structure that:

1. Can often be assembled in less than an hour,
2. Houses three generations under one roof,
3. Is easily replicated to accommodate a growing family,
4. Utilizes only locally available building materials,
5. Stores a family's equipment and food needs for up to six months at a time,
6. Withstands howling gale-force winds,
7. Keeps its occupants sufficiently warm to survive -40°F (-40°C) temperatures during winter,
8. Keeps its occupants sufficiently cool to survive 104°F (40°C) temperatures during summer,
9. Packs up to fit on the back of a horse or camel, and
10. Is light enough to be transported hundreds of kilometers away by horse or camel.

The circular shape of the yurt not only yields the most efficient living-area-to-materials-used ratio than any other shape, it is also inherently strong, and provides the base for one of the most small-scale, intensively utilized spaces ever designed by humankind. The conical roof is not only simple to construct, its shape and lack of eaves is smoothly aerodynamic—the howling winds slip around the dwelling.

Felt, made from the fleeces of the family's herd, provides a double layer of insulation in the cold months. It traps layers of air within its fibers and the tiny airspace between felt and the outer layer of the yurt, keeping in precious heat generated from the wood-and-dung-fired stove, which doubles as a heating and cooking tool. Tanned animal hides would have provided a waterproof outer layer in ancient times; modern yurts use a tough canvas material. During summer, only one layer of insulating felt is used, and on extremely hot days the bottom of the walls on the leeward side of the yurt are rolled up to create a cooling updraft.

"Borrow from cultures old and new, and with our imaginations, blend those borrowings to create new ways to live that are simpler, gentler, more generous, and beautiful."
—William Coperthwaite

Photo: Louis Crusoe (Creative Commons)

The design of the light wooden frame makes efficient use of a relatively scarce resource. The latticed wall frames fold into compact packages, while the rafter poles and main central support poles are tied in bundles for storage and transport. The central hoop, which supports all the rafters, sits comfortably on horseback and fits perfectly around the humps of a camel.

Students from Mongolia's inaugural permaculture design course applied permaculture design principles to modify and enhance the performance of the traditional housing structure, adapting an ancient culture to survive the changing social, cultural, and environmental patterns of modern times.

Reporting contributed by Matthew Lynch.

Ladakh Ecological Development Group

Ladakh, India

Despite the challenges of living at high elevations in the cold, dry Outer Himalayan plateau, the Ladakhi people have created a rich, harmonious, and sustainable culture from the sparse resources of their region. Much of Ladakh, which borders Tibet and is closely aligned with its culture, lies above 10,000 feet above sea level (3,000 meters). Traditionally, it was largely a self-sufficient agrarian economy; it produced an extraordinarily complete range and quantity of goods. Surplus barley was exchanged along the vast caravan routes for a few "luxuries," such as salt, tea, and stones for jewelry.

Traditional agriculture in Ladakh is connected to Buddhist values and the social network of village life. "Each [plot] is tiny, the very antithesis of broad scale agriculture, yet they produce yields higher than those of the West," Nick Wilson writes, in a piece discussing traditional Ladakh from a permaculture perspective.[9]

Ladakh, the northernmost part of India, was virtually independent until the mid-twentieth century, when the Chinese invasion of Tibet and other regional wars caused it to acquire strategic importance, which was followed by militarization and a "development" push, which is still ongoing. In the 1970s, outside economic pressures began undermining the local economy, and ills that were previously unknown—including pollution, crime, and family breakdown—began to take hold. Helena Norberg-Hodge, a linguist educated in Europe and the United States, who came to Ladakh in 1975, describes the change.

STACKING FUNCTIONS: A LADAKHI WOMAN STACKS BARLEY GRASS ON HER ROOF TO DRY OVER THE WINTER. IT WILL HELP INSULATE THE HOME BEFORE BECOMING FODDER FOR LIVESTOCK NEXT SEASON.

When I first arrived in Leh, the capital of 5,000 inhabitants, cows were the most likely cause of congestion and the air was crystal clear. Within [a] five minutes walk in any direction from the town centre were barley fields, dotted with large farmhouses. For the next twenty years I watched Leh turn into an urban sprawl. The streets became choked with traffic, and the air tasted of diesel fumes. "Housing colonies" of soulless, cement boxes spread into the dusty desert. The once pristine streams became polluted, the water undrinkable. For the first time, there were homeless people. The increased economic pressures led to unemployment and competition. Within a few years, friction between different communities appeared. All of these things had not existed for the previous 500 years.[10]

Norberg-Hodge founded the Ladakh Project in 1978 and has also helped with the establishment of several indigenous-run organizations in Ladakh, including the Ladakh Ecological Development Group (LEDeG) and the Women's Alliance of Ladakh. LEDeG, founded in 1983, works to counter the destructive "development" trends in Ladakh and to improve its culture from its own resources and ancient foundations. As an alternative to conventional development, the LEDeG has encouraged a path based on Ladakh's own values and its human-scale economy. The approach seems to be attracting attention at the highest levels of local policy making and is being taken up on a broader scale, with larger agencies adopting technologies such as photovoltaic panels, micro-hydro, and passive-solar design.

Traditionally, cooperative relations were cemented in society through systems for shared agricultural work and community support in difficult times. Small, formalized groupings of families tended to each other in times of need and nominated a member to the decision-making village council. These kinds of finely tuned systems erode and shift quickly when a culture is disparaged and young people are made to feel that the old way is backward. Nick Wilson writes about these changes:

The cash economy means an inevitable erosion in social relations; people cannot lend their ponies to a neighbor when they are being used to carry a trekker's bags. New divisions have appeared, between rich and poor, men ("breadwinners") and women, young and old, secular and religious, and Muslim and Buddhist. . . . Cultures have always evolved, but it is the sudden collision of two worlds that causes dislocation, wherever it occurs. Ladakh's small size, the fundamentally different modes of thinking between the old and new, the recentness of the situation and the Ladakhis' inadequate knowledge of the forces now shaping their lives (not seeing the myriad ecological and social problems of the West, for example) has made the process especially apparent in Ladakh.

TOOLS/TECHNOLOGY

Renewable Energy: The Ladakh Ecological Development Group has promoted appropriate technologies, such as parabolic mirrors (reflectors used to collect or project energy) and photovoltaic panels for heating, cooking, drying crops, and greenhouses. It has also spread the use of small-scale wind turbines and micro-hydro installations for grinding grain, producing electricity, and pumping water. Today, one or more of these technologies can be found in virtually every Ladakhi village.

BUILDING

Passive-Solar Construction: LEDeG has a demonstration campus with a workshop, greenhouse, and experimental farm. A passive-solar guesthouse hosts trainees and guests, powered on solar energy alone. The organization strives to bring attention to the sustainable aspects of indigenous society. It also runs a Rural Building Center just outside of the city of Leh.

THE TRADITIONAL, MULTISTORIED LADAKHI HOUSE IS MADE OF MUD, WOOD, AND STONE, WITH MASSIVE WALLS FOR THERMAL EFFICIENCY AND SPACE TO SHELTER ANIMALS IN WINTER.

The ecosystem of the steppe supports very few trees. Therefore, during winter, local residents often burn dung, roots, and brush to cook and to warm the space of one or two rooms of their house. Despite this, room temperatures often drop below freezing and even if families have plenty of time, the cold limits the possible activities. Furthermore, fuel collection takes up a significant part of summer and autumn labor for women, who often spend two to four hours a day collecting the 2 tons of fuel required to warm an average house during winter. Another drawback is the smoke that leaks from inferior stoves and fills the poorly ventilated rooms. The poor indoor air quality is responsible for the high rate of lung disease in Ladakh. Finally, the shortage of local fuel and the high price of imported conventional fuel result in a situation of energy vulnerability.

Passive-solar design is well adapted for the steppe, as the climate is very sunny, especially during the winter (see p. 110 for more on passive-solar design). LEDeG has promoted a passive-solar initiative to improve the energy efficiency and sustainability of Ladakhi homes. The group has raised funds for and implemented a variety of passive-solar techniques, both as new construction and retrofits. These include attached greenhouses, double-glazed windows, trombe walls, and thermal insulation with local materials. LEDeG has constructed or retrofitted over four hundred passive-solar houses in Ladakh since 2003, mainly as a partner with other organizations in a larger, regional effort. Impact studies reported by LEDeG show that passive-solar homes use 60 percent less fuel, there is less cold-related illness, and households greatly reduce their carbon emissions.[11]

Reporting contributed by Juliana Birnbaum. Photos by Craig Mackintosh.

LAND / NATURE STEWARDSHIP

DR. VANDANA SHIVA ON CLIMATE CHANGE

Photo: Kartikey Shiva

The Himalayan glaciers support nearly half of humanity. The mountains of snow have also been called the Third Pole, since they are the third largest body of snow on our planet, after the Antarctic and Arctic. Yet while melting snow and ice at the poles due to global warming and climate change is reported frequently, the melting of the Himalayan glaciers goes largely unreported, even though it impacts more people.

Over the past several years, the Navdanya research teams have worked with local communities in Uttarakhand and Ladakh to assess the impact of climate change on their ecosystems and economies and to evolve participatory plans for climate change adaptation (for more on Navdanya, see p. 140).

In Ladakh, the northernmost region of India, all life depends on snow. Ladakh is a high altitude desert

"You are not Atlas carrying the world on your shoulder. It is good to remember that the planet is carrying you."
– Dr. Vandana Shiva

with only about 2 inches (5 centimeters) of annual rainfall. Ladakh's water comes from the snow melt—both the snow that falls on the land and provides the moisture for farming and pastures, as well as the snow of the glaciers that gently melts and feeds the streams that are the lifelines of the tiny settlements. Climate change is changing this. Less snow is falling, so there is less moisture for growing crops. In villages where the snowfall on the fields was the only source of moisture, farming is ending.

Reduced snowfall also means less snow on glaciers and less stream flow. The shorter period of snowfall prevents the snow from turning into hard ice crystals, which means that more of the glacier itself is liable to melt when the summer comes. Climate change has led to rain, rather than snow, falling even at higher altitudes. This accelerates the melting of glaciers. Heavy rainfall, which was unknown in the high altitude desert, has become frequent, causing flash floods, which wash away homes, fields, trees, and livestock.

Climate change thus initially leads to widespread flooding, but over time, as the snow disappears, there will be drought in the summer. Glacial runoff in the Himalayas is the largest source of fresh water for northern India and provides more than half the water to the Ganges. The loss of glacier meltdown would reduce the Ganges's flow by two-thirds from July through September, causing water shortages for five hundred million people and 37 percent of India's irrigated land. Glacial runoff is also the source for other rivers, including of the Indus, the Brahmaputra, the Irrawady, the Yellow, and the Yangtze.

According to the Intergovernmental Panel on Climate Change (IPCC), "glaciers in the Himalayas are receding faster than in any other part of the world and if the present rate continues, the likelihood of them disappearing by the year 2035 and perhaps sooner is very high if the earth keeps getting warmer." According to the IPCC report, the total area of glaciers in the Himalayas is likely to shrink from 1,930,051 square miles to 38,000 square miles by 2035.

The lives of billions are at stake. The Navdanya network has mobilized to start a participatory process for Himalayan communities to engage in the discussion on climate change, including issues of climate justice, adaptation, and disaster preparedness. In terms of numbers of people impacted, climate change at the Third Pole is the most far-reaching. No climate change policy or treaty will be complete without including Himalayan communities.

Reporting contributed by Dr. Vandana Shiva and Dr. Vinod Kumar Bhatt.

PART 04

Temperate/Subtropical Climates: Humid and Highland Zones

Temperate climates, as defined here, are a broad category, including climates typical of the subtropics—areas adjacent to the tropics in both the northern and southern hemispheres—but not limited to these regions. The Köppen system defines these climates by the first letter C on the climate map (pp. 22–23). By this classification, the zone incorporates many of the world's most densely settled areas, covering most of Europe and populous areas of the United States, northern China, Korea, India, Australia, Brazil, and parts of Africa.

There is a lot of variation between different types of temperate climates. This part of the book includes two: subtropical humid and subtropical highland. Part 5 includes the two other major temperate climate types: Mediterranean and maritime.

The subtropical climates are primarily between latitudes twenty and forty degrees from the equator, but can appear in a broad range of latitudes—including the tropics themselves. The humid subtropical climate features hot, moist summers and warm to cool winters; it is found on the southeast side of all continents. In warmer subtropical climates, the winters are mild, with rare occurrence of frost or snow. Precipitation may be evenly distributed throughout the year, or there may be a winter dry season. These climates often support temperate broadleaf deciduous forests with tree species such as oak, maple, beech, linden, walnut, and chestnut.

The subtropical highland climate exists in mountainous locations in both subtropical latitudes and beyond. Despite the latitude, these higher altitude regions share characteristics with maritime climates.

The subtropics are expected to spread toward the poles as a result of climate change, with reduced precipitation and expanded desert regions.[1]

Photo: Sean Gold

FOOD SECURITY IS REAL SECURITY. A GRANDMA AND GRANDCHILD IN THEIR HOME GARDEN, NEAR TELULLA VILLAGE, SRI LANKA.

Lagoswatta Ecovillage

Kalutara District, Sri Lanka

DR. AHANGAMAGE TUDOR ARIYARATNE, FOUNDER OF THE SARVODAYA SHRAMADANA MOVEMENT

Lagoswatta is located in the fishing district of Kalutara, south of the Sri Lankan capital of Colombo; it is situated on a gentle slope and bordered by rice fields. It is one example of the Sarvodaya movement at work. Translated as "the awakening of all through shared labor," Sarvodaya Shramadana began in 1958 in a Rodiya village in the tropical backwoods. The Rodiya are one of Sri Lanka's "untouchable" peoples. The villagers lived in ramshackle wattle-and-daub houses, wore little or nothing in the way of clothing, and ate by harvesting wild yams and yam leaves, hunting in the forest, and begging in neighboring villages.

Teachers and students from several schools volunteered their time and labor for a joint effort to help the Rodiya, who were normally regarded as anathema. They dug wells and latrines dug, improved the houses, cleared land for cultivation, planted gardens, and held instructional programs to teach the people about the importance of sanitation, education, and self-employment.

One of the people involved was Ahangamage Tudor Ariyaratne, a young high school teacher in Colombo, who was the founder—and later the president—of the movement. He led forty students and twelve teachers from his school to participate in what he regarded as an "educational experiment." This experiment—and its success—was repeated in other villages, evolving separately from Sri Lanka's Department of Rural Development over the next couple of years and resulting in the establishment of what would ultimately become the largest development organization in Sri Lanka—the Sarvodaya Shramadana Movement. Within a few years, hundreds of schools were forming Shramadana camps. Since then, millions of people have become involved in what is effectively a large-scale democratic revolution that has a no-poverty, no-affluence ideal. Lagoswatta is unique in the organization, as it is Sri Lanka's first official ecovillage and was created as part of the relief efforts in the wake of the devastating 2004 tsunami.

LAND TENURE/COMMUNITY GOVERNANCE

Village Self-Reliance: The Sarvodaya students and teachers, along with their rural counterparts and community members, gifted their labor, knowledge, and resources for the common well-being of the villages they served. They built new access roads, water and irrigation systems, wells,

TEN BASIC HUMAN NEEDS

Basic health care	A clean and beautiful environment
An adequate supply of safe water	Communication facilities
A balanced diet	Energy
Minimum requirements of clothing	Total education related to life and living
Simple housing	Cultural and spiritual engagement

wattle-and-daub houses, preschools, and community centers in these camps without any cost to the government.

While most national governments aim for economic growth, globalized integration, so-called trickle-down economics, and—inevitably—more control, the Sarvodaya movement targets village-scale self-reliance, cultural and economic equality, and true bottom-up democracy.

When Ariyaratne and his colleagues began the project, they first sought to learn the basic needs of the villagers; they asked villagers to list ten, in order of priority. After surveying 660 villagers and averaging the results they came up with a list of ten basic human needs. "Sarvodaya has a vision of a poverty-free world," reads the organization's website, "[where] basic human rights are upheld and basic human needs are satisfied."[2]

When Lagoswatta began construction in 2005, an important aspect of the work was the involvement of the intended residents in the construction process itself. Their participation helped build a sense of ownership and self-determination for their future, while giving survivors a sense of purpose that helped them deal psychologically with the trauma of the tsunami, the loss of loved ones, and the subsequent dramatic change in their circumstances. Lagoswatta was designed with the technical advice and guidance of Australian permaculture experts Max Lindegger and Lloyd Williams, of Ecological Solutions Incorporated. The Global Ecovillage Network helped fund it. Lagoswatta has become an excellent model not only for Sri Lanka but for village development and disaster relief efforts worldwide.

The ideal for every Sarvodaya village is *Grama Swarajya,* "self-governance," where every community effectively becomes its own village republic. Villages enlisting with Sarvodaya go through a five-step process that begins with the hearts and minds of the individual participants. The five steps are psychological infrastructure development; social infrastructure development; basic community needs and institutional development; income, employment, and self-financing; and sharing with neighboring villages.

A CLEAN AND BEAUTIFUL ENVIRONMENT, ENERGY, AND SIMPLE HOUSING. FULFILLING SEVERAL OF SARVODAYA'S "TEN BASIC HUMAN NEEDS," EACH HOME IN LAGOSWATTA HAS ITS OWN GARDEN AND A SOLAR PANEL FOR ELECTRICITY. RESIDENTS ARE POSITIVELY ENCOURAGED AND TRAINED IN COMPOSTING, GARDENING, RECYCLING, AND MAINTENANCE OF THE SOLAR PANEL AND BATTERY THAT PROVIDE ELECTRICITY TO EACH HOME—SOMETHING MANY RESIDENTS NEVER HAD BEFORE.

BUILDING

Designing an Ecovillage: Lagoswatta is now home to fifty-five families, who originally came from three villages in the area. Each earth-brick home measures about 500 square feet (46 square meters) and consists of two bedrooms, a living room, a kitchen, and sanitation facilities, as well as a garden and a solar panel.

Water for drinking and irrigation is one of the biggest problems Sri Lankans face. Construction for Lagoswatta thus included fourteen rainwater-harvesting tanks to collect roof runoff, five drinking wells, and two communal bathing wells. The home design includes an underground biological soakage system for household gray water. Homes are equipped with a recycling receptacle, and on the edge of the village is a small recycling station, where materials are separated and stored for monthly collection.

HEALTH/SPIRITUAL WELL-BEING

Permaculture and Buddhist Principles: For Ariyaratne, village development and social improvement are not ends in themselves. The ultimate goal of the movement is *Sarvodaya,* "awakening for all." *All* here means the individual, the village, the country, and, ultimately, the entire world. Grounded in Buddhist values, this awakening, or enlightenment, is achieved through *Shramadana*—the selfless acts of sharing one's labor—and through this, gaining empathy with one another's experiences and sufferings. Ariyaratne has found a way to apply these principles (which are found in all the world's major religions) on a scale and in a way that peacefully but profoundly challenges the global industrial development model they are juxtaposed against.

A BURIED UNGLAZED CLAY POT, FILLED WITH WATER AND COVERED WITH A RAG, PROVIDES UNDERGROUND IRRIGATION, AS WATER SLOWLY PERCOLATES THOUGH ITS POROUS WALLS, WITH ALMOST NO EVAPORATION.

CULTURE/EDUCATION

Village-Level Independence: Nandana Jayasinghe, director of Sarvodaya's Agriculture Cluster and Development Education Institute, works to increase village-level independence by supplementing—but not supplanting—local knowledge with permaculture techniques suitable for their climate and culture. In recent years, Jayasinghe has been organizing annual Permaculture Design Certificate (PDC) courses with visiting international trainers.

According to Jayasinghe, about eighty villages within their network are specifically practicing permaculture, while the remaining villages almost universally reject conventional agrochemicals, due to the chemicals' disharmony with Sarvodaya's principles of prioritizing the health of their environment. The ethical basis of permaculture intersects very well with the Buddhist majority of Sri Lanka, whose

THIS VERTICAL LETTUCE RACK INCREASES YIELD PER SQUARE METER. BAMBOO IS HALVED TO FORM GROWING GUTTERS AND NAILED TO SUPPORTS. THE RACK IS PORTABLE, SAVES SPACE, AND CAN PROVIDE SHADE FOR SHADE-LOVING PLANTS.

worldview promotes a deep respect for the right to life of all creatures within the biosphere.

FINANCES/ECONOMICS

Microloans for Economic Development: Locally based economics, with a focus on low-tech solutions and voluntary simplicity, is another part of the Sarvodaya vision. Economic development in the Sarvodaya framework comes only after inner, personal development, with the goal of minimizing overly materialistic, ego-based ambition.

To facilitate local economic development, Sarvodaya created SEEDS (Sarvodaya Economic Enterprises Development Services). There are now more than five thousand SEEDS offices in Sarvodaya communities across the country—one for every three of Sarvodaya's over fifteen thousand villages.

If someone wants to provide people in the community with locally made ceramics, just getting started—by building or buying a pottery wheel and kiln—might be impossible without some financial assistance. This is where a microloan comes in. The SEEDS network provides startup capital for projects such as bakeries, small retail stores, and roadside market-garden stalls, and it helps people buy items such as sewing machines, garden infrastructure, and three-wheeler vehicles.

Most microloans are 3,000 to 4,000 Sri Lankan rupees ($27 to $36), with a maximum of 100,000 rupees ($900) for a small business. The SEEDS network measures requests for loans against the base ethics determined by the Sarvodaya communities themselves. Business proposals out of harmony with community-determined principles are rejected. In the Sarvodaya context, this means no support is given to businesses involving products or services deemed detrimental to the community as

COCONUT SHELLS MAKE EXCELLENT, BIODEGRADABLE PLANTERS. THE COIR (HUSK FIBER) IS EXTRACTED AND MIXED WITH SOIL TO BECOME A POTTING MIX WITH PARTICULARLY GOOD WATER RETENTION CAPACITY, BECAUSE IT REDUCES EVAPORATION.

PRODUCE NO WASTE: LAGOSWATTA'S BIOGAS SYSTEM USES THREE UNDERGROUND CONCRETE- LINED CHAMBERS IN A PROCESS THAT CONVERTS WASTE FROM COWS INTO A VALUABLE COOKING FUEL.

THE BLUE FLAME SHOWS THE EFFICIENT, CLEAN BURN THAT METHANE GAS PRODUCES. THE WASTE FROM THREE COWS IS MORE THAN SUFFICIENT TO KEEP THIS FIRE BURNING FOR THIS FAMILY OF EIGHT ALL DAY, EVERY DAY—COOKING GRAINS AND OTHER FOODS AND BOILING WATER, TO ENSURE HEALTHY DRINKING WATER.

LAGOSWATTA IS PART OF A NETWORK OF FIFTEEN THOUSAND SARVODAYA VILLAGES, CLOSE TO HALF OF THE TOTAL NUMBER OF VILLAGES IN SRI LANKA.

a whole, like alcohol, cigarettes, and gambling, or damaging to the environment.

Significantly, unlike faceless collateral-based loans from large centralized banks, SEEDS loans are made at the community level, among people who have a relationship with one another. Securing a loan is hence based more on connection and trust than on collateral security.

TOOLS/TECHNOLOGY

Biogas: Biodigestion is a permaculture design technique that is practical and rewarding. Some home gardeners use biogas to meet one of their energy requirements in a closed loop. Families that have enough land to keep a few cows—and with about $100 for the initial installation of equipment—can easily supply enough methane gas from a biogas system to fuel all their cooking requirements.

The biogas installation pictured here (middle) consists of three concrete-lined chambers. The one on the right is about 2 feet deep. Cow manure is shoveled into water in that first chamber. The slurry flows through an underground pipe into the center chamber, about 12 feet deep and 3 feet wide (3.5 meters by 1 meter). Methane gas builds up in this chamber and flows through the small hose you can see running toward the house; it goes directly into the kitchen (pictured bottom left). Overflow from this central chamber goes into the chamber at left; it is later shoveled out and mixed into composts.

Across the kitchen is the wood burning stove, what they had to use before the biogas installation. The gas cooker saves a lot of time that was once spent collecting firewood, which was often scarce and which produced smoke that choked lungs and the atmosphere. Dead wood can now be composted or used in construction, and carbon emissions are reduced, because biogas burns cleaner than wood. To date, there are about sixty to seventy such biogas installations working efficiently within the Sarvodaya network.

Reporting and photos contributed by Craig Mackintosh. For more, see "Letters from Sri Lanka" at permaculturenews.org.

Bija Vidyapeeth and Navdanya

Doon Valley, Uttarakhand, India

Photo: Navdanya

NAVDANYA'S SEED BANKS HONOR NATURE'S SLOW PROCESS OF CROSS-POLLINATION AND HYBRIDIZATION, PRESERVING A RICH GENETIC LEGACY THAT TOOK MILLIONS OF YEARS TO CREATE.

The state of Uttarakhand lies on the southern slope of the Himalayas, between the Ganges and Yamuna rivers. Climate and vegetation here vary greatly with elevation, from glaciers at the peaks to subtropical forests at the lower elevations. Bija Vidyapeeth is located outside of Dehradun, in the Doon Valley, and has the humid subtropical climate typical of the Himalayan foothills.

Bija Vidyapeeth is a biodiverse, highly productive, organic 45-acre (18-hectare) farm and orchard. The farm's regenerative practices are restoring soil that was desertified by conventional monoculture. The farm now produces more than 1,500 varieties of plants, including 600 types of rice, 160 types of wheat, and diverse varieties of millet, pulses, oilseeds, vegetables, and medicinal plants. It is nestled within the larger campus of the Earth University, a hub of the Navdanya network.

Founded by world-renowned environmentalist, physicist, and activist Dr. Vandana Shiva (see pp. 128-129), Navdanya began as a participatory research initiative. It was born out of a search for a nonviolent farming approach. It has been promoting organic farming, saving seeds, and creating awareness on the hazards of genetic engineering since 1984. At its core, the organization is about balancing the needs of healthy ecosystems and people, especially those relying on the land as their source of livelihood. Navdanya is a network of seed keepers and organic producers spread across sixteen states in India. The foundation has helped set up fifty-four community seed banks across the country and has trained over five hundred thousand farmers in food sovereignty and sustainable agriculture over the past two decades.

In 1996, the Navdanya foundation acquired land on the outskirts of Dehradun and established the seed bank in order to bring resources to local farmers and help them diversify their crops. Bija Vidyapeeth, which loosely translates to "School of the Seed," was established by Satish Kumar and Vandana Shiva after the 9/11 terrorist attacks in New York, promoting "a vision of holistic solutions rooted in deep ecology and democracy as an alternative to the current world order."[3] It is located on Navdanya's biodiversity conservation and organic farm in Doon Valley. Prior to the establishment of the school and farm, the land was a toxic desert—an aftermath of eucalyptus monoculture.

The efforts of the residents, teachers, and students have nursed the plot back to health and rejuvenated the soil. Utilizing the Bija Vidyapeeth farm campus, the Earth University was created to inspire local farmers to learn more about agricultural diversity and ecological processes. It also hosts interns from around the world, offering them a unique, immersive learning experience.

In the past decade, Dr. Shiva and the Navdanya network have been responsible for bringing the notion of biopiracy—the exploitation of indigenous knowledge of nature for commercial gain without permission—to the forefront of discussions of globalization. The campaign ties in with the ethos of protecting low-income farmers and indigenous knowledge and, consequently, food rights and food sovereignty in the face of industrial agriculture.

Navdanya operates on multiple scales and in various realms. Most broadly, it aims at integration: reconnecting people with natural cycles and working from the seed to the table. Within the political arena, it links the farmers' fields to governmental policy. As a cultural movement, it strives to connect ancestral knowledge to the future, for the sake of children and grandchildren.

Regenerative design strategies in use on the Bija Vidyapeeth campus:

Use of solar energy for supply of warm water and electricity

Rain and gray-water harvesting for irrigation purposes

Biogas production for cooking purposes

Using bulls for farming practices such as hulling instead of machinery

Compost production for soil fertilization

Consumption of mostly farm or local products

Using companion planting in order to promote biodiversity and enhance yields by using the natural synergy among plants

Photo: Navdanya

HEALTHY COOKING CLASSES AT BIJA VIDYAPEETH.

CULTURE/EDUCATION

Empowering People: The focus on seeds has set Navdanya apart from other environmental organizations. A main goal is to empower farmers with knowledge of heritage seed varieties and issues related to genetically modified seeds (such as the long-term effects of using the high-yielding corporate seeds that were promoted so broadly during the South Asian Green Revolution). They have battled corporations, including Monsanto, over the issue of biopiracy, and won major legal victories related to the patenting of traditional varieties of rice and the medicinal uses of the neem tree.

Through grassroots conservation efforts, awareness campaigns, and cultural festivals, Navdanya works to protect the biodiversity of India. The festivals strengthen the network's efforts by bringing people together and helping them to recognize that nature and biodiversity are the basis of the cultural and material sustenance of their lives.

The Earth University program is within the biodiversity conservation farm of Bija Vidyapeeth; it aims to spread knowledge about holistic ways of life and livelihood, respectful of both the environment and the people. It recognizes that the land is the source of income for a large percentage of the population of India, and it aims to teach farmers how to get the most out of the land while keeping in line with what is best for the land.

The courses held at Bija Vidyapeeth have mainly been based around biodiverse and organic farming, earth democracy, Gandhian philosophy, and human rights in the face of economic globalization dominated by big companies. All in all, the overarching goal of all these courses is to create awareness and help the participants to "be the change that [they] wish to see in the world" (as Gandhi said) by becoming better local and global citizens. The program is run in association with Schumacher College in the United Kingdom, and lecturers have included the physicist Fritjof Capra and Anita Roddick, the eco-social entrepreneur and founder of the Body Shop.

HEALTH/SPIRITUAL WELL-BEING

Ecology of the Earth and the Body: According to Dr. Shiva, the philosophies of Gandhi are a driving force behind the network, helping it to stay grounded and to define its actions more clearly. Gandhi's teaching of *swaraj*, "self-rule," or "responsibility for one's own domain," has an overarching presence—be it water sovereignty, food sovereignty, or seed sovereignty.

Navdanya is a Hindi word that means "nine seeds." These nine seeds represent India's food security, connoting a diverse ecological balance at every level—from the ecology of the earth to the ecology of our bodies.

Photo: GandhiMedia.org

MOHANDAS GANDHI PROMOTED A DECENTRALIZED, INDEPENDENT SOCIETY, CAPABLE OF MEETING ITS NEEDS BY LOCAL MEANS. EMPLOYING NONVIOLENT CIVIL DISOBEDIENCE, GANDHI LED INDIA TO INDEPENDENCE AND INSPIRED MOVEMENTS FOR CIVIL RIGHTS AND FREEDOM AROUND THE WORLD.

The nine seeds are:

Yava (barley) represents Aditya (the sun)

Shamaka (millet) represents Chandra (the moon)

Togari (pigeon pea) represents Mangala (Mars)

Madga (mung bean) represents Budha (Mercury)

Kadale (chickpea) represents Brihaspati (Jupiter)

Tandula (rice) represents Shukra (Venus)

Til (sesame) represents Shani (Saturn)

Maasha (black gram) represents Rahu (north lunar node, where the moon crosses the sun's path)

Kulittha (horse gram) represents Ketu (south lunar node or shadow planet)

Reporting contributed by Muneezay Jaffery.

Auroville Township and Ecovillage

Viluppuram District, Tamil Nadu, India

Photo: AurovilleOutreachMedia

AT THE CENTER OF AUROVILLE STANDS THE MATRIMANDIR, THE "TEMPLE OF THE MOTHER." IN THE MIDDLE OF THE ADJACENT AMPHITHEATER, A LOTUS-SHAPED URN CONTAINS THE AUROVILLE CHARTER AND SAMPLES OF EARTH FROM ALL OVER INDIA AND THE WORLD, A GESTURE OF NATIONAL AND GLOBAL HUMAN UNITY.

The "city of dawn," Auroville, is on a low-lying plateau in a humid, subtropical zone on the Bay of Bengal in southern India. Auroville has grown to be a model city for harmonious and environmentally sustainable living with a population of around 2,300. The layout of the site, designed by architect Roger Anger, mimics a spiraling galaxy and embodies the ethos of unity and integration with nature that is alive there. The collaborative efforts undertaken by communities and volunteers at the township resonate with permaculture principles and have resulted in remarkable achievements, such as reforestation, efficient resource management, and community cohesion. Just over 40 percent of the residents are Indian, with the remainder originating from nearly fifty different countries.

"Auroville has always embodied sustainability as a theme," says Bill Sullivan, a resident of the township since 1974 who is currently involved in the community's zero-waste initiative. "An inspiration to live to a higher calling is enough to sustain people living here."[4]

In the mid-twentieth century, founder Mirra Afassa (a.k.a. "The Mother"), inspired by the teachings of spiritual leader Sri Aurobindo and with the assistance of an offshoot of his ashram, which carries his name, conceived the idea of establishing a "universal township." The vision was born into reality in 1968, when an inauguration ceremony brought together representatives from 124 nations to officially found the settlement. The representatives brought soil from their homelands to be mixed in a white marble urn in the shape of a lotus bud, now a focal point in the community's amphitheater and a symbol of the township's purpose: the realization of human unity in diversity.

Photo: Sergio Lub

DUE TO DEFORESTATION, THE RESIDENTS FOUND A PARCHED, BARREN LANDSCAPE WHEN THEY ARRIVED IN THE LATE 1960S. THEIR EFFORTS TO REPLANT AND REHYDRATE THE LANDSCAPE HAVE PAID OFF.

Sri Aurobindo (1872–1950) was an Indian nationalist and freedom fighter, as well as a yogi, prolific poet, spiritual teacher, and writer. Auroville can be viewed as an effort to manifest his vision of integral yoga—a "yoga of synthesis" geared toward the evolution of a practitioner's life into a "life divine." Aurobindo wrote, "Man is a transitional being. He is not final. . . . The step from man to superman is the next approaching achievement in the earth evolution. It is inevitable because it is at once the intention of the inner spirit and the logic of Nature's process."[5] The goal of this practice is to transform the self in order to bring together the disparate elements of humanity toward living harmoniously as members of one universal family.

Hundreds of years ago, forests covered the land that is becoming Auroville, but when the first residents arrived, they found a parched and barren landscape. Deforestation, floods, and winds had rendered the land unsuitable for farming. Starting small, the residents dug wells, began designing irrigation systems, and planted the area. They put in nitrogen-fixing hedges and built up the soil using biomass to make compost and mulch. To contain the monsoon rains that washed away topsoil, the residents created earthen embankments and small dams, water-collecting technologies that held water until it was needed in the dry season for irrigation and allowed it to replenish underground aquifers.

The concerted efforts of the residents have paid off, and today over two million native hedges, fruit trees, and fuelwood trees have been planted in Auroville. The trees have restored the land for productive agriculture by preventing erosion and returning necessary nutrients to the soil.

LAND TENURE/COMMUNITY GOVERNANCE

Zoning and Civic Participation: The concept of universal suffrage applies at all levels of decision making at Auroville. Accepted members of Auroville are entered in the register of residents who collectively form the Residents Assembly. Working groups take part in all forms of community activities, ranging from land-resource management to budget control to new member applications.

Peace Area: At the heart of the site are gardens, the Matrimandir temple, an amphitheater, and a hundred-year-old banyan tree at the geographical center of Auroville.

The Residential Zone: Covering an area of over 400 acres (189 hectares), the residential zone is an area for community and individual housing. It also includes dining facilities, community kitchens, social gathering areas, gardens, and libraries. The zone has been designed to be 45 percent built surface and 55 percent green space.

The Industrial Zone: The smallest of the four main zones, the industrial zone covers an area of 360 acres (109 hectares) and includes all the business and commercial units—the cottage industries and manufacturing units operating in Auroville. Impacts on the environment are meticulously taken into consideration before a commercial unit is established.

The Cultural Zone: The hub for education, art, and cultural activities. It includes schools, sports fields, a music studio, and a center for performing arts. An artists' settlement in this zone offers various workshop spaces and a theater.

The International Zone: An area within the township dedicated to collaborative work between countries around the world, expressing Auroville's philosophies of unity and universality.

The Green Belt: The outermost zone surrounding the central township; it promotes efficient environmental management by protecting the land, conserving water, and enriching biodiversity. Sections of this zone are also used to experiment with conservation and food-growing techniques.

CULTURE/EDUCATION

Unending Education: The cultural zone in Auroville includes a number of schools offering full primary and secondary education, adhering to a curriculum that recognizes and works on the development of four aspects of every child, the mental, physical, emotional, and psychic. Students are also prepared for entering universities around the world. Children between the ages of two and four can be sent to crèche, or preschool (there are three operating in the community).

One of the philosophies behind Auroville, included in its charter, is the concept of "unending education"—that there are no age limits to education. Learning can be gained from various research centers, such as the Center for Scientific Research, and also by taking classes in a host of topics, including languages, cultural studies, yoga, and healing.

The Auroville Volunteering, Internships, and Studies Program is a testament to the community's philosophy of unending education. This course allows people from all over the world to come to the township to experience its teachings and way of life and to learn from the land and nature first-hand.

BUILDING

USING ON-SITE RESOURCES—COMPRESSED STABILIZED EARTH BLOCKS, EMPLOYED FOR VAULTS AND DOMES, SAVE IMMENSE QUANTITIES OF STEEL AND CONCRETE. STABILIZED EARTH MORTAR IS USED AND THE WALLS EXPOSED TO RAIN ARE PLASTERED WITH LIME STABILIZED EARTH PLASTER.

Auroville Earth Institute: The Auroville Earth Institute researches, develops, promotes, and transfers earth-based building approaches that are cost and energy effective. Founded in 1989 by the Indian government, the institute evolved into its current form in 2004. Its main technology is Compressed Stabilized Earth Blocks, which are approved by the government for disaster resistance. The institute is part of a worldwide network, along with the International Centre for Earth Construction, ABC Terra in Brazil, and a number of Indian NGOs.

Satprem Maini, who cofounded the institute, was drawn to the intersection of spirituality and architecture. He is currently developing a one- to two-year program for both trained and lay earth builders to learn appropriate technologies, water systems, and earth-building strategies. "The first condition for sustainable development is the proper management of human resources," Maini says.[6]

FINANCES/ECONOMICS

Phasing Out Cash: Auroville functions as a collective economy with minimal cash exchange between individuals and groups. Instead, there are two forms of funds operating: the City Services Fund and the Unity Fund.

In the 1980s, Auroville established the Maintenance Fund (now known as the City Services Fund) to gradually phase out all cash transactions in the entire township including purchases in shops and restaurants. They achieved this by first setting up cash accounts for all the registered commercial/business units and registered residents in Auroville—guests are provided temporary accounts. In order to make payments, the local bank authorizes transfers between the relevant accounts. Members of the community who are working full time in any of Auroville's community projects are given a monthly maintenance that goes directly into their (personal) maintenance account and can be considered a salary. Members who have an income from outside Auroville are able to pay this into their maintenance account as well.

ONE OF THE AIMS OF THE AUROVILLE EARTH INSTITUTE IS TO EMPOWER PEOPLE TO CREATE HABITAT FOR THEMSELVES, USING THE RESOURCES THAT ARE READILY ACCESSIBLE, LIKE THE EARTHEN BLOCKS. THE INSTITUTE SEES THIS AS A FORM OF SOCIAL ACTIVISM.

SPIRULINA PRODUCTION IN NADUKUPPAM, ONE OF THE MANY COTTAGE INDUSTRIES RUN BY THE PITCHANDIKULAM BIO-RESOURCE CENTRE IN AUROVILLE. WHILE MAKING A PROFIT, THE ETHIC OF EARTH CARE IS HELD ALOFT HERE. IMPACTS ON THE ENVIRONMENT ARE TAKEN INTO CONSIDERATION BEFORE A COMMERCIAL UNIT IS ESTABLISHED.

SOLAR ENERGY IS ONE OF THE MOST ABUNDANT RESOURCES IN SOUTHERN INDIA. THIS "SOLAR BOWL" COOKS TWO MEALS A DAY FOR 1,000 PEOPLE. THE STATIONARY BOWL FOCUSES THE SUN'S RAYS ON A CYLINDRICAL BOILER THAT FOLLOWS THE SUN'S PATH WITH THE USE OF A COMPUTER-DRIVEN HELIOSTAT.

The other fund operational at Auroville is the Unity or Central Fund. Established in 1989, it is at the core of all economic activity taking place in Auroville and ensures community services and activities, which residents don't pay for directly, run smoothly. Some of the regular sources for this fund are international grants and donations, plus income from the community itself. The commercial enterprises at the ecovillage are required to contribute 33 percent of their annual surplus income to the fund, and each household in the ecovillage makes a monthly contribution of 1,500 rupees ($27).

This form of communal economy is successful at Auroville because of its small size. This also allows a large number of community activities to be free of charge and conveys a strong message about the value of social and spiritual participation at the township.

LAND/NATURE STEWARDSHIP

Food Sources and Systems: In the main township area, meals are served in communal dining halls, and there are a number of restaurants and cafés in the residential zones of the village. Most food expenses in the dining areas are covered by the monthly payments made by registered residents.

Auroville is moving toward greater self-reliance in its food systems. At the moment, the green belt produces just 2 percent of the community's total rice and grain requirements and about 50 percent of its total fruit and vegetable requirements. Since Cyclone Thane, a new space for the ecovillage's farmers to put forth their needs has been opened at the monthly financial meeting to help the larger community understand how agriculture can best be supported there. This could include seed supply, subsidizing food production, and also increasing the demand for locally grown food by keeping costs low for the consumers.

A small proportion of the green belt on the outskirts of the site is used for agricultural activities, where organic, biodynamic, and permaculture techniques are tested. Foraging for fruits, especially berries, is being promoted by communities like the Sadhana Forest (see p. 151). The community is planting "seed hubs" (trees or bushes that bear fruit easy to eat immediately) along walking trails in order to encourage growth of the forest. The idea is people walking along the trail will pick the fruit from these seed hubs and spit out seeds as they walk further along the trail, resulting in growth and diversification of forest cover.

Water Sources and Systems: Water in this area is predominantly sourced from groundwater storage in the form of aquifers. In order to meet the township's water needs without overexploiting underground water sources, they have developed a horizontal gravel filter that incorporates the root zones of plants such as canna and gladiolus, through which gray water is cycled for reuse. Given its location—in a fairly dry part of southern India—communities and researchers in Auroville are perfecting numerous examples of water projects, techniques, and methodologies. The research units established here are at the forefront of devising sustainable, environmentally friendly techniques for water resource management. This includes water treatment, distribution, storage, and accessibility.

The Auroville Water Harvest unit is described as "an integrated water development agency" that aims to "develop efficient and sustainable

THE SEVENTEEN-UNIT "REALIZATION" APARTMENTS COMPLEX EMPLOYS SEVERAL ENERGY-CONSERVATION SYSTEMS. MOST INNOVATIVE WAS AN EARTH COOLING TUNNEL THAT PULLS HOT AIR THROUGH A PIPE THAT RUNS THROUGH THE BOTTOM OF A MASSIVE RAINWATER-HARVESTING TANK, ALLOWING IT TO COOL BY HEAT EXCHANGE, BEFORE THE AIR IS PUMPED INTO RESIDENTIAL UNITS. BOTH DEPENDENCY ON CHEMICAL COOLANTS AND CONSIDERABLE ELECTRICITY INPUTS ARE TRANSCENDED BY THIS INNOVATIVE **STACKING OF FUNCTIONS**.

re-mediation techniques based on deep understanding of the surface and groundwater systems." They work on battling saline water intrusion, which takes place when overexploitation of groundwater from coastal aquifers results in seawater entering and contaminating the aquifers. This is also a social concern, as the water can no longer be used by humans and income-generating activities, such as farming. This Auroville Water Harvest unit has designed decentralized wastewater treatment plants and systems for rainwater harvesting. An interdisciplinary approach enables them to focus on the social aspects and environmental concerns related to water-resource management. Sociological research is incorporated, as the group believes that perceptions of water are closely linked to how it is used.

Another research unit operating here is Aqua Dyn Auroville. The unit is based on the Vedic and Dravidian concept of *thaneer pandall*, "the gift of water." Aqua Dyn views fair access to clean water as integral to a just culture, echoing the simple ethics at the foundations of permaculture: earth care, people care, and fair share (see p. 15). Reliable supplies of pure, clean, potable water are scarce in many parts of the world, especially degraded areas, like this part of Tamil Nadu, and this unit strives to provide water infrastructure for villages without access to a clean water supply

Reporting contributed by Muneezay Jaffery.
Photos contributed by Satprem, courtesy of Auroville Earth Institute, unless otherwise noted.

Photos courtesy of Sadhana Forest

SADHANA FOREST COMMUNITY

In 2003, the Sadhana Forest community was established within Auroville by Yorit and Aviram Rozin. A century before, this area of roughly 70 acres (28 hectares) was covered in tropical, dry evergreen forest. Deforestation of the area wiped out nearly all of the indigenous trees, essential nutrients leached out of the land, and the water cycle needed for growing was disrupted. The process of desertification was gradually taking over the surrounding land.

Sadhana Forest's aim is to assist the land in reverting back to a healthy state and to reestablish the naturally occurring, healthy, closed-loop cycles within this ecosystem. Members of the community have introduced permaculture principles for effective land- and water-resource management, referring to the entire process as ecological revival. Another goal is to enable and empower the local rural villages to cultivate their own food and become more self-reliant through reforestation. "The main aim of this ecological project is to support the local rural villages: by retaining water and filling the aquifer, Sadhana Forest allows the villagers to cultivate their food and prevents exodus towards nearby city slums," Aviram says.

"BY RETAINING WATER AND FILLING THE AQUIFER, SADHANA FOREST ALLOWS VILLAGERS TO CULTIVATE THEIR FOOD AND PREVENTS EXODUS TOWARD NEARBY CITY SLUMS."

Some unique aspects of Sadhana Forest are:

Its volunteer base: The project is carried out entirely by volunteers, both residential and temporary visitors to the community, estimated to number about one thousand per year, from over fifty countries.

Its economic self-reliance: The tasks carried out are not reliant on outside funding. This makes it cost effective and constant, and it also brings out the right message to the people.

Replicability: The aim has always been to "create a grassroots movement that can be achieved by replicating itself." They are now looking into replicating the project in Morocco and Haiti.

Experimentation: "Sadhana Forest intends to explore new ways of doing old things," Aviram explains. Putting new ideas into action using onsite material has resulted in innovative techniques with nature and people at the forefront.

According to the founders, understanding the needs of the land was essential, and they soon realized that their first priority was to increase the soil fertility. They added nitrogen-fixing hedges of beans and legumes, which have been successful in restoring the nutrient content of the soil. They also added biomass and compost to the ground to create an organic mulch layer, which acts as a protective layer of topsoil and assists in retaining moisture and nutrients.

Despite the progress they were making, they still needed to develop protection from climatic risks such as monsoons, which hit this part of India every autumn with torrential rains. The lack of forest cover was one of the main reasons for soil erosion. They needed to take measures to reduce the amount of surface flow and topsoil erosion that followed the monsoon rains. The community residents constructed a number of features using earth materials, including comprehensive embankments, known as bunds, and small dams. Both have worked well for collecting water and also demonstrate the sustainable use of earth material for construction. These earthworks hold water until it is needed for irrigation during the dry season, and a small amount percolates down to the water table, replenishing underground aquifers. One of the greatest achievements of this project has been to replenish the previously dry aquifer to full capacity.

While Sadhana Forest started as an environmental project focused on reforestation, gradually the focus has become regeneration from a broader, systems-level standpoint. The project's acceptance of feedback and subsequent evolution has been essential to its work—insight and input from volunteers from a variety of backgrounds adds to the knowledge base, and techniques are tested out. Collectively, the participants bring "not just expertise, but optimism," says Aviram.

Reporting contributed by Shelini Harris.

Photo: Willam Yu

RICE TERRACES, CULTIVATED BY THE HANI PEOPLE FOR MANY HUNDREDS OF YEARS IN THE DUOYISHU VALLEY, YUNNAN PROVINCE, CHINA.

TERRACING: AN ANCIENT TECHNIQUE ESSENTIAL TO MODERN PERMACULTURE

Terrace agriculture is a method of maximizing growing space on mountainsides achieved through the construction of graduated field platforms on contour with a landscape. This type of agriculture has been practiced for centuries throughout Asia and around the world, a picturesque example of the permaculture approach to rainwater: slow it, spread it and sink it. Terracing increases infiltration of rain and irrigation water and reduces surface runoff, thus preventing excessive soil erosion and water loss. Though labor-intensive to create, it is easier to plough, sow and harvest on the level terraces than on an incline. As the effects of climate change become more apparent with erratic monsoons and rapidly depleting groundwater reserves, ancient techniques such as terracing take on a new relevance. Terrace systems demonstrate the permaculture approach of ***stacking functions***, where one design element creates multiple benefits. A number of other permaculture principles are apparent here as well: terraces are designed ***from patterns to details*** and successfully ***catch and store energy*** in the form of water, soil and labor.

O-Farm and Hong Kong's Agriculture

Hong Kong, China

Photo: Benjamin Gottlieb

THE "ECO-MAMA" ROOFTOP FARM BRINGS A LITTLE GREEN TO THE CONCRETE OF HONG KONG'S QUARY BAY DISTRICT.

Hong Kong is one of the most densely populated cities in the world, with roughly seven million residents packed into a sea of apartment buildings, making urban farms practically impossible anywhere other than on the rooftops. Beyond the logistical challenges of planting crops in a city void of open space, many of Hong Kong's agriculture pioneers are frustrated by the local government's lackluster support of urban farming. Despite these roadblocks, food forests continue to be established on rooftops and in the few open lots sprinkled throughout a region that imports more than ninety percent of its food. O-Farm is one of these: an organic community garden where very small spaces—86 square feet (8 square meters) on average—are rented by Hong Kong residents. O-Farm is one of an estimated three hundred urban farming projects that now occupy the spaces between and atop the megacity's high-rises, joining the broader, global movement of food sustainability projects in city settings.

IN KEEPING WITH THE **SHARE THE SURPLUS** ETHIC, YIP TSZ SHING AND HIS WIFE, SHIRLEY, MAKE A CUSTOM OF SHARING THEIR WINTER MELON HARVEST WITH ALL MEMBERS. THE BIGGEST MELON WEIGHED SIXTY-EIGHT POUNDS!

O-FARM IS AN ORGANIC COMMUNITY GARDEN THAT OFFERS CITY-DWELLERS A FEW SQUARE METERS OF EARTH THOUGH WHICH THEY CAN RECONNECT TO THEIR FOOD AND EACH OTHER; THE SOCIAL INTERACTION WITH OTHER "O-FARMERS" IS A BIG DRAW.

Some members of O-Farm travel long distances to garden fresh organic food and have social interaction with other community gardeners. The miniature farm produces its own natural fertilizer and has a few small, super-efficient rocket stoves used for cooking food on site. Concerns about the safety of practices at mainland Chinese farms, where the majority of Hong Kong's produce comes from, have fueled the growing appetite for organics. A number of highly publicized scandals involving industrial chemical use by farmers prompted more consumers to pay higher prices for certified organic produce.

"There are food forests and productive trees in amongst small vegetable gardens, small but very productive and diverse by nature. There are hundreds of different innovative techniques being implemented for things such as bird scaring, tool storage, food drying, trellises and compost systems, along with intricate watering systems," observes permaculture teacher Geoff Lawton on a visit to O-Farm. "Then there are the lovely little personal decorative touches that you can see all around—for example in the different fences. There are small competitions held amongst gardeners for the most productive [garden], the most diverse and of course the prize for the largest [vegetable] of its kind."

A small neighboring farm has now also become organic, influenced by the success and popularity of O-Farm, which hosts lectures and discussions on environmental and health issues and has a shop selling organic products. Despite this encouraging trend, Chan Choi-hi, a member of the Hong Kong district council, said the Hong Kong government must do more to build a viable urban-agriculture policy.

"There is no policy, no vision and no idea of how to do urban farming in Hong Kong from the government. It's not even in the agenda," Chan says. "So first of all, we are trying to push this idea from an economic angle." The economic angle, Chan says, may be the only way to convince top government officials to invest time and resources into bolstering Hong Kong's nascent urban farming movement. Farming makes up just a fraction of Hong Kong's current GDP, however, and employs just 4,700 residents,

NATURE'S ALTERNATIVE TO CHEMICAL SNAIL-KILLER. APPLE SNAILS ARE SERIOUS PESTS IN CHINA, DAMAGING AGRICULTURE AND NATURAL ECOSYSTEMS. DUCKS KEEP THE SNAILS IN CHECK WHILE ADDING FERTILITY TO THE SOIL.

according to Hong Kong's Agriculture, Fisheries, and Conservation Department, less than one-tenth of 1 percent of the population. Only 1.6 percent of land is farmed, most of it in the New Territories, on the city's far northern rim—and even that acreage is under threat from developers. A government proposal to develop the New Territories threatens to remove about 242 acres of farmland, according to a joint statement issued by green groups. This accounts for about 13 percent of Hong Kong's active farmland, they say.[7]

The government has set up roughly thirty urban farm plots across the territory, but many are found in the median strip between highways or in remote locations of the city, rendering them both unattractive and inconvenient for residents, says Sam Hui, an architecture and engineering professor at Hong Kong University. "If we really want to see the maximum benefits of urban farming here we have to create more rooftop farms," says Hui, whose research focuses on sustainable agriculture and green roof use.

"There are a lot of empty, leftover rooftops that could easily be transformed into fields," confirms Osbert Lam, a local entrepreneur who, in 2011, started City Farm, fourteen stories above the street. For just $15 per month, Lam rents out toolbox-sized planter boxes to businessmen, elderly couples, and families alike, and even runs horticulture classes. He mixes soil imported from Germany with moss, sand, and compost

Photo: Benjamin Gottlieb

THE BEGINNING OF A POSITIVE TREND? AS OF 2012 THERE WERE ABOUT ONE HUNDRED CERTIFIED ORGANIC FARMS IN HONG KONG; SEVEN YEARS EARLIER, THERE HAD BEEN NONE. BUT WITH THREE HUNDRED URBAN FARMING PROJECTS IN A CITY OF SEVEN MILLION, THE PERMACULTURE IDEAL OF A DECENTRALIZED, LOCAL FOOD SYSTEM IS STILL A WAY OFF.

to fill his planters, and lets the humid, subtropical climate do the rest.

"Twenty years ago, locals thought the soil here was dirty," says Simon Chau, founder of Produce Green Foundation, which manages Hong Kong's first urban farm, in Tsuen Wan. "Now, after twenty years, people have started to realize that it is rewarding and meaningful to grow something themselves and to eat it."

Beyond convincing politicians, Chau says Hong Kongers themselves have historically been resistant to the idea of farming as a suitable pastime. "It is the lowest of our traditional caste system. In traditional Chinese culture, if you're good at nothing else, you work on the farm," Chau says. "Also, Hong Kong is a very money-minded place. . . . Land is also very expensive in Hong Kong, so people don't spend time worrying about growing their own food."

Despite the many challenges facing urban agriculture in the region, Osbert Lam is optimistic that his vision of a megacity capped with green gardens will be realized. "I believe you can build a community of rooftop farmers here in Hong Kong."[8]

Reporting contributed by Benjamin Gottlieb and Geoff Lawton. Photos contributed by Geoff Lawton, unless otherwise noted.

Fuzhou Wastewater Treatment Project

Fuzhou, Fujian, China

THE BAIMA CANAL IN FUSHOU EVENTUALLY EMPTIES INTO THE MINJIANG RIVER AND WAS CHOSEN FOR A PILOT REMEDIATION PROJECT AS IT WAS HIGHLY POLLUTED, WITH AN INFLUX OF ALMOST 750,000 GALLONS OF UNTREATED DOMESTIC SEWAGE PER DAY.

A LINEAR RESTORER WITH TWELVE THOUSAND PLANTS OF OVER TWENTY NATIVE SPECIES WAS INSTALLED. THE PLANT ROOT ZONES AND FABRIC MEDIUM OF THE RESTORER PROVIDE THE BIOPHYSICALLY DIVERSE SURFACE AREAS NECESSARY FOR EFFECTIVE BIOLOGICAL TREATMENT OF WASTEWATER.

Fuzhou, a city of over seven million people, is the capital of Fujian province in southeast China. With its coastal location and the Minjiang River snaking through it, the city is an important seaport and economic center, with food processing industries and companies that make paper, textiles, and chemicals. Before 2002, domestic sewage, industrial waste, and effluents were all being disposed of untreated in the Minjiang River, via an array of canals throughout the city. This network of canals, nearly 50 miles (80 kilometers) long, began to exhibit characteristics of dangerous pollution, such as odors and floating solids, along with suspended and dissolved chemicals. The city government recognized this as an immediate health risk for the inhabitants of both Fuzhou and the fishing villages located downstream, and it began to search for a solution.

Wastewater treatment is a necessary part of urban infrastructure, ensuring that sewage does not enter rivers and lakes and contaminate the water system. Treatment commonly results in gray water, which is considered safe for disposal or for reuse as fertilizer in farms and public green spaces. The conversion of "black" water to "gray," however, is conventionally achieved through the use of a range of chemicals that emulate the nitrogen cycle.

Ecological treatment of black water and the subsequent use of treated water has become a burgeoning field within the sustainability movement. One of the trailblazers in this field is John Todd, a biologist who has ventured into the world of ecological design and applied technologies. His work recognizes the functionality and behavior of plants, and his treatment method uses plants to purify wastewater.

In an early project, Todd built a greenhouse wastewater treatment plant. He ran sewage through a series of tanks in the greenhouse, with plants suspended in the flowing waters, and constructed artificial marshes made of sand and gravel. No chemicals were added, but plenty of plants and aquatic creatures—from microorganisms to snails to small fish—were used at different stages to clean the waters. He regarded his concept of Eco Machines as a start toward "embracing a new relationship with the natural world which can sustain us all."[9]

Variations of Todd's installations are being put into action worldwide. The Living Machine in use at Findhorn is one of his inventions (see p. 274). A recent project in the United States, near the birthplace of the American industrial revolution in Massachusetts, is using his design to clean a canal polluted by crude oil. That Massachusetts project uses similar technology to that has been put in place at the Urban Municipal Canal Restorer in Fuzhou, China.

The Fuzhou city government was interested in an affordable and low-maintenance wastewater treatment process that could take place within the existing canal system. The Baima Canal was chosen for a pilot project, because it was the most polluted and because an elementary school and a number of temples and residential blocks are located fairly close to it, making the area a perfect setting for a major investment cleanup. The city government was interested in an on-site solution—one that didn't involve installing an additional pipeline and pumping water to an outside treatment facility.

In the summer of 2002, a 546-yard (500-meter) linear restorer with thousands of plants was installed. Permaculturists often use the strategy of "increasing the edge effect" in designing integrated systems that thrive through diversity, since the edge, or "ecotone"—where two biological systems meet—is a zone of greater variety and density of natural resources than each of the contributing communities (see p. 206).

The restorer works as follows. Wastewater entering the end of the canal is rerouted to the start of the system for treatment. Water first passes through an anoxic zone (a layer devoid of oxygen), which allows for removal of toxic nitrates, can cause eutrophication. As the wastewater moves through the system, a fine-bubble aeration system distributes air along the canal from blowers located on a central floating barge. Low-intensity and uniformly distributed aeration circulates the water, forcing it past biologically active zones. The restorer adds beneficial bacteria to the system at two locations, using species known for their ability to digest sludge and grease, essential for treating industrial waste, as well as for nitrogen removal.

The restorer system successfully met the goals set by the city of Fuzhou. The clarity of the water in the canal has increased from less than 6 inches to several feet, and the water now meets standards for treated wastewater. The restorer system reduced odors, eliminated floating solids, and drastically improved the aesthetics of the neighborhood. The canal has become a local common space, with a walkway that attracts pedestrians, and the improvement has had a positive impact on social interaction in the community. Furthermore, this technology reduced the negative impact of the pollutants in the canal on downstream aquatic ecosystems, which especially benefitted the local fishing industry.

Reporting contributed by Muneezay Jaffery. Photos contributed by John Todd.

Zaytuna Farm and PRI

The Channon, New South Wales, Australia

THE SWALES AND EARTHWORKS OF ZAYTUNA FARM DEFINE THE SITE'S NATURAL CONTOURS CLEARLY.

Zaytuna Farm and the Permaculture Research Institute is a 66-acre (27-hectare) research site and education center that was formerly a beef and dairy ranch. It has several narrow valleys in a state of reforestation with native eucalyptus regrowth and a camphor laurel emergent rainforest. The open pasture areas are partially dominated by fire-response weeds, due to the continuous burn-maintenance practices of the previous owners. Designed by Geoff Lawton, student of Bill Mollison, it has been under constant development as a demonstration site since 2001. Today it welcomes a steady stream of students from around the world, who come to study permaculture hands-on at the world headquarters for the Permaculture Research Institute (PRI), which Lawton founded in 1997, at Mollison's request upon retirement. PRI has expanded and is now a network of international permaculture institutes, with branches in the United States, Turkey, Greece, Jordan, Chile, Kenya, and New Zealand.

☼ LAND/NATURE STEWARDSHIP

Food and Water Systems: There is an extensive series of fifteen dams (valley dams, ridge point dams, contour dams, and aquaculture fish ponds) and several kilometers of water-harvesting swales that help to drought-proof the property during the dry winter season and to raise the overall potential for aquaculture.

Multispecies food forests have been established and are continuously being extended, and there has been some rehabilitation of the forest creek edge. The food forests have citrus, passion fruit, tamarillo, guava, custard apple, climbing pumpkin, and much more. Chickens and ducks free-range in the forest, keeping it free of pests and weeds—as well as keeping it well fertilized. Over thirty species of bamboo have been planted for various uses including fresh shoots for food; material for natural building, weaving, and fishing rods; living hedges that serve as erosion control and windbreaks; and forage for animals.

A variety of kitchen gardens growing diverse vegetables and herbs are maintained, with well-drained raised beds and sunken semiaquatic beds for Asian crops (taro, bananas, coco yam galangal, Vietnamese mint, turmeric). One garden is designed to demonstrate urban-gardening techniques, complete with a closed-loop aquaculture system and pond. The main garden in the central valley specializes in the cultivation of bulk crops (amaranth, corn, salad mallow, potatoes, broad beans, peas, kale, squash, melons, sweet potato, and cassava).

There are dairy cows, which are milked every day, and beef cows and workhorses, which play an integral part in the management of the farm. There is a small herd of Saanan-Nubian cross goats, bred for both meat and milk, which forage on weeds; these are milked every other day.

The farm has a nursery shade house and polytunnel system, which has on its own solar-powered drip-irrigation system and an automatic humidifier. All of the site's vegetables, fruit trees, legume trees, forest trees, and bamboo are started in this nursery. There is a plan to expand it into a retail plant nursery, which would also have a weekly farm market, where local people can buy any surplus produce grown on the farm.

Compost, natural anaerobic/probiotic ferments, and worm castings are the main sources of fertilizer for the farm, and there is extensive composting system connected to the nursery.

The site employs several cooks to keep students and visitors fed (serving about 25,000 meals

THE KITCHEN GARDEN IS NADIA LAWTON'S BABY—AND A VERY PRODUCTIVE ONE—SUPPLYING THE BULK OF THE 25,000–30,000 MEALS SERVED EVERY YEAR.

MOST MEAL INGREDIENTS COME FROM THE FARM. ZAYTUNA GROWS ABOUT 65% OF ITS OWN FOOD.

a year). The head chef, Ish, reports that the farm provides about 65 percent of its own ingredients for its meals. Considering that the farm focuses on education and producing eager permaculturists and teachers rather than on food production, this is not an insignificant figure and demonstrates the farm's commitment to food self-reliance.

BUILDING

Using Local Materials for Insulation: All of the main buildings on the farm were built using straw-bale construction methods, with cob and earth chaff render and natural lime plaster. Wheat straw, rice straw, sugar cane, and bamboo have all been used as in-fill bale construction.

A student common room provides some study and social space for the evenings, and there are plans for a whole new student complex, including showers, toilets, kitchen, and accommodations.

TOOLS/TECHNOLOGY

Energy, Waste, and Water Cycles: A rocket-stove water heater and a gray-water reed-bed filtration system provide not only an excellent supply of hot water and gray-water treatment, but are also a good demonstration of appropriate low-input, low-tech elements that work. All drinking water on the site is harvested from rooftop rainwater catchment. All toilets are dry composting.

The electricity needs for the entire farm are met by a large solar power station with the copper-indium-selenium panels attached to the most up-to-date charge controller inverter system and a state-of-the-art battery bank storage unit. All of the common-room appliances are labeled with their power consumption to help students appreciate the real implications of turning on the switch.

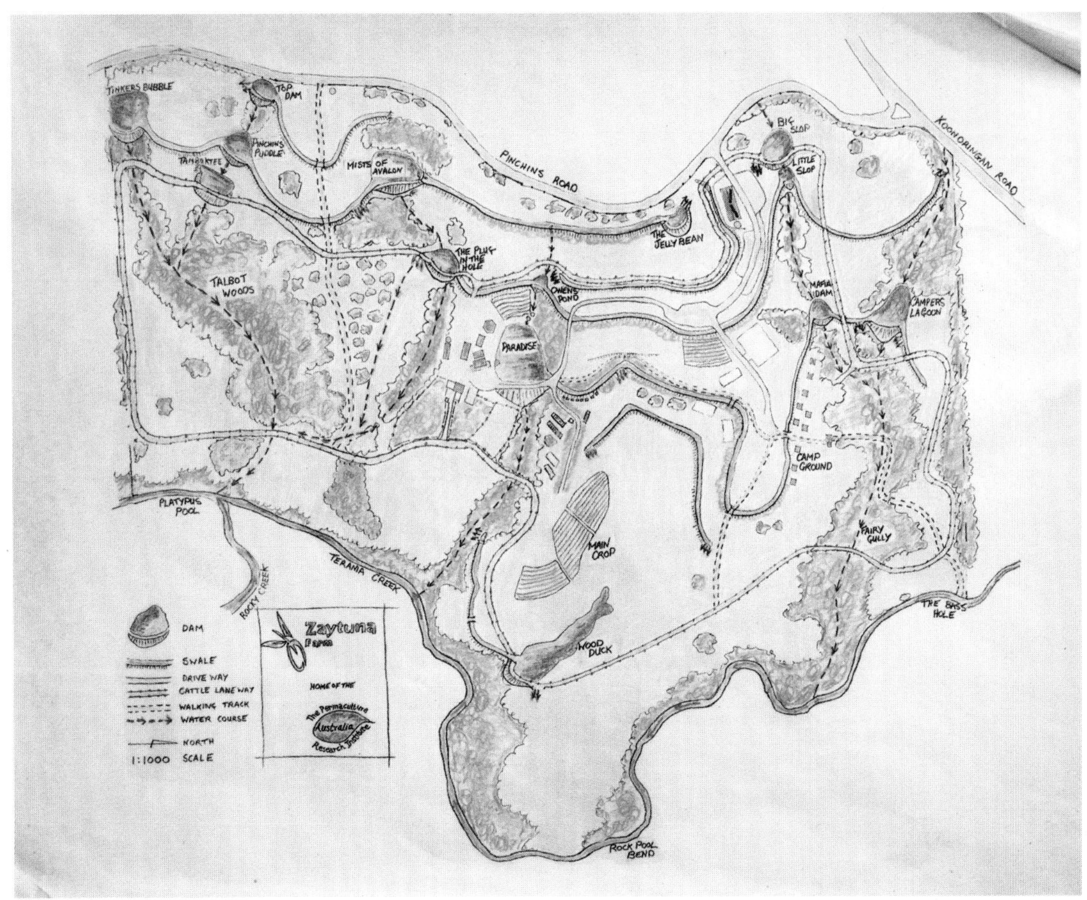

CULTURE/EDUCATION

Hands-On Experience: A stay at Zaytuna Farm gives a practical permaculture experience in forestry, crop gardens and nursery management, animal husbandry, general farm maintenance, water systems, consultancy, alternative energy systems, natural building methods, and surveying, as well as the experience of communal living. Projects around the farm are progressive, working with both the development of the students as well as the property as a whole.

PRI Australia offers four full design courses yearly, and Zaytuna hosts ten-week internships that include subjects such as surveying, earthworks, aid-project establishment and management, farm forestry, nursery systems, animal systems, main crops, food forests, fuel-wood production, urban systems, gardening agriculture, architectural design, energy systems, waste systems, aquaculture, community group establishment, and composting systems.

"All the world's problems can be solved in a garden."
— Geoff Lawton

ZAYTUNA'S FOUNDER, GEOFF LAWTON, AT THE FARM'S ENTRANCE. GEOFF STARTED STUDYING WITH BILL MOLLISON BACK IN 1983 AND HAS SINCE BECOME ONE OF PERMACULTURE'S FOREMOST TEACHERS.

THE PRINCIPLE OF **CATCH AND STORE ENERGY** CAN'T BE DEMONSTRATED IN A MORE OBVIOUS WAY THAN A BEEFED-UP SOLAR SYSTEM LIKE THIS ONE.

LAND TENURE/COMMUNITY GOVERNANCE

Permaculture Hamlet Land Trust: Zaytuna Farm is currently home to Geoff and Nadia Lawton (when they are not traveling internationally as permaculture design consultants) and hosts groups of about twenty interns at a time. There are plans to change the ownership of the farm and turn the farm into a permaculture hamlet land trust with multiple occupancy. Ownership will be divided into eight shares, with the Lawtons holding one and PRI another, and the remaining six shares will be available on a leasehold basis, in which other people can lease a section of the land. People leasing part of the farm will benefit from being a part of the infrastructure of the farm, and the overall new ownership system will grant the farm an extreme degree of resilience.

Reporting contributed by Craig Mackintosh and Geoff Lawton. Photos by Craig Mackintosh.

Djanbung Gardens and Jarlanbah

Nimbin, New South Wales, Australia

UNDER A NEW FORM OF LAND TENURE CALLED COMMUNITY TITLE, THE FORTY-THREE RESIDENTIAL LOTS OF JARLANBAH HAVE FREEHOLD / INDIVIDUAL OWNERSHIP, WITH JOINT OWNERSHIP AND MANAGEMENT OF 22 ACRES OF COMMUNITY LAND. A SET OF BYLAWS IN THE LAND TITLE'S MANAGEMENT STATEMENT DIRECT LAND USE AND GOVERNANCE, AND ARE LEGALLY BINDING.

Situated on the edge of Nimbin village in the lush subtropics of northern New South Wales (NSW), this community comprises two adjoining developments designed by regenerative design pioneer Robyn Francis in the early 1990s. Djanbung Gardens, permaculture's first purpose-designed education center and demonstration farm, is home to Permaculture College Australia and has innovated sustainability education and training. Jarlanbah was the first permaculture-designed ecovillage project in NSW and broke new ground in the planning profession as part of the National Strategy for Ecologically Sustainable Development.

☼ LAND TENURE/COMMUNITY GOVERNANCE

Community Title: Jarlanbah was the first neighborhood designed under Community Title, a new form of land tenure introduced in 1990 in NSW. The residential lots at Jarlanbah have freehold ownership, with joint ownership of community land. The community land has bylaws to guide sustainable management and stewardship based on permaculture principles and is divided into specified land-use systems: woodlots, conservation forest, water bodies, sustainable agriculture, and the community center. The community meets regularly and elects an executive committee to manage legal and financial affairs, and residents volunteer for management committees to take care of the different land-use systems.

Djanbung Gardens is owned by Robyn Francis and is leased to Permaculture College Australia, a nonprofit association with a membership of Djanbung residents and key individuals within the college's Bioregional Campus support network.

ROBYN FRANCIS'S DJANBUNG GARDENS AND JARLANBAH HAVE BECOME A VALUED, INTEGRAL, AND DYNAMIC NEIGHBORHOOD WITHIN THE NIMBIN AREA, WHICH IS ESSENTIALLY MADE UP OF A NETWORK OF OVER FORTY INTENTIONAL LAND-SHARING COMMUNITIES.

☼ LAND/NATURE STEWARDSHIP

Regenerative Design: The concept plans of both Djanbung and Jarlanbah were developed to ensure the protection and regeneration of the natural environment and to promote biodiversity and a harmonious coexistence with wildlife. In 1991, both properties were degraded, cleared pastureland. They now support a diverse abundance of wildlife and over eighty bird species. Jarlanbah bylaws require domestic animals to be confined to the owner's lot to reduce impact on wildlife.

Engagement with local Bundjalung indigenous heritage is important to both projects. Bundjalung elders gave the name Djanbung (*djanbung* means "platypus") to the site, together with a story and totem for healing the rift between people and their environment. *Jarlanbah* means "place of the rainbow," and residents contribute a percentage of their taxes to local Aboriginal community initiatives.

At the ecovillage, the landscape code encourages edible landscapes and food production on residential lots. Levity Gardens, an organic collective and CSA on Jarlanbah's main community agriculture lot, includes a citrus orchard, market garden, chickens, and a living soil laboratory that makes compost and cultivates effective microorganisms. Water is supplied courtesy of the sky as rainfall—neither Djanbung nor Jarlanbah is connected to municipal water. Dams are designed for aquatic production with native fish and water plants, including lotus and waterlily.

Djanbung Gardens devotes over 20 percent of its land to native species for fuel, habitat, food, medicine, and crafts. The remaining landscape models a wide range of permaculture techniques, creating diverse microclimates and small-scale interconnected systems:

- A warm temperate orchard on the lowland supports thirty types of fruit and nut trees that can withstand winter frost, and is managed by a happy flock of ducks that fertilize the trees and control weeds and pests.

- A subtropical food forest grows in a frost-free microclimate as an example of multitiered agroecology of tropical legume, fruit, and nut trees with coffee, pineapple, and tropical spices in the understory.

- Vegetable production systems demonstrate organic methods and permaculture techniques to provide a year-round supply of fresh food for residents and for visitors taking courses there. The gardens are central to the training programs, together with postharvest storage and preserving techniques. Long-term students have access to individual plots in the student community garden.

- Chickens, turkeys, ducks, and two pet pigs process garden and food waste into compost ingredients.

- Firewood and building materials are produced in the outlying zone 4 to 5 forest system and a collection of fourteen species of clumping bamboos are harvested annually.

BUILDING

Pioneering Codes for Ecological Design: The houses at Jarlanbah are diverse in design and demonstrate different approaches to energy-efficient housing for this climate. The first approved domestic wastewater treatment systems using wetland filtration and purification in NSW were installed at Jarlanbah and Djanbung Gardens in 1994.

Djanbung demonstrates a range of solar design, and natural and sustainable building techniques. The classroom is a hexagon made of pressed-earth bricks with natural air-conditioning ventilation systems for summer cooling. Other building materials include "saw-ment"—waste sawdust from local timber mills that has been pressed to create durable wall panels with the insulating properties of wood. Three old railway carriages were recycled to provide student accommodation. Bamboo structures, fences, and screens are found throughout the property. Social considerations have also been a critical factor in the design of buildings at Djanbung Gardens.

Both properties use rainwater-catchment to provide drinking water, and all wastewater is treated and reused on site. Composting toilets, along with water-conserving appliances and behavior adjustment, dramatically reduce water consumption.

TOOLS/TECHNOLOGY

Powering Down: While connected to the grid, both Djanbung and Jarlanbah have exceptionally low electricity consumption and generate a substantial percentage of their own power from solar panels, the only viable renewable energy source for this location. At Jarlanbah, households are restricted to a 20 amp feed (30 percent of the standard Australian household), which powers basic appliances but will not support energy-hungry appliances such as electric stoves, space heaters, and air conditioners. A number of houses have feed-in solar arrays, which reduces Jarlanbah's electricity demands from the grid. The key focus, however, has been on reducing the need for electricity, wherever possible, through good design, energy efficiency, and use of nonelectrical appliances.

Djanbung Gardens integrates appropriate technologies into everyday life, with careful consideration given to tools and appliances for domestic and garden functions. Students are introduced to cob oven, rocket, and TLUD (top-lit updraft) stoves, as well as solar ovens for outdoor cooking. For gardening and building, there are sickles, scythes, and an array of other hand tools. The few power tools here are used sparingly.

ALL JARLANBAH LOTS WERE DESIGNED FOR MAXIMUM SOLAR ACCESS, AND THE LANDSCAPE CODE ENSURES THAT RESIDENTS' SOLAR RIGHTS ARE RESPECTED. IT IS THE FIRST DEVELOPMENT IN AUSTRALIA TO CREATE BYLAWS ENSHRINING PASSIVE-SOLAR DESIGN, ENERGY CONSERVATION, RAINWATER COLLECTION, CONSERVATION, AND BIOLOGICAL WASTE TREATMENT.

As it is located just a little over a half-mile (1 kilometer) from the well-serviced village of Nimbin, most residents can meet their daily transportation needs through walking and cycling, substantially reducing the dependence on and use of private motor vehicles.

CULTURE/EDUCATION

A Living "Learn-Scape": Education was the key driver of Djanbung Gardens' design as a living classroom, or "learn-scape," that bridges the gap between theory and practice. Permaculture College Australia manages the living classroom and training programs, which include the classic permaculture design course, plus vocational training and community education in permaculture and skills for sustainable living. Since 2005, Accredited Permaculture Training (APT) has been offered at Djanbung. The program also offers professional development courses for permaculturists in design, teaching, community facilitation, and sustainable aid work.

Djanbung and Jarlanbah interact closely with the wider community of Nimbin and its bioregion, operating local businesses and being active

TWO PET PIGS HAPPILY PLOW THE MAIN CROP BEDS FOR SEASONAL PLANTING OF TROPICAL TUBERS AND PUMPKIN IN SUMMER, AND GARLIC IN WINTER. THE PIGS ALSO ENJOY WALKS TO CLEAN UP WINDFALL FRUIT AND TO PLOUGH UP SPECIFIC GARDEN PLOTS. ANIMAL SYSTEMS ARE INTEGRATED TO SUPPORT PLANT PRODUCTION, PROVIDE ECOSYSTEM SERVICES, AND ENSURE WELL-BEING AND A HAPPY LIFE FOR ALL.

in a number of organizations and programs. Nimbin has been a focal area for sustainability and alternative lifestyle since the 1970s—a coevolving sanctuary of sustainability, celebrating cultural and human diversity. Djanbung is used for numerous events, meetings, and celebrations, including seasonal ceremonies throughout the year. Students are encouraged to engage with the wider community, undertaking project work and volunteering with the numerous excellent local initiatives, including farmers' markets, vegetable gardens in local schools, the Food Security Group, Sustainable House Project, Environment Centre, Indigenous Cultural Centre, and LETS (Local Exchange and Trading Systems—for more on this alternative currency, see p. 256).

Reporting and photos contributed by Robyn Francis.

Huehuecóyotl Ecovillage

Tepotzlán, Morelos, Mexico

HUEHUECÓYOTL IS ONE OF LATIN AMERICA'S FIRST ECOVILLAGES, AND AN INTERNATIONAL PIONEER IN PERMACULTURE, COMMUNITY LIVING, AND SUSTAINABILITY EDUCATION.

Huehuecóyotl Ecovillage is named for a mythical coyote from Aztec culture, the god of music and dance, a wisdom-carrier who represents the meeting of the old and the new. Nestled between the craggy cliffs of Tepotzlán, about an hour and a half from Mexico City, in a dry, temperate ecosystem, the community was formed in 1982 by an international group of artists and educators, many of whom had traveled the world in a nomadic theater group known as the Illuminated Elephants Traveling Gypsy Theatre.

During the community's early years, many members lived in their vans and converted buses while the communal structures and individual family homes were built. Huehuecóyotl is currently home to about twenty members and has a large extended community that visits and participates in events and workshops. After many years of experimenting with a shared, communal economy, today community members all have their own ways of earning a living and contribute dues toward the maintenance and improvement of the ecovillage. Many community members earn at least part of their income through activities offered

"The ideal of a single civilization for everyone, implicit in the cult of progress and technology, impoverishes and mutilates us."
—Octavio Paz, Mexican poet, "The Labyrinth of Solitude" (1967)

VALUING DIVERSITY AND LEADERSHIP, HUEHUECÓYOTL HAS BEEN SOMETHING OF AN INCUBATOR FOR SUSTAINABILITY TRAILBLAZERS. A NUMBER OF MEMBERS HAVE GONE ON TO BECOME LEADERS OF GROUPS SUCH AS THE GLOBAL ECOVILLAGE NETWORK, GAIA UNIVERSITY, THE VISION COUNCIL, GUARDIANS OF THE EARTH, THE INTERNATIONAL INSTITUTE FOR FACILITATION AND CHANGE, ECOBARRIOS MEXICO CITY, AND THE RECENTLY CONCLUDED RAINBOW PEACE CARAVAN.

on-site, such as courses and training in topics such as ecovillage design and leadership development. Some members spend significant amounts of time traveling the world as educators, trainers, and artists, while others work in nearby Mexico City, running a program called EcoBarrios, which aims to integrate permaculture practices into urban neighborhoods.

At each phase of the community's growth, members have made great efforts to find the most ecologically appropriate solutions to the questions of natural resources and water and waste management. Constructions are generally of adobe with clay-tile roofing, an ancient building technique common throughout Mexico. The houses at the ecovillage put a creative spin on this traditional design with beautiful woodwork, stained-glass windows, and spiral and circular designs.

The water table is too low for a well, so the entire year's water supply must be harvested during the rainy season. A dry creek bed on the site becomes a beautiful waterfall in the rainy season that the

INTEGRATE RATHER THAN SEGREGATE: FOUNDERS KATHY SARTOR AND GIOVANNI CIARLO—THE MUSICAL GROUP SIRIUS COYOTE—INTEGRATE WORLD MUSIC AND STORYTELLING WITH ECOLOGICAL AND COMMUNAL TEACHINGS.

ARTISTIC SENSIBILITY IS EMBEDDED IN MOST EVERY ASPECT OF THE HUEHUECÓYOTL COMMUNITY, FROM THE ARCHITECTURE TO THE MUSICAL ACTIVITIES THAT SUPPLEMENT WORKSHOPS AND TRAININGS. THEY USE THE ARTS TO DISSEMINATE THEIR MESSAGE AND CULTURE OF ECOLOGICAL RESPONSIBILITY.

community channels to a large cistern, the main water catchment and storage. This is supplemented by individual cisterns at the family homes. Gray water is an important resource, in some cases passing through constructed wetland systems before watering gardens, and in other cases being piped directly into community orchards.

Composting toilets turn human waste into a resource, increasing fertility around the property, and a recycling center ensures that the maximum amount of reusable materials is saved from the landfill. A communal composting system collects organic matter and produces a rich fertilizer for the communal gardens, which provide a steady supply of fresh produce for residents and visitors.

Almost all Huehuecóyotl residents have some creative practice, including theater, poetry, sculpture, storytelling, music and music production, filmmaking, and painting. This is seen throughout the community, from the intricate murals adorning the community gathering space to the music and activities that are part of the site's workshops. Odin Ruz gives workshops that unite the art of drumming with community-building dynamics and values. Toña Osher, one of the founding members, recently produced a series of paintings of corn and Mexican culture as part of a national campaign for food sovereignty.

More than any one example or practice, Huehuecóyotl has played an integral role in the creation of a modern earth-honoring culture based on ecological sustainability, cultural diversity, and the reencounter of ancient traditions in a present context. This "Culture of Peace" as dubbed by Alberto Ruz, another founding member, was taken on the road for thirteen years as the Rainbow Peace Caravan (see following page).

Photos and reporting contributed by the Común Tierra Project.

CULTURE / EDUCATION

THE RAINBOW PEACE CARAVAN

The Rainbow Peace Caravan *(Caravana Arcoiris por la Paz)* was a project of traveling community, performing arts, and education that began in 1996 in the ecovillage of Huehuecóyotl in Mexico (see accompanying profile). Founded by Alberto Ruz and a group of volunteer artists and activists from around the world, the project sought to cross the Americas to connect with the diverse cultures of Latin America and foster a culture of peace, ecology, and care of the earth. During its thirteen years of activity, the caravan community included more than four hundred volunteers, about twenty to forty at any one time, and facilitated hundreds of activities, including theater; art and dance workshops and performances; dynamic participatory events; and large gatherings, such as the Consejo de Visiones (Vision Councils) in Peru and Brazil. They mounted their roaming "Peace Village" everywhere they went, including implementing the model at the millennial World Social Forum in Porto Alegre, Brazil.

Recognized across the region for their innovative approach to sustainability education, the Caravan was invited to participate in a national project organized by the Ministry of Culture of Brazil. They visited cultural groups and communities throughout the country, exchanging knowledge and experiences. In late 2009, after thirteen years of inspiring people across the Americas and birthing many related projects (including Atlantida Ecovillage, see profile p. 40), the Caravan suspended its journey.

Photos and reporting contributed by the Común Tierra Project.

Qachuu Aloom Association

Rabinal, Baja Verapaz, Guatemala

JULIAN VASQUEZ CHUN AND HIS MOTHER, PAULINA, PROUDLY TEND THEIR FIELD OF AMARANTH. GUATEMALA'S SPANISH INVADERS ONCE MADE IT ILLEGAL TO GROW AMARANTH UNDER PENALTY OF DEATH; TODAY THE QACHUU ALOOM ASSOCIATION IS CHAMPIONING TRADITIONAL PRACTICES SUCH AS THE CULTIVATION OF THIS HIGHLY NUTRITIOUS GRAIN.

High in the mountains, a serpentine five-hour drive north of Guatemala City, lies the small town of Rabinal. Founded in 2003, a local association called Qachuu Aloom (Mother Earth) has successfully revived historical (and permacultural) values within the Achi Maya community. By building alliances, practicing seed saving, and developing a network of social and economic opportunities, this Maya-run organization is rebuilding communities in the aftermath of the country's brutal civil war. It strives to strengthen cultural identity by restoring traditional farming and building practices. One of their main initiatives has been the reintroduction of amaranth cultivation and preparation to Guatemala.

AMARANTH

The amaranth plant was sacred to the Maya, given the importance of its life-sustaining properties. It was used in ceremony and constituted a major part of the diet. Amaranth is an extremely healthful grain, containing high levels of essential nutrients such as protein, calcium, magnesium, and iron. During the Spanish conquest, the Spanish banned amaranth and burned amaranth fields—and they punished those they caught growing it by cutting off one of their hands, or even by executing them. As a result, the grain nearly became extinct, except in remote areas. Among the Achi Maya, the cultivation of amaranth for cereal and flour was virtually lost over the past century, as lifestyles modernized and more food was bought from stores.

The organization offers courses in permaculture, access to a seed library, and microloans to local initiatives. The seed library is simple and effective: families "borrow" seeds and cultivate them with assistance from more experienced growers. They save seeds from their year's crop, return the "borrowed" seeds to the library, keep some of the food they grow for their families, and sell the rest to the association, which packages it for market and sells it to fund the group's programs. About three hundred families in the region are members of Qachuu Aloom, and there are nine full-time staff members.

Most people assume that all of Guatemala was colonized by the Spanish. The Achi Maya of Rabinal, however, successfully resisted the conquistadors and continued to live self-sufficiently in the region for centuries. The pressures of economic globalization and the violent political throes of the Guatemalan nation, however, gradually forced change and assimilation. In the early 1980s, Rabinal was targeted by the Guatemalan military, which had a policy of genocide against the indigenous Maya population. The community endured some of the worst violence of the civil war, and they were left with a shattered population and without access to basic resources, such as clean drinking water and medical care.

New Mexican Sarah Montgomery founded Qachuu Aloom with Cristobal Osorio Sanchez, a local farmer who had lost members of his family in the notorious Rio Negro massacres. These massacres claimed up to five thousand lives over a two-year period, sparked by protests over a hydroelectric dam project in which a total of thirty-eight communities were forcibly relocated close to Rabinal.

✡ LAND/NATURE STEWARDSHIP

A Quiet Revolution: "We used to work the land using chemicals, but thank God we were brought information about the negative health and environmental effects of using them," says Juana Raxcaco, an organizer with the project. "We started this practice of seed saving, packaging and selling, and have seen great results. We used to buy very expensive chemicals, making our production so expensive that we didn't even make any money. Now we are cultivating without having to buy anything, as we get seeds from the association, and we are making a profit from selling them back and are also growing healthy foods for our families, without contamination."

The seed bank, amaranth cultivation, and natural growing techniques are central to Qachuu Aloom's philosophy. It maintains a demonstration garden site, which had been a degraded cattle pasture and is surrounded by unimproved plots that look like dusty soil wastelands. The garden is bursting with a polyculture of medicinal and edible plants and has an overstory of fruit trees. Terraces were constructed out of rocks and tires as a demonstration of mountain agriculture. *Canavalia* beans are planted as a nitrogen-fixing cover crop and can also be used as an inexpensive coffee substitute. The planting is done in a minimal-till style, using live soil fixers to hold the soil and prevent erosion. "It's a quiet revolution," Montgomery observes. "People are defending their own seeds from aid organizations wanting to bring in GMO seeds. It's about changing people's minds."

THE SEED BANK IS MADE OF ADOBE AND STAYS COOL IN HOT WEATHER. ADOBE COATED WITH LIME PLASTER WAS A TRADITIONAL BUILDING MATERIAL, NOW OFTEN REPLACED WITH CINDER BLOCKS AND CEMENT BECAUSE THEY ARE SEEN AS MORE MODERN, EVEN THOUGH THE HOUSES GET MUCH HOTTER. CRISTOBAL OSORIO SANCHEZ SAYS, "THE STATUS OF THE CEMENT HOUSE IS BEING RECONSIDERED."

BUILDING

Traditional and Modern Technologies: The association built an ecological demonstration center using cob and bamboo construction, which has a facility for seed storage, a medicinal plant garden, and a vermicomposting system. Solar energy is used to power a dehydrator and the pump for the well. There are model rainwater-catchment and gray-water systems that have been duplicated at a number of association members' homes. In other ways, people are returning to traditional building materials like adobe, which stays cooler than modern cinder blocks. "Many houses also have tin roofs, which also end up making houses get hotter," Sanchez explains. "We have seen people replace them with clay tiles after taking our courses."

ASSOCIATION MEMBERS WEIGH *CANAVALIA* SEEDS, USED AS A COVER CROP TO ENRICH SOIL AND AS A CHEAP COFFEE REPLACEMENT. "IN ONE SMALL VILLAGE THE MOVEMENT HAS BEEN GROWING AND WE NOW HAVE FIFTEEN FAMILIES WITH GARDENS—WE STARTED WITH TWO. WE CONSUME WHAT WE GROW, AND ALSO SAVE THE SEEDS FOR OURSELVES AND TO SELL."—JUANA RAXCACO, PROJECT ORGANIZER

CULTURE/EDUCATION

Permaculture as a Way of Living: Qachuu Aloom offers courses in permaculture design and workshops in seed saving, homesteading skills, and related topics. They also run a successful youth program and an exchange program with native communities in North America. The association's newest program is geared toward youth education and involves an innovative, yearlong course on permaculture, natural building, and Mayan culture and language. Sarah Montgomery explains that most local children go to conventional school these days, but they can emerge feeling that their traditional lifestyles are out of date, and they find few job options. "The idea is to pick young people who really identify with our mission, and find out what their interests are, in order to connect them with ways of studying them," she says. "Teachers [in the association's new program] will be both elders and fellow youth, from within the culture, people who will be inspiring to [the young people]. We hope to integrate permaculture and Mayan cosmology, so when we talk about water systems, for example, we will also talk about water's traditional symbolism and role."

HEALTH/SPIRITUAL WELL-BEING

Empowering Women: The women's circle within Qachuu Aloom was inspired by a community from the Chimaltenango region of Guatemala. The women from a town called San José Poaquil had found a strong variety of amaranth growing in the garden of an elder woman; they planted it, saved the seeds, and created a collective that became very successful, selling amaranth all over the country. They were invited to come to Rabinal and teach the local women of Qachuu Aloom.

"I think we were so successful with [our] program because the women came and shared their stories—often stories of the violence that many of them experienced. They all cried together, and also shared their success," says Montgomery. Following the war, when people were targeted and even murdered for organizing, there was a lot of fear and mistrust in the community that greatly affected the project. "At the beginning, the women would hardly talk, and now some of them are out there speaking in front of large groups, presenting about our association. What made it work was that we were organizing with leaders who were from the community and trusted."

Qachuu Aloom is also a force for eating healthy, local foods, an idea that swims against the stream of fast-food franchises pouring into the region. At group lunches, traditional foods are usually served, in an effort to revalue indigenous foods and reeducate people about their preparation. Program director Edson Xiloj, of the K'iche' Maya, comes from Chichecastenango in another part of Guatemala. He studied conventional agriculture at university before coming to Qachuu Aloom as an intern and realizing that he wanted to work with permaculture. Xiloj says that when he asked his grandmother why people used to live so long, she told him it was from eating the indigenous "weeds"—like amaranth.

"OUR GRANDPARENTS GREW THEIR FOOD WITHOUT CHEMICALS, AND NOW AGAIN WE ARE REVIVING THOSE PRACTICES THAT WERE THROWN OUT WHEN INDUSTRIAL AGRICULTURE CAME THROUGH."

FINANCES/ECONOMICS

Microloans: Qachuu Aloom offers microloans to its members to begin small-scale enterprises or improve the infrastructure of their homes or gardens. The potential within even the most modest of microloans is great: Qachuu Aloom loaned $20—which goes a long way in local currency—to a single mother to start making shampoo. She has developed her own mixtures and now sells her shampoo in two municipalities, enabling her to support her children.

The Garden's Edge, a nonprofit organization based in New Mexico, in the United States, is run by Sarah Montgomery and other social and environmental activists. It has helped to fund the Guatemalan association, to arrange cultural exchanges between Pueblo and Maya leaders, and to establish permaculture projects. Currently, the Garden's Edge is funded mainly by grants and individual donors, but they are working toward raising more and more of their budget through the sale of seeds.

Reporting contributed by Juliana Birnbaum. Photos by Louis Fox.

I'jatz Association

San Lucas Toliman, Lake Atitlán, Guatemala

Established in 1994, I'jatz is a small, thriving permaculture center located on 1.7 acres (0.7 hectare; 1 *manzana*) of land in San Lucas Toliman, a village on Lake Atitlán in Guatemala. The local population is mainly Tzutujil and Kakchiquel Maya. I'jatz (seeds in the local language) closely links permaculture principles to traditional Mayan methods of working with land. A demonstration food forest teaches systems for growing edible plants in small spaces. Hundreds of local people have planted gardens using permaculture techniques learned at I'jatz, and the center run courses regularly for indigenous and *campesino* (farmer) groups from throughout Mesoamerica. The center also organizes a women's group and a small farmers' cooperative.

In 1994, a regional group called Permacultura America Latina held Guatemala's first permaculture design course in San Lucas Toliman. Soon after, the Associacion I'jatz was formed to produce and distribute ancestral Mayan heirloom seeds. Rony Lec, a Kakchiquel anthropologist who had studied permaculture, came and collaborated with the local church congregation, which donated the land for the site. These groups joined forces to design the site, with the special goal of managing rainwater. The plantings have grown into a multistoried food forest, now the only remaining forest in the town.

CULTURE/EDUCATION

The Story of Our Grandparents: I'jatz offers workshops in local schools, the towns surrounding Lake Atitlan, and villages in the region. Volunteers from abroad come regularly for the six-month apprenticeship program. Four staff members are certified permaculture designers who teach regular courses.

I'jatz is a member of a national network promoting organic agriculture, and the project has empowered many local families to grow food organically. Locals visit the site to take workshops and get plants, animals, and materials to implement the techniques they learn in their own homesteads. San Lucas is an area that lends itself to growing a diversity of foods.

"We are picking up the story of our grandparents, who were more involved with planting seeds," explains Francisca, president of the women's group at I'jatz. "Today, because of the type of education they are getting, our children don't want to dedicate themselves to seeds. But I think it is something that they need to keep practicing, how to grow their own vegetables. It has cost something, this global change, because the soil has become weak and contaminated, unable to produce without the use of chemicals. We hope that the change that you can see here will help benefit people's health as well as the environment."

THE I'JATZ WOMEN'S GROUP COOKS FOR AN EVENT. THE PRINCIPLE **INTEGRATE RATHER THAN SEGREGATE** HAS SOCIAL APPLICATIONS AS WELL. THE WOMEN INVOLVED ARE MAINLY THOSE WHO HAVE BEEN WIDOWED OR SEPARATED FROM THEIR HUSBANDS, AND HERE THEY CAN SUPPORT EACH OTHER AND COLLABORATE ON PROJECTS TO MEET THEIR NEEDS.

LAND/NATURE STEWARDSHIP

Taking Up Old Ways: The I'jatz site has a weblike network of swales that wind and turn around the garden beds, known as *chinampas*, to slow the water (see p. 48). The swales are practically a river in the rainy season and are full of sediment that enriches the soil. This system of controlling the water flow is connected to permaculture but is also similar to traditional agroecological farming systems

THE RAINWATER-CATCHMENT TANK IS A SECOND SOURCE OF WATER AVAILABLE ON THE SITE. GUILLERMO CAMPA WORKS THE TANK'S HAND-OPERATED ROPE PUMP, MADE FROM RECYCLED MATERIALS AND NOT DEPENDENT ON ELECTRICITY. PERMACULTURE REMINDS US TO BUILD REDUNDANCY AND RESILIENCY INTO OUR SYSTEMS, ESPECIALLY PARTS WITH CRITICAL FUNCTIONS, LIKE THOSE THAT DELIVER WATER.

in the surrounding countryside, according to Guillermo Campa, president of I'jatz. The *chinampas* design is an ancient one in Mesoamerica, sometimes called "floating gardens." The site also has a medicinal plant garden, incorporating seventeen different plants with various traditional uses, such as treating fever or stimulating milk production in mothers after birth.

There are forty banana circles that filter and hold water. This popular permaculture design allows farmers to integrate other moisture-loving plants, such as sweet potato, comfrey, and mint, and it increases the amount of organic matter that goes into the soil. I'jatz cultivates green and yellow bamboo as a construction material, and it helps to hold the soil in place, avoiding erosion.

The organic compost made at the site has increased in value tremendously over the past decade. The compost, as well as the planting of nitrogen-fixing plants, has dramatically improved the soil on the parcel.

"The seventies saw an excessive use of chemicals

"I THINK THAT TRADITIONAL PEOPLE PRACTICED PERMACULTURE. OUR ANCESTORS USED ALL OF THE PARTS OF A PLANT FOR DIFFERENT PURPOSES; THEY KNEW ABOUT MICROCLIMATES AND RAISED FRUIT TREES APPROPRIATE TO THEIR SITE. THROUGH THE MODERNIZATION OF AGRICULTURE, THIS TRADITIONAL KNOWLEDGE HAS BEEN LOST, BUT LITTLE BY LITTLE, PEOPLE ARE TAKING UP OLD WAYS AGAIN—LEARNING HOW TO AVOID POLLUTING THE WATER AND TO CONSERVE THE SOIL."—GUILLERMO CAMPA, PRESIDENT OF I'JATZ

on this soil, the results of which we are working to reverse through permaculture techniques," Campa says.

"There is a cooperative of organic coffee growers in the I'jatz network that use the compost, and they have had good results," Campa reports. "The concept of ecological agriculture is not only social and ecological, but also has to be economical. People sometimes only focus on the ecological aspect, but it also has to be socially beneficial. This is an area of extreme natural beauty, but of extreme poverty."

The I'jatz farmers' cooperative decided to focus their energy on the production and commercialization of organic coffee. I'jatz's founder, Rony Lec, and his wife, Rebecca, however, wanted to continue work on the protection of genetic diversity, both locally and throughout Mesoamerica. In 2000, the Lecs founded the Mesoamerican Permaculture Institute, or IMAP. The two associations continue to collaborate and support each other.

In the decade since its founding, IMAP has organized local growers to produce vegetables organically, helped to create fair-trade markets and seed banks, and set up a center that trains local and international students. They responded to Hurricane Stan in 2005 with low-tech water-treatment systems, soil-conservation practices, community gardens, and other appropriate-technology approaches to disaster relief.

Reporting contributed by Juliana Birnbaum and Comùn Tierra project. Photos by Louis Fox.

FINANCES / ECONOMICS

ACHÉ GUAYAKÍ FOREST PRESERVATION

The Aché Guayakí people are hunter-gatherers in the Atlantic Forest; a region of tropical and subtropical rainforest that extends along the Atlantic coast of Brazil and inland to Paraguay and Argentina. Intense deforestation began there in the 1970s and the Aché were confined to smaller and smaller sections of forest until less than 10 percent remained. Food became scarce as animal habitat and vegetation was destroyed. The Aché, forced to find food elsewhere, began to target ranchers' cattle. They became viewed as a menace and suffered a tragic genocide. Now a North American enterprise, called Guayaki (with permission from the Aché people to use that name), has partnered with the tribe and other indigenous communities in the region. Guayakí is pioneering an innovative business model that preserves what remains of the endemic forest, replants the region with native hardwood species, provides living wages, and supports the self-reliance of the Aché people.

GUAYAKI, A NORTH AMERICAN ENTERPRISE, IS PARTNERED WITH THE ACHÉ GUAYAKÍ TRIBE. TOGETHER THEY HAVE CREATED A VIABLE MODE FOR MARKET-DRIVEN FOREST RESTORATION.

CULTIVATING MATE TREES IN THE SHADE OF THEIR ANCESTRAL FOREST HOME IS THE BEST WAY THE ACHÉ GUAYAKÍ PEOPLE HAVE FOUND TO PROTECT IT.

THE GUAYAKI COMPANY PROVIDES TECHNICAL ASSISTANCE TO THE TRIBE IN BUILDING NURSERIES FOR BOTH MATE AND NATIVE HARD-WOOD TREES, ALLOWING FARMERS TO REPOPULATE THEIR RAINFOR-EST, WHICH RESTORES THE LAND TO A BIODIVERSE STATE.

This model is centered on the shade-grown cultivation of yerba mate. Like coffee, yerba mate is mostly cultivated with chemical- and amendment-laden monocultural practices in tropical and subtropical regions, where clearing forest for soy, corn, cattle grazing, and other industrial agriculture uses have resulted in massive losses of biodiversity (93 percent in the region) and habitat for forest-dwelling indigenous populations. Guayaki recognized the opportunity to create a new model for cultivation of yerba mate under canopy shade that keeps the rainforest intact.

Earth Care and People Care

The Kue Tuvy Preserve sustains thirty-five families of the Aché Guayakí and is protecting 12,500 acres of the Atlantic Forest (home to over 336 bird and mammal species). In June of 2009, the Aché harvested their first crop of yerba mate, five years after planting the locally collected and propagated seed.

Guayaki approaches tribes like the Aché with care and humility. "We build a relationship with them just like a relationship formed around the gourd circle. We do not look at them as inferior. We are not telling them what is best for them. We share dreams, emotions, share necessities. We learn from each other, we learn from difference and see if there is a path of mutual support. That is what guarantees collaboration, empowerment, health, and education—caring for one another and caring for the earth," says Alex Pryor, founding partner of Guayaki Yerba Mate and leader of their South American team.

The partnership developed by Guayaki with the Aché people has provided the Aché with enough income to meet their needs, supporting the opportunity to organize and plan for their future. Guayaki helps curate planning processes by convening gatherings with all community stakeholders—including the tribe's elders, women, and children; the nearby *campesinos;* the loggers; and NGOs in the region—for conversations and planning for mutual support. "We are simply connectors. Yerba mate represents sharing, connecting, generating dialogs, creating community," says Pryor. Guayaki has also created a community fund, a percentage of gross revenues that is collectively administered by the community itself.

Deeper resilience is growing. Integrating the community around the yerba mate cultivation is yielding local self-reliance. For example, the Aché have begun sharing techniques for cultivating shade-grown yerba mate with local *campesinos,* who, in turn, share food-growing techniques and seeds with the Aché. And interest has grown in other sources of income and food, such as honey, fruits, and nuts. When the Aché began selling yerba mate to the export market through the Guayaki enterprise, the government began to officially recognize them as an organized people, which led to the Aché receiving land title to their ancestral home forest.

Ethical Enterprise?

Permaculture land-use ethics invite us to protect intact ecosystems where they remain and, where ecosystems have been destroyed, to help restore them. Permaculture design also suggests that we take care of earth while taking care of people. The Aché Guayakí enterprise model showcases how land use that both preserves and restores can support community development.

"We are simply connectors. Yerba mate represents sharing, connecting, generating dialogs, creating community."
– Alex Pryor, founding partner

Photo: Mateo Sluder

OVER THE YEARS, GUAYAKI HAS CAREFULLY DEVELOPED A MARKETPLACE DEMAND IN NORTH AMERICA FOR ORGANIC, SHADE-GROWN YERBA MATE. STRIVING TO ESTABLISH A CARBON-NEGATIVE BUSINESS MODEL, THEY ARE ACTIVELY PROMOTING AND EMPHASIZING THE CULTURE OF BREWING LOOSE-LEAF MATE WHILE STILL MEETING MARKET DEMAND FOR PACKAGED, CANNED, AND BOTTLED BEVERAGES. LOOSE-LEAF DISTRIBUTION GREATLY REDUCES PACKAGING AND SHIPPING.

Guayaki does not hide the reality of the energy and carbon emissions involved in the global trade of yerba mate. They have calculated that when yerba mate is grown in shade of an intact polyculture forest, the carbon sequestered in growing the yerba mate exceeds the carbon emissions generated in bringing it to market.

Permaculture Principles Applied to Enterprise

Guayaki has committed to a model of small and slow growth. They primarily grew their business revenues from operations rather than taking venture capital they were offered, which would have both enabled and required the company to grow much faster and yield higher financial returns. Taking that route, they feel they would not have been able to maintain their ethical practices and intentions.

Guayaki could, even today, choose to work with plantation-style yerba mate producers to increase yields and profit margins. Instead, they work with a decentralized network of smaller farms and tribes to create the stacked function of social and environmental yields. "We are constantly working to innovate to internalize costs into our company to be of greater benefit to the community," said David Karr, cofounder of Guayaki. Its long-term mission is to restore almost 150,000 acres (60,000 hectares) of South American Atlantic rainforest and provide living-wage jobs for a thousand families.

Reporting contributed by Kevin Bayuk. Photos by Celine Frers, unless otherwise noted.

The Farm

Summertown, Tennessee, U.S.A.

Photo: Albert Bates

COMMUNITY MEMBERS PLANT A LIVING ROOF ON THE STRAW-BALE GREENHOUSE AT THE FARM'S ECOVILLAGE TRAINING CENTER.

The Farm, established in 1971, when approximately 320 "flower children" set out to revise the American Dream, is one of the nation's few 1960s-era back-to-the-land, experimental utopian communities still in operation today. The founders pooled their resources and bought a 1,750-acre (708-hectare) tract of land atop a plateau in Tennessee. The land was being farmed and earlier had been a Native American hunting ground. Founder and spiritual leader Stephen Gaskin dubbed the community the "Technicolor Amish." The community's story of "voluntary peasantry" stands in stark contrast to the larger trajectory of mainstream U.S. culture, and has been chronicled in numerous media outlets. The community has survived significant changes to its structure, population, and governance over the past forty years—that it exists today is a testament to its ability to adapt to change.

AT A TIME WHEN PEOPLE WERE SIMPLY DROPPING OUT OF SOCIETY, STEPHEN AND INA MAY GASKIN FOUNDED THE FARM. STEPHEN REFERRED TO IT AS "UTOPIA WITH A ZIP CODE."

Photo: Albert Bates

THE FARM'S SWIMMING HOLE IS POPULAR ALL SUMMER.

AT THE FARM SCHOOL, CHILDREN ENJOY THE STIMULATING ENVIRONMENT OF THE WHOLEO DOME, BY ARTIST CAROLING GEARY.

Although many residents do not specifically identify with permaculture, the community's commonly held values—pacifism, natural birth, right relation with the earth's resources, and social outreach—mirror the core permaculture ethics of earth care, people care, and fair share. During its apex, from the 1970s to early 1980s, The Farm grew to become a self-sufficient society with approximately 1,200 residents in Tennessee and in satellite communities doing outreach around the world. Today, the ecovillage is home to 160 residents, and there is a wider circle of thousands who are connected with the community. It also features a world-renowned birth clinic (see Midwifery on The Farm, p. 193)

One of the most famous communes born out of the 1960s counterculture movement in the United States, The Farm was formed at a time when anti–Vietnam War sentiment and dissatisfaction with the status quo was so powerful that thousands of Baby Boomers chose to "drop out" of society and seek alternatives. Their efforts resulted in a flowering of hundreds of communes across the nation. In 1971, spiritual teacher Stephen Gaskin and two hundred young followers left San Francisco's Haight-Ashbury district in search of a simpler, better life, close to the land. They sailed east across the country in a caravan of sixty converted school buses, adding about one hundred more participants along the way.

The journey ended on a plateau of scrub Blackjack oak and deep rhododendron hollows, littered with abandoned moonshine stills, in the heart of the Tennessee hills. In an adventurous spirit reminiscent of the early American pioneers, the cadre of middle-class college students of varying ethnic backgrounds established a community based on shared values of natural childbirth, a vegan diet, pacifism, and care for each other and for the earth.

From the beginning, Farm members were more committed to building a spiritual community—-what Gaskin called "utopia with a zip code"—than simply dropping out of American society. Everyone took a vow of poverty and shared homes and belongings, with the exception of the "tools of one's trade." They met each Sunday morning for meditation in an open meadow.

Within four years, the community had blossomed into an efficient rural village, with a gatehouse, bathhouse, flour mill, bakery, medical clinic, free store, bank, school, soy dairy, motor pool, book publishing company, radio station, and solar power technology company. They raised crops for their vegan diet and established the nonprofit relief agency Plenty International, which today continues to work with indigenous and underserved populations globally.

Farm residents have tried to live true to their values while simultaneously showing the world (via music, self-published books, speaking tours, and outside media coverage) that it was possible to live a life of peaceful cooperation, veganism, planet-friendly solar power, political activism, and altruistic work with people in need. In a Mother Earth News interview, Gaskin said, "We have it within our power to voluntarily assume a simpler lifestyle which can be so graceful and so much fun that it will just naturally spread of its own accord. We can do this . . . not as individuals, but as a culture."[10]

The community's connection to permaculture can be traced back more than thirty years to the Right Livelihood Award (which some refer to as the Alternative Nobel Peace Prize). The first recipients of the award, in 1980, were Stephen Gaskin—representing The Farm and its global nonprofit, Plenty International—and an Egyptian architect named Hassa Fathy. Bill Mollison was one of three award recipients the following year. Plenty's Albert Bates and Mollison formed a friendship at a gathering of recipients.

Some of the specific permaculture techniques being implemented on The Farm include the recent installation of an edible forest garden at the school, plans for neighborhood ponds, mass-brewing compost teas, encouraging more rainwater collection and storage, and establishing ecologically sensitive standards for all new homes built there.

BUILDING

From Commune to Training Ground: The Farm has sixteen residential roads, approximately sixty single and multifamily homes, and twenty-five public buildings, including businesses, a school, community center, store, and a guesthouse. There is also a new experimental farming operation and an organic community garden. Horses graze in pastures that have recently been keylined (an agricultural design system involving landscaped water harvesting and soil building) and supplemented with injected biochar and compost tea slurries.

Within The Farm, where residents of the former commune now live, is the Ecovillage Training Center (ETC). The ETC has been a hotbed of permaculture education, earth-based architecture, and natural design systems since the mid-1990s. Created and led by longtime Farm resident, permaculture innovator, and author Albert Bates, the ETC is designed to immerse apprentices and visitors alike in an experience of earth-centered architecture and permaculture techniques that inspire and mimic a village setting.

JASON DEPTULA AND ALAYNE CHAUNCEY'S HOME IS A CUTTING-EDGE EXAMPLE OF A BUILDING MADE FROM ACCESSIBLE TECHNOLOGIES AND MATERIALS (CORDWOOD, COB, AND TIMBER FRAME, AMONG OTHERS). THE HOUSE IS DESIGNED TO GENERATE ALL OF ITS OWN ENERGY NEEDS AND POWER THE FAMILY'S GOLF CART.

Today the site is experiencing a flowering of permaculture-specific activity in the soil of the larger community. Bordering The Farm is Spiral Ridge Permaculture, an innovative homestead of recently clear-cut land on a ridge top, purchased by Cliff Davis and Jennifer Albanese. They are building a closed-loop system using an annual gardening approach inspired by Masanobu Fukuoka's natural farming method. Their hope is to create a living example of a permaculture homestead from which both The Farm residents and bioregional residents can learn.

Within The Farm, Jason Deptula and Alayne Chauncey's locally-sourced home is one of the village's examples of building with eco-technologies and materials. The house features a living roof that keeps the house cool and radiant floor heating using solar power.

LAND/NATURE STEWARDSHIP

Water Harvesting: When Bates gives a tour of the ETC, he often includes a water tour, leading visitors past a 400-square-foot (36-square-meter) catchment roof and 5,000-gallon (18,971-liter) pressurized holding tank that feeds water to the main building and other structures. Hillside swales and contour drains divert water to fruit trees and into downhill ponds, lawns, and gardens.

Halfway down the hill, water from the swales and ponds overflows and joins rain catchment and gray water from the solar showers. This, in turn, feeds into a lagoon and duck pond system. Water from these ponds trickles down into the subsoil beneath the central garden's root zone, and it is used topically as "duck water" on raised beds. From the garden ponds, eco-hostel showers and kitchen, and the barn roof, the water flows into an 11,000-square-foot (3,385-square-meter) constructed wetland, where it is held, pulsed downhill, and treated naturally—with water plants and reedbeds—before ending up at the bottom of the site in a bamboo vernal pond. The bamboo growing in the basin is the final step in this estuary system. It is harvested and used in construction of the greenhouses and other areas; it is also used as a feedstock for biochar. Wetland plants, rich with the nutrients of the human food chain, are harvested, composted over winter, and added to the gardens in the spring, closing the cycle. Additionally, there are several other large tanks that store rainwater from roofs at the ETC, and there are composting toilets that feed urine into the reedbeds and return humanure to fruit and nut trees.

Protecting and Restoring Biodiversity: Directly adjacent to The Farm is a 1,400-acre (566-hectare) preserve called the Big Swan Headwaters Preserve, which was established by Swan Conservation Trust, a Farm-based nonprofit that works to protect and restore native hardwood forests, biodiversity, wildlife habitat, and water quality in the bioregion. The trust has another 100 acres (40 hectares) called Highland Woods Preserve, which is also adjacent to The Farm. The Tennessee Nature Conservancy donated an additional 20 acres (8 hectares), known as the Langford Branch State Natural Area, in 2002. According to Bates, The Farm's forest stands today at 2,940 acres (1,750 at The Farm itself, so the annual rate of sequestration is 5,750 to 6,900 tons of carbon per year. He calculates that The Farm is using only about 15 percent of its forest to offset its total carbon emissions.

NO CHEMICAL FERTILIZER ON THIS TRACTOR. THAT'S COMPOST TEA IN THE BLUE BARRELS. BRIAN BANKSTON, THE "KEYLINE COWBOY," IS INJECTING THE TEA AND A MIXTURE OF BIOCHAR AND ROCK MINERALS USING A KEYLINE SUBSOIL PLOWING METHOD TO NATURALLY BUILD FERTILITY IN THE SOIL.

Evolving Food Systems: During The Farm's development, two core philosophies of pacifism (not killing animals for meat and using the earth's resources efficiently) resulted in a strictly vegan diet of homegrown foods. One of the community's most influential publications, *The Farm Vegetarian Cookbook,* features the community's soy-based diet, which makes better use of earth's resources by decreasing human dependence on cows for meat. Though most of its fields are kept in fallow reserve or rotating pasture instead of crop production, a majority of the homes on The Farm have backyard gardens where organic vegetables are grown in the spring, summer and fall. Winter production in bioshelters is also common. Some members, like Doug Stevenson, are committed to moving toward greater food security and are developing more elaborate systems. "It is not uncommon for us to have meals made up entirely of food we have grown," he reports.

Mark Hubbard, who was born on The Farm, and his wife—with help from community members—have begun a project to grow ten types of beans and grains in a field that once yielded enough food to feed hundreds of people. Food security is his primary purpose for the creation he dubs Unity Farm. He says, "I am concerned with the collapse of our system of production and consumption and I have no faith in the longevity of the food production and distribution system. I definitely think it's going to collapse within my lifetime, so one of my main thrusts is to get sustainable if I need to."

TOOLS/TECHNOLOGY

Renewable Power: The Farm was an early champion of solar power and has opposed nuclear energy for decades. One of the community's main businesses is S. E. International Inc., which has been manufacturing and selling digital and analog ionizing radiation detection devices and Geiger counters to both individuals and government agencies since 1979.

The Farm gets its electricity from the Meriwether Lewis Electric Cooperative, which buys wholesale from the Tennessee Valley Authority (TVA). About 80 percent of Farm residents spend an extra $8 per month to purchase green power (wind and hydropower) via a program called Green Power Switch. There are three major solar arrays on and adjacent to The Farm that feed power back to the TVA Green Power Grid. The TVA requires power generated to be sold back to the TVA (at a rate of 12 cents per kilowatt) instead of directly powering homes. In the event of an emergency situation that might cause the entire grid to go down, The Farm could conceivably generate its own power by feeding its solar electricity directly into a microgrid.

CULTURE/EDUCATION

Raising a Permaculture Army: For years, the ETC has offered workshops, programs, and apprenticeships such as shiitake mushroom growing basics, solar installation, biochar stove camp, natural building, herbal medicines, bamboo cultivation and construction, ecovillage design, and permaculture.

Bates says his game plan for teaching, both on The Farm and around the world, is to raise a permaculture army. The ETC is a project of the Global Village Institute (GVI) and is affiliated with the Global Ecovillage Network and with Gaia University, which offers college credit for several of its programs. Doug Stevenson's Green Life Retreats host retreats in Belize and on The Farm, the most popular of which is the Experience Weekend in Tennessee.

Permaculture is one of many alternative subjects being taught by Jennifer Albanese and Jessie Smith at The Farm School. "We are co-constructing a responsive curriculum that fits our natural ways of being and learning," says Farm School director Peter Kindfield. "Our Enchanted Edible Food Forest functions both as an experiential context for learning about permaculture and a place where children can learn in a way that fits their inner nature."

FINANCES/ECONOMICS

A Creative Collective Economic System: After nearly thirteen years of dreaming big and living poor, Farm members confronted the realities of financial mismanagement, idealism, medical debt, the farming crisis, and the inflation of the early 1980s. In 1983, The Farm moved from being a fully communal economy to a collective in which each family became responsible for their own finances. According to Doug Stevenson, the "Changeover" required all members to provide for their families individually and to pay dues for the "operation and management of the community and its property." Hundreds left. The total accumulated debt was estimated to be well over $400,000, and eventually was found to be as much as $600,000. The community's remaining residents retired that debt by 1989.

A system of community-based microloans allows Farm members to develop the property, since traditional banks will not arrange loans for building projects on the collectively owned land. Adult members of The Farm community pay approximately $100 per month in dues. These dues pay for community expenses such as water and the upkeep of community buildings and paved roads.

HEALTH / SPIRITUAL WELL-BEING

MIDWIFERY ON THE FARM

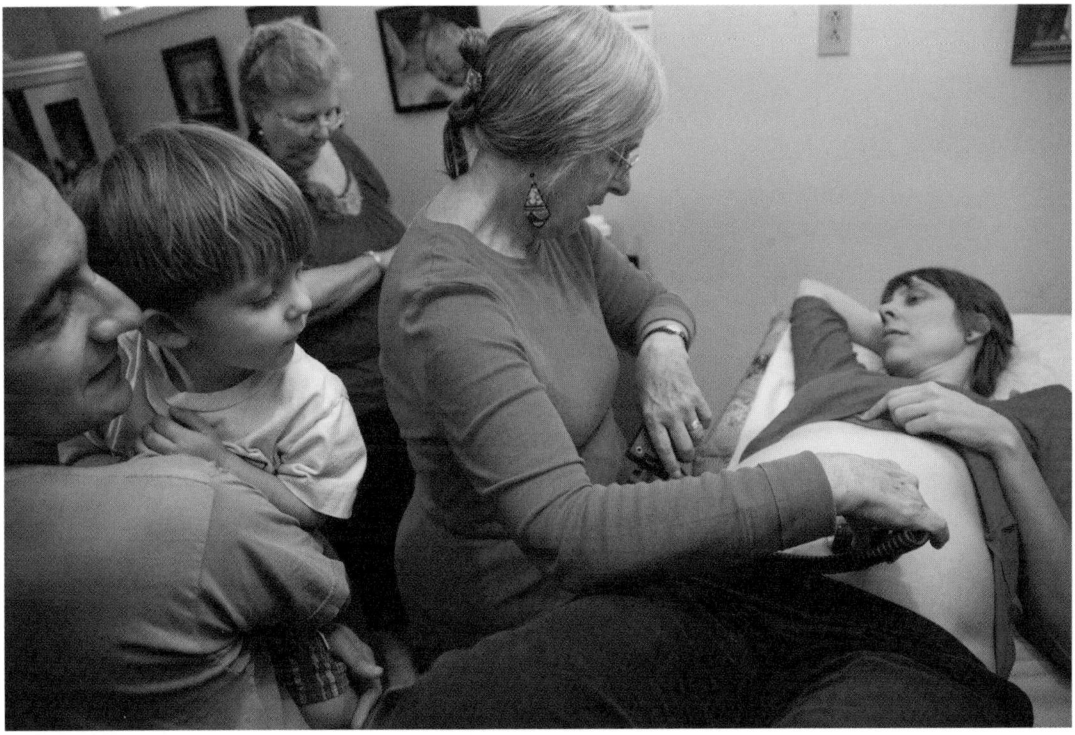

Photo: Susanna Frohman

THE PERMACULTURAL PERSPECTIVE OF **WORKING WITH NATURE** ALSO APPLIES TO BIRTH AND DEATH, THE MOST DRAMATIC OF LIFE'S PROCESSES. BILL MOLLISON SAYS, "AIDING THE NATURAL CYCLES RESULTS IN HIGHER YIELD AND LESS WORK. A LITTLE SUPPORT GOES A LONG WAY." THE FARM'S MIDWIVES, THOUGH NOT SELF-IDENTIFIED PERMACULTURISTS, HOLD A VERY SIMILAR PERSPECTIVE ON NATURAL BIRTH.

About two miles from the entrance to The Farm community is a clinic that houses The Farm Midwifery Center (FMC), established in 1971 as a service for the growing village. Under the tutelage of a local physician who had for years provided obstetric home-birth services for an Old Order Amish community, The Farm midwives began their work in an area in which there were essentially no midwives.

It is widely recognized that birth workers on The Farm have helped to bring midwifery back from the brink of extinction in the United States. Together, under the tutelage of Ina May Gaskin, author of the internationally best-selling *Spiritual Midwifery,* they have safely birthed more than three thousand babies naturally, with a cesarean-section rate of less than 2 percent. This pioneering work resulted in Ina May Gaskin being named one of four recipients of the Right Livelihood Award in 2011 and induction into the National Women's Hall of Fame in 2013.

Ina May Gaskin and The Farm midwives advocate for and provide safe, natural birthing options for families. They have shown that empowering birth experiences are possible for mothers well prepared for labor, well cared for in pregnancy, and surrounded by love, patience, and continuous support during the birth. Citing unnecessarily high rates of cesarean section, labor induction, and maternal death in the United States, The Farm midwives work to educate women in how to avoid unnecessary medical intervention in the home or hospital. Gaskin says, "Our birth outcomes clearly demonstrate that well-prepared, healthy women, aided by skilled midwives with good relationships with the local medical community can safely give birth in out-of-hospital settings."

Many apprentice-trained midwives around the country, as well as several of The Farm midwives, have been actively involved in getting midwives recognized as medical professionals. Several of The Farm midwives were active in establishing the North American Registry of Midwives (NARM), which issues the Certified Professional Midwife (CPM) credential.

Through political advocacy by midwives on and off The Farm, twenty-seven states now recognize the CPM credential. Legislative campaigns for state licenses are taking place in an additional eleven states. The application for certification office for NARM is located on The Farm. Since 1994, when the first CPM credential was issued, more than 2,200 women have been certified as Certified Professional Midwives. "The practice of moving midwifery forward in general is just a continuation of believing that women should have the option of choosing a skilled midwife who is able to work in an out-of-hospital setting. In providing such options, we know that there are midwives all over the world who are engaged in the same work that we do," says, NARM Board Member, founding Farm member and CPM Carol Nelson.

In addition to attending births, teaching, and lecturing worldwide, Gaskin also spearheads the Safe Motherhood Quilt Project, which features the names of every American woman whose death from pregnancy-related causes can be documented since 1982. The project is aimed at lowering the currently rising maternal death rate through the establishment of a system of consistent and mandatory reporting, counting, classifying, reviewing, and analyzing the causes of maternal deaths in the United States.

Reporting contributed by Susanna Frohman. Logo, above, courtesy of The Farm Midwifery Center. Opposite page: all photos by Sarah Boccolucci, coloradobirthphotos.com, except middle left, by Emily Weaver Brown and bottom right, by Louis Fox.

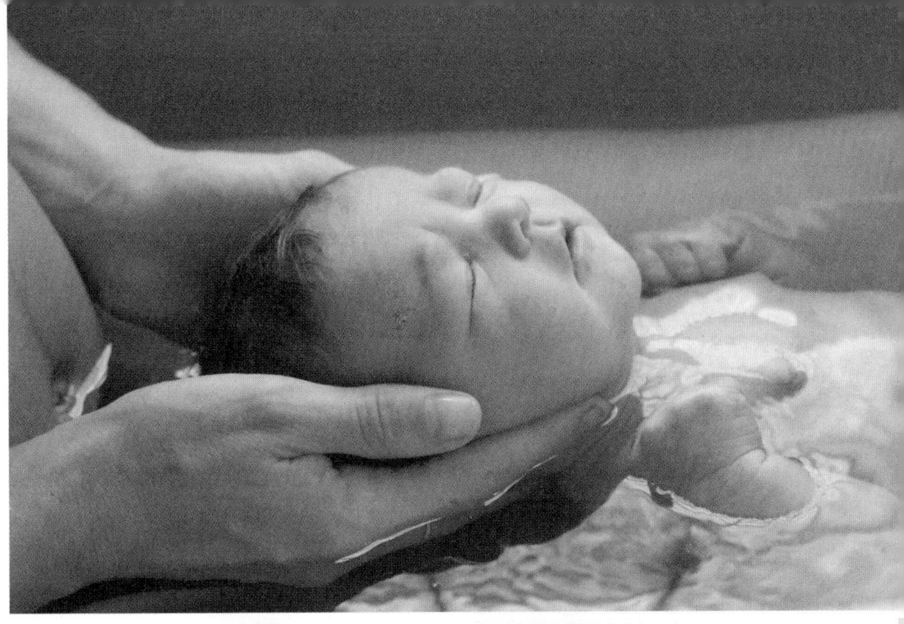

"MANY OF OUR PROBLEMS IN U.S. MATERNITY CARE STEM FROM THE FACT THAT WE LEAVE NO ROOM FOR RECOGNIZING WHEN NATURE IS SMARTER THAN WE ARE."—INA MAY GASKIN, *BIRTH MATTERS: A MIDWIFE'S MANIFESTA*

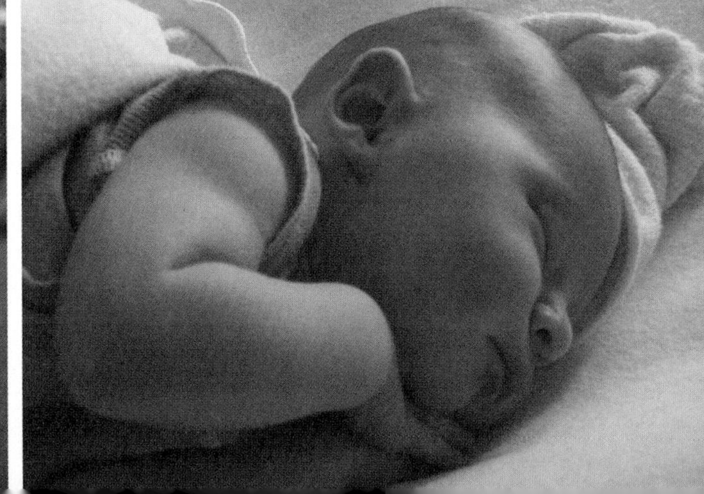

POLITICAL OUTREACH ON THE FARM

Plenty International, The Farm's global nonprofit, has worked for decades toward the protection, stewardship, and distribution of global resources. It also assists economically underserved and indigenous community groups with projects that promote local food, water, energy, health, and economic self-sufficiency. Plenty works in Haiti, the Mississippi Gulf Coast, Native American reservations, Guatemala, and Nicaragua. During the late 1970s, Plenty provided free ambulance service to residents of the Bronx, New York, because local medical services considered it too dangerous to respond to calls.

Plenty also works locally. Kids to the Country is one of their most successful local efforts. Over the past twenty-five years, it has enabled approximately five thousand children from the inner city of neighboring Nashville to spend a week each summer in the woods at The Farm.

One of the most interesting organizations led by a former founding Farm member is the Farmer Veteran Coalition, which works today to "mobilize the nation's food and farming community to create healthy and viable futures for America's veterans by enlisting their help in building a green economy, rebuilding rural communities, and securing a safe and healthy food supply for all" while training a new generation of farmers to replace the aging farmer population. Founder and executive director Michael O'Gorman says, "While I learned the mechanics of growing food on the Farm, what really made me successful in my farming career was learning about community. Farming was traditionally a communal event and I got to learn how to harness the excitement and joy that we shared when working together and growing food together. That was a skill that made me thrive when managing hundreds of Mexican farm workers—people close to those communal roots. And it is similar skills that I am now passing on to new farmers, fresh from their experience of war. Food sustains those we feed, but the act of producing it sustains us," he says.

After 9/11, members of the greater Farm community started a nonprofit called Peace Roots, which later became the Peace Roots Alliance (PRA). The organization is geared toward stopping the root causes of war.

More than Warmth is a Farm-based educational project for American students to learn about world cultures. Founded by long-term Farm member Judith Biondo Meeker, the program has helped more than 15,000 students nationwide with social studies, art, and literature projects and has resulted in the creation and distribution of approximately 1,500 handmade quilts to students by students in fifty countries, including Afghanistan and Iraq.

Susanna Frohman

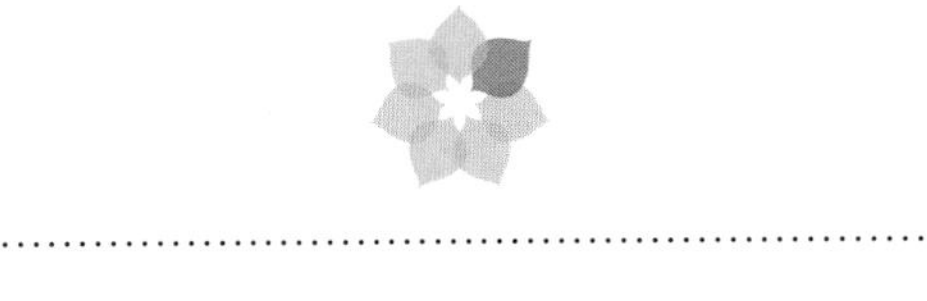

TOOLS / TECHNOLOGY

BIOCHAR

Biochar is a kind of charcoal that is incorporated into agriculture, providing a mechanism for carbon sequestration, soil improvement and water retention. It is produced by cooking organic matter in a low-oxygen environment (pyrolysing).

According to Albert Bates, author of *The Biochar Solution,* the use of charcoal as a soil additive goes back thousands of years and was the basis for ancient agriculture in areas of poor soil. To understand how biochar works, we need to understand the chemistry of carbon and the different forms carbon can exist in, also known as allotropes. There are two broad categories of carbon that cycle through the atmosphere and through the soil. The organic compounds in soils are the core components of the carbon cycle, formed through the decay of organisms. The other form is inorganic carbon or recalcitrant carbon—a hard, crystalline form that does not break down easily. An examination of this inorganic carbon under a microscope reveals a structure composed of millions of pores, resulting in a huge surface area. When inorganic carbon is added to soil, the pores fill up with microbiota, amoebae, nematodes, and fungal hyphae. The piece of charcoal effectively becomes a biological store that feeds nutrients into the roots of plants. The pores can also act as caches for water. In all, it helps make the garden grow by providing ample nutrition, balancing soil chemistry, soaking up heavy rainfall, and ensuring a slow release of moisture during dry periods. Carbon in its biochar state is unable to cycle back as carbon dioxide or methane, remaining in the soil for thousands of years as biomass. This is where the geo-engineering aspect of biochar comes into play. Agricultural or wood wastes that are turned into biochar provide a way to store large amounts of carbon in the ground.

This ability to sequester carbon places biochar on the radar of corporations looking for engineered solutions to climate change. To make biochar a worthwhile carbon sink, however, we would need to take about 10 gigatons of carbon from the atmosphere annually. The process would need to be rolled out on a large scale, but the implications of mishaps or the misuse of practices can be frightening. The industrial-scale deployment envisioned by some would replace slow-growing forest ecosystems and their indigenous populations with genetically modified biomass plantations controlled by transnational conglomerates.

Permaculture advocates small-scale solutions and accepting feedback as essential. The science backs permaculture's approach to the use of biochar: studies of energy and externalized costs indicate the industrial model is noncompetitive and a waste of investment. The farther you separate the farmer and the production of biochar, the less cost-effective the process becomes. But at the farm or community level, biochar is an excellent soil additive that can be used to generate power, heating, and air-conditioning.

Muneezay Jaffery.

The GreenHouse Project

Johannesburg, South Africa

MAKING SURE THAT ALL ITS INITIATIVES HAVE AN INCOME-SAVING OR INCOME-GENERATING ASPECT, THE GREENHOUSE PROJECT HELPS THE LOCAL INNER-CITY COMMUNITY MEET ITS IMMEDIATE SURVIVAL NEEDS WHILE ADDRESSING GLOBAL ENVIRONMENTAL ISSUES.

The GreenHouse Project is a South African permaculture demonstration center, located in the inner-city environment of Johannesburg, that is demonstrating urban regeneration strategies and spreading successful ideas in the region. Joubert Park, where the project is based, is sandwiched between crowded residential areas (including Hillbrow, notorious for crime and unemployment) and the main business district. Johannesburg has a subtropical highland climate, with mild temperatures, due to its high elevation of 5,751 feet (1,753 meters).

Initiated in 1993 by Earthlife Africa Johannesburg, in partnership with city officials, the GreenHouse Project has taken over an old park utility depot and transformed its sheds, hothouses, and grounds. The main facility is a project office and resource center that is off the grid, using photovoltaic panels to provide solar power. It is surrounded by small plots for community gardening and teaching. The site has a dry composting toilet and recycles or composts its trash as much as possible. Gray-water systems recycle water from sinks for the garden irrigation systems.

The GreenHouse Project teaches courses in renewable energy, sustainable water and sanitation management, zero waste, organic food, medicinal plants and landscaping, and green building. The project is now the hub of an effective education program on nutrition and empowers people to establish their own organic gardens—at least one hundred families in the townships now have portable barrel gardens. The permaculture gardeners at the site undertake training of the extensive flatland community in the Hillbrow district, including preschool children.

THE PORTABLE BARREL GARDENS HAVE BECOME ONE OF THE GREENHOUSE PROJECT'S MOST POPULAR TECHNIQUES. FOR DORAH LEBELO, ONE OF THE INITIAL LEADERS OF THE PROJECT, IT WAS IMPORTANT TO ADDRESS THE FALLACY THAT BLACK PEOPLE DON'T CARE ABOUT THE ENVIRONMENT.

The members of GreenHouse realized early on that to achieve their aims, they had to be relevant to people living around the park, who are often more focused on issues of day-to-day survival than on saving the environment. The project's initiatives therefore also have immediate benefits such as income generation and resource saving. The recycling and urban organic agriculture initiatives, for example, are run by cooperatives that are supported by GreenHouse. The urban organic agriculture cooperative has twenty-two members: two from GreenHouse and two each from ten other community-based projects around Johannesburg.

According to outreach officer France Maleme, when it comes to climate change, not much has been done at the grassroots level to educate locals about the threat—and this is where GreenHouse comes in. Instead of showing graphs and other abstract scientific information that is difficult to understand, they have organized a roadshow that has been very successful, showing visuals and films to get the message across, and spread dialogue about solutions.

Reporting contributed by the Berkana Institute. Photos by Elias Koch, The Global Oneness Project.

Chikukwa and CELUCT

Chimanimani, Zimbabwe

BEFORE THE CREATION OF CELUCT, THE LANDSCAPE AROUND THE VILLAGES WAS HEAVILY DENUDED AND SUFFERED FROM CHRONIC EROSION.

Chikukwa is a community nestled in a gap between mountain ranges on the border with Mozambique and was a route for Zimbabwean guerrillas during the colonial liberation struggle. After Zimbabwe's independence in 1980, the same paths were used by Mozambicans in their bitter civil war. Up until 1990, Chikukwans often slept in the bush to avoid the violence. War—together with Chikukwa's remote situation—limited development in this area. The six Chikukwa villages are on steep slopes and erosion is a key problem; there is only one flat area, next to a small river. Twenty years ago, the majority of the villagers were trying to survive by selling monoculture crops on the global market, and deforestation was increasing. Chikukwa

"Water that can be spoilt can also be purified."
—Shona proverb

TODAY THE CHIKUKWA VILLAGES' LANDS ARE AN ABUNDANT POLYCULTURE. STANDING ON A HILLTOP, YOU CAN SEE THE HOUSES NESTLED AMONG ORCHARDS, THE EARTH BANKS (BUNDS) WITH VETIVER GRASS IN THE CROPPING FIELDS, AND THE EXTENSIVE WOODLOTS. ALL ARE TYPICAL OF THE PERMACULTURE DESIGN STRATEGY THAT THE COMMUNITY BEGAN TO DEVELOPING HERE IN 1992.

was once home to a subtropical forest, but it had been almost totally cleared since the colonial era when, ironically, the area was delineated as a Tribal Land Trust. In 1992 the villagers started an initiative to turn things around using the permaculture design approach. Today, their effort has restored their water supply, helped the community to deal with social issues, and brought back polyculture food-growing systems.

"Not only have they managed to stay food secure and peaceful during the last conflict ridden years in Zimbabwe, but they have also managed to retain strong and joyful community relations with plenty of

A LUSH POLYCULTURE PROVIDES YIELDS OF BANANAS, COFFEE, AND BIOMASS WHILE PROVIDING A MOISTURE-RETAINING GROUND COVER AND RESILIENCE AGAINST CROP FAILURE AND EROSION. CONCENTRATING ON SUBSISTENCE RATHER THAN COMMERCIAL PRODUCTION HAS BEEN A DISTINCTIVE FEATURE OF THIS PROJECT, ENABLING THE PROJECT TO PAY ATTENTION TO PRACTICAL STRATEGIES TO STRENGTHEN FOOD SECURITY RATHER THAN PIPE DREAMS OF COMMERCIAL SUCCESS.

heart-warming laughter, singing, dancing and celebration," writes Permaculture Research Institute Kenya director Elin Lindhagen.[11]

In the early 1990s the main spring that fed the Chikukwa villages dried up—a wake-up call to a people that had been trying to survive mainly on cash-crop farming. The spring's flow fed the village not only physically but spiritually, and traditional beliefs dictated that the water spirits of the spring be restored to revive the health of the community. A group formed calling itself *Nyuchi Dzakasimba*, which in Shona, the local language, means "strong bees," pointing to their commitment to hard work.

The group worked together to reforest the area and restore the community's water supply, and through this process, they started to learn about permaculture. They invited people to come to teach workshops, out of which the villagers developed a larger design plan that started a transformation process. The result has controlled soil erosion on their steep slopes, improved food security, and empowered communities to mediate conflicts. Their original gardening club became CELUCT (Chikukwa Environmental Land Use Community Trust). Though they began with barren hills and a trend toward desertification, the area is now verdant and lush, with houses set in orchards and gardens, cropping fields stepped with contour banks planted with vetiver grass, and hilltops and gullies planted with forests and woodlots.

"To use permaculture lingo, Chikukwa can be described as a real edge, both in terms of ecology, culture and language," Lindhagen says, "and the edge effect has certainly produced something rich. The community here has a sense of being both somewhat innocent and progressive at the same time. It is as if they skipped the industrialized phase and went straight into becoming a sustainable community." (See p. 206 for more on the edge effect in permaculture.)

LAND/NATURE STEWARDSHIP

Water, Food, and Forests: Following permaculture principles, the villagers of the Chikukwa clan reuse water from their kitchens and rooftops for their gardens and orchards, irrigating their cropping fields using bunds and swales to slow and redirect water. They have built their topsoil with green manure, mulches, and compost and have managed their livestock to collect manure and consume garden waste. The communities have reforested the hilltops to secure their rainwater catchments and to protect the hills from cattle and deforestation. At the same time, they have planted woodlots to ensure a plentiful source of wood for building and cooking fuel. They have restored their water supply by putting in check dams and planting the gullies with indigenous trees, fencing the critical areas.

Using these technologies, the Chikukwa villages have been able to diversify their food production through their own gardens and work on a number of community farms. The rich diet of the Chikukwa villagers today is rare in rural Africa and ensures adequate protein, vitamins, and minerals, as well as essential carbohydrates. Virtually every household has small livestock; an orchard; a vegetable garden; cropping fields with systems integrated to make use of available sun, water, and wind; and laborsaving design principles. The village landscape is a mosaic of wood lots and small pockets reserved for cattle grazing. While primarily a subsistence farming community, Chikukwa's successful adoption of permaculture techniques has proved effective economically as well. When Zimbabwe suffered drought-related food shortages, buyers came to Chikukwa, where food remained abundant.

THE LEADER OF THE PERMACULTURE CLUB IN HIS VILLAGE, MAI MATSEKETE, HOLDS THE FUTURE.

HEALTH/SPIRITUAL WELL-BEING

Indigenous Worldviews and Permaculture: The permaculture framework complements the spiritual beliefs of the Chikukwa people. In their tradition, the natural world is revered. As one of the first moments of this transformation, traditional leaders invoked the spirits of their ancestors and performed rituals when the springs were reclaimed. They decreed the protection of the sacred forests

MAI MATSEKETE AND HIS FAMILY CONSTRUCTED THESE SWALES ON CONTOUR TO PREVENT EROSION IN THEIR FIELD AND TO DIRECT WATER TO THE ORCHARD ON THE LOWER SIDE OF THE HOUSE. ALMOST LIKE MAGIC, SWALES CAN BRING A COMMUNITY'S SPRING BACK TO LIFE.

WHEN ZIMBABWE SUFFERED DROUGHT-RELATED FOOD SHORTAGES, BUYERS CAME TO CHIKUKWA, WHERE FOOD REMAINED ABUNDANT.

that were being replanted around these springs. These forests correspond to permaculture's zone 5 (wild nature as an essential aspect of a constructed human agricultural system).

Kevin Chikukwa, a spiritual leader in the community, explains the link between permaculture and their traditional spiritual knowledge. "We are in line with CELUCT in the use of organic agriculture. We are not supposed to use artificial fertilizers, because it damages the soil. Also in our tradition, we encourage our committed members to work in harmony with nature." Linking the protection of the land, soil, water, and plant life, these traditional spiritual leaders support permaculture for the care it gives to the land and the spirits that reside there.

VILLAGERS FIXING A GULLY WITH A ROCK BUND, VETIVER GRASS, AND INDIGENOUS TREES. THIS PROJECT FOLLOWED A CONFLICT-RESOLUTION WORKSHOP THAT ADDRESSED THE COMPETING INTERESTS OF DIFFERENT HOUSEHOLDS AROUND THIS GULLY, WHICH WAS ERODING SOME FIELDS AND DEPOSITING RICH SILT IN OTHER FIELDS.

☼ LAND TENURE/ COMMUNITY GOVERNANCE

Grassroots Representational Structures: The organizational structure of CELUCT also increases local participation and democracy by including community members, traditional leadership, and professional staff in bottom-up decision making. The community is mobilized and empowered by the grassroots, representational structure of CELUCT, with committees responsible for local and institutional decisions. The committees review financial accounts and record minutes at their meetings, adding to the legitimacy of each committee and ensuring the transparency and accountability of the central organization. If villagers require assistance with education and training in a particular issue, they consult the local club that addresses that issue (for example, the permaculture club or the women's society). Representatives from the club then approach the CELUCT management to assist the local organizations in developing a response. From their early focus on food security and land care, CELUCT has branched out to create programs for women, youth, and people living with HIV, developing solutions for conflict mediation and preschool education. These are all organized via bottom-up participatory management, pioneered through their initial permaculture-based efforts.

Reporting and photos contributed by Terry Leahy and Monika Goforth.

DR. JOANNE TIPPETT ON THE EDGE EFFECT

From a permaculture perspective, one of the most important aspects of understanding patterns is that of the "edge effect." In nature, there are no rigid borders; the edge is more of a diffuse region of exchange, an interchange of elements, and a net for new information—in the form of nutrients, seeds, or cultural exchange. Edges are extremely important. They are the most productive areas in terms of both species and actual physical production. At the edge of two ecosystems, one finds species from both systems, along with special species adapted to the conditions of the edge.

The edge is very important in terms of biodiversity and production of biomass. At the edge, there is an increased cycling of materials and information. There is a possibility for increased synergism—the mutually beneficial relationships between elements of a system. The edge increases possibilities for creativity, as it is the point for merging, change, and new ideas.

The edge effect can be understood by considering the edge of water and woodland systems. Water has many beneficial effects on land: sunlight reflection is increased, and climate is moderated, warming up less quickly but staying warm for longer. Productive edge plants (such as sweet rushes, reeds, blueberries) thrive there. The water also benefits from the edge with the land, due to the increase in highly productive margin plants and enrichment by nutrients from the land. Tree leaves fall into the water; land animals and birds visit and deposit the richness of their fertilizer.

The edge of woodland is also highly productive. Species are able to receive more light; soft fruits, vegetables, and herbs thrive on the additional nutrients and moisture provided by the trees. Many native cultures have learned how to benefit from the edge of forests. In New Guinea, the Tsembaga people practice agriculture in forest clearings. "A Tsembaga gardener is almost as irritated when a visitor damages a tree seedling as when he heedlessly tramples on a taro plant. The Tsembaga recognize the importance of the regenerating trees; they call them collectively *duk mi,* or 'mother of gardens.'"[12] Agroforestry offers unparalleled opportunities for increasing the beneficial edge effect between crops and trees.

Dr. Joanne Tippett, excerpt printed with permission from the author, from "A Pattern Language of Sustainability: Ecological Design and Permaculture," BA dissertation, Lancaster University, 1994[13]

Durban Botanic Gardens

Durban, KwaZulu-Natal, South Africa

STUDENTS FROM A NEIGHBORING SCHOOL WATER THEIR SEEDLINGS AFTER PLANTING THEM INTO A NEWLY CREATED BED USING A NO-DIG, SHEET-MULCHING METHOD. SMALL GARDEN BEDS USING THIS METHOD CAN BE SEEN ALL ALONG THE PERIMETER OF THE PERMACULTURE TRAINING GARDEN AT DURBAN BOTANIC GARDENS.

Set on 30 acres (12 hectares) in a major city on the east coast of South Africa, Durban Botanic Gardens (DBG) was founded in 1849 for the introduction and trial of agricultural crops and is now home to a burgeoning environmental education program guided by the ethics and principles of permaculture. Through progressive leadership, partnerships, and a commitment to building local ecological literacy, it has become a successful example of permaculture within the botanic garden structure.

DBG's Permaculture Training Centre, designed by Gabriel Mngoma, is on land that formerly was a sports field. The permaculture program engages participants in a structured, interactive learning experience that invites discovery and observation of ecological systems. School groups who participate in a DBG permaculture program often go on to create permaculture gardens at their own schools.

While the garden hosts approximately five hundred thousand visitors each year—and the permaculture program grows through local outreach—the engagement continues beyond Durban. DBG has a partnership with Woza Moya, a community center located two hours southwest, in a village affected by one of the highest HIV/AIDS rates in the world.

Woza Moya is dedicated to providing support services for families affected with HIV, AIDS, and poverty throughout the surrounding Ufafa Valley, and DBG provides permaculture courses and support for village women to grow their own food. This is a tremendous source of empowerment, and it can mean the difference between eating or going hungry. These women then multiply the program's reach by teaching their neighbors how to start their own permaculture gardens, with the goal of increasing food security through the Ufafa Valley, one woman at a time.

Reporting and photos contributed by Erin Marteal.

PART 05

Temperate/Subtropical Climates: Mediterranean and Maritime Zones

This section includes temperate/subtropical climates of the maritime and Mediterranean variety. These climates are both typical of the west coasts at the middle latitudes of most continents, and generally feature warm, but not hot, summers and cool, but not cold, winters: a relatively narrow annual temperature range. Along with the climate zones featured in part 4, they are part of the Temperate/Subtropical Group C classification on the Köppen map (see p. 22).

In Europe, the maritime climate reaches further inland and predominates the continent up to the Alps. Also called "marine west coast or oceanic," it appears in coastal northwestern North America, portions of southwestern South America, and parts of Africa, Australia, and New Zealand, among other locations. These areas typically have abundant, regular precipitation and moderate temperatures that support dense forests, including conifers, and a wide variety of plant life.

The Mediterranean climate is located in bands between thirty and forty degrees north and south of the equator, and though temperatures are relatively mild, winter and summer extremes can vary greatly between different regions. These zones occur on the coast of California, the coastal areas of the Mediterranean Sea, the coast of Chile, the Cape region of South Africa, and coastal Australia. Flora usually consists of regions of tall, dense shrubs with leathery leaves or needles, interspersed with some woodland (scrub oak). There are also a number of areas that fall into a transition zone between the Mediterranean and maritime climate types or are categorized differently according to different systems of classification.

Mediterranean ecosystems are among the most endangered on earth. Though they cover only a little over 2 percent of the planet's land surface, they tend to be densely populated and have a long history of human activity, especially in agriculture. They support about 20 percent of the world's plant species and are susceptible to rapid loss of biodiversity due to development and climate change.[1]

Photo: Sean Gold

Torri Superiore Ecovillage

Liguriza, Italy

Photo courtesy of Terri Superiore

WASTE NOT WANT NOT: ONCE ABANDONED, THIS MEDIEVAL SETTLEMENT HAS A COMPACT, STURDY DESIGN THAT SURVIVED SEVEN CENTURIES, MAKING IT A WORTHY HOME FOR PEOPLE WHO VALUE SUSTAINABILITY. BY USING THE SITE'S ORIGINAL HIGH-DENSITY, VERTICAL STRUCTURE, NEW RESIDENTS ENJOY FIVE ACRES ALMOST ENTIRELY FOR AGRICULTURE AND OPEN SPACE.

The medieval hamlet of Torri Superiore is on a hillside between the Alps and the Mediterranean and consists of three main buildings with over 160 vaulted rooms, linked by an intricate labyrinth of stairways, covered walkways, and terraces. In 1989, a small group of like-minded people formed an association to purchase the hamlet, with the aim of restoring it according to permaculture principles and reinhabiting the 5-acre (2-hectare) site as an ecovillage and cultural center. The Torri Superiore Cultural Association now has about thirty members, both resident and nonresident, from Italy, Germany, France, and Australia. Torri Superiore Ecovillage hosts courses in permaculture and other subjects, and the ancient buildings have largely been restored, creating a home for a new generation of villagers.

In many ways, the hamlet lent itself well to ecovillage design, in that the compact structure is inherently energy efficient and built of local stone and lime. Also, it was, in fact, truly created for communal living, as evidenced by the large hall, which was probably a common kitchen, the open-air oven, and the densely knit hive of rooms and terraces. Over seven centuries, many hands built Torri Superiore, and it continues to be a work in progress, with several community members dedicated full time to the continuing restoration.

In the late thirteenth century, a period of intense social and religious unrest likely motivated a group of people to begin building Torri Superiore, whose name means "upper towers" on a hillside above the Bevera River. The initial settlers were seeking protection by choosing to live communally within the fortress-like structure, which eventually came to rise several stories and became a labyrinth of rooms.

As the region is too mountainous to support large-scale agriculture, the first settlers fished, grew grapes and olive trees on the terraced slopes for wine and olive oil, and traded. The last levels of the structure, which by that time had grown to the three connected buildings, appear to have been built around Napoleon's time, when the hamlet also reached its highest population. Napoleon annexed Liguria, where Torri Superiore is located, to France, but soon it came under the control of the Sardinians. Eventually Liguria became part of modern-day Italy (the Ligurian language, though presently in danger of dying out, is still spoken today). The hamlet of Torri Superiore was gradually abandoned as locals migrated to urban centers, leaving the towers to decay.

By 1989, Torri Superiore was falling into ruin, with collapsed vault ceilings and debris blocking the many rooms and hallways, which is when a small group approached the site with the hopes of restoring it in line with ecological principles and respecting its unique character. Despite the obvious draws of the beautiful site—located in what is known today as the Italian Riviera—restoring the medieval structure carried its own set of unique challenges. Italy's ancient land-ownership system meant that even a few square meters of land can be owned. Therefore, different parts of the building were in the names of different people who had to be tracked down.

"The complexity of the building and the absence of any detailed map forced us to spend the first three years in observation, study, and map-drawing to understand what exactly we were buying from the multitude of different owners," writes founding member Lucilla Borio.[2] "Most of the buildings had big cracks in the walls, some vaults were damaged or fallen, heaps of debris and rubbish were blocking the access to half of the rooms, and the general picture was rather discouraging." Small local firms, supported by volunteer efforts of all members and residents, did a large part of the building and restoration work, all in accordance with permaculture philosophy.

☼ LAND/NATURE STEWARDSHIP

Restoring the "Local Gold": Evidence of the long-term process of urbanization in the region is prevalent in the valley surrounding Torri Superiore. Many of the traditional agricultural terraces are eroding away, and the ancient rows of olive trees the ecovillagers took on were extremely overgrown. Borio compares the unkempt old trees to a hidden treasure, calling them the "local gold." The community

has worked to improve the soil through intensive composting and other permaculture techniques. Beneath the olive trees, they plant green-manure plants, such as mustard greens, peas, fava beans, and oats, which increase soil fertility.

The community produces olive oil, grapes, and other produce, and they try to source as much organic and local food as possible. Homemade products include bread, *pasta fresca,* olive oil, goat cheese, honey, jams, yogurt, and ice cream. They use no prepared products, frozen foods or genetically modified foods. By keeping their food production local, the ecovillage is slowly reintroducing an ancient, sustainable system. The aim is to revive the traditional, intimate Italian relationship with eating, which many locals fear is being lost through the rise of modern, ultra-processed food.

The simple method of hand-harvesting olives entails shaking the tree and swatting at its branches with a long stick, causing the ripe olives fall onto a fine net spread over the ground beneath. Some modern olive growers use a mechanized harvester, but that tends to damage both the trees and the olives. It takes 9–11 pounds (4–5 kilos) of olives to produce about a quart (1 liter) of olive oil.

Currently, the community makes about 60 percent of the olive oil it uses, including some used by Borio to make body lotions and soaps. The olive cycle is one of the community's best closed-loop cycles. Goats eat the foliage from olive tree pruning, and the villagers use the pruned branches to make furniture, as chips for the goats' bedding, or as fuel in wood stoves. They spread the wood ashes under the trees to add potassium to the soil.

BUILDING

Renovating an Ancient Cohousing Hamlet: The original building presents a uniquely compact layout: three five-story buildings connected in an exceptionally dense, hive-like structure—a design feature that has preserved it to some extent and helped it survive the injuries of time. Narrow passageways and staircases create a web of interwoven rooms with vaulted ceilings (both barrel and cross vault). The structure's 162 rooms include a common kitchen, bathrooms, several dining areas, living rooms, playrooms, a shop, offices, a library, and a yoga/practice space. They are on eight levels and have been redesigned to create a cultural center with an attached guesthouse and twenty small private apartments.

For restoration work, the community members use local stone, natural lime, and natural insulation, which creates breathable walls with excellent air quality. All the doors and windows are wood, and only eco-friendly paints are used.

TOOLS/TECHNOLOGY

Energy and Waste: One of the major benefits of building with stone and terracotta is that in the warm, dry Mediterranean climate, the thick stones are cooled at night, keeping the building comfortably cool by day. Along with these ancient technologies, the community has integrated a hydronic heating system for heat during the winter months, fueled by wood stoves and solar panels. The water runs through tubes under the terracotta floors for radiant heat or, in some rooms, through

DEFORESTED CENTURIES AGO, THESE ANCIENT TERRACES ON CONTOUR CONTINUE TO CONTROL EROSION.

panels on the walls. As some rooms have limited headroom and stone floors, the radiant tubes are inset into the walls and plastered over. The group has also experimented with cork panels and vermiculite as an additive to the plaster to increase the insulating value of the walls.

"Banning cement plaster, Styrofoam panels, aluminum windows, and synthetic paints made us look like foolish eco-idealists, but it paid off in the end," writes Borio.[3] Solar panels are used to provide hot water, and there is a low-temperature heating system throughout the village and in the private houses (with a maximum of 64.4°F [18°C]). The community buys renewable energy from the grid, through an Italian system that allows consumers to choose green energy.

Curbing waste production is another way of living economically and in accordance with permaculture principles. All of their food waste is used to feed the animals or is composted. The community has a separate collection for other waste materials, and they reuse, refurbish, and recycle as much as possible. They also have a couple examples of composting toilet designs (one indoor, one outdoor).

☼ LAND TENURE/COMMUNITY GOVERNANCE

Collective and Private Ownership: Ecovillage residents meet once a week, and consensus decision making is observed at these meetings. During the decision-making phase, a resident can hold three positions: ***giving consensus*** means that one approves of the proposal and is available to participate in the action directly; ***standing aside*** means that one agrees with the idea but will not participate for personal reasons; ***blocking*** means that one thinks the proposal should not go forward. To block a proposal, a resident must explain his or her reasoning openly to the whole group. One block is enough to stop the proposal.

Half of the rooms belong to the Torri Superiore Cultural Association, the collective that originally bought the site, and the other half to individual members who have converted them to apartments of varying sizes.

A YOUNG COMMUNITY MEMBER SHOWS OFF HER PROJECT IN THE COMMUNAL DINING TERRACE.

LUCIA BORIO MAKES AND SELLS OLIVE OIL SOAPS AND LOTIONS, ONE OF THE COMMUNITY-BASED INCOME STREAMS.

CULTURE/EDUCATION

A Broad Spectrum: The ecovillage offers courses year-round on topics related to sustainability, communal living, crafts, and care of people and of the environment. They have also offered permaculture design courses since 2000. Their ceramics workshops produce hand-cast tableware, colored with *engobe* (colored clay) or enamel. Recent educational offerings include biochar, basket weaving, vegetarian cooking, holistic communication, herb crafting, yoga, biodynamic gardening, faciliating consensus, and Transition training (see p. 252 for more on the Transition movement).

FINANCES/ECONOMICS

Communal and Individual Economies: Torri Superiore is unique in that some members choose to pool their income and expenses while others are financially independent. Most residents work within the community, at the guesthouse or on the restoration work. Others work outside jobs, in this modern incarnation of an ancient community.

Reporting by Juliana Birnbaum. Photos by Louis Fox.

Peace Research Village Tamera

Alentejo, Portugal

Photo: Simon du Vinage

In Portuguese, the phrase "deserted landscape" can mean two things: abandoned by people, or turning into a desert. For the Alentejo, the largest district of Portugal, both are true. Vast areas are depleted after decades of intensive monoculture and deforestation; many farmers have given up, due to the hard and dry conditions; in the villages, only older people remain. In spite of its hospitable Mediterranean climate and original beauty, this has become one of the regions in the world that tell the story of scarcity.

In 1995, a small group of German researchers (Sabine Lichtenfels, Dieter Duhm, and Charly Rainer Ehrenpreis) created the Peace Research Village Tamera in the Alentejo. Today 160 people live, work, and study on 370 acres (150 hectares). They are striving to create a "model for the future"—an example that can be replicated worldwide. While it remains under construction and development, the permaculture lakes and terraces of Tamera, its straw-bale buildings, futuristic solar mirrors, and the influx of young people from around the world are already demonstrating that sustainable abundance is possible—not only in the Alentejo, but anywhere on the globe.

TOOLS/TECHNOLOGY

Test Field for a Solar Village: "Water, food and energy will be freely available for all of humankind if we follow the logic of nature and not the laws of capitalism," says Dieter Duhm, one of the cofounders. The teams for ecology and technology at Tamera have taken on the challenge of this statement through scientific research.

With the amount of sunshine in southern Portugal, future generations may wonder how the population could have experienced a scarcity of energy. Yet most of the energy consumed in the nation today is produced from oil and hydropower from big dams. Tamera's technology team wants to show that regional energy autonomy is possible even without large industry.

Solar collectors and photovoltaics produce most of Tamera's electricity and warm water. An experimental micro-biogas plant, lovingly called Hulda the Cow by the researchers, is fed food waste and compost and provides the energy needed at night and on rainy days. In the solar kitchen, a Scheffler Reflector (a parabolic mirror that can be used indoors) and different solar cookers produce the heat needed to prepare meals for about forty people at a time in the communal kitchen.

The technology team, led by German inventor Jürgen Kleinwächter, runs a laboratory for decentralized production and storage of solar energy. They are testing and improving an energy greenhouse with lenses to focus the sunlight, a Stirling engine to transform temperature differences into electrical and mechanical power, and a solar pump.

Barbara Kovats, coordinator of the SolarVillage test field, says that as long as large corporations control the supply of energy, water, and food, there will be injustice and war. "We want to show how regional, community-based autonomy in food and energy can work." The community develops and tests these techniques, Kovats says, and once they have been tested, "they can be applied by communities worldwide, especially in crisis areas where in cases this knowledge can decide about survival."

LAND/NATURE STEWARDSHIP

Reestablishing the Water Cycle: The image of the Alentejo as a desert is shattered when one encounters Tamera's landscape, where the typical brown of the region has been transformed into many shades of green. Ecologically designed lakes and ponds, surrounded by terraces and edible landscapes, look as if they have always been there. In fact, they were built just recently, showing the core of Tamera's ecological work: a new way to treat and understand water.

One hundred years ago, Austrian water researcher Viktor Schauberger stated that decoding the secret of water will lead humanity out of scarcity and capitalism and into abundance and

Photo: Thomas Lüdent

Photo: Simon du Vinage

WITH PERMACULTURE EXPERT SEPP HOLZER, TAMERA'S ECOLOGY TEAM DEVELOPED A CONCEPT FOR LANDSCAPE HEALING TO STORE ALL RAINWATER THAT FALLS ON THE GROUND. THE WATER-RETAINING LANDSCAPE IS BEING USED AS A MODEL FOR OTHER COUNTRIES SUCH AS ISRAEL-PALESTINE, BRAZIL, AND KENYA. GOVERNMENTAL ORGANIZATIONS HAVE ALSO SHOWN INTEREST IN TAMERA'S EXAMPLE AS A POSITIVE "BOTTOM-UP STRATEGY" FOR ADAPTING TO CLIMATE CHANGE.

justice for all. He observed what he called "the full rainwater cycle." Many landscapes today show only half of this original cycle. The cycle is interrupted when monocultures and overgrazing harden the ground so that it cannot absorb rainwater. As a result, rainwater flows off the landscape, washing away the fertile topsoil and leaving behind depleted, dusty earth, and thus causing droughts, floods, and desertification. Tamara is reversing that through rainwater catchment. Bernd Mueller, responsible for the water management at Tamera, reports, "In 2007, we built the first water retention space, the so-called Lake One. The following April a new [natural spring] emerged, which since is flowing steadily all year through—something very rare in southern Portugal."

Since then, Mueller and his team have built many more retention spaces of up to about 7 acres in size, along with swales and terraces, and planted ten of thousands of trees—knowing that the best means for water retention and erosion control is vegetation. Wildlife, such as otters and birds, has returned, and fruit and vegetables grow in abundance on the shores.

Gardens in Cooperation with Nature: The edible landscape around the lakes of Tamera is dense with diverse fruit trees, berry bushes, herbs, and vegetables that feed the community. These shoreline gardens require less irrigation, due to the natural moisture of their location, and supplemental water needed in summer can be pumped from the lakes using solar energy. The food forests are crossed with shaded trails for walking. There is only one part of the garden where visitors are asked not to pick fruits or flowers: the colorful seed garden. Seed autonomy is an important principle in permaculture, especially with today's widespread loss of biodiversity. In order to sustain regional varieties and to become independent from global seed corporations, the ecology team saves and stores its own seeds and exchanges them with seed networks.

CULTURE/EDUCATION

The "Heart Place": Clearly, the ecological and technological systems underway at the ecovillage cannot be maintained by people who live in separation, distrust, and competition with each other. On a hill in the very center of Tamera's site is the "heart place," a stone circle with shining white marble stones. Founder Sabine Lichtenfels was inspired by the ancient stone circle in Évora, Portugal. The stone circle serves the Tamera community as gathering place and a space for meditation and prayers. Beyond this, it is an artistic monument to the most important research topic of Tamera: community.

Tamera members believe that social sustainability, with trust between the genders and generations, is the true key to abundance. Today, the founders have gathered their decades of experience in community into training courses offered through the Tamera Peace University. A basic course focuses on the philosophy of a sustainable culture of peace, and there are follow-up seminars on community-building skills. Every year several hundred people take part in the basic semesters and the "School of the Future," an internet-based educational network of people connected to Tamera's work of developing a healthy, self-reliant community—part of the larger "Global Campus" of the ecovillage.

Tamera understands the world is in transformation. "Under the layer of wars and conflicts humanity desires a planetary community: as a unity whose organs don't fight, but support each other. Global compassion—the ability to feel the need, the pain and also the healing impulses of others—opens the way to the planetary community," community member Leila Dregger writes.

Through the Grace Foundation, initiated by Sabine Lichtenfels, Tamera has organized annual

IF PERMACULTURE IS ABOUT WORKING WITH RELATIONSHIPS BETWEEN ELEMENTS IN A SYSTEM TO CREATE SUSTAINABLE ABUNDANCE, WHAT DOES IT OFFER IN THE REALM HUMAN RELATIONSHIPS? ALONG WITH SUSTAINABLE SOLUTIONS FOR FOOD, WATER AND ENERGY, FOR YEARS TAMERA HAS BEEN DEVELOPING AN INTERPERSONAL SCIENCE, BECAUSE HUMAN BEINGS THEMSELVES ARE OFTEN THE MOST CHAOTIC ELEMENT IN THEIR SUSTAINABLE SYSTEMS.

peace pilgrimages in crisis areas like Israel-Palestine and Colombia, to form community with people from all sides; to listen to victims and perpetrators alike; help overcome pain, anger, and fear; and discover the powerful longing for peace running under the surface of hostility. Through these walks, the participants have formed deep friendships and collaborations with peace workers and communities all over world.

The Institute for Global Peace is based at Tamera and has built strong connections with various initiatives for global change. It hosts an annual Summer

Photo: Starhawk

University and symposia on special topics relevant to planetary transition, such as water, education, and food systems.

Sustainability in Love: "There will be no peace on earth unless the war in love has ended," Duhm wrote in his books *The Sacred Matrix* and *Eros Unredeemed*. Tamera believes that a holistic model for sustainability has to address love and partnership. "The social vessels that society offers for love and sexuality—like marriage, secret affairs, or abstinence—don't reflect our full longing. The core of Tamera's community research is to create new social vessels for our deep wishes for intimacy and partnership, embedded in the trustful atmosphere of community," writes Lichtenfels, Duhm's life partner, in her book *Temple of Love*.

"Trust guarantees sustainability," Monika Berghoff says. "This is why the Tamera community puts so much emphasis on this issue."

HEALTH/SPIRITUAL WELL-BEING

Ethics and Design Principles: Tamera and its international network want to manifest a big vision: to establish a lifestyle for the future by creating models that are distant from fear, violence, or mistruths. Friendship and cooperation between people and nature is part of the vision, as is solidarity and trust between people—in particular between men and women.

"LONG AGO, ALL PEOPLE ON EARTH LIVED IN TRIBES AND EXTENDED FAMILIES. COMMUNITY IS THE ORGAN OF HUMANKIND WHICH HAS BEEN WOUNDED THE MOST. IF WE KNEW HOW TO LIVE TOGETHER IN PEACE AND TRUST, NOBODY WOULD LIVE ON ONE'S OWN." —SABINE LICHTENFELS

"A society will be sustainable when it is coherent with the cosmic processes which have created the planet, its mountains and forests, its oceans, rivers, animals, plants and human beings," writes Monika Berghoff, of Tamera's political department. "Tamera and its international partners envision a global society of peace. In all its working fields Tamera follows the principle of abundance instead of scarcity."

FINANCES/ECONOMICS

Creating Abundance: The principle of abundance present in nature and its gift economy inspired Tamera in the development of its economic system. "Just like every tree gives away its seeds, its shade, and its leaves as compost, and won't charge for it or calculate what it gets back, Tamera's community members give each other their work without being paid," writes Ehrenpreis, one of the cofounders of the ecovillage. "Tamera's economy overcomes the pattern of exchange—of asking 'what do I get for what I give.' This principle requests a lot of trust, which only can be created in community. When community 'works' well, you will never really lack something you need. There is always somebody to help you, and there is always somebody whom you can help."

Reporting contributed by Leila Dregger.

Hava & Adam Eco-Educational Farm

Modi'im, Israel

Established in 2003 on 8 acres (3.23 hectares) in central Israel, toward the southern edge of the Mediterranean climate zone, the Hava & Adam Ecological Farm aims to serve as a community center and a model for sustainable living. With a small core group of residents, the farm hosts about twenty volunteers at any given time, providing space for a dynamic and diverse community of experiential learners who study permaculture and similar techniques. The farm provides the majority of vegetables consumed by its residents; is completely off the energy grid; and includes a greenhouse, bakery, store, recycling unit, arts workshop, and a variety of natural buildings.

"*Hava* is the original Hebrew name for Eve—the Bible's first woman and the original mother. *Hava* also means 'farm' and is closely related to the word *havaya,* meaning 'experience.' At the Hava & Adam Farm, Hava comes before Adam for at least two reasons: the first is because we emphasize the feminine, nature-based aspect of life, and the second is because we understand the value of first-hand experience," the community's website explains.[4]

CULTURE/EDUCATION

Working the Land, Not Fighting over It: Hava & Adam is a peace center, in that it is open to people of all faiths to share knowledge about working in harmony with the land and to gain a deeper understanding of each other in the process. "The problem here is the policy of separating people, not just isolating the Palestinians, but preventing Israelis from communicating with Palestinians. The Israelis don't learn Arabic and many Palestinians don't learn Hebrew, people can't communicate, which will only increase the fear" founding member and former resident Petra Feldman says.

Chaim Feldman, Petra's husband and one of the original directors of the center, works with Palestinian farmers on reintroducing traditional agricultural practices and bringing in appropriate permaculture strategies. The Palestinians have shared irrigation techniques as well as heirloom seeds that can grow with little water, and have learned permaculture techniques that allow them to grow more intensively in smaller spaces, essential in an era where land use has become so restricted. The collaboration began when Chaim met a Palestinian ecologist at a peace demonstration, who has, since then, networked with Arab farmers and helped to bring interested participants to the farm.

Hava & Adam is federally sponsored, which gives participants the opportunity to work there for a year or more as part of their national service, as an alternative to military service. The center also attracts international interns from Europe, America, and other countries. It holds a popular "work weekend" where potential volunteers come and try out being on the farm, and then the center selects those who seem to be the best fit for the work there and who have a passion for it.

The Eco-Israel program, based at the center, welcomes international students for semester- or summer-long courses of study, focused on permaculture, sustainability, communal living, and Jewish/Israeli peoplehood. Participants receive a Permaculture Design Certificate at the end of the course.

School groups visit about six times a week to participate in hands-on learning activities. There are about ten local teachers with school gardens who bring groups regularly to educate students about permaculture techniques. There are also a number of other groups that visit on ecotours or other programs. Workshops have been held in the art studio on topics such as weaving with recycled materials like cloth and plastic; making mosaics with scrap ceramics; mud and clay ceramics; and producing medicinal herbs, oils, and creams.

LAND/NATURE STEWARDSHIP

Feeding the Community: The volunteer-run garden provides 70 to 80 percent of the vegetables needed to feed the community, and there are several additional plots for farming experiments. They have had good results integrating geese to patrol for pests and to provide fertilizer through their waste. Other animals on-site include chickens, which provide eggs; and goats and sheep, which provide milk and cheese. A rainwater-catchment system provides water for irrigation in the summer.

Photo courtesy of Hava and Adam

TAL IS ONE OF THE YOUNG ISRAELIS WHO WORKS AT THE FARM IN PLACE OF MILITARY SERVICE. FAR FROM SEEING THIS AS A SHIRKING OF THEIR DUTY TO THEIR COUNTRY, THEY BELIEVE THAT BUILDING LOCAL FOOD SECURITY AND HUMANISTIC CONNECTIONS BETWEEN PEOPLE (RELIGIOUS AND SECULAR, IMMIGRANT AND NATIVE, ISRAELI AND PALESTINIAN) TO BE THE MOST IMPORTANT THING THEY CAN DO FOR THEIR NATION AND THE REST OF PLANET.

"WE WORK THE LAND TOGETHER INSTEAD OF FIGHTING ABOUT IT."
—PETRA FELDMAN

DANNY, AN ECO-ISRAEL PARTICIPANT, TENDS TO A LEMONY CULINARY HERB KNOWN AS JERUSALEM SAGE. HE SAYS IT'S THE BEST PLANT IN HIS GARDEN FOR ATTRACTING POLLINATORS AND REPELLING PESTS.

TOOLS/TECHNOLOGY

Energy, Water, and Waste Cycles: The site is off the grid, using photovoltaic panels to capture solar energy. The goal is zero waste: all organic matter is composted, a gray-water system allows for reuse of water, and paper and plastic are recycled. The remaining waste is often repurposed as building insulation and material. Because of the hot, dry climate, the composting toilets break down waste very quickly and can process liquids and solids together. The humanure is used for fertilizing trees.

"This is where civilization started, so it could be the best place for a turning point," Petra Feldman says. "Israel is a very small country which is quickly filling up with buildings and roads. Water aquifer levels are dropping dramatically, which is very problematic, so we really have to change our course."

Reporting contributed by Juliana Birnbaum. Photos by Jacob Goldberg, unless otherwise noted.

Los Angeles Eco-Village

Los Angeles, California, U.S.A.

Just off of one of the most congested traffic corridors in Los Angeles, tiled with a mosaic of fast-food chains, nail salons, and dollar stores, lies a little green oasis: the Los Angeles Eco-Village (LAEV). Three miles west of downtown Los Angeles, it is a place of urban regeneration and innovation in the warm Mediterranean climate of Southern California. LAEV was born out of the civil unrest expressed in the Wilshire Center/Koreatown neighborhood after the Rodney King verdict. Established in 1996, the ecovillage includes about fifty apartments and acts as a central hub for many green activities and campaigns in the city.

Two blocks of 1920s-era apartment buildings have been retrofitted through a nonprofit organization guided by a permaculture approach to problem solving. Within its grounds, LAEV has facilitated technology and lifestyle changes, such as installing solar panels and composting facilities, as well as providing rent reductions for people who live car-free. It has transformed its courtyard into a 7,000-square-foot (650-square-meter) garden that provides fruits, herbs, and vegetables, as well as a lush common area to sit and relax in. LAEV has also incubated businesses like the Bicycle Kitchen—a shop that repairs bikes and that trains neighborhood children in bicycle maintenance skills. Perhaps most importantly, the community has influenced the broader political process of Los Angeles. This has ranged from lending support to "green" mayoral candidates to engaging in public planning processes, such as the restoration of the Los Angeles River and local redevelopment.

The origins of LAEV are connected to the explosive 1992 Rodney King verdict, which prompted demonstrations and riots in which fifty-three people died and a number of buildings burned to the ground. One area badly affected by the riots was Wilshire Center/Koreatown, a multiethnic, working-class neighborhood where Lois Arkin, a founder of the ecovillage, had lived for thirteen years. She was part of a group interested in forming an ecovillage and that had been looking for a spare plot of land on which to build a new facility. In the wake of the 1992 events, they felt moved to work together to restore the community and retrofit an existing block. They established an organization called Cooperative Resources and Services Project (CRSP), which bought the two apartment buildings, which had fallen into disrepair and had a low occupancy rate. She and collaborators talked to neighbors, organized events, and "created positive gossip." This was the start of a long process, one that continues to evolve. "We are ecovillages in process, aspiring ecovillages. We have a long way to go to create completely closed-loop systems," Arkin says.

Gradually the group attracted new residents, people who were interested in supporting and being a part of the ecovillage, while still maintaining space for those existing residents who wished to stay on without being involved in the ecovillage itself. This mixture of people and openness to different perspectives created a system where social and economic diversity was welcome. "Diversity is essential to healthy systems in permaculture," Arkin says.

TOOLS/TECHNOLOGY

Energy: Given its urban setting, LAEV's founding members did not set out with the intention to become completely autonomous and self-reliant, but instead pledged to dramatically reduce reliance on unsustainable energy sources. Air conditioners were replaced with wooden blinds and natural shading (though a few ceiling fans have had to be installed in the second-floor apartments to cope with the summer heat). Other attempts to reduce energy reliance include the gradual addition of photovoltaic panels and solar water heaters to units. The village places particular emphasis on car sharing, biking, and walking, both to reduce the use of gasoline and to make more streets car-free.

BUILDING

Transforming Conventional Housing: LAEV is made up of forty-eight individual apartments of varying size, between 400 to 1,000 square feet (37 to 92 square meters). Several of these have been turned over to the community: a large meeting room with adjoined kitchen, a bike store, a laundry, and a bulk food room (where members can buy shares of rice, coffee, pasta, and other foods from

THE BLOCKS STAND OUT FROM THEIR SURROUNDINGS WITH THEIR ABUNDANCE OF GREENERY, WITH FRUIT TREES AND FLOWERS EDGING OUT TOWARD THE ROAD.

Photo: Louis Fox

URBAN CULTURE AND PERMACULTURE MIX IN THE MURALS THAT BRING THE WALLS OF L.A. ECOVILLAGE TO LIFE.

large storage boxes). Communal use is made of the large lobby, which is also used for events, and the courtyard, where with inviting chairs and tables sit in the shade of a magnolia tree. At the back of the blocks, several garages have been converted into workshops. The apartments are at varying stages of eco-renovation, with some of the residences unchanged, others in the process of being radically transformed. The majority of the renovation uses natural materials, such as ceramic tiles, bamboo, and cork floors. Common spaces use carefully chosen materials as well, such as the recycled tire flooring used on the stairs. Residents have also installed five gray-water recycling systems, which only recently became legal in the building code in the state of California.

✪ LAND/NATURE STEWARDSHIP

Edible Forest: Despite being in a highly urban space, LAEV has placed a particular emphasis on expanding local food sources. The apartment blocks stand out from their surroundings with their abundance of greenery, with fruit trees and flowers edging out toward the road. The courtyard is now a garden, providing tomatoes, herbs, peppers, chard, borage, bananas, peaches, apples, apricots, figs, mint, and comfrey. A flock of chickens is integrated into the garden; honeybees are housed on the roof.

Arkin explains, "We have a foot of mulch in the courtyard: we call the soil our future, our wealth." The courtyard not only uses every inch of space to grow food, but facilitates interaction between neighbors and greater responsibility for looking after, sharing, and enjoying the space. Fruit trees shade hidden nooks, chairs, and hammocks, and colorful murals bring life to the walls. The outside space is just as utilized as the courtyard is, extending the ecovillage's reach beyond its formal boundaries. Members recently secured permission to grow macadamia nut trees along the sidewalk and are in the process of establishing a learning garden across the road, where they will run workshops for school children.

Ecovillage residents are also striving to make

CHICKENS ARE INTEGRATED INTO THE GARDEN SYSTEM, AS WELL AS HONEYBEES, WHICH ARE HOUSED ON THE ROOF.

"WE HAVE WORKED WITH [LOCAL OFFICIALS] TO GREEN THE NEIGHBORHOOD, WORKING WITH DIFFERENT DEPARTMENTS ON THINGS LIKE THE SIDEWALKS AND TREE PLANTING."—LOIS ARKIN

use of every inch of space for slowing and storing water. "We broke up the concrete and created the first permeable sidewalk in L.A., mulched the pathways of our courtyard, and are harvesting rainwater from roof feeds," Arkin says. "We cooperated with a local youth center to create an eco-park with a stream fed by a storm drain, and a gravel bed that allows storm water to return to the water table."

FINANCES/ECONOMICS

Transitioning to a Cooperative Model: The original group established the nonprofit organization CRSP in order to buy the apartment blocks, and for many years the blocks were owned by CRSP and rented to individuals. The group is now in the process of incorporating as a limited-equity housing cooperative, with a Community Land Trust owning the property. The affordability of the apartments has always been central to the project (*affordable* meaning that 30 percent or less of your income is spent on housing costs). In this way, the village will gradually be able to convert the housing in the neighborhood from rental to affordable cooperative ownership.

This district of Los Angeles is currently a "rent-burdened" area, which means that many residents pay an inordinate percentage of their income for housing—what is often substandard housing. Current rents at the village are between $455 and $730 per month (depending on the size of the living space), which makes them several hundred dollars cheaper than equivalent places in the area.

LAND TENURE/COMMUNITY GOVERNANCE

Accepting Feedback: There are two aspects to LAEV's community approach that have helped it to succeed as a village and as a larger neighborhood movement. First, they accept feedback and try new methods to improve their internal governance and decision-making systems. New tenants have to pass

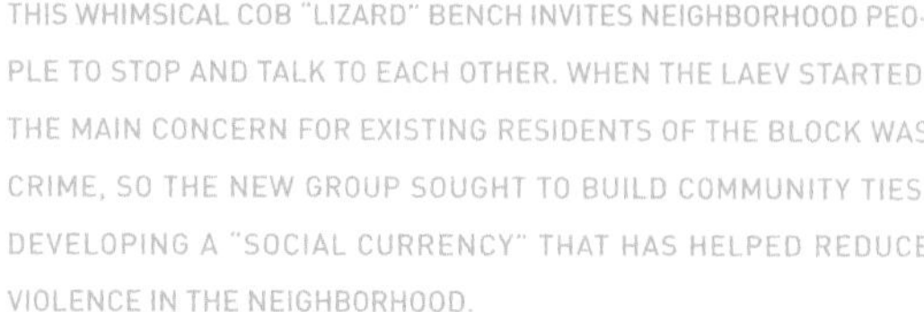

THIS WHIMSICAL COB "LIZARD" BENCH INVITES NEIGHBORHOOD PEOPLE TO STOP AND TALK TO EACH OTHER. WHEN THE LAEV STARTED, THE MAIN CONCERN FOR EXISTING RESIDENTS OF THE BLOCK WAS CRIME, SO THE NEW GROUP SOUGHT TO BUILD COMMUNITY TIES, DEVELOPING A "SOCIAL CURRENCY" THAT HAS HELPED REDUCE VIOLENCE IN THE NEIGHBORHOOD.

A MIXTURE OF PEOPLE AND OPENNESS TO DIFFERENT PERSPECTIVES CREATED A SYSTEM WHERE SOCIAL AND ECONOMIC DIVERSITY WAS WELCOME. "DIVERSITY IS ESSENTIAL TO HEALTHY SYSTEMS IN PERMACULTURE," SAYS LOIS ARKIN.

a rigorous eighteen-month membership process to become part of the community. At weekly meetings, consensus is used to make group decisions.

Second, they have a real and practical concern for the community as a whole, well beyond the boundary of their apartment blocks. For Arkin, one of the aims of an ecovillage is to sprout projects that work outside the village's borders, such as organic businesses, cottage industries, and nonprofit organizations.

At LAEV these initiatives reach out into the community in a number of different ways. There are bicycle-rights groups, an organization that packs and distributes boxes of organic vegetables, and a group seeking to revitalize the Los Angeles River. There is constant pressure on the city to improve the public transit network, and the ecovillage now has excellent access to public transport. Furthermore, as an entity, the ecovillage tends to get lobbied to give its support to certain initiatives or support mayoral candidates.

Living here is also about changing relations within communities. As in many big cities, it is common for people to live next door to each other for years and never speak. Part of the goal of the ecovillage is to enhance local friendships, encourage people to talk to each other, and make the community feel safer, so that people will allow their children to play outside. They do this both within the confines of the village and beyond.

Reporting contributed by Juliana Birnbaum, Jenny Pickerill, and Erik Assadourian.
Photos by Jenny Pickerill, unless otherwise noted.

The People's Grocery

Oakland, California, U.S.A.

Photo: Mark Virata

Since 2003, the People's Grocery has sought to address West Oakland's health and food security issues through a highly localized, on-the-ground transformation of the food system. Along with its main mission—to establish a supply of fresh foods from within the community—the organization strives to create jobs within the local food industry, support local food businesses, and train people in jobs for the "green" economy.

The People's Grocery's California Hotel Garden is located at a historic hotel in West Oakland that currently provides low-income, single-occupancy housing for about forty residents. In 2009 the People's Grocery took over the small garden that had been abandoned by residents since 2003 and turned it into full-fledged community garden.

Inner-city West Oakland: twenty-five thousand residents, fifty liquor stores, and zero grocery stores selling fresh produce. Yet in the early 1940s, this area was a thriving cultural hub and industrial center, driven

Photo: Mark Virata

MAX CADJI SEES THE GARDEN AS A VENUE FOR CONNECTING LOCAL PEOPLE—THE SPACE IS USED FOR COMMUNITY EVENTS, SUCH AS BARBEQUES, OPEN TO THE WHOLE NEIGHBORHOOD. THE GOAL IS TO CREATE A PLACE WHERE RESIDENTS WANT TO SPEND TIME AND ARE DRAWN TO LEARN MORE ABOUT SKILLS THAT COULD LEAD TO NEW CAREERS IN THE LOCAL FOOD INDUSTRY.

by wartime prosperity. It was the West Coast headquarters for Marcus Garvey's African American rights movement and filled with happening music venues playing jazz and the blues. Built in 1934, the California Hotel served the African American community during the last decades of the Jim Crow era, when musicians were not allowed to stay at the hotels where they were playing. It hosted such famous acts as Sam Cooke and Little Richard. Today the California Hotel is still famous in the neighborhood, a monument to the cultural hotspot that West Oakland once was.

After the Depression and World War II, the tides of urbanization and the war-based economy began shifting; today West Oakland is the poorest neighborhood in the Bay Area. Nearly 30 percent of its residents live below the poverty line, many suffering from increasing rates of malnutrition and chronic disease.

West Oakland—deemed "food insecure" for decades—has been served for almost twenty years by a variety of food-justice organizations with missions to expand the availability of healthy food (see accompanying article, p. 235 for more on the pioneering work of Mo' Better Foods). The groups use creative and place-based strategies for providing resources to people with the highest need and the least access.

CULTURE/EDUCATION

Community Restoration, Food Security: The California Hotel Garden harnesses the history of the building and the neighborhood as a vehicle for growing community. The food grown in the garden is available to any of the hotel or neighborhood residents. Every Friday the residents come down for distribution of eggs from the chickens. One of the residents is on staff and sells plants from the garden once a week at the local farmer's market. Max Cadji, the garden's coordinator, explains that community restoration is its true objective, leveraging food as a development strategy. Because many of the hotel's residents are elders who lived during the hotel's heyday, resurrecting this history is a way of engaging the community and connecting people to its vibrant past.

CATCHING AND STORING ENERGY THROUGH EDUCATION. SHARING KNOWLEDGE IS ONE OF THE BEST WAYS TO BANK HARD-WON LESSONS AND ENRICH A COMMUNITY. PEOPLE'S GROCERY NOW HAS YOUTH AND ADULT OUTREACH PROGRAMS AND WEEKLY COOKING CLASSES. THE GARDENS ARE MORE THAN JUST PLACES FOR GROWING FOOD; THEY ARE COMMUNITY CENTERS AND CLASSROOMS.

Art is an important part of the garden's presence in the community. The mural that stands as a colorful backdrop to the green vegetable beds was conceived by a group of residents and is a tribute to the various facets and marginalized demographics of West Oakland's past. The sides of the wooden vegetable beds are painted with quotes by famous minority activists such as Cesar Chavez and Marcus Garvey, reminding visitors of the neighborhood's history of engagement in social justice.

People's Grocery offers a number of educational programs, including one in urban agriculture, food justice, and nutrition education that has become a training ground for West Oakland residents to become nutrition demonstrators at hospitals, schools, public events, and other community gatherings.

Expanding from gardening into education and outreach, People's Grocery launched the Collards & Commerce Youth Program in the summer of 2003, including urban-gardening courses, community outreach, business classes, and cooking and nutrition workshops. In August of 2003, the founders and their first crew of youth launched what has become the flagship enterprise of the organization, the Mobile Market.

The People's Grocery now has a 2-acre farm, various outreach programs, and cooking classes. Another initiative has been the establishment of a network of urban food forests around the city of Oakland. The farm, the food forests, and the California Hotel Garden provide a source of fresh food for the organization's Grub Box program, a highly successful program delivering weekly boxes of fruits and vegetables to participating families. But these gardens are more than just places for growing food; they are community centers serving as classrooms for People's Grocery's urban-agriculture educational programs.

Oakland has become an epicenter for urban

homesteading—home-scale practices for increasing the self-reliance of city dwellers, including growing food, saving seeds, small animal husbandry, and the mastery of heirloom kitchen skills like canning, fermenting, and drying the harvest. Urban homesteading—permaculture-style—includes careful water, waste, and energy use, as well as expanded efforts toward community education and resilience. An exemplary project in this movement is K. Ruby Blume's Institute of Urban Homesteading, a home-based folk school offering sixty to seventy-five classes per year in small-scale urban self-sufficiency, including raising goats, growing medicine, making cheese, and organic gardening in small urban spaces. It's important to note that projects like the Institute of Urban Homesteading, which mostly serves Oakland's white population, are preceded by more than twenty years of African American activism for food security, healthy communities, and job creation in the neighborhood. The creation of a healthy food system is a task that calls for numerous iterations of educational and inspirational projects to serve each demographic in the neighborhood.

LAND/NATURE STEWARDSHIP

MAKE USE OF BIOLOGICAL INTELLIGENCE: GIVEN ITS LOCATION CLOSE TO HEAVY INDUSTRY AND THE FREEWAY, THE SOIL AROUND THE CALIFORNIA HOTEL GARDEN WAS REPLETE WITH LEAD, ARSENIC, AND HEAVY METALS. IMPROVING THE SOIL WAS CRITICAL; THEY USED PERMACULTURE TECHNIQUES LIKE VERMICOMPOSTING—LETTING THOUSANDS OF WORMS IN LARGE BINS DO MOST OF THE WORK OF MAKING COMPOSTABLE WASTE INTO SOIL.

Improving Soil: Not surprisingly, given its urban location, close to industry, the earth at the California Hotel Garden was badly degraded. Improving soil is, as Cadji puts it, "the essence of urban agriculture." The gardeners used vermicomposting and have had great success in using a method inspired by Cuban-style *organoponico*. First, the bottom of the bed is filled with potting soil mixed with compost, then a layer of coffee grounds is laid on top. Next come the worms, more coffee grounds, more compost, and finally, seeds. This technique, along with thinning out the plantings, has enabled the gardeners to harvest thirty bunches of greens in two months from just one bed. The site has also recently incorporated a beehive and is teaching beekeeping. A rainwater-catchment system on the roof provides water for irrigation.

Reporting contributed by Kelly Egan and Rachel Kaplan. Photos by Ananda Wiegland, unless otherwise noted.

MO' BETTER FOODS
OAKLAND, CALIFORNIA

Since 1996, Mo' Better Foods has been promoting ways to recruit the African American community to feed itself by making connections with African American–run farms throughout California and bringing what they grew back into the neighborhoods where people needed it most. They founded a farmer's market and a cooperative grocery store in the mid-1990s. The strategy of rebuilding relationships between farmer and eater is part of a larger healthy economics campaign put forth by Mo' Better Foods.

With fresh food hard to find in the neighborhood, and so many mom-and-pop markets converted to liquor stores with no produce, the need for "real" food was apparent. Empowering people to feed themselves was part of the group's mission, but finding African American farmers was even harder than finding healthy food in the food deserts of West Oakland. Mo' Better began to make connections with African American farmers throughout California, marketing and helping to distribute their produce.

David Roach, the founder of the group, explains that one of its intentions is to encourage educated youth to stay in their community and to inspire others to further their studies. "While we agree that the tactics of teaching cooking or starting urban gardens and farms have some benefits, we believe they are a band-aid approach to solving the health disparities we face in our communities today. The effects of the 'double blow' (banks red-lining African American neighborhoods and the years of African American farmers being discriminated against by the USDA and other agencies) will not be resolved by converting lots into a community garden, or teaching youth how to cook. . . . [It's about] rebuilding the food system that once existed between African American farmers and the communities where we live."[5]

Rachel Kaplan.

OAEC/Sowing Circle

Sonoma, California, United States

Photo: Louis Fox

UPON ITS FOUNDING IN 1994, OAEC WAS ALREADY OFF TO AN AUSPICIOUS START. AS PART OF THE PROPERTY, ITS MEMBERS INHERITED ONE OF THE FIRST CERTIFIED ORGANIC GARDENS IN THE UNITED STATES, WHICH NOW PRODUCES 65 TO 85 PERCENT OF THE FRESH FRUIT AND VEGETABLES CONSUMED BY RESIDENTS AND COURSE PARTICIPANTS. IN ADDITION, THESE BARREL-VAULTED ROOF HOMES WERE DESIGNED BY SUSTAINABLE-ARCHITECTURE PIONEERS SIM VAN DER RYN AND PETER CALTHORPE IN THE MID-1970S.

Sowing Circle is a limited liability company (LLC) and consensus-based group of ten members with a vision for social change. They steward the Occidental Arts and Ecology Center (OAEC), a nonprofit organization that is a core part of their vision. OAEC is an ecovillage for living, demonstration, and training and is a think tank where thousands come to reflect and strategize. It combines practical, experiential programs with on-site models of sustainable land and water management, food and farming systems, and human dwellings—all infused with artistic expression. The goal is to train and support whole communities, emphasizing techniques for self-organizing, to solve complex ecological, cultural, and economic problems.

While established in 1994 as Sowing Circle and OAEC, the organic garden at the site (one of the first certified in United States) and sustainable building projects began in 1970s under various auspices—the most famous was known as the Farallones Rural Center. It currently has twenty-five residents and ten full members, and it employs forty to fifty people. The center is located on 80 acres (32 hectares) just outside the small town of Occidental, near the coast of Northern California's Sonoma County. It has a transitional Mediterranean-maritime climate.

LAND/NATURE STEWARDSHIP

Wildlands, Water, and Food: Potable water comes from a hybrid system of well water and a rainwater-harvesting system. There are two 40,000-gallon (150,000-liter) storage tanks with gutters that allow them to self-fill off of their own roofs. The agricultural water supply is 100 percent from rainwater harvesting; a pond 25 feet (7.6 meters) deep supplies water for the exceptionally long dry season. Earthwork systems harvest runoff water, including a quarter-mile of hand-dug swales on contour, numerous rain-gardens, and several ephemeral ponds that recharge groundwater. The water is chlorine-free, treated with a carbon filter and UV light.

VALUING AND PRESERVING BIOLOGICAL DIVERSITY: IT'S ESTIMATED THAT NEARLY 90 PERCENT OF HISTORIC VARIETIES OF FRUITS AND VEGETABLES IN THE UNITED STATES HAVE GONE EXTINCT, MOSTLY IN THE PAST CENTURY. TO COUNTER THIS TREND, OAEC MAINTAINS A SEED COLLECTION OF ABOUT THREE THOUSAND OPEN-POLLINATED HEIRLOOM VARIETIES OF VEGETABLES.

Just 3 to 4 acres (out of the 80 acres at OAEC) are being intensively managed for production of annual vegetables, along with perennial crops, flowers, and fruits such as apples, peaches, kiwis, and grapes, with a focus on heirloom varieties. The drastic loss of historic varieties of fruits and vegetables is a worldwide problem.[6] Most of the land is a wildland interface with a habitat pond that breeds fish, snakes, newts, frogs, and insects.

"There's an intensive agriculture piece—these gardens are double-dug, biointensive," Founding member Brock Dolman says, "Is that permaculture or not? . . . I think it can be appropriately applied as an element within a permaculture system at the right scale, in the right location. There's never been a mechanical piece of equipment that's worked this soil, it's all hand done."

BUILDING

Getting Permits for Natural Building: On-site residences were designed by architects Sim van der Ryn and Peter Calthorpe and built with state funding in the mid-1970s, when California had an Office of Appropriate Technology (before it was closed, under the Reagan years). OAEC is home to

OAEC'S CHICKEN TRACTOR GIVES THE BIRDS A STABLE HOME BASE WHILE THEY ROTATE BETWEEN FORAGE AREAS ON THE PROPERTY.

"WITH THIRTY YEARS OF ORGANIC COMPOST AND COVER-CROPPING, THIS SOIL'S BEEN CALLED THE BEST IN SONOMA COUNTY." —BROCK DOLMAN

the first permitted light straw/clay building in the state, and it has other structures that showcase a number of forms of natural building—wattle and daub, rammed earth, cob, and straw bale. Residences are heated and cooled by passive-solar technologies, each with slightly different designs that were monitored for research purposes to perfect the techniques.

CULTURE/EDUCATION

Spreading Ecological Literacy: Courses are offered throughout the year that include many aspects of permaculture techniques and design, as well as visual arts. Hundreds of local schools, both rural and urban, participate in the OAEC ecological literacy program.

TOOLS/TECHNOLOGY

Overlapping Energy Sources: OAEC has a 10-kilowatt photovoltaic system that is intertied with the grid. They estimate that it produces about 50 percent of their electricity. In addition, for three months of the year, a micro-hydro system produces enough electricity that OAEC sends power back to the grid—making the meter go backward! Propane is used for cooking and some of the water heaters. When a solar hot water system was installed on the bathhouse, they achieved an 83 percent reduction of propane use.

Reporting contributed by Juliana Birnbaum. Photos by Ananda Wiegand, unless otherwise noted.

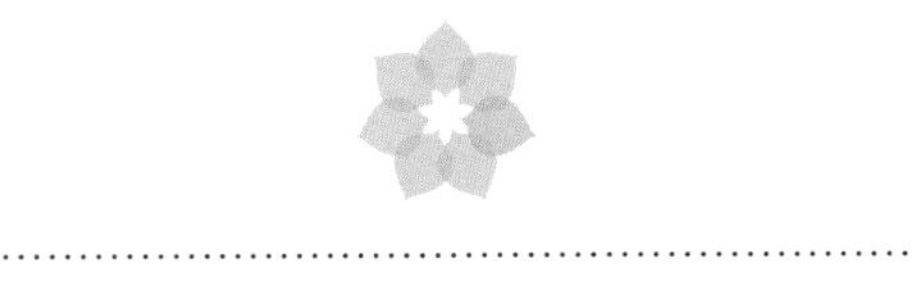

AN INTERVIEW WITH OAEC'S BROCK DOLMAN

Photo: Kerry Brady

Brock Dolman: When you get into what they call the ego-system side of this question, we're working one of the experiments. Two of our founders teach trainings on starting and sustaining intentional communities. We've got some big brains who have worked this whole game out. My feeling is that the intentional community is the most permacultural thing going here, it's the most cultural piece. If you don't figure out the residential, land-owning, and educational business side of this game, you're not going to have the integrity and cultural connectivity to actually have a model that works. All the gray-water systems, [composting] toilets, photovoltaics—that stuff comes and goes, those are itinerant elements, and they're not permaculture. They are applications of tools if you nest them within a framework that can hold them. I think people get too hung up on the nouns, the things, and they don't understand the verbs, the flows, the communication. So they think, "if I sheet mulch my lawn and plant a fruit tree and have gray water, I'm doing permaculture." I don't think they understand what that means on a deeper level.

Juliana Birnbaum: So the actual permaculture is in you, in your sustainable relationships.

BD: Some people use that phrase as a synonym for *permaculture*—"mutually beneficial relationships" is a phrase that you'll often hear. Permaculture, to me, is just a design methodology for regenerative human settlement patterns. All it is, is a design method. What are we designing? It better be regenerative, because we've got to make up for lost time. "Sustainable" ain't cutting it. Human settlement is what we're up against, which means [that] *settlement* includes human endeavors like forestry, ranching, agriculture, urban, suburban, rural industry. And then there's pattern. How do we read natural patterns and then make our settlements behave . . . in harmony with how natural flows of earth, air, water, fire, and other biological cycles work. If sustainability is about our ability to sustain the cycles of life—if you design a settlement that compromises the cycles of life, hydrologic cycle, fire cycle, phosphorus cycle, then your capacity to sustain your presence in that place for a long time, intergenerationally, is very likely not to succeed.

The *culture* word in *permaculture* is the ego-system *restory-ation*. How do you *re-story* the ego-system? What's the story it believes in? If greed is what drives it, we'll be sunk. Are you a part of it or apart from it? That's an ecological literacy challenge.

Our modern era, I think, is the most ecologically illiterate expression of humanity the planet has ever known. The culture part of permaculture—how do we create containers of culture that support right livelihood, right relationship, reciprocity, reverence, but literally feed you and give you water. Permaculture, if the designers do it well, creates conditions for this convivial, communitarian container. . . .
How can we create a revolution that's more engaging and nourishing to spirit and body than what's being offered to it by the mechanistic, industrial culture. We've got to win people over.

JB: What's the secret to the success of the ego-system here?

BD: I think that it was a primary design agenda—that it was very clear that we were coming together as a community. Creating containers for participatory decision making, putting the right people in the right circle to make the right decision. There's a commitment to that relationship.

JB: How do you see yourself as part of the larger global community?

BD: We're trying to be an example within American culture. We have partnerships, collaborations with other permaculture centers around the world. We've had lots of international gatherings with social-justice organizers; we see ourselves as a center for such organizing. OAEC is the leading nonprofit for Californians against genetic engineering.

Permaculture is encouragingly fringe. In certain communities, it's more recognized. In many indigenous communities—maybe they don't need to be taught the word—they just need the corporations to get off their back so they can go back to doing it. But in the overdeveloped world, those of us who are strung out on our dependency on fossil fuels. . . . I think that the reality check is going to be really hard in our communities collectively.

What I've found in the permaculture world is a lot of deeply rooted people trying to instill this knowledge and its application in their community to build resiliency in advance of the coming "Great Turning," as it meters out differently in different nations, different communities. There are, in so many countries, these little nascent permaculture seeds that are starting to garden out.

All of us who came together in community here, we're all earth-based folks, with a general sense of humility and respect for being part of a larger system and a deep sense of social justice. The thread that tied us all together was social-justice work, ecological justice. There's no dogma or practice—the spiritual practice that we do is, we come together twice a month and do consensus-based, collective decision making! That's where our church is, if we've got a church *[laughs]*.

From an interview with Juliana Birnbaum, OAEC, October 2009.

City Repair

Portland, Oregon, U.S.A.

Photo: Kai Sawyer

City Repair (CR) is a community-led urban regeneration movement rooted in "placemaking." It started in 1996, spread throughout neighborhoods of Portland, Oregon, and is now moving beyond. From transforming street intersections into public gathering places to planting urban food forests for public grazing, the diversity and scope of the CR movement is extraordinary. Through a collaborative mix of permaculture, green building, art, and celebration, a growing number of empowered citizens are "reclaiming urban space to create public place." CR defines placemaking as "a multi-layered process within which citizens foster active, engaged relationships to the spaces which they inhabit, the landscapes of their lives, and shape those spaces in a way which creates a sense of communal stewardship and lived connection."

The movement sprouted in a backyard teahouse made from recycled material and piled with cushions,

which hosted weekly potlucks and festivities. Cofounder Mark Lakeman recalls that "it was just a place for neighbors to sit down, say hello and interact." The gatherings grew to several hundred people before the city condemned the illegal structure. This government intervention helped catalyze the first CR action, known as "intersection repair," where a community transforms an urban intersection into a public square.

Failing to gain city hall's understanding and permission, residents decided to reclaim an intersection by getting together to paint an enormous mandala and build functional structures on each of the corners. Children inspired the beehive-shaped cob dispenser for the local newspaper (the *Bee*) and a kids' clubhouse, where toys can be exchanged, built from driftwood. Residents also built a twenty-four-hour tea station, a community bulletin board, a little library, a stage, and a family-sized cob bench. The city government then saw the benefits of intersection repair (all without spending any tax money) and legalized the process. Since then, several dozen intersection repairs and over three hundred placemaking projects have since been accomplished in Portland and elsewhere, some in other states. These projects include installing gardens and cob benches in schools and the construction of the Portland's first straw-bale dwelling at Dignity Village, a community of formerly homeless people. Many of these projects are accomplished during the annual Village Building Convergence (VBC) that began in 2000.

THE PLACES CREATED BY CITY REPAIR, LIKE THIS NEIGHBORHOOD TEA STATION, ENCOURAGE BENEFICIAL INTERACTION, JUST AS INSECTARY PLANTS DO IN A GARDEN. "WHAT WE WERE DOING WAS WE WERE SEEDING A GARDEN OF THE VILLAGE, WE WERE REGROWING THE VILLAGE HEART, WITH ALL OF THE FUNCTIONS AND AMENITIES THAT YOU'LL FIND."—MARK LAKEMAN

CULTURE/EDUCATION

Community Workshops: City Repair hosts various community workshops throughout the year through what it calls the Placemakers Academy. Once a year, they organize the ten-day Village Building Convergence (VBC) where free workshops are held in conjunction with neighborhood improvement projects throughout Portland. Concurrently with the VBC, the Village Building Design Course is offered, which explores concepts such as collaborative design, community-building skills, and participatory group facilitation.

BUILDING

Taking Back the Commons: City Repair emphasizes low-cost, low-tech, and ecologically sustainable building techniques such as cob, straw bale, light straw clay, and timber frame. Several living roofs have been installed, and passive-solar gain strategies have been utilized. Whimsical and artistic structures are also encouraged, such as a mermaid cob bench, the chicken and cat palace, and a beehive shaped newspaper dispenser. Helping build structures is an important opportunity for acquiring new skills, and volunteers help build as they learn green building techniques.

LAND/NATURE STEWARDSHIP

De-Pave City Repair has reclaimed paved spaces for gardens, and has sprouted food forests throughout Portland, from sidewalks to schools. Some participants now have aquaculture systems and are raising bees, chickens, and rabbits in their backyards, thanks to inspiration and resources gained through City Repair and its programs.

Reporting contributed by Kai Sawyer. Photos by Adelaide Nalley, unless otherwise noted.

Bullock's Permaculture Homestead

Orcas Island, Washington, U.S.A.

THE BULLOCKS' CAREFUL STUDY OF THE LAND ALLOWED THEM TO ISOLATE TINY MICROCLIMATES IDEAL FOR PARTICULAR SPECIES. THEIR PLANTINGS CONSIST OF HUNDREDS OF FOOD-PRODUCING SHRUBS, VINES, TREES, AND PERENNIALS FROM AROUND THE WORLD AND INCLUDE MULTIPLE VARIETIES OF POPULAR SPECIES.

Through a combination of acute observation skills, a passion for homesteading, a love of hard work, and a stream of helpers, the Bullock's Permaculture Homestead (BPH) functions as a home to the Bullock family, a thriving nursery, and a training site for skilled and inspired permaculture practitioners from around the world. From the extensive utilization of "waste" to the homestead culture of joking, love of food, and generosity, there is much that can be learned about living sustainably at the site. BPH is located on Orcas Island, one of the San Juan Islands, which lie in the rain-shadow of the Olympic Mountains and are near the northernmost extension of a cool maritime/Mediterranean climate zone. The property features a variety of preexisting microclimates and soil types, including rocky, dry south-facing hillsides; a marsh; and a wet valley bottom. Since acquiring the original 5 acres in 1982 and an additional 5 acres a few years later, the Bullocks have transformed this piece of land from one dominated by briars across much of the arable land into an innovative, productive, and verdant paradise.

TOOLS/TECHNOLOGY

Energy Redefined: Instead of thinking about energy solely in terms of amps and watts, the Bullocks take a permaculture approach, which broadens the conventional definition to include "energy flows," feedback loops, human and animal labor, and other various forms of energy utilized through the organization of overlapping systems. Recognizing that the cheapest form of energy comes from tasks being built into the natural flow of the property, feeding the chickens or going out to pick a favorite fruit becomes an opportunity to ***stack functions***. While the larger goal might be eating a delicious peach, along the way they are able to actively engage with their system. By doing this, they are able to achieve greater efficiency, because their system continues to be finely tuned. The Bullocks consider these energies (such as animals free-ranging on the farm) to be vital to developing closed-loop cycles, because they translate into an overall reduction of inputs needed from more traditional methods, such as tractors to move manure.

For heat and electricity, the site is mainly solar powered and wood heated, with a small amount of energy coming from the grid. Electricity for domestic use and agricultural water pumping is generated by a few large solar arrays. A small generator is used when electricity is needed remotely.

ASIDE FROM ANIMAL PRODUCTS, LIVESTOCK IS INCORPORATED INTO THE FARM ECOLOGY TO INCREASE SOIL FERTILITY AND KEEP VEGETATION AND PESTS IN CHECK.

Water is stored in tanks and ponds in as many locations as are available—and as high in elevation as possible. These reservoirs are fed using photovoltaic pumps, with a gasoline-powered pump serving as backup. Water stored high in the landscape is a reserve for regular agricultural watering for times when the sun isn't shining—eliminating the use of regular solar well pumps—and the reservoirs also act as an emergency supply of water in the event of a fire. The distribution of water through piping from source to storage is divided regionally, partially

Photo: Colette Schmitt

DOUG BULLOCK AND ONE OF MANY EXTENSIVE PLANT AND TREE NURSERIES AT THE HOMESTEAD.

to protect against total system failure in the event of a leak, but also because the Bullocks' practice of scavenging for equipment has led them to use smaller pumps of the sort common in the early part of the twentieth century. These pumps have lower power, but they are a good match for the "array direct" format of water pumping used on the property. These regional water systems are linked by valves, so water can be fed from one to another when needed.

The greenhouse at the BPH is an instructive example of how energy can be generated and stored creatively through a ***stacking of functions***. During the winter, residents use the greenhouse as their kitchen, dining/living room, workshop, shower, propagation space, and so forth. Cooking, activity, and the woodstove provide heat. The woodstove can also heat an attached sauna, which doubles as a food-dehydration room. A wood-fired water heater is used for needs in the kitchen and for showers in the winter (solar showers are used in the warmer months). Propane and wood are mainly used for cooking, although the Bullocks have been looking for a way to cook with local fuel, and are experimenting with rocket stoves and gasification stoves.

☼ LAND/NATURE STEWARDSHIP

Creating a New Culture around Food: Food is a central element of the Bullock's Permaculture Homestead, and much thought and enjoyment is put into every part of the food cycle: planting, harvesting, preparation, consumption, and waste. The Bullocks take the permaculture principle ***share the surplus*** to heart by frequently hosting large meals with the skill builders and weekly potlucks for the surrounding community. Skill builders operate on a schedule that allows each builder to take part in cooking for the rest of the group.

Although the homestead is not self-sufficient in terms of food, it is full of many practical examples for food security and serves as a "plant bank" for their region. The Bullocks are passionate about fruit and nut trees and have a diverse collection of edible, medicinal, and special-interest trees. Since the property sits in a rain shadow, which creates slightly drier conditions than most of western Washington, they are able to grow a wide range of plants, some requiring maximum heat exposure and others needing a moderated position. For instance, several dozen varieties of apples and plums serve to lengthen the harvest season, bolster resistance to pests and diseases, diversify uses (e.g., preserving, cooking), and enhance snacking experiences.

Extensive use of grafting allows for quicker harvests and other desirable properties. *Malus fusca,* commonly known as Pacific crabapple, grows like a weed on the property and the fruit is usually unappealing. Since these trees thrive in the area and have established root systems, however, the Bullocks have utilized them by grafting tastier varieties of apples onto them. They also have experimented with inter-genus grafts, for example, tasty pear varieties are grafted onto the tops of the prevalent hawthorn bushes, which have the advantage of being deer resistant and not requiring irrigation, planting, or fencing.

While planting trees for current and future generations of people, the Bullocks are also providing habitat for animals. Brush, stone piles, and small zones are left wild throughout the property to create habitat for the snakes and lizards that work to keep pest populations down. The birds have the abundant fruit trees and shrubs (local birds prefer smaller fruits) to snack on in the early summer. With nut trees continuously being planted around the property the Bullocks have also seen a large rise in the squirrel population; they are trying to come up with a solution to this problem. The marsh, used by previous owners for cattle grazing and growing potatoes, is now teeming with life and is a popular spot for bald eagles and great blue herons. In the marsh and along the bank, the Bullocks have built *chinampas*—which were developed originally by the Aztecs (see p. 48)—from prunings and excavated soil to create productive islands that further increase the biological activity of the marsh.

The continued success of BPH is due to the spirit of observation, experimentation, and accepting feedback infused into the culture of the farm. They are constantly trying novel approaches on the homestead—some fail horribly and some succeed dramatically. Innovation often comes from combinations of seemingly disparate elements.

CULTURE/EDUCATION

Learning through Experimentation: Although originally intended as a private home for the Bullocks families, the homestead has evolved into an educational space with regular visitors, a "skill builder" program, and two regular courses each year. Visitors are welcome most weeks of the growing season to experience permaculture by living along with the skill builders. Each year, the seven-month skill builder program hosts twelve participants, who learn gardening, composting, grafting, plumbing, building, welding, teaching, and communal living. Each skill builder is assigned several garden beds, which provide them an opportunity to experiment with vegetable varieties and gardening techniques, such as chicken tractors and natural farming. As education is usually associated with the work needs of the homestead, skill builders learn by doing. An intensive three-week design course, taught by a team of highly experienced permaculture instructors, focuses on the fundamentals of permaculture, systems thinking, and integrated living. Shorter sessions, often led by visiting practitioners, cover subjects like animal tracking, permaculture in public schools, and urban and social permaculture, among others.

BUILDING

Take Advantage of What You Can: When making decisions, the Bullocks brainstorm all of their possible needs, stacking as many functions as possible into each new component of their system. This is reflected in the structures built there, complete with food storage, propagation areas, and passive-solar heating. In replacing the failing foundation of one existing home on the land, they took advantage of the opportunity and constructed a bedrock-cooled root and wine cellar. A variety of natural building styles are employed, including one home built with salvaged lumber, insulated with light-straw clay walls, and finished with natural plasters.

The Bullocks adjust living arrangements according to the seasons, as some months are warm and dry, while others are cold and rainy. During the warmer months, which have long days and Mediterranean-style, temperate dry weather, most aspects of life can be conducted outside or in the simple, open-air structures for maximum comfort. In the summer, the family and skill builders set up outdoor kitchens and a tipi-style gathering space called the Aloha Lodge, where meetings, meals, and lectures take place. Permanent structures, built for year-round residents, are designed small to contain heat and conserve resources; they are heated the use of woodstoves, insulation, and double-paned windows oriented toward the winter sun.

Reporting contributed by Scott MacDonald and Kai Sawyer. Photos by Kai Sawyer, unless otherwise noted.

O.U.R. Ecovillage

Shawnigan Lake, Vancouver Island, British Columbia, Canada

A RESIDENT ELDER AND AN INTERN FROM PERU SHARE A QUIET MOMENT IN THE HERB GARDEN.

Shawnigan Lake has a cool, mild climate and is in a transition zone between temperate rainforest and boreal forest. The lake's name was adapted from the First Nation Hunquminum name for the lake, Shaanii'us, and the village is mostly a summer recreation area for islanders. It is located approximately 30 miles (48 kilometers) north of Victoria. O.U.R. Ecovillage—O.U.R. is an acronym for One United Resource—is a sustainable living demonstration site and education center located on 25 acres (10 hectares) of land in Shawnigan Lake. It is known for the pioneering work its members have done to rezone their land to be more inclusive of alternative building models. This work with regulatory authorities brought in major support from the provincial government. The O.U.R. pioneers began working with engineering and regulatory teams on topics such as earthen construction and wastewater systems, exploring how they could be used within approved building codes.

GROWING UP IN AN ECOVILLAGE GIVES CHILDREN THE OPPORTUNITY TO BE EDUCATED BY A DIVERSE RANGE OF ADULTS.

SEVEN ACRES OF ORCHARDS, GREENHOUSES, AND GARDENS FEED GUESTS IN THE "ZERO MILE MEAL EATERY."

LAND TENURE/COMMUNITY GOVERNANCE

Revolution through Rezoning: Inspiration for the ecovillage came in the 1990s, when O.U.R. was a citywide youth program and was linked with an intentional community house in Victoria. Approximately fourteen individuals became the development team, known as the "Creation Team," and began the process of creating O.U.R. Ecovillage in 1999. The former owner, who sold them the land, donated one third of the original asking price in the spirit of helping to create a vibrant, environmentally aware ecovillage.

Since then, the group has established O.U.R. Community Association, a nonprofit guided by a primary principle: by the community, for the community, and through the community. They have partnered with a vast number of local and international NGOs, academics, a variety of government departments, the Cowichan Community Land Trust, and the Land Conservancy of British Columbia to do a flora and fauna species map.

In 2007, O.U.R. Ecovillage Cooperative was formed to provide a legal model for the collective ownership of the land and a governance structure that would bring together all interested parties. It is the primary decision-making body for the community, and both individual members and member organizations participate in its governance.

O.U.R. rezoned its property by creating a precedent-setting, permaculture-based Sustainable Land Management Design, making the ecovillage an integrated land-use zone including a conservation area, educational activities, an organic farm, and a cluster of off-the-grid homes. The land was surveyed and mapped along ecological lines, and visioning workshops involved planners, agrologists, permaculture designers, educators, lawyers, and health professionals, as well as government representatives. The rezoning application called for an entirely new designation, and the process concluded in 2004 with what is called a "Rural Residential Comprehensive Development Zone."

O.U.R. is developing the property as an environmental classroom, with four sectors. The Woodlands/Wetlands Conservation sector includes

THIS UNIQUE STRUCTURE WAS THE FIRST NATURAL BUILDING IN CANADA TO BE PART OF A CLIMATE-CHANGE DEMONSTRATION PROJECT.

O.U.R. VISION: SUSTAINABLE WELL-BEING FOR THE LAND, OURSELVES, AND OUR WORLDWIDE VILLAGE.

sensitive ecosystems, woodlot management areas, and nature trails. The Agricultural sector combines organic agriculture and animal husbandry. The Ecological Education and Infrastructure sector provides a central gathering area for community educational activities. The Residential sector will have clustered housing with units of various sizes.

Dynamic Governance: The ecovillage works within a Dynamic Governance model (known as sociocracy in Europe and Latin America—see Atlantida Ecovillage, p. 41) to create a fluid and efficient integration of the many contributions required to maintain the village with the core values of equality and respect for diversity. Dynamic Governance was developed in the 1960s by Gerard Endenburg at his company in the Netherlands, and it has evolved into a model (also known as Circular Organizing) used by many organizations worldwide.

There are various ways to participate in the village, resident or not, but all members are part of a team that is connected to the central decision-making hub, the General Circle. Roles are assigned and chosen with respect for each person's vision and talent, and good communication within the circle creates a sense of responsibility and accountability for long-term outcomes.

CULTURE/EDUCATION

Skill-Building: The ecovillage offers full summer internship programs annually on a variety of subjects, such as natural building, as well as permaculture design certificate courses and advanced teacher trainings. O.U.R. also hosts a wide range of ongoing workshops on subjects such as youth empowerment, consensus decision making, conflict resolution, nonviolent communication, alternative resource usage, organic horticulture, permaculture, sacred ecology, and forest gardening.

Reporting contributed by Lori Henry. Photos courtesy of O.U.R. Village, unless otherwise noted.

Transition Norwich

Norwich, East Anglia, U.K.

SEEN AS THE FLAGSHIP PROJECT OF TRANSITION NORWICH, THE NORWICH FARMSHARE IS A COMMUNITY-OWNED FARM OUTSIDE THE CITY AND THAT DELIVERS VEGETABLES WEEKLY TO MEMBERS.

The Transition Initiative is a broad international network of cities and towns that have responded to climate change, peak oil, and economic instability with an ideology of community empowerment, re-localization, and resiliency. The movement is based largely on permaculture principles. *The Transition Manual,* a guiding framework for any group interested in incorporating the ethic, encourages citizens to make small and steady change that reduces their energy use and carbon footprint. Being unified within the Transition network supports and trains communities as they self-organize around the model, developing locally based solutions. Officially the world's first Transition city, the Norwich initiative brings issues of sustainability and climate change to the urban landscape, demonstrating the movement's capacity to shift policy in larger population centers.

The Transition concept emerged from work that permaculture designer Rob Hopkins did in writing an "Energy Descent Action Plan" with Kinsale College students in Ireland. The plan looked at creative adaptations in the realms of energy production, health, education, economy, and agriculture as a road map to a sustainable future for the town. Two of his students, Louise Rooney and Catherine Dunne, set about developing the Transition Town concept further and presented the Energy Descent Action Plan to Kinsale Town Council. To their surprise, the council decided to adopt the plan and work toward more independence from fossil fuels. The concept then spread to Totnes, England, Hopkins's hometown, where he and Naresh Giangrande developed the idea in 2005 and 2006.

Photo: Albert Bates

THE TOWN OF TOTNES WAS FOUNDED WELL BEFORE THE OIL ECONOMY (CA. 900 CE); THANKS THE TRANSITION MOVEMENT, IT WILL LIKELY OUTLIVE IT. "THE ELEMENTS OF FUNCTIONAL COMMUNITY THAT EXISTED IN TRADITIONAL SOCIETY STILL EXIST MOST STRONGLY IN SMALL TOWNS AND VILLAGES, NOT IN OUR CITIES" –DAVID HOLMGREN

In 2008, responding primarily to the global economic downturn, four hundred residents of Norwich came together to resuscitate an alternative grassroots economy based on small family businesses and local produce. Whereas other ecovillages and intentional communities gather people in close proximity, Transition Norwich operates via social-media outlets—virtual organizing is essential to the mobilization of bodies for actions and events around the city. It calls itself an "affiliation of ordinary citizens who are actually excited about the idea of a post-oil based Norwich."[7]

FINANCES/ECONOMICS

Community Farming and Local Currencies: The Norwich FarmShare is set up as a community-owned cooperative, which enables all the income from sales to be put back into the farm—to pay growers, buy equipment, and cover any other costs. Funds from this pool are also set aside for future growth plans, such as purchasing chicken coops, more land, or seeds.

A number of Transition locations have introduced a local currency, including Totnes, Bristol, and London, which has a currency called the Brixton Pound. The benefits of these currencies include building resilience in the local economy, encouraging more local exchange, and reducing the carbon footprint by keeping business local. The concept is being expanded to incorporate an online banking system, which that includes time-banking and enabling trade between Transition communities. Transition

Photo: Jim Wileman

TRANSITION MOVEMENT FOUNDER, ROB HOPKINS, APPLIES PERMACULTURE PRINCIPLES TO PLACE-BASED, COMMUNITY-LED EFFORTS IN RESPONSE TO CLIMATE CHANGE, PEAK OIL, AND ECONOMIC UNCERTAINTY.

currencies have thus far been backed by British sterling, but there is talk of finding alternative backing such as kilowatt hours or underutilized assets (see accompanying article on local currencies).

CULTURE/EDUCATION

Transition Circles: Central to the Transition Town movement is the idea that a life without oil could, in fact, be far more enjoyable and fulfilling than the present. "By shifting our mind-set we can actually recognize the coming post–cheap oil era as an opportunity rather than a threat, and design the future low-carbon age to be thriving, resilient and abundant—somewhere much better to live than our current alienated consumer culture based on greed, war and the myth of perpetual growth."[8]

The Streets-Wise model for motivating individuals to make personal changes that reduce their carbon footprint started with 450 households in Totnes and was originally called Transition Streets; it has been successful in several ways. The approach brings people together in groups to support each other and share resources as they brainstorm ways to change their behavior and reduce their energy use. While it had practical goals, such as funding photovoltaic panel installation for low-income households, one of the more surprising results was that participants reported that the main benefit was "building good relationships with neighbors."[9]

In Norwich, a less formal approach, called "Transition Circles," was formed out of a second wave in the initiative. A core group of Transitioners made a decision to radically cut their carbon emissions in the key areas of home energy, transport, food, and "stuff." The second motivation was to start up intentional communities in different neighborhoods, bringing people together to create and celebrate a low-carbon culture.

The groups have been meeting regularly and have since broadened their focus to include larger practical initiatives, such as co-ops to buy food in bulk and child-care circles. For Norwich participants, finding a path toward personal carbon reduction is a defining element of what Transition looks like in an urban context.

EATING LOCALLY REDUCES "FOOD MILES" AND THUS "EMBODIED ENERGY" (THE SUM OF ALL THE ENERGY REQUIRED TO PRODUCE GOODS OR SERVICES), AS WELL AS CARBON POLLUTION AND RELIANCE ON FOSSIL FUELS.

☼ LAND/NATURE STEWARDSHIP

FarmShare: Norwich FarmShare is a community-owned farm growing vegetables and delivering them weekly to members. It is located just outside the city, on land that previously was sugar-beet monoculture. The farm has a goal of cultivating one hundred varieties of vegetables. Permaculture strategies are in place to attract beneficial insects and pollinators, as well as birds, and a community beekeeping group maintains a hive at the edge of the woodland nearby.

☼ TOOLS/TECHNOLOGY

Norfolk Car Club: The Car Club is a pay-as-you-go car-share operating in the region, reducing car ownership and associated carbon emissions. Car Club cars are parked in designated parking spots located all over the city. People can sign up for the service for free; members reserve a car online and use a "smart card" to unlock the car. The user pays by the hour, and cars are available all the time.

Reporting contributed by Muneezay Jaffery. Photos courtesy of Tony Buckingham, unless otherwise noted.

CHARLES EISENSTEIN ON LOCAL CURRENCIES

A sacred way of life connects us to the people and places around us. That means that a sacred economy must be in large part a local economy, in which we have multidimensional, personal relationships with the land and people who meet our needs, and whose needs we meet in turn. Otherwise we suffer a divide between the social and the material, in which our social relationships lack substance, and in which our economic relationships are impersonal. It is inevitable, when we purchase generic services from distant strangers and standardized products from distant lands, that we feel a loss of connection, an alienation, and a sense that we, like the things we buy, are replaceable. Local currency is often proposed as a way to revitalize local economies, insulate them from global market forces, and re-create community. At present, there are thousands of them around the world, unofficial currencies issued by groups of ordinary citizens. In theory, local currency offers several economic benefits:

1. It encourages people to shop at local businesses, since only they accept and use the local currency.
2. It increases the local money supply, which increases demand and stimulates local production and employment.
3. It keeps money within the community, since it cannot be extracted to distant corporations.
4. It allows individuals and businesses to bypass conventional credit channels and thus offers an alternative source of capital, for which the interest (if any) will circulate back to the community.
5. It facilitates the circulation of goods and services among people who may not have sufficient access to national currency but who may have time and skills to offer.

Experiments in Local Money: Proxy Currencies

The first kind of local currency considered here is the dollar (or euro) proxy currency, such as the Chiemgauer or the BerkShare. You can buy a hundred BerkShares for $95 and buy merchandise at the usual dollar price; the merchant then redeems a hundred BerkShares for $95 at participating banks. Because of this easy convertibility, merchants readily accept them, and the 5 percent discount is well worth the extra business volume. However, the same easy convertibility limits the currency's effect on the local economy. In principle, merchants receiving BerkShares have a 5 percent incentive to source merchandise locally, but in the absence of local economic infrastructure, they usually won't bother.

Proxy currencies do little to revitalize local economies or to expand the local money supply. They provide a token of desire to buy local but a very small economic incentive to do so. Since BerkShares originate as dollars and are convertible into them, anyone with access to the former also has access to the latter. The international equivalent is found in countries that adopt a currency board. We call these dollarized economies, because they have effectively surrendered any monetary independence. Proxy currencies like BerkShares are useful as a consciousness-raising tool to introduce people to the idea of complementary currencies, but by themselves they are ineffectual in promoting vibrant local economies.

Complementary Fiat Currencies

More promising than proxy currencies are fiat currencies, such as Ithaca Hours, that actually increase the local money supply. Many Depression-era scrips fall into this category. Essentially, someone simply prints up the money and declares it to have value (e.g., an Ithaca Hour is declared equal to $10). For it to be money, there must be a community agreement that it has value. In the case of Ithaca Hours, a group of businesses, inspired by the currency's founder, Paul Glover, simply declared that they would accept the currency—in effect, backing it with their goods and services. During the Depression, scrip was often issued by a mainstay local business that could redeem it for merchandise, coal, or some other commodity. In other cases, a city government issued its own currency, backed by acceptability for payment of local taxes and fees.

The effect of fiat currencies is much more potent than that of proxy currencies, because fiat currencies have the potential of putting money in the hands of those who would otherwise not have it.

Such currencies are often called "complementary," because they are separate from and complementary to the standard medium of exchange. While they are usually denominated in dollar (or euro, pound, etc.) units, there is no currency board that keeps reserves of dollars to maintain the exchange rate. They are thus similar to a standard sovereign currency with a floating exchange rate.

In the absence of local government support, because complementary fiat currencies are not easily convertible into dollars, businesses are generally much less willing to accept them than they are proxy currencies. That is because in the current economic system, there is little infrastructure to source goods locally. Locally owned businesses are plugged into the same global supply chains as everyone else. Regrowing the infrastructure of local production and distribution will take time, as well as a change in macroeconomic conditions driven by the internalization of costs, the end of growth pressure, and a social and political decision to re-localize. Noneconomic factors can influence the social agreement of money. The idealism of a few that sustains local currency today will become the consensus of the many.

Time Banking

There is one resource that is always locally available and always needed to sustain and enrich life. That resource is human beings: their labor, energy, and time. Whereas local currencies are viable only to the extent that producers are making goods and services that are consumed locally by people who, themselves, produce locally consumed goods and services, human beings are always "producers" of our time (by the mere act of living), and there are many ways to give this time for the benefit of others. Therefore, time-based currencies (often called "time banks") offer great promise, without needing huge changes in economic infrastructure.

When someone performs a service through a time bank, it credits his or her account by a single "time dollar" for each hour worked, and it debits the recipient's account by the same. Usually there is some kind of electronic bulletin board with postings of offerings and needs. People who could otherwise not afford the services of a handyman, massage therapist, or babysitter thus gain access to help from a person who might otherwise be unemployed. Time banks tend to flourish in places where people have a lot of time and not much money. It is especially appealing in realms requiring little specialization, in which the time of any person is, in fact, equally valuable. A prime example is the famous *fureai kippu* currency in Japan, which credits people for time spent caring for the elderly. Time banking is also used extensively by service organizations in America and Britain. It can also apply to physical goods, typically by way of a dollar cost for materials and a time dollar cost for time.

The fundamental idea behind time banks is deeply egalitarian, both because everyone's time is valued equally and because everyone starts out with the same amount of it. If there is one thing that we can be said to truly own, it is our time.

When time-based currency replaces monetary transactions, it is a great equalizing force in society. The danger is that time currency can also end up transferring formerly gift-based activity into the realm of the quantified. The future, perhaps, belongs to nonmonetary, unquantified ways of connecting gifts and needs. Still, at least for a long time to come, time banks have an important role to play in healing our fragmented local communities.

Reclaiming the Credit Commons

Another way to foster local economic and monetary autonomy is through the credit system. When an economic community applies formal or informal mechanisms to limit the acquisition of credit and, consequently, the allocation of money, the local economy can maintain its independence just as if it had instituted currency controls. To illustrate this point, consider an innovation commonly mentioned in discussions of complementary currency: mutual-credit systems, including commercial barter rings, credit-clearing cooperatives, and local exchange trading systems (LETS). When a transaction takes place in a mutual-credit system, the account of the buyer is debited and the account of the seller is credited by the agreed-upon sales price—whether or not the buyer has a positive account balance. For example, say I mow your lawn for an agreed price of twenty credits. If we both started at zero, now I have a balance of +20 and you have a balance of -20. Next, I buy bread from Thelma for ten credits. Now my account is down to +10 and hers is +10.

This kind of system has many applications. The above scenario exemplifies a small-scale, locally based credit system often called LETS. Since its inception in 1983 by Michael Linton, hundreds of LETS systems have taken root around the world. Mutual credit is equally useful on the commercial level. Any network of businesses that fulfill the basic requirement—that each produces something that one of the others needs—can form a commercial barter exchange or credit-clearing cooperative. Rather than issue commercial paper or seek short-term loans from banks, participating businesses create their own credit.

Mutual-credit systems reclaim the functions of banking for a local community, a business community, or a cooperative entity. They foster and protect the internal economy of their members, insulating it from external shocks and financial predation in the same way that local currencies do. Indeed, local currencies will never be able to expand beyond marginal status unless they have a credit mechanism that protects them from the speculative runs that numerous national currencies have suffered in the last twenty years. Local and regional credit-clearing organizations can exercise capital control functions similar to those that wiser nations imposed when developing their economies through import substitution. The most famous mutual-credit system, Switzerland's WIR, provides a rather extreme model for this principle: once you buy into it, you are not permitted to cash out. On a local level, this would force foreign investors to source components locally.

The decision of how to allocate capital on a large scale is more than an economic decision; it is a social and political decision. Even in today's capitalist society, the largest investment decisions are not always made on considerations of business profits. Putting a man on the moon, building a highway system, and maintaining armed forces are all public investments that do not seek a positive return on capital. In the private sector, though, bank profit determines the allocation of capital, which is the allocation of human labor, creativity, and the riches of the earth. What shall we, humanity, do on earth? This collective choice is a commons that has been privatized and shall be restored to us all in a sacred economy. That does not mean removing investment decisions from the private sector, but rather changing the nature of credit so that money goes to those who serve the social and ecological good.

Excerpted with permission from Charles Eisenstein from ***Sacred Economics: Money, Gift, and Society in the Age of Transition****, (Berkeley, CA: North Atlantic Books, 2011).*

Tinker's Bubble Eco-Community

Little Norton, Somerset, U.K.

Tinker's Bubble is an eco-community established in 1994 in southwest England that manages 40 acres (16 hectares) without the use of fossil fuels or internal combustion engines. The aim of the community's ten to fifteen residents is "to derive their livelihoods from the sustainable management of the land and its resources."[10] After a long battle for permission from the local planning board, it is now a legal and established site (though with restrictions as to what they can build).

TOOLS/TECHNOLOGY

Energy without Fossil Fuels: Community members have several photovoltaic panels and a wind generator that together generate electricity for the community. Combined these generate 1.4 kilowatts, which does not all get used in summer, but is sometimes not quite enough in winter. All the houses have electric lighting and electronics like stereos and laptop computers.

There is an abundance of wood on-site, which they use as fuel for heating and cooking. Dining facilities are communal, and there is both an indoor and an outdoor kitchen. They use scythes to cut crops and hay and a steam-powered sawmill to prepare planks for building. Dolly, the workhorse, is used in farming and to help move material around the site. The lack of loud engine noise adds to the residents' quality of life.

BUILDING

Experimenting with Natural Building: Each of the buildings at Tinker's Bubble is different—a thatched round house, a straw-bale insulated house, and other buildings using a variety of construction techniques: cob, cordwood, straw bale, pallet, roundwood, and Douglas fir shingle (or shake); there's even a metal roof. The houses do not have high thermal mass and do not benefit from passive-solar gain (because of trees). Their main eco-features are that they are mostly made from natural material, through a process of experimentation, and they're built on-site by the people who will live in them. There are no rules as to how a house should be built; the only rule is that new

A LITTLE OF THE OLD, A LITTLE OF THE NEW— BUT NO FOSSIL FUELS...

building projects need communal agreement.

Tinker's Bubble is about true low-cost eco-housing, using local, often free, natural materials. Members feel it is important buildings are temporary—that having a low impact is also about being able to remove a house easily. Thus, the houses should not be too solid or too robust, as that would compromise their temporary design.

The houses are compact in size; some might consider them too small, but once inside, it becomes clear that they are well designed for the needs of the inhabitant, with space for a chair, desk, bed, and fire. Often the beds are in a loft, close to the roof, creating fun sleeping platforms that also free up living space down below. One inspiring house belongs to a resident named Charlotte, who built a straw-bale, cordwood, cob, and pallet house by herself in eleven months, without any prior experience in building. Inside it has a large living space and two sleeping platforms on different levels. Dan, another resident, built a green-painted house/workshop with a curved metal roof. It sits wonderfully in the forest like a colorful bunker; it looks cozy and purposeful at the same time.

There is also a barn under construction, being built from large sawn timbers pegged together with no metal fixings—a proper timber-framed building. It will be clad and roofed with the community's own wood and sits on a foundation of local stone, using no cement or mortar.

☼ LAND/NATURE STEWARDSHIP

Food and Water Systems: Three-quarters of the land comprises woodland, forest, orchard, and a stream (from which the land draws its name). It has a very peaceful and English feel—rolling green hills, apple blossoms, wildlife, and changeable maritime weather. Much of the focus on the community is to live successfully and sustainable from the land. Thus great energy is put into growing food, rearing animals, and caring for the land.

There is a communal garden, but most of their food comes from the residents' extensive private gardens. Through the use of polytunnels and their own skills, and with a significant amount of work, they provide a large percentage of their fresh food from the land. In addition, the community has a cow, chickens, and geese for milk and eggs. They store the milk in the stream to keep it cool and often make cheese. They purchase additional dried goods and staples (such as rice and lentils) in bulk from an organic wholesaler.

They source all water from a local spring. A hydraulic ram pump, powered by the flow of the stream, brings the water to the top of the hill. From there it is distributed to the communal round house, bathhouse, and some of the residences. Toilets are all dry composting, using no water. In other places, like the outdoor kitchen, water and waste from the sink is filtered through a colander, and a piece of guttering directs the water down toward the gardens.

FINANCES/ECONOMICS

Cash and the Collective Fund: Given that the aim of Tinker's Bubble is to allow residents to live off the land, members require very little additional cash income. All residents, however, must pay into the collective food and equipment fund. Residents generate this income in different ways, either selling their own organic vegetables or products (such as elderberry syrup) or working for one of the community's collective enterprises. The community also has a forestry business and they produce organic apple juice.

LAND TENURE/COMMUNITY GOVERNANCE

Residency and Becoming a Shareholder: Although residents have separate dwellings, Tinker's Bubble has a communal structure. Members share meals and one main bathhouse. As with most communities, there is a reasonable turnover in members, who include several long-termers and various newer residents who have been there just a few years, with an average of about ten adult residents and several children. Each adult has to work a "domestic" day every fortnight (when he or she cooks the evening meal and does the washing up). They make a list of all the other jobs that need doing, and people sign up. Other than that, there is great autonomy is how people choose to live their lives and spend their time. Effectively, there are only two clear rules: no fossil fuels and no internal combustion engines. As long as people pay their share and meet their work requirements, they are free to do what they like, so long as it fits within the objective of a land-based livelihood.

New arrivals must be accepted by consensus at the monthly meeting, and then residency is assured for only three months. The process is repeated every three months until someone becomes a shareholder (the land is owned in the form of shares, with six of the thirteen owned by one of the original founders). After two years of residence, members either begin the process of purchasing a personal share of the land or move on. Through this process, the residents are gradually buying the land in shares, ensuring that ownership is spread across many individuals. They hope that land ownership will be transferred completely over to the community within the next few years.

Reporting and photos contributed by Jenny Pickerill.

Findhorn Ecovillage

Moray, Scotland, U.K.

Findhorn Ecovillage, according to research done in 2006,[11] has the smallest ecological footprint of any community studied in the industrialized world, and its residents have about half the impact of a typical citizen of the United Kingdom. First famed for its "miracle garden," it is now the largest ecovillage in the country and a major teaching center—approximately three thousand participants from around the globe take part in a range of workshops, programs, and events each year. The concept of regenerative relationships between humans and nature has been central to its activities since its establishment at a trailer park, where the founders initially settled in 1962. Today, the community has approximately three hundred residents of diverse nationalities and religious and spiritual backgrounds.

Findhorn had humble beginnings. The founders, Peter and Eileen Caddy, arrived at a trailer park, were

"As it is in permaculture: work with nature, not against nature."
—Pioneer member, Craig Gibsone

Photo: Findhorn Foundation

CATCH AND STORE ENERGY, THEN SHARE THE SURPLUS! FINDHORN'S FOUR WIND TURBINES PRODUCE ENOUGH POWER FOR THE ECOVILLAGE, AND THEY EXPORT A SUBSTANTIAL AMOUNT OF CLEAN ENERGY TO THE GRID.

joined by a friend, Dorothy Maclean, and—inspired by the countercultural reawakening of the 1960s—began an adventure into sustainable living and spiritual exploration. They started a garden, and, to their surprise, the beach soils of Findhorn Bay began supplying them with a huge array of vegetables, herbs, and flowers.

Skeptics have named factors such as the microclimate of Moray and the use of copious amounts of horse manure, provided by nearby farmers, to explain Findhorn's incredibly fertile garden, but many called it a miracle, exhibiting a unique cooperation with nature. Many visitors were attracted to the area, became part of the spiritual-ecological community, and decided to stay and get more involved.

Photo: Findhorn Foundation

THE HOMES IN THE "BARREL CLUSTER" ARE MADE OUT OF USED DOUGLAS FIR WHISKEY BARRELS FROM A LOCAL DISTILLERY—ENSURING MINIMAL WASTE OF MATERIAL AND EMBODIED ENERGY.

"The project has changed in size and structure, yet the essence of the place is still the same," says a pioneer member, Craig Gibsone. "In the beginning, Findhorn was more spiritual, but worked very intensely with the forces of nature. As it is in permaculture: work with nature, not against nature." In the context of increasing global awareness about climate change and peak oil, Findhorn's achievements and evolution are taking on ever-greater significance.

BUILDING

Ecological Design: A comprehensive eco-design building code was developed for the site, which all new buildings must adhere to. Some features of this code include efficient and effective natural insulation (especially since this part of the United Kingdom is very cold); organic paints; and sustainable, all-natural building materials, such as clay tiles. Other design approaches include low-energy design features for lighting and heating, locally sourced building materials and—in certain housing areas—communal areas for cooking and relaxing. A large number of houses utilize a southerly orientation to make maximum use of solar panels and passive-solar heating. Many residences, businesses, and community buildings use compact fluorescent light bulbs.

Some of the ecological building styles include:

Bag End Cluster: The first cluster of eco-housing at Findhorn, developed in the 1980s. The architects took on an experimental approach in order to identify suitable materials and most effective use of space. They created compact, well-lit flats, the first in the United Kingdom to use cellulose fiber insulation. Although they imported some materials, they prioritized energy conservation, organic paints, and non–animal based glues.

Whiskey Barrel or the Barrel Cluster: A group of round houses constructed with wood from Douglas Fir whiskey barrels made in the 1920s and used at a local distillery for almost sixty years. This technique was first introduced in 1986, creating cozy living spaces; since then extensions and roof variations have allowed for expansions.

Straw bale: This method was first used for a family home constructed in 2002 by local builders using a timber frame and straw bales for insulation and a lime-based mortar. These "breathing" walls allow a controlled exchange of air and vapor to moderate humidity and ensure air quality. A number of houses built in this style are part of the area called Field of Dreams, which includes a number of ecologically designed residences.

LAND/NATURE STEWARDSHIP

THE GARDENS ARE AS MUCH A SOCIAL FOCAL POINT AS THEY ARE AN AGRICULTURAL ONE, SERVING AS MEETING PLACE FOR RESIDENTS—BE IT FOR FESTIVALS OR FOR GARDENING—AND ENABLE CHILDREN AND ADULTS TO APPRECIATE AND DEVELOP AN INTERDEPENDENT RELATIONSHIP WITH THE NATURAL WORLD. VOLUNTEERING AT THE GARDENS ALSO EARNS MEMBERS AND GUESTS MEAL TICKETS FOR THE COMMUNAL DINING HALLS.

Pioneering CSA in the Miracle Gardens: Findhorn was a pioneer in community-supported agricultural systems, introducing a cooperative box scheme that has since become a cornerstone of the local food movement. Findhorn's community dining halls offer vegetarian meals, and the common meal structure minimizes food waste. Organic waste from these kitchens is added to compost piles at homes or in the main gardens.

The original "miracle gardens," called Cullerne Gardens, that first brought recognition to Findhorn are still thriving, dedicated to growing vegetables, herbs, and fruit. They also grow flowers for tinctures. The community maintains a woodland habitat to ensure sustainable ecosystem succession. The incorporation of a woodland area encourages biodiversity and natural biological cycles to maintain fertility and also control pests.

Cullerne gardeners have always used techniques that could be called "permaculture," but have begun to identify specifically with the approach over the past several years. They use a number of strategies:

They experiment with different species and establishing a perennial forest garden, to complement the woodland area.

They use permaculture-based mulching techniques and incorporating of green manure into the soil, such as clover, as well as leaf mulch and cooked food.

They use raised beds in the polytunnels, a no-dig approach, and German mounds for growing outside the polytunnels.

They are moving toward more diversity and polyculture, away from a production-oriented, monoculture approach.

They've installed a vermicomposting system, fed primarily by kitchen waste.

Photo: Findhorn Foundation

FINDHORN'S LIVING MACHINE, DESIGNED BY JOHN TODD, IS NOT ONLY CAPABLE OF MEETING TOUGH NEW SEWAGE OUTFLOW STANDARDS BUT USES NO CHEMICALS AND IS RELATIVELY INEXPENSIVE TO OPERATE.

They use a chicken tractor to work the soil and fertilize it. The eggs are used at the community kitchens and sold to neighbors.

Food systems at Findhorn are providing a living education on nature and the environment, as well as feeding the community.

FINANCES/ECONOMICS

Local Currencies: Since 2002, a local currency, the Eko, has been in place. There are roughly £20,000 worth of Eko notes in circulation and issuing them has enabled Ekopia, the community development trust, to make low-interest loans and donations to support various initiatives. These businesses allow surplus wealth to remain within the Findhorn community through reinvestment. An assessment of the economic impact of Findhorn estimated that the community is generating over four hundred jobs and £5 million of business annually.[12]

More than 60 percent of Findhorn's income comes from conferences and educational and training courses. The remainder comes from rent paid by residents and donations made by residents and visitors. Expenditures at the foundation are few, as many services are provided within the community, and energy is created on-site. Because many resources are shared, including tools and maintenance equipment and laundry and dining facilities, ecovillagers annually consume about half the products of the average U.K. citizen.

Reporting contributed by Muneezay Jaffery. Photos by Graham Meltzer, unless otherwise noted.

Svanholm Collective and Ecovillage

Skibby, Zealand, Denmark

Photo: Toke Stjernholm (Creative Commons)

Svanholm is an ecovillage that has pioneered the organic farming movement in Denmark and achieved a remarkably productive, self-reliant food system. Based on a large medieval estate near the fjords west of Copenhagen, it was established as an organic farming collective in 1978. Approximately eighty adults and forty children collectively own and manage 988 acres (400 hectares) of farm and woodland. Svanholm (Danish for "swan islet") was not specifically designed as a permaculture community, but is aligned with the approach and demonstrates a number of its principles. Its shared economy allows for a continually evolving system, and today the collective boasts a number of successes, including food and energy production, financial sustainability, education, and self-governance.

The Svanholm estate is first mentioned in historical documents in 1346, when it was owned by the

BEYOND YIELDING DAIRY PRODUCTS, MEAT, AND WOOL, SVANHOLM'S SHEEP MOW THE FIELDS AND IMPROVE THE FERTILITY OF THE LAND THROUGH MANAGED GRAZING IN THIS COOL-COLD TEMPERATE CLIMATE.

knight Niels Knudsen Manderup. Today, the community shares the old manor house and about twelve other structures on the farm. Community members are fully engaged in cultivating their own produce, which is enough to meet their needs year-round. Beyond this, the community tends to their own cows and sheep, which they raise for meat and milk. They produce some organic products in surplus, including root crops, grain, milk, and meat, which they process and pack on-site and sell at Danish markets.

The community employs about half of its members on-site, and all residents put 80 percent of their income into the communal economy, which covers all basic needs; they keep the remaining 20 percent for personal use. They make decisions by consensus, as their website explains:

Because of our common economy, we're not tied up by only having to look at the profitability of production. We can also put emphasis on the human or ecological factor, that which is helping us further on toward a sustainable life. It is of great importance that we have these common funds, so we can allow ourselves to experiment and take some chances. That way we can start different projects and let them run for a period of time, till we can judge if they meet our demands. If we are to find new and realistic suggestions to sustainable solutions, it is very important to have this possibility.

Photo: Christina Jensen

The Svanholm community is working toward carbon neutrality and currently produces about 70 percent of its own electricity and heating. They have two wind generators and a wood-chip furnace fueled primarily from sustainably harvested trees from their land. During the summer, passive-solar technology is used heat water for the community.

Svanholm members cohere around common ideals relating to ecology, communal living, and participatory self-governance. *Selvforvaltning* is a Danish word that is hard to translate into English. "It's rooted in modern Danish culture, and is used in the development of educational and management ideas," Svanholm's website reads. "It represents the ideas of stimulating people, pupils and workers to be more involved in decision-making and feel responsible for the outcome. *Self-government* is the English word we thought would be the closest."

The self-government principle extends to the community's approach to raising and educating its children, and every common meeting starts with news from them and allows the opportunity for parents and children to directly participate. Whereas in most of Denmark both parents work outside the home and children are in government-sponsored, age-delineated school, activities, or daycare for the majority of the week, at Svanholm, the emphasis is on integrating young people into the daily life of the multi-generational ecovillage. While formal education happens outside the community, when the children are not in school they are usually free to participate in ecovillage activities, and some teenagers choose to join in the work on the farm. "We try to help them find their own rhythm and interpret their own needs—which is difficult if you have to spend all of your childhood in the very regulative environment of an institution," the website continues. Interestingly, the broader Danish discussion of its educational system has recently focused on children's individuality and autonomy, issues that have been at the core of Svanholm's approach to childrearing since its start.

Reporting contributed by Nicollette Constante. Photos courtesy of Svanholm, except where otherwise noted.

Rainbow Valley Farm

Matakana, New Zealand

THE FOUNDERS OF RAINBOW VALLEY FARM CHOSE TO START WITH DEGRADED LAND: THE TREES HAD BEEN CUT, THE SOIL WASHED AWAY, AND THE VEGETATION DESTROYED BY WILDFIRES. THEY WAITED A FULL YEAR TO SEE HOW THE LAND AND SUN CHANGED WITH THE SEASONS BEFORE STARTING WORK ON WHAT WOULD BECOME SOME OF THE MOST FERTILE 20 ACRES IN NEW ZEALAND. THE FARM HAS SINCE BECOME A WORLD-FAMOUS EXAMPLE OF WHAT CAN BE ACHIEVED WITH PERMACULTURE.

Joe Polaischer and Trish Allen bought a small property in the Matakana area, north of Auckland, New Zealand, in 1987. They chose land so degraded it was said to be useless, but the steep slopes of the valley reminded Polaischer of his native Austria, and the land was dirt cheap. The couple arrived in their house truck and parked it at the bottom of the valley.

The first challenge was bringing the soil back to life. The heavily eroded clay soil—subsoil, really, as there was no topsoil—turned to boot-yanking muck in winter and caked into hardscape ceramic in summer. They rented earth-moving equipment and dug swales, terraced, and built dams. By hand, the two dug raised

"Through the land people will be nourished.
Through the people the land will be nourished." —Maori proverb

beds for the vegetable garden and planted over six hundred fruit and nut trees, grown from seeds and cuttings. They rotated their dairy cows through the terraces on the hillsides and added ducks and geese to the orchards for pest control.

Within a few years, Rainbow Valley Farm became about 85 percent self-sufficient for their food. WWOOFers (volunteers from the Willing Workers on Organic Farms) arrived from Japan, Europe, and Africa. Polaischer and Allen began teaching permaculture courses and drew their graduates into a local permaculture guild in northern New Zealand. Both traveled and lectured, showing slides of what they had done.

JOE POLAISCHER AND TRISH ALLEN BUILT THEIR PASSIVE-SOLAR, EARTH-SHELTERED HOME OF ADOBE BRICKS, WITH SALVAGED WOOD FOR WINDOWS, DOORS, AND THE ROOF BEAMS. THE GREEN ROOF GOES INTO THE SIDE OF THE HILL, SO FREE-RANGE CHICKENS, DUCKS, AND GUINEA FOWL CAN FORAGE AND BUILD NESTS IN THE ROOF'S LONG GRASS. HONEY, STRAWBERRIES, HERBS, GRASSES, EGGS, AND FLOWERS GO FROM THE ROOF TO THE TABLE.

In 2009 Polaischer passed away, and Allen moved into Matakana, selling the farm to a Maori permaculture family, Wiki Walker and Cedric Hockey, who created the Rainbow Valley Farm Whanau (*whanau* means "family" in Maori). The *whanau* ethos, according to Walker and Hockey, means that—beyond being owners—they consider themselves caretakers and cultivators of the land. Hockey says that Polaischer and Allen left some big shoes to fill and that he still hasn't identified all the species of trees that were planted on the property. With repairs to the water system, the installation of living roofs, and a road upgrade, however, the family has been able to reopen the farm to visitors and classes.

The *whanau* has added a mudroom at the back of the house. They have eight full-time residents and usually another four WWOOFers. The house garden design was rebuilt in a traditional *koru* shape, with an aquaponic feature. Hockey explains, "There is no prescription for what is the 'right way' only the best way for you within the resources you have available to you. A *koru* is a Maori design that imitates the early growth stage of the native frond. The spiral represents new beginnings, fertility, and growth. Spiral designs can also found in permaculture. We felt that this was an appropriate symbol and technique, which resonated with us as a Maori family. It is also a very beautiful pattern which looks really lovely."

Rainbow Valley Farm is an icon of New Zealand permaculture and a growing testament to the transformation possible when a couple of people with inspiration and knowledge take on a bare, eroded hillside.

Reporting and photos contributed by Albert Bates.

Photo: Francesco Vicenzi

STARTED IN 1982 ON A LOT IN MELBOURNE THAT WAS LITERALLY TRASHED (A DECOMMISSIONED QUARRY AND LANDFILL), CERES IS ONE OF THE PIONEER PERMACULTURE PROJECTS. BECAUSE OF ITS TENURE AND ACCESSIBLE URBAN LOCATION, ONE CAN SEE CERES AS AN EXAMPLE WHAT A FUTURE PERMACULTURE SOCIETY MIGHT LOOK LIKE.

Photo: Elia Petzierides

CERES

Melbourne, Australia

The Centre for Education and Research in Environmental Strategies (CERES) is at the forefront of a community-based movement in Australia that works toward greater self-reliance in food and energy systems. It is an award-winning urban sustainability center and community park providing positive, hands-on education on subjects such as environment, energy, food and water, and low-tech solutions for a post-carbon world. CERES is located on 10 acres (4 hectares) along the edge of the once-polluted Merri Creek in Melbourne, the second-largest city in Australia. It boasts an impressive array of programs and systems that range from community gardens (where there is a fifteen-year waiting list to get a small plot) to one of the world's most energy- and water-efficient freestanding aquaponic systems. The center welcomes an impressive seven hundred thousand visitors per year.

The concept of permaculture was born in Australia. With only about 5 percent of Australia's total land area classified as suitable for dryland or irrigated agriculture and 25 percent of it desert, this land necessitates a smarter approach to food production. In the past decade, with food prices rising by an astonishing 43 percent, Australians are now more than ever looking for creative and efficient strategies for putting more food on the table.

CULTURE/EDUCATION

The Commons: There is an easiness that permeates the rambling creek-side acres. One can hear the tall gum trees rustle softly in the wind, the calls of native birds, the fallen leaves that crunch underfoot on the walk around the cafe, the hiss of the coffee machine, the soft sounds of cutlery touching plates in between bites of food, and pieces of conversation spoken in a variety of languages.

CERES is a busy place. Locals with a bike in need of a tune-up show up at the Bike Shed; those with surplus lemons trade at the Urban Orchard; the Bee Group boasts eight hives and offers beekeeping courses. Egg lovers can join the Chook Group, where fourteen families take turns looking after the fifty chickens—each family on duty one day every two weeks. Their reward is to be able to take home all of the freshly laid organic eggs for that day.

CERES offers an array of courses. While cheese making is their most popular course, all post-carbon skills are very popular, such as pickling, canning, and beer making. According to Chris Ennis, the organic farm manager at CERES, the popularity of these courses seems to be based on a need to reconnect with nature and environment. "People feel disconnected—so screen based, citified. Most people don't have a connection with country anymore."

Another way for locals to get reconnected with nature and with each other is through the Urban Orchard program. It is a food swap based on the "take what you think is fair" system. This low-tech "trestle table market" has become popular around Australia and serves as a social outlet where people

can make friendships and share knowledge.

The well-known Sustainable Schools Program welcomed its one-millionth schoolchild in 2010. The Honey Lane teaching garden, the first certified organic city farm in Australia, has wide paths flanked by burgeoning rows of veggies and is home to two hundred or so chickens and their welcome by-products. This natural and practical environment gives the children exposure to where their food comes from in a relaxed way. The Sustainable Schools Program has relationships with three hundred schools in the state of Victoria and wrote the curriculum that is currently being rolled out on a national level.

TOOLS/TECHNOLOGY

Green Tech: The CERES Green Tech team has put into action a number of energy-related projects that embody the core principles of permaculture. A shade structure on the site is an example of Building-Integrated Photovoltaics and is the first of its kind in the world, with the capacity to generate 1.44 kilowatts of energy from the sun. A solar concentrator, called a Scheffler Dish, tracks the sun throughout the day and concentrates its rays at one hundred times their intensity, creating temperatures

of up to 1,472°F (800ºC). The energy is then used for cooking, producing electricity, heating, the generation of steam for laundries, and more.

✪ LAND/NATURE STEWARDSHIP

Aquaponics: CERES also has in operation a free-standing, commercial aquaponic system that produces 450 to 750 bunches of herbs per week with only 270 watts of electricity (the equivalent of three incandescent light bulbs).

Just north of Melbourne, the Murray-Darling Basin is where Australia's two largest rivers join; it is also Australia's food-bowl. Seventy percent of the country's irrigation takes place there, and it produces 40 percent of the agricultural output, while only receiving 6 percent of the country's rainfall. In recent years, over-extraction has led to an artificially extended drought, beyond the capacity of the environment to withstand. Recent attempts at legislation to curb water usage have sparked fiery protests from farmers.

The politics of developing alternative farming methods are complicated, but from the perspective of Steve Mushin, a sustainable designer working on aquaponics, "an unexpected outcome of

STEPHEN MUSHIN LED THE CREATION OF ONE OF THE WORLD'S MOST ENERGY- AND WATER-EFFICIENT FREESTANDING AQUAPONIC SYSTEMS. EVEN THOUGH AQUAPONIC SYSTEMS REQUIRE CONSIDERABLE MANAGEMENT AND KNOWLEDGE OF BOTH FISH AND PLANT CULTIVATION, IN A WATER-POOR TERRITORY, THEY ARE AN APPROPRIATE TECHNOLOGY BECAUSE THEY USE LESS THAN 1 PERCENT OF THE WATER A TRADITIONAL FARM OF SIMILAR SIZE WOULD. IN PERMACULTURE, THE DECISION TO APPLY A CERTAIN TECHNIQUE IS ALWAYS BASED ON THE SPECIFIC CIRCUMSTANCES OF THE SITE.

the aquaponic project is that now engineer-types who visit CERES are getting interested in farming too." CERES has come a long way since its modest beginnings, yet it remains humble and doesn't overly boast of its place in permaculture history. "Permaculture is just low-tech good sense," Ennis says.

Reporting contributed by Rebecca Williams. Photos courtesy of CERES, unless otherwise noted.

Melliodora

Hepburn Springs, Victoria, Australia

MELLIODORA IS THE PERSONAL HOME OF DAVID HOLMGREN AND SU DENNETT, AS WELL AS A LIVING TOOL FOR PERMACULTURE RESEARCH, TRAINING, AND COMMUNITY DEVELOPMENT.

As the co-originator of permaculture, David Holmgren wanted to practice what he preached. After several years of living in the fast-paced city of Melbourne, Holmgren and his partner, Su Dennett, wanted to get back to the land and put their ideas on sustainable design to practice. They chose Hepburn Springs, a small town with a temperate, inland climate. They purchased a bare, 2.5-acre (1-hectare) plot in 1985 and named it Melliodora, after the yellow box eucalyptus *(Eucalyptus melliodora)* that populates the area. They wanted their home and lifestyle to serve as a living tool for permaculture research, training, and community development, focusing on local, small-scale solutions.

THE SITE HAS A PASSIVE-SOLAR HOUSE MADE FROM MUD BRICK AND PRODUCTIVE MIXED FOOD GARDENS AND ORCHARDS INTEGRATED WITH DOMESTIC ANIMALS. A SYSTEM OF WATER CATCHMENT IRRIGATES THE LAND, AND THE CREEK HAS BEEN REGENERATED ON THE PUBLIC LAND THAT BORDERS THEIR PROPERTY. THE FAMILY HAS BEEN ABLE TO IMPROVE THE HEALTH OF A DEGRADED LANDSCAPE THROUGH REGENERATIVE DESIGN STRATEGIES, WHILE ALSO ACHIEVING LOCALLY BASED MEANS TO MEET THEIR BASIC NEEDS.

LAND/NATURE STEWARDSHIP

Zoning the Site: Designed explicitly with permaculture principles, the property was divided into different zones of production based on natural contour, soil type, and the relationship to the house. Melliodora includes three major zones of production. Zone 1, the area closest to the house, has the greenhouse and an intensive vegetable garden. This area requires the most labor but yields the majority of food throughout the year. Zone 2 contains extensive orchards, with over 120 fruit and nut trees; chickens; and two dams, which provide fresh water and fish. Goats graze amid intensive orchards in zone 3. These orchards extend into the land further afield that borders the site, zone 4, which consists of a creek and public lands that are managed jointly by the family and local community, allowing for regeneration after a long history of degradation from gold mining.

"The climate was always somewhat extreme [here], and it's intensified over the past twenty years with climate change," Holmgren writes in his book on Melliodora.[13] Building diversity and variety into systems helps mitigate those effects.

Perennial planting systems have been crucial for the success of Melliodora. An abundance of perennial trees and plants can achieve a variety of functions at once, including soil improvement, windbreaks, and the provision of food and animal fodder.

Soil Building and Water Systems: The initial poor soil quality and intensive demands of the many growing systems create a need for constant soil building. Over the years Holmgren has used a variety of techniques to replenish minerals and

restore the balance of soil nutrients. He maintains that such attention is essential to plant health and is constantly experimenting with new strategies, such as choosing mulch appropriate to the mineral balance of the particular plant species.

The effective implementation of water harvesting and management at Melliodora was crucial in the design process. Not only was this important for the success of food production and the improvement of soil quality, it acts on a more practical level toward fire safety, money savings, and long-term sustainability. This is especially important in the notoriously dry continent of Australia. The combination of lack of water and poor soils, combined with human impact and climate change, are increasingly difficult challenges. "Failure to manage water resources to optimize the biological productivity of the land is a fundamental cause of land degradation symptoms as diverse as acidification, erosion, salinity, water logging and tree decline." Holmgren writes.

Holmgren installed two large dams to maximize water capture in the rainy months. Water is then pumped to a large cement tank above the house for gravity-fed irrigation below. Holmgren placed irrigation lines on the contour lines of the sloping property to maximize absorption into the landscape. The house itself has a 951-gallon (3,600-liter) tank that collects rainwater from the roof for house use, which is always given priority over the town water for cooking and drinking. The rest of the roof runoff flows into the dams. A well is used as a last resort, when other harvesting sources are low.

CULTURE/EDUCATION

Local and Global Outreach: Thousands have visited Melliodora from the local community and beyond to learn design tools and specific techniques appropriate to the climate and landscape. The documentation of their meticulous planning and efforts in the book *Melliodora: A Case*

Study in Cool Climate Permaculture has acted as a valuable tool for other permaculture enthusiasts—they can see a complete design process from inception to "completion" (which incorporates the principle of accepting feedback and making modifications over time).

BUILDING

SU DENNETT AND TONY SOCCIO UNROLLING FOIL SACKING OVER ROOFING BATTENS. VISIBLE ARE CARDBOARD APPLE PACKING SHEETS BEING USED AS BAFFLES TO CONTAIN CELLULOSE IN THE INSULATED SECTIONS.

Permaculture Approach to House Design: Before purchasing the land at Hepburn Springs, Dennett and Holmgren weighed guidelines for the house design and materials. Holmgren warns of the potential danger in developing design criteria too extensively before actually finding and working with the land. There is, however, benefit to having a good conceptual framework that can help guide decisions about purchasing land and materials. Dennett and Holmgren had a tall order when considering their major building material. They wanted something with a low production cost, high thermal yield, and low toxicity, yet something structurally sound and energy efficient. In the end, locally made mud bricks worked to fulfill all their building guidelines. For the structural and finish timber, they gave consideration to what would be of least environmental impact and assessed the pros and cons of all available sources. They cut joinery wood from reclaimed, fire-damaged cypress and blackwood and used locally forested hardwood varieties for the structural components. Whenever possible, they got other pieces from local and salvaged building materials to support the local economy and reduce waste.

Holmgren and Dennett attempted to stack functions with each design element, in the house, whenever possible, extracting multiple benefits from each strategy. The plan focused on creating integrated, dynamic spaces that have multiple functions to allow for wall sharing and decreased use of overall materials needed. By making passive-solar gain a design priority, Holmgren and Dennett—as well as the environment—benefit from minimal use of electrical lighting; they get natural heating through the large double-glazed windows and maximize indoor sunlight in an otherwise cloudy climate (see p. 110 for more on passive-solar design). This has also allowed them to meet most of their heating needs through intelligent design. On the coldest days, they use a high-efficiency, slow-combustion radiant heater..

The heart of the house is the kitchen, which extends into the outdoor working and food-producing areas, including a multifunctional greenhouse. The inclusion of the greenhouse is crucial for Melliodora's food production needs in the cool and cloudy climate. It serves many functions, including food production year-round and a place to start plants for the more limited outdoor growing season in summer. It also is a crucial temperature regulator for the house, storing solar heat in the winter and helping to cool the house in the summer. Because the family knew that storing food from the garden would be important, they included details like a "cool cupboard" in the kitchen, which keeps produce cool without refrigeration.

Every detail of the house's design and construction embodied the family's desire to live true to their value systems, rooted in permaculture. "Private properties reflect personal responsibility, skills, and idiosyncrasies and have a special value in promoting permaculture, because they show how real people have integrated their ideas into their lives." Holmgren writes. This was, indeed, a major reason why they built Melliodora: the family saw the need to translate the initial ideas behind permaculture to the practical, domestic scale.

LAND TENURE/ COMMUNITY GOVERNANCE

Integrate Rather than Segregate: Melliodora achieves a balance between self-sufficiency and connection with local community resources. By having their home in the "urban-rural fringe" area of Hepburn Springs, the Holmgren-Dennett family can benefit from community utilities and facilities while also maintaining a type of rural lifestyle. "One of the learnings from a lot of the early efforts of individual and collective 'going back to the land' is that it works better to be closer to or part of small settlements and villages," Holmgren says. "Practically and logistically . . . there are all those practical and sustainability reasons why clustered settlements make sense. But it's also the connection in as part of a very clear identification with the traditional community. Elements of functional community that existed in traditional society still exist most strongly in small towns and villages, not in our cities."

ONE OF THE ONLY FRUIT TREES ON THE PROPERTY WHEN THEY ARRIVED, THE "OLD PEAR TREE" IS ONE OF THE LARGEST OF ITS KIND IN VICTORIA AND HAS SERVED THE FAMILY AS A LIVING REMINDER OF WHAT "SMALL AND SLOW SOLUTIONS" CAN ONE DAY YIELD.

The idea of maximizing the edge effect of two systems, in this case rural and urban, is an idea central to permaculture (see p. 206). Choosing a town-based location improves quality of life through social and cultural interaction (which Dennett and Holmgren considered fairly essential for their teenage children). It also improves the potential for income-generating networks and trading and bartering. Melliodora has given back to the community via permaculture training; attracting visitors, who

HOLMGREN AND HIS FAMILY EAT ENTIRELY IN SEASON. "YOU CAN CHANGE YOUR YIELDS EVER SO SLIGHTLY BY ADJUSTING GROWING TECHNIQUES TO PUSH THE LIMITS OF YOUR SEASON, BUT YOU CAN CHANGE YOUR HUMAN CONSUMPTION BEHAVIORS MUCH MORE," HOLMGREN EXPLAINS.

boost the local economy; and advocacy and sharing ideas on local environmental issues.

"Commitment to our local community has paralleled our increasing self-reliance and wider role in permaculture education," Holmgren writes. "Community self-regulation and governance is a natural extension of the principle of self-reliance. The local ratepayers' association, LETS system [see p. 259 for more on LETS] and community management of public lands have been some areas of our most active involvement in our local community." Such a commitment to reciprocity at a local level is an essential part of the permaculture value system. Through principle 8—integrate rather then segregate—mutual benefit is the result and greater change is possible (see inset piece for Holmgren on the commons, land tenure, and community governance).

Reporting contributed by Colette Schmidt and Rebecca Williams. All photos courtesy of Holmgren design.

LAND TENURE / COMMUNITY GOVERNANCE

AN INTERVIEW WITH DAVID HOLMGREN

Photo: Anne Marie Brookman

I think there has always been a strong crossover between the household- and community-level design in permaculture. From the beginnings of permaculture in the 1970s, there was a close connection to the "back to the land" movement and the counterculture. Within that broad movement, intentional communities and ecovillages were major themes. Many intentional communities around the world have been strongly influenced by permaculture, and some—such as Crystal Waters in Australia and Gaia ecovillage in Argentina—are centers for teaching and demonstrating it. Although permaculture focuses a lot on self-reliance and household economy, there has always been a recognition that some functions need to be done on a larger scale. Intentional communities have been a way of experimenting with some of those aspects of permaculture that weren't so easy to do at the personal or household level.

In places like Denmark, where collective ownership has been well established, intentional communities and cohousing are almost mainstream, but in English-speaking countries, there has been a prevailing view that personal autonomy was more important than collective capacity and that freehold title to land is almost like natural law—a given that we don't question.

Permaculture in its broadest application involves redesign of everything we do according to ecological principles. The question that started permaculture: "What would agriculture look like if we redesigned it using ecological principles—as if we were starting from scratch?"

And it's the same with society. Intentional communities are based on a premise that we have to consciously redesign society from the bottom-up processes of household and community life. This same premise informed earlier waves of intentional communities, in the 1930s and 1890s, reacting against industrialized society that had isolated people in households of nuclear families.

Another connection between permaculture and intentional communities has followed from peoples' difficulty in attempting personal and household self-reliance. The idea of being a self-reliant individual, a jack-of-all-trades, reflecting how traditional rural people used to live, not only requires up-skilling and hard work, it also requires a simplification of requirements and expectations. People have learned either by direct experience or as cultural learning across generations that they need moral, practical, and technical support. This has highlighted the idea

THE QUESTION THAT STARTED PERMACULTURE: "WHAT WOULD AGRICULTURE LOOK LIKE IF WE REDESIGNED IT USING ECOLOGICAL PRINCIPLES—AS IF WE WERE STARTING FROM SCRATCH?"

that collective reliance (rather than self-reliance) in community may be more attractive.

The cost of land has been another element that pushes people toward collective endeavors. In countries like Australia, the United States, Canada, and New Zealand, until recently, people have been able to use savings to buy themselves a piece of land, but in Europe, the costs (and often the land-use planning laws) have made rural resettlement very difficult. Ironically, land prices in Australia are now [in 2013] prohibitive, because the property bubble has not yet burst.

Land reform and debt reform are arguably the two most important political issues worldwide that don't get discussed enough. A debt jubilee for poor countries (to reduce pressure to built export economies) and redistributing land to rural people could increase food production and local economies, avoiding the carrots and sticks driving people into megacities. In affluent countries, debt jubilee is also relevant to deal with the debt crisis and refocus investment on productive land use.

In every society before fossil fuels, the amount of land that was held privately was quite small. There was some collective structure for managing most land in common. In some cases, this was feudal, but more often than not, the commons were managed for mutual benefit. One of the cornerstones of industrialization was the enclosure (privatization) of the commons. It's still going on around the world today.

Permaculture—from its beginnings—said that if you want to design from ecological principles to survive, you look at the models in nature and societies that existed on a renewable energy basis, rather than ones that consume capital (e.g., fossil fuels), because these later ones don't last once their capital assets are exhausted. All the societies that are based on income (i.e., renewable resources) have this pattern of integrated land use, and overlapping land rights, on commonly owned land. This suggests there's a very strong connection between land tenure (how land is owned and how it is used) and long-term societal sustainability.

The freehold land-tenure model we take for granted can only achieve a patchwork of alternate land uses without the synergies of integration. On large feudal estates, integration was the norm to support both the internal economy of the estate and the export wealth that accrued to the owner.

The other way to achieve this integration is some type of common ownership and collective governance structure with overlapping enterprise use. Use rights (license)—rather than just the lease of a patch—encourages integration and stacking of functions within the landscape, which is necessary for permaculture productivity. Thus the forester manages all of the trees in the landscape—whether in avenues or steep catchment forests, it's all silviculture. And the rancher manages the grazing animals everywhere, including into the forested land. It's very hard to do that with the freehold tenure system; it just doesn't work—or it works only to an extremely limited extent.

A big influence on my thinking on broadacre and landscape permaculture was working with Hakai Tane in New Zealand in 1979. Hakai is a land-use planner and resource ecologist, quite an extraordinary person, and my second (permaculture) mentor. He persuaded me that the permaculture vision of integrated broadacre landscapes of field crops, tree crops, grazing, forestry, and aquaculture depended on a land-tenure and settlement pattern different from the conventional freehold-ownership structure that we take for granted. He argued that new land-tenure models (body corporate/condominium) have the potential to create new, integrated land-use patterns using collective ownership and governance, which would include more limited and transferable private ownership of houses and gardens.

At a more practical level, Hakai Tane and I agreed that every broadacre grazing and cropping property needed at least 20 percent tree cover, and most farmers don't have the time or skills to manage trees. It's a completely different skill set and a completely different culture: silviculture. So you need a forester. Every large property also needs a beekeeper, and every farm landscape (excepting arid areas) should have significant water so it can support a livelihood in aquaculture. The cultural difference between traditional cropping farmers and ranchers is ancient—a really different culture and skill set. So, all of these things need to happen together; integrated land uses and livelihoods occupying the same land but carried out by different people.

Intentional communities are effectively pioneering alternative ways of owning land. Most intentional communities, however, haven't got very far with broadacre land use, for all sorts of reasons. Few intentional communities generate much of their livelihood from their land. There is often a conservation and land-restoration ethic, which may be quite valid. On the other hand, it can be an excuse around a consensus to do nothing is easier than a more interventionist plan. Seeing these failures to effectively manage common land has stimulated my own thoughts and modest contributions to modeling common land management both within ecovillages and within the larger public land commons.

From an interview with Rebecca Williams, Melliodora, January 2010.

PART 06

Snow Climates: Continental and Taiga Zones

Continental climates are typified by a broad annual variation in temperature. They usually occur in the interior of continents or on their east coast, north of forty degrees latitude in the Northern Hemisphere. Köppen's map (pp. 22–23) labels these group D climates as snow regions, as they are characterized by snowy winters, with average temperatures in the coldest month dropping to freezing or a few degrees below, though some continental climates have hot summers. In the Southern Hemisphere, continental climates are extremely rare, existing only in some highland locations, due to the lack of land area in corresponding latitudes.

Warmer continental climates support grasslands or mixed deciduous/coniferous forests and a great deal of agricultural activity. The coldest of these climates, known as ***boreal*** or ***taiga*** zones, mainly lie between fifty and seventy degrees latitude in the Northern Hemisphere. Taiga is the world's largest terrestrial biome, covering approximately 17 percent of earth's land. Its range includes most of inland Canada and Alaska, as well as Scandinavia, much of Russia, northern Mongolia, and the northernmost parts of Japan. The term ***boreal forest*** is sometimes used to refer to the more southerly part of the taiga biome, which is a closed-canopy, mainly conifer forest with some deciduous trees, such as maple, elm, and oak. The northernmost part of this biome is called ***lichen woodland*** or ***sparse taiga,*** with smaller, stunted tree species.

Continental climates are experiencing warming that is expected to bring increased winter precipitation, including heavier snowfalls and rainstorms, and more frequent droughts in summer. The average temperature of Wisconsin, in the American Midwest, for example, is expected to increase 8°F–18°F in summer and 6°F–11°F in winter by the end of the century.[1]

Some boreal forest and taiga zones are undergoing a climate shift that is causing noticeable changes in their vegetation. This could create a feedback loop that causes yet more warming by altering the types of trees that grow in the region. When evergreen trees replace species that drop their needles or leaves, as is happening in the Russian boreal forest, more sunlight is absorbed rather than reflected, increasing the ground-level heat retention. If the permafrost covering parts of the taiga melts, its frozen, carbon-rich soil could release large quantities of carbon dioxide into the atmosphere.[2]

Photo: Sean Gold

EcoVillage at Ithaca

Ithaca, New York, U.S.A.

THE CENTRAL CORRIDOR BETWEEN HOMES IS CAR-FREE, SO THAT FRONT YARDS OPEN UP ONTO COMMUNAL SPACE, WHICH NOT ONLY ALLOWS FOR NEIGHBORS TO COME INTO MORE CONTACT BUT MAKES PLAY MUCH SAFER FOR CHILDREN, WHO CAN EXPLORE THE INDOOR AND OUTDOOR SPACES OF THE ECOVILLAGE FREELY.

Founded by two single mothers, Joan Bokaer and Liz Walker, in 1991, EcoVillage at Ithaca (EVI) was the first cohousing community to be established in the eastern United States. It includes three neighborhoods on 176 acres (71 hectares), where a developer had initially planned 150 conventional subdivision homes. The first two neighborhoods have thirty attached homes each; at the time of this writing, the latest neighborhood is developing forty units, which will create a resident population of about five hundred. Ithaca, located two miles from the ecovillage, is a medium-sized city that is home to several universities. The region has the hot summers and cold, snowy winters typical of a continental climate.

"The ultimate goal of EVI is to redesign human habitat by creating a model community that will exemplify sustainable systems of living—systems that are not only practical in themselves but replicable by others," reads the ecovillage mission statement.[3] The project demonstrates the feasibility of a site design that provides housing, energy, social interaction, and food production while supporting natural ecosystems. The ecovillage includes a community-supported agriculture plot that feeds about one thousand subscribers in the growing season and a pick-your-own berry farm with five varieties of berries.

The cohousing movement began in Denmark in 1968, inspired by a newspaper article, "Children Should Have One Hundred Parents." Planned, managed, and owned by residents, cohousing communities are made up of private homes and shared facilities like a kitchen, classrooms, playrooms, gardens, and a laundry. Today, hundreds exist in Denmark and northern Europe, with about 300 in the Netherlands, 120 in the United States (and about 100 more in the planning stages), and a number in Canada, Australia, and the United Kingdom. Cohousing is designed to maximize social interaction between residents, who often share meals and other activities. While these communities can be rural, suburban, or urban, housing is clustered to allow more open land for shared use and residents often park cars on the periphery of the development.

THE PRINCIPLE OF **CREATIVELY USE AND RESPOND TO CHANGE** IS WELL ILLUSTRATED BY THIS PERGOLA, WHICH IS SHADED BY GRAPE LEAVES IN SUMMER BUT ALLOWS FOR SOLAR GAIN IN WINTER WHEN THE LEAVES FALL.

TOOLS/TECHNOLOGY

Catching and Storing Energy: On average, households at the ecovillage use about half of the energy and half of the water of a typical American house. A number of homes have rainwater-catchment and/or gray-water systems, and photovoltaic arrays on the rooftops meet about half of the community's energy requirements.

"EVI takes a pragmatic approach to ecological sustainability. Rather than opt for the sexiest (and often most expensive) appropriate technologies, we put our money into energy reduction measures first," cofounder Liz Walker writes. "Some of those measures are not easy to spot (super-insulated homes that have been oriented for maximum solar exposure are less visibly 'ecological' than are windmills and solar panels, for example), but that doesn't mean they aren't effective. Taken together they add up. We are building a 'green' community and culture, rather than individual state-of-the-art 'green' buildings."

LAND TENURE/COMMUNITY GOVERNANCE

A Hybrid Model of Land Ownership: Like most cohousing communities, EVI is a hybrid of private and communal ownership. Individuals or families own the housing units, while the land is owned separately, similar to a condominium structure. In this case, the nonprofit educational organization that started the project owns the majority of the land, while the homeowners collectively own the land immediately surrounding the housing through a group called the Village Association.

We make decisions by consensus, a process in which all points of view are taken into account. Objections get raised and solutions are proposed to address them. Facilitators help us work toward achieving a "group mind," in which commonly-held values lead to a clear consensus. After much discussion the community as a whole comes to a decision with which everyone can agree. Sometimes an individual may disagree with the decision but still agrees to abide by it—an acceptable choice within the consensus process. If someone feels very strongly that a group decision is wrong, then the consensus process allows a person to "block" it. Since proposals only come to the floor for a decision after weeks of discussion, proposal writing, and committee meetings, blocking a decision is a very serious step. And usually a very rare one.[4]

"WHEN I CAME, THERE WAS ALREADY A DECISION TO MAKE IT A MAINSTREAM-ORIENTED MODEL THAT WOULD DRAW IN THE MIDDLE CLASS AND SHOW PEOPLE THAT IS WAS POSSIBLE TO LIVE A MORE ECOLOGICAL LIFESTYLE AND STILL BE COMFORTABLE."—ELAN SHAPIRO, FOUNDING RESIDENT

"ONE OF THE THINGS I LIKE ABOUT HAVING A KID HERE IS THAT SHE GETS TO GO OUT TO THE CHICKEN HOUSE TO GATHER THE EGGS, OR CLIMB A CHERRY TREE AND EAT CHERRIES. . . . SHE'S GROWING UP ABLE TO RUN AROUND WILD, WITH A REALLY NICE SET OF EXPERIENCES, NOT JUST SUPERVISED PLAYDATES."

CULTURE/EDUCATION

Learning in a Village: "Child-rearing in our cohousing neighborhood differs from the mainstream. Most kids seldom if ever watch TV—they are far too busy participating in the day-to-day activities of the village community. At EVI children learn conflict resolution skills from the earliest age. And the six- to twelve-year-olds participate in a 'Kids Council,' where they take part in developing their own behavioral guidelines and doing fun projects, such as building a bike trail," explains Walker.

The ecovillage offers community meals nearly every other day in one of the common houses, which have a common kitchen and workshop space, as well as offices, a playroom, and shared laundry facilities.

"At the start, we were not so focused on sustainability and self-sufficiency, but times have changed," observes Elan Shapiro, one of the founding residents, who teaches sustainability at local universities, holds retreats and trainings at the ecovillage, and organizes and networks for urban community gardens in low-income neighborhoods. It's the role that we play in the movement, to show people that it can be done."

An educational center offers courses in the social and ecological aspects of cohousing to residents, visitors, and students at the local colleges. As one of the pioneer ecovillages in the United States, EVI has played a major role in showing how it's done to people interested in building similar communities nationally and around the world.

Reporting contributed by Juliana Birnbaum.
Photos by Louis Fox.

Growing Power

Milwaukee, Wisconsin, U.S.A.

Photo: Peter DiAntoni, courtesy of Yes! magazine

WILL ALLEN AND HIS DAUGHTER, ERIKA, FIGHT "FOOD RACISM" WITH A NETWORK OF PROJECTS, INCLUDING THIS AQUAPONIC GREENHOUSE IN MILWAUKEE. THE SPROUTS IN THE FOREGROUND LIE ABOVE A FOUR-FOOT DEEP, WATER-FILLED TRENCH HOLDING TEN THOUSAND TILAPIA AND YELLOW PERCH.

At the northern outskirts of Milwaukee, in a neighborhood of boxy post–World War II homes near the sprawling Park Lawn housing project, stand fourteen greenhouses arrayed on two acres of land. This is Growing Power, the only land within the Milwaukee city limits zoned as farmland. Founded by MacArthur Foundation Fellow Will Allen, Growing Power is an active farm producing tons of produce each year; it's also a food-distribution hub, organic soil–production facility, and a training center. It's the home base for an expanding network of similar food centers as well, including a Chicago branch run by Allen's daughter, Erika. The farm is located in a food desert, a part of the city devoid of full-service grocery stores but lined with fast-food joints, liquor stores, and convenience stores selling mostly soda, processed snacks, and sweets. Growing Power is an oasis in that desert.

☼ LAND/NATURE STEWARDSHIP

Urban Agriculture and Aquaculture: Since 1993 Allen has focused on developing Growing Power's urban-agriculture project, which grows vegetables and fruit in its greenhouses, raises goats, ducks, bees, chickens, turkeys, and—in an aquaponic system designed by Allen—tilapia and Great Lakes perch. Altogether, it grows 159 varieties of food.

Growing Power also has a 40-acre (16-hectare) rural farm in Merton, outside Milwaukee, with about an eighth of the space devoted to intensive vegetable growing and the balance used for sustainably grown hay, grasses, and legumes, which provide food for the urban farm's livestock.

Growing Power composts more than six million pounds of food waste a year, including the farm's own waste, material from local food distributors, spent grain from a local brewery, and the grounds from a local coffee shop. Allen counts as part of his livestock the red wiggler worms that turn that waste into "Milwaukee Black Gold" worm castings.

Allen designed an aquaponic system, which he built for just $3,000, a fraction of the $50,000 cost of a commercially built system. In addition to tilapia, a common fish in aquaculture, Allen also raises yellow perch, a fish once a staple of the Milwaukee diet, before pollution and overfishing killed the Lake Michigan perch fishery. Growing Power will soon make this local favorite available again. The aquaponic system has ten thousand fingerlings, which grow to market size in as little as nine months.

Photo: Mercedes (Creative Commons)

JUST AS SOME PERMACULTURALISTS STRIVE TO CULTIVATE EDIBLE ABUNDANCE IN REMOTE DESERT LANDSCAPES, SO DOES WILL ALLEN IN THIS MILWAUKEE NEIGHBORHOOD—WHAT HE CALLS A "FOOD DESERT."

But the fish are only one product of Allen's aquaponic system. The water from the fish tanks flows into a gravel bed, where the waste breaks down to produce nitrogen in a form plants can use. The gravel bed supports a crop of watercress, which further filters the water. The nutrient-rich water is then pumped to overhead beds to feed crops of tomatoes and salad greens. The plants extract the

Photo: Ryan Griffis, temporarytraveloffice.net

PRODUCE NO WASTE, AND STACK FUNCTIONS FOR MULTIPLE YIELDS. WILL ALLEN SHOWS THE FISH IN ONE OF GROWING POWER'S 4-FOOT-DEEP, 10,000-GALLON AQUAPONIC TANKS. WASTE FROM THE FISH FEEDS GREENS AND TOMATOES. THE PLANTS PURIFY THE WATER FOR THE FISH. THE FISH EVENTUALLY GO TO MARKET.

nutrients, while the worms in the soil consume bacteria from the water, which emerges virtually pristine and flows back into the fish tanks. This vertical growing system multiplies the productivity of the farm's limited space.

FINANCES/ECONOMICS

Green Employment in a Job Desert: Growing Power also provides thirty-five good-paying jobs in an area of high unemployment. The staff at Growing Power is highly diverse—a mixture of young and old, African American, white, Asian, Native American, and Latino, with remarkably varied work histories. Some are former professionals who left the high-stress environments of corporations, social work, and other fields. Others are former blue-collar workers, farmers, or recent college graduates.

HEALTH/SPIRITUAL WELL-BEING

Dismantling Racism in the Food System: Allen also works on the Growing Food and Justice Initiative, a national network of about five hundred people that fights what he calls "food racism"—the structural denial of wholesome food to poor African American and Latino neighborhoods. "One of our four strategic goals is to dismantle racism in the food system. Just as there is redlining in lending, there is redlining by grocery stores, denying access to people of color by staying out of minority communities."

The store at Growing Power's Milwaukee farm is the only place for miles around that carries fresh produce, free-range eggs, grass-fed beef, and locally produced honey. Even in winter, customers find the handmade shelves and aging coolers stocked with fresh-picked salad greens. "Low-quality food is resulting in diabetes, obesity, and sickness from processed food," Allen maintains. "Poor people are not educated about nutrition and don't have access to stores that sell nutritious food, and they wind up with diabetes and heart disease."

Growing Power supplements its own products with food from the Rainbow Farming Cooperative, which Allen started at the same time as Growing Power. The cooperative is made up of about three hundred family farms in Wisconsin, Michigan, northern Illinois, and the South. The southern farmers, who are primarily African Americans, make it possible to offer fresh fruits and vegetables year-round. The produce goes into Growing Power's popular Farm-to-City Market Baskets—a week's supply of twelve to fifteen varieties of produce costs $16. A $9 "Junior/Senior" basket, with smaller quantities of the same produce, is also available.

Photo: Justin Leonard (Creative Commons)

PUTTING A FARM RIGHT IN A CITY IS A GREAT EXAMPLE OF **INTEGRATE RATHER THAN SEGREGATE.** IT REDUCES "FOOD MILES," CREATES MEANINGFUL JOBS, RECONNECTS URBAN DWELLERS TO NATURE, AND INCREASES FOOD SECURITY.

Each Friday, Growing Power delivers 275 to 350 Market Baskets of food to more than twenty agencies, community centers, and other sites around Milwaukee for distribution. Bernita Samson, a retiree in her sixties with eight grandchildren, picked up the Market Basket habit from her brother and late mother. "I get the biggest kick out of what I get in my bag each week," she says. "At Sunday dinners my grandkids say, 'Oh, Grandma, this is good!' They really like what they call the 'smashed potatoes.' "

For Samson, Growing Power provides not only healthy food but also a vital source of community.

"Sometimes it's so crowded at the [Growing Power] store on Saturdays you can't even get up in there. Going there gives you a chance to meet people and talk."

CULTURE/EDUCATION

Hands-on Learning: Four middle schools and high schools bring students to Growing Power to learn about vermiculture (raising worms) and growing crops—and to eat the food they've grown. The program provides year-round gardening activities for children and teens at its Milwaukee headquarters and offers summertime farming experience on its parcel in Merton, which is adjacent to the Boys and Girls Club's Camp Mason. Growing Power recently leased 5 acres at Milwaukee's Maple Tree School and built a community garden in partnership with the school. Growing Power also assists school gardens at the Urban Day School and the University School of Milwaukee.

"For kids to make their own soil, grow their own food, and then get to eat it, that's a very powerful experience," Will Allen says. "There's nothing like hands-on experience for kids who are bored with school. They get excited about what they're learning and then take it back to their classes."

Every year, ten thousand people tour the Growing Power farms. In addition, about three thousand youths and adults from around the world participate in formal training sessions, learning how to build aquaponic systems, construct hoop houses (low-cost greenhouses covered by clear plastic), use compost to heat greenhouses, use worms to turn waste into rich fertilizer, and all the other low-tech, high-yield techniques that Growing Power has developed or adapted. The center also hosts an annual National-International Urban & Small Farm Conference, which has brought together thousands of participants to share ideas about building more resilient, community-based food systems.

"Growing Power is probably the leading urban-agricultural project in the United States," says Jerry Kaufman, a professor emeritus in urban and regional planning at the University of Wisconsin–Madison. "Growing Power is not just talking about what needs to be changed, it's accomplishing it."

Reporting contributed by Roger Bybee, from "Growing Power in an Urban Food Desert, originally printed in YES! magazine, Spring 2009

The Federation of Damanhur

Piedmont, Italy

HUMAN BEINGS CRAVE AESTHETIC SURROUNDINGS AND UNIQUE EXPERIENCES. CREATIVE INSPIRATION AND TALENT CAN BE SEEN AS LEGITIMATE RESOURCES AND THE RESULTING ART AS A VALUABLE YIELD IN BOTH A SPIRITUAL SENSE AND ECONOMIC SENSE. DAMANHUR'S TEMPLE COMPLEX BRINGS A STEADY STREAM OF TOURISTS, THOUGH THAT WASN'T THE PURPOSE OF THEIR CONSTRUCTION.

A community of one thousand thrives in the foothills of the Alps of northern Italy, known as the Federation of Damanhur ("the city of light"), named after an ancient Egyptian city. Its citizens live in diverse, multifamily dwellings they call *nucleos,* scattered throughout the Valchiusella Valley and including approximately 1,200 acres (485 hectares) of land. The Piedmont region has a unique ecosystem: sheltered by the Alps to the north and west and the Mediterranean Sea to the south, it has cold winters and warm, dry summers; it is considered a continental climate. Damanhur has productive organic farms, schools, healing and arts centers, over sixty diverse businesses, an alternative currency, and laboratories for scientific research—illustrating many principles of thriving, living systems. Its stated purpose is to learn, practice, and share ways that humans might live sustainably on the earth. Already several decades into its quest, Damanhur is committed to exchanging understandings with others through leadership in the Global Ecovillage Network, the School of Meditation, and workshops that attract thousands. Related centers have been established in other parts of Italy and Europe, Japan, and the United States. Visitors come to visit the amazing underground, hand-dug temples and to learn about Damanhur's rich culture and ambitious work in ecological, spiritual, and social realms.

DAMANHUR'S TEMPLES WERE AN IMMENSE LABOR OF CREATIVE AND SPIRITUAL DEDICATION, HELPING FORM A COHESIVE COMMUNITY.

In the mid 1970s, two dozen Italians coalesced into a community in the Valchiusella Valley, thirty miles north of Turin. Inspired by their multifaceted leader, Oberto Airaudi ("Falco," 1950–2013), they focused their energies on the seemingly impossible task of excavating an underground cavern. It was tedious work, carving into the rock entirely with hand tools, but they shared a common vision and were inspired to accomplish their goal together. They concealed their work from the public for fourteen years, hiding more than two million buckets of earth and rock, integrating it into other buildings and structures. As underground rooms were completed, their project changed from construction to art and creative expression; they covered walls, floors, and ceilings with ornate and beautiful mosaic images, symbolic and full of meaning. The intricate series of temple rooms spreading out in the depths of hewn caverns became canvasses for the talented and inspired artists. The daunting physical challenge of the project was the social glue that created a cohesive community, and the process of working together for a common vision became a pattern for the further evolution of the Damanhur community.

Photo: Louis Fox

Photo: Louis Fox

Years later, the excavation came to the attention of regional authorities, who initially called the excavation a hazard and planned to destroy the work. When they saw the temples, however, with their quality workmanship and engineering and the exquisite beauty of the architecture and artwork, they declared them a regional treasure. Thousands of tourists visit the site yearly, which generates significant income for Damanhur. The temples, however, are only an outward indication of the spiritual depth that is core to the community's existence.

HEALTH/SPIRITUAL WELL-BEING

Shared Community Superconsciousness: While Damanhur is a leader in the Global Ecovillage Network and it has many of the features of secular ecovillages, it considers itself foremost a spiritual community. The founders chose the location because they believed it lies at the intersection of multiple "synchronic lines" of spiritual energy. They constructed (and are still expanding) the temples in part to be connected to that underground energy of synchronic lines. Damanhurians spend much of their time in ritual and spiritual practice, seeking a shared community consciousness. Their School of Meditation teaches these practices to citizens, as well as to interested people globally, believing this "superconsciousness" is key to human sustainability on the planet. Damanhurian teachings derive from past civilizations and practices and utilize esoteric research and technologies for healing and incorporating health into daily existence.

LAND TENURE/COMMUNITY GOVERNANCE

Nucleos: As Damanhur has grown through the years, it has evolved a unique structure—a "holarchy" with a large system containing subsystems, analogous to the patterns of natural systems. When a group of Damanhurians purchase an old farmhouse for renovating, it becomes a new living unit they call a *nucleo*. There are over thirty *nucleos*, each with about two dozen residents, who become a "family" that creates agreements and lives together as a close-knit, interdependent

COMBINING A CENTRALIZED AND DECENTRALIZED MODEL, DAMANHUR IS ORGANIZED INTO ABOUT THIRTY SEMI-AUTONOMOUS COLLECTIVES CALLED *NUCLEOS*, WHICH GOVERN THEIR DAILY AFFAIRS, WHILE THE FEDERATION COORDINATES THE OVERARCHING VISION. THE FARM PICTURED HERE IS PART OF PRIMA STALLA, ONE OF THE MAIN FOOD-PRODUCING *NUCLEOS*.

community. That is an appropriate size to foster the daily relationships necessary for shared decision making and the housekeeping needed to live harmoniously. Each family eats together, shares costs, and has weekly meetings to discuss issues of the *nucleo* and the larger Federation of Damanhur.

Each *nucleo* has a unique focus, such as a business or service that benefits the federation. There are different options for citizenship at Damanhur, with differing degrees of financial commitment and benefits. The federation owns the buildings and land in common and distributes financial contributions according to *nucleo* and broader needs.

Federation governance is involves a written constitution and three elected "guides" who work with the *nucleo* captains to make decisions for the federation, with weekly citizen meetings for feedback and discussion. The original founder, Falco, took on an advisory role throughout his life, meeting with the entire community on a weekly basis to answer and discuss questions of spiritual and local importance. In all, the unit subsystems of *nucleos* are of a scale that favors daily relationships, while the federation is on a scale that supports the common focus of community sustainability in all its aspects: financial, spiritual, ecological, and social.

In 1985 a group of Damanhurians undertook a yearlong experiment in complete self-sufficiency, the "Olio Caldo Project." The intention of the project was to live entirely on what they produced or could trade for within the community—shelter, food, clothing, shoes, tools, bags, energy, and furniture. The yearlong experiment morphed into a long-term goal for the entire community of Damanhur.

LAND/NATURE STEWARDSHIP

Ecological and Climactic Balance: From the beginning, when the first land was purchased and designated as the Sacred Forest, Damanhurians have been committed to understand and connect with the natural world. Native-plant restoration occurs in the forest preserve and elsewhere to stress the value of connecting to the spirits of the earth, plants, and animals. They generally do both the commercial-scale farming and home-scale gardening using organic or biodynamic methods, rather than with permaculture-specific practices, though this may be shifting. There is a growing appreciation and practice of permaculture food-production systems in some of the more experimental *nucleos,* such as pond aquaculture and *hugelkulturs* (a permaculture technique that was traditional to Eastern Europe, in which layered garden beds are created using "waste" biomass, including fallen logs).

FINANCES/ECONOMICS

Developing a Local Economy: One way Damanhur supports its local economy is with its own currency—the minted ***credito*** coins, which are accepted by Damanhurian businesses (for more on local currencies, see p. 256). The *credito* is actually a proxy currency, since it can be exchanged one-to-one for euros, which means that local economic "energy" can escape outside the community. There is an emotional benefit associated with *credito* use within the community, however, and there were serious proposals to discontinue the *credito*/euro exchange during the global economic crisis of 2008. The community has also discussed sharing the *credito* as a common complementary currency among other members of the Global Ecovillage Network.

Photo: Hildur Jackson

DAMANHUR'S OWN CURRENCY, THE *CREDITO*.

Damanhur has made a considerable investment in their main production farm, Prima Stalla, a *nucleo* on valley bottomland. Food from fields, greenhouses, and a herd of beef cattle is sold to other *nucleos*. Most *nucleos* also have their own greenhouses and gardens, but gardening depends on labor outside of citizens' day jobs. As prices of produce escalate, it is becoming more feasible for Damanhurians to quit their day jobs and garden to lower food costs.

"DAMANHUR AND ITS TEMPLES OF HUMANKIND ARE A BEACON OF POSSIBILITY FOR THE FUTURE." —ALEX GREY, PAINTER

BUILDING

Renovated Farmhouses and New Buildings: Most of the *nucleos* incorporate some aspects of sustainability in their built environment. A key contributor to energy conservation is the shared housing in large farmhouses, which reduces the community's carbon footprint. Both renovated farmhouses and new buildings use energy-saving technologies. Space- and water-heating systems use large-scale furnaces with sustainably harvested local wood. Sun orientation, window placement, and construction materials maximize energy efficiencies, and most buildings have photovoltaic panels and solar water heaters. A number of Damanhurian businesses work in the fields of solar technology and energy-efficient renovation. Many *nucleos* have water catchment and storage systems, and some are experimenting with natural building methods, including straw-bale and earth-bag houses.

TOOLS/TECHNOLOGY

A Community of Innovators: Damanhur excels in experimenting with alternative technology innovations. Some *nucleos* are working with solar-tracking collectors for water heating, geothermal heating systems, and algae-based energy production systems. Today, the federation provides 70 percent of its hot-water supplies through passive-solar installations; 35 percent of its electricity from photovoltaics and small hydroelectric turbines, and 90 percent of its own heating requirements through sustainably harvested wood. In addition, 35 percent of Damanhurians use biodiesel cars (there is a supply pump on-site) and 40 percent have cars that run on methane or liquid gas.

Reporting contributed by Chuck Estin and Juliana Birnbaum.
Photos courtesy of Damanhur Federation of Communities, unless otherwise noted.

Kovcheg Ecovillage

Kaluga, Russia

ELENA LAZUTINA WITH WHEAT HARVESTED THE TRADITIONAL WAY, BY HAND. AN UNQUANTIFIABLE BENEFIT OF GROWING, HARVESTING, AND PREPARING ONE'S OWN FOOD IS THE DEEP SENSE OF CONNECTION AND APPRECIATION ONE GAINS FROM SOMETHING AS ROUTINE AS EATING.

Kovcheg Ecovillage was founded in 2001 when four families leased just under 300 acres (120 hectares) of former agricultural land from the government—a forty-nine-year government lease at no charge. The plot is located 87 miles (140 km) southwest of Moscow, in the Kaluga region. The establishment and setup of this community is characteristically Russian, a culture that highly values closeness with nature and the seasons; 70 percent of Russians are gardeners (see p. 314 for more on Russia's home gardens).

Kovcheg—the name means "ark"—was inspired by the Anastasia movement associated with Vladmir Megre's Ringing Cedars of Russia book series, which offers details on principles for living close to the earth in a self-sufficient village of "kin's domains," or family homesteads. The Anastasia movement is named after the books' central character, who lives in simple and harmonious relationship with the woodland forest around her. The books describe framework and design strategies that have many similarities to permaculture philosophy and have sparked a neo-homesteading movement that combines spiritual ecology with traditional family values quite different from the countercultural lifestyle associated with the 1960s-era back-to-the-landers (see inset for more on the crossover between permaculture and the Anastasia movement). Anastasia centers can also be found in Australia, Belarus, Bulgaria, Canada, Croatia, Czech Republic, Germany, Ireland, Israel, Kazakhstan, Kyrgyzstan, Latvia, Lithuania, the Netherlands, New Zealand, Romania, Slovakia, Slovenia, Switzerland, Tajikistan, Ukraine, United Kingdom, and the United States.

KOVCHEG PRINCIPLES

Every member or family unit is allocated 2.5 acres (1 hectare)

Decision making at community meetings by 75 percent majority

Permanent residence at the ecovillage is encouraged

Only organic gardening allowed

No smoking or alcohol

All toilets are composting

No animals kept for meat

No constructed fences between plots

BUILDING

Simplicity and Minimalism: In accordance with the principles of the Anastasia movement, the permanent families in Kovcheg live on 2.5-acre (1-hectare) homesites. Seventy-nine plots include homes, personal gardens, and beehives, with a large central area reserved for common use and a circle of farm and woodland on the perimeter. Similar to the zones approach in permaculture, this pattern is emulated by many communities that prefer to grow food in larger quantities on the outskirts of the ecovillage. Along with the shared infrastructure, such as bucket-drawn wells, the community collectively owns some tools and heavy equipment, such as a tractor, excavator, grader, and large truck.

Since inception in 2001, the Kovcheg members have built more than a hundred houses of varying sizes. They built most of the houses by themselves, at a rate of twelve to twenty per year. They mostly used lumber milled on-site and insulated the houses from the winter cold with clay-straw walls. Shared facilities include a traditional Russian sauna, a school, a sustainability video library, and a large building that functions as a place for gathering and holding events.

Photo: Leonid Sharashkin

THE COMMUNITY CENTER—THE FIRST BUILDING ERECTED IN KOVCHEG—NOW WITH A SCHOOL ANNEX.

CULTURE/EDUCATION

Teaching Sustainable Living Skills: Kovcheg offers courses in ecovillage living, natural building, and sustainable beekeeping. In 2005 they produced an instructional video, "How to Build a Warm Winter Home with Light Clay-Straw," geared toward the below-freezing temperatures of Russia. They have hosted three ecovillage gatherings. In February 2009 sixty visitors from twenty-five other ecovillage projects in Russia and other former Soviet countries came for four days of workshops and networking. The village common house, in the center of the settlement, is the hub for community culture—whether it is art, language, or music classes.

HEALTH/SPIRITUAL WELL-BEING

Holistic Lifestyle: Kovcheg members strive for a holistic, healthy lifestyle. Asked about their reasons for moving to Kovcheg residents mention common themes, including the ability to devote more time

TALENT IS A KOVAHEG ON-SITE RESOURCE. THOUGH THE VILLAGE IS 140 KILOMETERS [ABOUT 87 MILES] FROM THE METROPOLIS OF MOSCOW, ITS OWN COMMUNITY CENTER IS THE POPULAR HUB FOR CULTURE. RESIDENTS GIVE BACK THROUGH TEACHING OR OFFERING THEIR PROFESSIONAL SKILLS IN SOME WAY

to one's family, a desire to leave the expense and money-orientation of city life, and the opportunity to be one's own boss. Also cited are the desire to live in closer community with neighbors; a better sense of safety and security; and environmental factors, such as cleaner air, soil, and water. The ecovillage is free of drugs, cigarettes, and alcohol.

☼ LAND/NATURE STEWARDSHIP

Deep Ecology: Collectively, the residents of Kovcheg appear to be deeply connected to their forest surroundings. The deep, ecological philosophy elaborated in the Ringing Cedars *Anastasia* books (see p. 312) underpins decisions made at the village. The perspective transcends simple aesthetic appreciation; the residents embrace the resources presented by the forest and strive toward a holistic

KOVCHEG RESIDENTS BELIEVE THAT CREATING HEALTHY AND NURTURING ENVIRONMENTS FOR CHILDREN'S DEVELOPING BODIES AND MINDS IS KEY TO A POSITIVE FUTURE. BILL MOLLISON TALKS ABOUT THE PRINCIPLE OF **SUCCESSION:** "RECOGNIZE THAT CERTAIN ELEMENTS PREPARE THE WAY FOR SYSTEMS TO SUPPORT OTHER ELEMENTS IN THE FUTURE."

management approach. They employ numerous techniques, such as careful pruning, clearing underbrush, planting new trees, and halting illegal woodcutting by others, to ensure the forest around them thrives. In order to sustainably manage the woodland—and to provide some income—the residents operate their own sawmill and a woodworking shop.

"We log ill trees and take them away," says biologist and village cofounder Fedor Lazutin. "The bushes and small trees keep growing, so the forest can recover. Many trees don't adapt well to the increasingly hot summers. So we are logging more and more diseased trees to save the forest." According to Lazutin, the forest was once mixed coniferous and broadleaf trees, but was replanted with coniferous only. These trees are not adapting well to warm summer temperatures, which are on the rise, due to climate change.

KOVCHEG RESIDENTS ARE AVID BEEKEEPERS. AT SEMINARS, THEY SHARE THEIR KNOWLEDGE OF BEEKEEPING WITH MINIMAL INTERVENTION AND WITHOUT DRUGS OR SUGAR WATER. THE SYMBIOTIC RELATIONSHIP HUMANS CAN CULTIVATE WITH BEES EXEMPLIFIES MANY PERMACULTURE PRINCIPLES: **AIDING NATURAL CYCLES, USING SMALL AND SLOW SOLUTIONS, USING AND PRESERVING BIOLOGICAL RESOURCES AND INTELLIGENCE.**

☼ LAND TENURE/COMMUNITY GOVERNANCE

Gradual Growth: Not all of the homes at Kovcheg are insulated enough to be able to withstand the harsh winter conditions in Russia. Because of this, Kovcheg has become a seasonal retreat for many; with the summer population reaching roughly two hundred people. There are forty families (about 120 people) who live in Kovcheg year-round and form the core of this ecovillage, making it one of the successful Anastasia-style ecovillages in Russia.

The ideology behind the settlement is straightforward and easy to replicate. The first priority is to identify the vision and principles that will serve as the foundation for the community. The next step is gradual growth that encourages sustainability.

Though they share similar worldviews, the residents of Kovcheg are a diverse mix. One of the founders is a former successful businessman who moved from the city to the country for the sake of his child. He now wórks as a beekeeper and gardener. Other residents include former wrestlers, fashion models, and opera singers. Many would agree that this variety of cultural and occupational backgrounds gives the community its own personality.

Kovcheg members devised a set of clear guidelines that helped considerably in their establishment as a government-approved settlement. These include agreements for drafting meeting agendas and running meetings efficiently. The community is governed via whole-group meetings four or five times per year, using a 75-percent supermajority vote for significant decisions and a majority-rule vote for simpler items. Specific committees for various agendas and activities manage the ecovillage the rest of the year.

Kovcheg has a two-year provisional membership period, and requires new residents to move to their plot permanently during this time. Although members can sell their plot and leave the ecovillage, the buyer must be approved by the group. If a member violates the community's agreements, depending on the severity or consistency of the violations, the community is able to exclude that member from using the common facilities, such as roads, effectively rendering them unable to access their plot. So far the community has not had to use this provision.

THE BEEHIVES BUILT BY KOVCHEG COFOUNDER FEDOR LAZUTIN WEATHER THE COLD RUSSIAN WINTER.

FINANCES/ECONOMICS

Transparent Systems: A formal, detailed accounting system has been put into place for all money matters. "Trust and check" is an old Russian proverb, and since tradition is a strong factor at Kovcheg, finances are well managed. There is full transparency in the use of common funds and, instead of having a single leader, responsibility is shared among all members. The ethos here is simple: if you don't like the way a job is being done, show a better way and contribute to the solution. The economy is partly supported by the educational programs and the sale of artisanal crafts, but most people commute into the city one or two days a month to supplement their incomes.

Reporting contributed by Muneezay Jaffery.
*Photos courtesy of **Keeping Bees with a Smile** by Fedor Lazuti, unless noted otherwise.*

THE ANASTASIA MOVEMENT

The Anastasia movement is publicly aligning itself with and promoting the philosophy and design strategies of permaculture. Many tried-and-true permaculture techniques can be recognized in the Anastasia material published by Ringing Cedars. Here are a few similarities:

• Multipurpose hedgerows: One of the distinctive features of Anastasia's "kin's domains" is that each domain is surrounded by a hedge of trees and shrubs, which provide privacy, windbreak, shade, shelter, habitat, food, and medicine for humans, similar to many permaculture designs.

• Natural building methods: Anastasia stresses that people should build their own homes to the extent they are physically capable. Natural, local materials predominate and a high level of craftsmanship is displayed; each house is highly individualized.

• The integration of animals into agricultural systems: Anastasia texts mention chickens and dairy and meat animals (This reflects the real-life situation on the ground. In Russia, 60 percent of the meat and 49 percent of the dairy products are produced at the home scale.

• Forest Gardens: Anastasia literature strongly emphasizes fruit production. The descriptions leave no doubt that they are referring to species-rich, multistory polyculture. The typical Russian gardener grows thirteen different kinds of vegetables and seven different fruit, berry, and nut crops on the same small plot.

• Inclusion of minimally managed wildlands into human settlements: Anastasia stresses that creating a habitat for a wide biodiversity of birds, insects, bees, and butterflies—think pollinators, predators, and checks and balances—is part of a healthy human-wildlife interface.

But Anastasia is far from a dry text on permaculture techniques—the books read more like fantasy novels, with elements of the supernatural and the spiritual, and there is some debate over whether the events are real or fictional. Vladmir Megre, author of the series, describes a chance encounter with a young woman named Anastasia on the bank of the River Ob in 1994. She reportedly led him deep into the Siberian taiga, where she revealed her philosophy on humanity's relationship to nature, the

"THERE ARE HUNDREDS OF THOUSANDS WHO ARE DISCOVERING MORE AND MORE TRUTH WITHIN THEMSELVES AND ARE CHANGING THEIR WAY OF LIFE AT THE CORE." —ANASTASIA

universe, and God, as well as on lifestyle, education, nutrition, spirituality, love, family, sexual relations, and plants.

Anastasia is what some would call a "fully realized human being," or even a superhuman being. In the novels, she has the ability to translocate her body, not only to other places on the earth, but to other planets in other solar systems. She has the ability to see at a distance, as well as many other extraordinary abilities. Anastasia is deeply in love with the earth. She connects with all the life-forms around her. She can communicate with the wild animals, and they willingly serve her. "To be healthy, one must feed one's self with lovingly grown produce," she advises.[5] Throughout the texts, she points out many times that eating food grown on corporate, mechanized farms is not good for our health or our spirit.

The word **permaculture** is mentioned in Megre's text several times, and Dr. Leonid Sharashkin (see his article on the following page), the English-language editor of the nine Anastasia books, has produced a video called "Reconnecting to Nature through Spiritual Permaculture," which ties together agroforestry, permaculture, and the Anastasia principles.

Reporting contributed by Michael Pilarski. ***Anastasia*** *cover art courtesy of Ringing Cedars of Russia (www.ringingcedarsofrussia.org). Art by Alexander Razboinikov.*

LAND / NATURE STEWARDSHIP

THIRTY MILLION PERMACULTURISTS: RUSSIAN HOME GARDENS

Photo: Rob Lee (Creative Commons)

What Russian industry produces more wealth than steel manufacturing; more than electric power generation; more than the chemical and pharmaceutical sector; more than forestry, timber, pulp, and paper industries put together; or more than manufacture of building materials? What Russian industry contributes a greater share to gross domestic product (GDP) than the oil refining, natural gas, and coal industries combined? The answer is—as mind-boggling as it may sound—the family food gardens.

Today, just as a hundred years ago—or a thousand years ago—the majority of Russia's agricultural output is coming not from large-scale, commercial, industrialized operations, but from family gardens. Russia's food gardens currently produce over half of the country's food and represent one of the largest sectors of the country's economy, involving two-thirds of the population.

According to official data, over thirty million Russian families engage in food gardening and, collectively, are more productive than the farming sector, while using less than 6 percent of agricultural land in the country! Russian gardeners produce up to forty times more value per acre than commercial farmers. These bountiful harvests are all the more amazing given the government's long-standing policy of allocating only the least productive, marginal lands for community gardens.

During the Soviet period, when all land was government-owned, Russian families could only get minuscule plots. This, however, promoted extremely intensive growing practices and the proliferation of highly diverse, multistoried permaculture gardening techniques, where a large number of perennial crops (fruit-bearing trees and shrubs) were interplanted with annual vegetable crops. There was simply not enough land at people's disposal to do it any other way.

Research on the economic, agricultural, social, and spiritual dimensions of family gardening in one of Russia's oldest provinces (the Vladimir region, east of Moscow) showed that 95 percent of families either tend their own garden or benefit from the gardens of others. These highly diverse, predominantly organic operations include, on average, thirteen different vegetable crops and seven different perennial fruit, nut, and berry crops grown on the same small plots—veritable microscale permaculture gardens with predominantly organic methods.[6]

According to government data, Russia's gardening families grow over, 11.5 million tons of vegetables, and 3.2 million tons of fruit and berries, which represent about 80 percent of Russia's total output of these crops. With over $14 billion of produce annually, the *dacha* ("garden") movement represents almost 2.5 percent of Russia's gross domestic product (GDP).[7]

The resulting degree of food security and true independence is remarkable. Even during the difficult 1990s, following the collapse of the Soviet Union, when Western powers were using their taxpayers' money to send food aid to Russia, Russia actually continued to be more food-secure than Western Europe or Japan—all thanks to its tens of millions of food gardens.

One might think that Russians simply have to grow their own food due to economic hardship. But, interestingly, researchers found that participation in food gardening does not decrease with growing income. This means that the produce is but one of the benefits of food growing. The gardeners, who share strong agrarian ethics, see in working the land a symbol of self-reliance, a family space, an opportunity for informal interaction with neighbors, contact with living nature, and a continuation of a millennia-long tradition of living in union with Mother Earth.

Indeed, the Russian word *dacha* derives from the verb meaning "to give." This highlights the ancient Russian tradition—still very much alive today—to see food growing not as wrestling from nature higher and higher yields, but rather a way of communing with Mother Earth.

Today, gardening continues to be Russia's primary agriculture, both in its economic significance and as a practice based on a millennia-long tradition of living a simple and self-sufficient, land-based life. Not only that, but there is a growing body of evidence confirming that small-scale growing methods are far more advantageous even on purely economic grounds, which calls for a reassessment of our outlook on agriculture and offers a vision of a sustainable and beautiful agriculture of the future.

Reporting contributed by Dr. Leonid Sharashkin.

Sólheimar Ecovillage

Grímsnes- og Grafningshreppur, Iceland

THE BIRTHPLACE OF THE ORGANIC FARMING MOVEMENT IN SCANDINAVIA, SÓLHEIMAR IS IN THE GEOTHERMAL HOTSPOT OF ICELAND, WHICH ALLOWS IT TO SOURCE ALL OF ITS HOT WATER AND MUCH OF ITS ENERGY DIRECTLY FROM UNDERGROUND SPRINGS.

STARTED IN 1930 AS A HOME FOR CHILDREN IN NEED, TODAY THE ECOVILLAGE IS HOME TO APPROXIMATELY ONE HUNDRED FULL-TIME RESIDENTS AND IS KNOWN FOR ITS ARTISTICALLY AND SOCIALLY INTEGRATED ATMOSPHERE.

The unique village of Sólheimar (a name that means "the home of the sun") is situated on a large parcel of boreal birch forest and alpine tundra of 618 acres (250 hectares) in size, formally known as "Hverakot," approximately 62 miles (100 kilometers) southeast of Reykjavík. About one hundred people live here, ranging from toddlers to the elderly and including those with serious illnesses or disabilities.

In 1930 Sesselja Hreindisar Sigmundsdotter, a pioneering young Nordic woman, founded the small village of Sólheimar as a home for orphaned and disabled children. From the start, the project set its focus on cultivating the health and relationship between humanity and nature, inspired by the ideas of Rudolf Steiner. Today, the Four Pillars of Sólheimar's foundation—community, work life, nature, and culture—can be traced back to the seeds of Sigmundsdotter's original vision.

As a way to take into account their economic, social, and environmental impacts on society, Sólheimar places its emphasis on sustainable construction, organic farming, creating products from natural and recycled materials, and energy self-sufficiency (through geothermal sources—Iceland has the largest renewable-energy production per capita in the world, due to the volcanic activity on the island).[8] The nonprofit organization that owns the land in the ecovillage also incorporates six independent companies, including Nærandi, an organic bakery that also provides food service to the ecovillage; Ölur, a reforestation center and tree nursery; Sunna, an organic greenhouse; Guesthouse Sesseljuhus; and Græna Kannan, an organic café. The community currently welcomes thirty to thirty-five thousand guests every year.

SEVERAL BIODYNAMIC TECHNIQUES ARE USED IN THIS ORGANIC GARDEN. PERMACULTURE IS HIGHLY COMPATIBLE WITH BIODYNAMIC FARMING, AN INVENTION OF RUDOLF STEINER, WHOSE TEACHINGS STRONGLY INFLUENCED SÓLHEIMAR'S FOUNDER.

Photo: Albert Bates

"CATCHING" THE ENERGY AVAILABLE ON-SITE. A NETWORK OF GEO-THERMALLY HEATED SUNNA GREENHOUSES HELP TO MAKE IT ONE OF THE LARGEST PRODUCERS OF ORGANIC VEGETABLES IN ICELAND YEAR-ROUND.

LAND/NATURE STEWARDSHIP

Birthplace of Organic Farming: Sólheimar is considered the birthplace of the organic farming movement in Iceland and Scandinavia. The first form of employment offered here was solely in agriculture and horticulture, and a diet based on organic vegetables was one of the foundational concepts of the original children's home. Today, the geothermally heated Sunna Greenhouse network houses the village's primary food system. The farm cans and stores its harvest, and it sells its surplus to other local markets. Nærandi, one of Sólheimar's business units, is in charge of all food production and service at the ecovillage.

BUILDING

Construction: All building plans address the impacts on both human health and the environment. They constructed Sesseljuhus, the environmental center, completely free of PVC. The building is clad with driftwood from the shores of Iceland. The paint used inside is made from organic vegetable oils. The walls are insulated with Icelandic lambswool, and the ceilings with recycled paper. The site also includes a church, a sports center, swimming pool, and both private and shared residences.

OVER SEVENTY CHICKENS ARE KEPT AT SÓLHEIMAR, WHICH PRODUCE LOTS OF ORGANIC EGGS FOR THE COMMUNITY.

A MICRO-HYDROELECTRIC POWER PLANT—THIS OUTLET FROM A CONSTRUCTED POND TURNS A WATERWHEEL, PROVIDING YET ANOTHER RENEWABLE ON-SITE SOURCE OF ENERGY.

LAND TENURE/COMMUNITY GOVERNANCE

Integrating Living and Working: Most residents live and work at Sólheimar, and many have lived in the village for the majority of their lives. A board of representatives governs the nonprofit organization that owns the land and enterprises housed there. The ecovillage provides employment for most residents, as well as for long-term visitors.

CULTURE/EDUCATION

Artisan Collective: Art and culture have long been important parts of the work in Sólheimar, and there are several creative-arts workshops in the village. All of the products are sold in the grocery store and art gallery located in the village, as well as at various stores in neighboring towns and cities. The workshop facilities include candle making, woodworking, weaving, herbs, ceramics, and arts and crafts. Sólheimar also has a sculpture garden, which officially opened in 2000 and includes works by pioneers of Icelandic sculpture made between 1900 and 1950. A famous theater group is active in the village year-round.

The ecovillage offers classes to residents and, in partnerships with outside institutions, in neighboring communities. At Guesthouse Sesseljuhus, the ecovillage hosts educational exhibits in various fields of environmental science throughout the year. Music has always been a significant part of the social life here, and the village woodworking workshop makes many instruments by hand. In 1989 a choir was established, with the addition of a permanent music teacher to the staff.

"A system that works is worth gold."
—Icelandic proverb

TOOLS/TECHNOLOGY

Energy and Waste Systems: One of Iceland's first natural waste-processing wetland systems was developed here and is able to generate a good deal of its power independently. The Sesseljuhus building is mainly powered by solar cells and wind turbines. The village sorts and recycles all garbage, if possible, and they compost food scraps to fertilize the soil in the greenhouses and forests. Cardboard and paper are recycled into works of art, clothing into rugs, and scrap wax into new candles.

The geothermal heat source underneath the ecovillage is used for hot water heating. "We have also a pool here . . . it's not very big but it's really warm," said member Cees Meyles in a 2005 interview for a Radio Netherlands documentary: "We have turned the nature a little bit upside down here in Iceland: mostly people go to the swimming pool to cool themselves, but here it is very good to be in a hot tub with the weather really crazy, snowing on you."

Reporting contributed by Briana Dickinson. Photos courtesy of Sólheimar, unless otherwise noted.

GOOD TIMES
山梨100
23-13

Fuji Eco Park Village

Kawaguchiko, Yamanashi, Japan

FUJI ECO PARK VILLAGE SITS AT THE FOOT OF THE MAJESTIC MOUNTAIN IT'S NAMED AFTER.

Fuji Eco Park Village stands as a stunningly picturesque model for the burgeoning permaculture community in Japan and for dwellers in colder climate zones worldwide. The 1.5-acre (0.6 hectare) site, nestled snugly at the base of the iconic Mt. Fuji, is located three hours by car from Tokyo and has become a popular ecotourism destination since its establishment in 2000. It welcomes thousands of domestic and international visitors every year. Owner and founder Masaharu Imai sees Fuji Eco as a respite from the stresses of Japanese city life and a way to engage the public on how Japan can—and must—change from the bottom up.

LAND/NATURE STEWARDSHIP

Food and Water Systems: The village features numerous examples to assist the public in learning more about organic and sustainable farming. There are models of compact urban gardens, herb planting designs, and garden layouts, as well as permaculture-inspired systems for integrating animals into agriculture.

"Near Fuji there is only about one meter of soil. Under that is all rock. Most people in this area are cattle ranchers, so growing vegetables here is considered a bit strange," says Kazuo Obuchi, a volunteer through Willing Workers on Organic Farms (WWOOF). The most successful harvest has been daikon (Japanese radish), and experiments continue in other crops that are suited to this high-altitude, fertile, misty site. The site utilizes organic, no-dig farming methods, and companion planting.

Drinking water is sourced from a well through the area's typically tough, volcanic rock. This rock poses challenges for water retention in the soil. Fuji Eco has a number of methods for water conservation and recycling. There are large swales that keep moisture in the vegetable beds. A biotope pond design utilizes microorganisms, other animal life, and plant life to purify wastewater and sewage, which is then used to water the vegetable beds. Another ingenious watering system for the vegetable beds features the use of a 264-gallon (1,000-liter) water tank that catches rainwater and then slowly waters the soil in dry spells. Lastly, comfrey, a dynamic accumulator of essential soil nutrients, such as silica, nitrogen, magnesium, potassium, calcium, and iron, is left to soak in the tank to create a compost tea used as a natural fertilizer.

LARGELY BUILT BY VOLUNTEER AMATEURS OVER A PERIOD OF TWO YEARS, THE FRAME OF THE MAIN HOUSE IS CONSTRUCTED FROM RECLAIMED WOOD AND RAILROAD SLATS AND INSULATED WITH LOCAL ORGANIC MATERIALS.

BUILDING

Creative and Traditional Construction: Fuji Eco features a main house, constructed from old railroad slats and reclaimed wood from a *kayabukiya,* a type of traditional Japanese house. The walls are earthen bricks that were fashioned of mud mixed with straw, hemp, kudzu, rice husks, and other local organic materials. The massive interior wood beams are coated with a traditional dye called *kakishibu,* made from fermented persimmon, which acts as natural insect repellent. According to Masaharu Imai, the house took two years to build, from disassembling the original structure to completion, by a "community of amateurs with the occasional pro." The main house features passive-solar heating for the cold winter months and benefits from high ceilings and open-air passageways for optimum air circulation in the summer.

The ecovillage includes a number of small bungalows and is seeking community-minded people to build second homes on the property.

LOCAL COWS, LOCAL MILK—PCCJ MAKES USE OF ALL ITS RESOURCES AT HAND AND NEARBY.

STOKING THE COMMUNITY'S WOOD-FIRED TRADITIONAL *ROTENBURO* (OUTDOOR COMMUNAL BATH).

LAND TENURE/COMMUNITY GOVERNANCE

The Communal Spirit: "I want to expand the community by giving people the freedom to build small houses on the land and let them use the main house as a common space," says Imai. His vision is rooted in the reality that it is difficult for the average Japanese family to move to the countryside, given the countryside's lack of employment opportunities. He imagines Fuji Eco as a city-dweller's second home, which provides land free of cost and allows community access to the main house and all amenities for a small fee. He stresses that building here is economical (about $10,000, compared to $100,000 in the city), and the site comes ready with a community and the communal spirit—both essential components for any permaculture project. "People participate in permaculture events for the community more than anything else," explains a visitor. "There are lonely people in the cities."

Imai started the project with the simple desire to create an energy-efficient house. A dozen years

THE "SHEEP RING" IS A BEAUTIFUL APPLICATION OF **INTEGRATING RATHER THAN SEGREGATING.** THE CIRCULAR ENCLOSURE IS DIVIDED INTO THREE EQUAL SECTIONS, AND A ROTATION OF USES (GRAZING/FERTILIZING, RESTING/COMPOSTING, AND PLANTING) IS CYCLED THROUGHOUT THE YEAR. THE HEXAGONAL BARN IN THE CENTER REMAINS HOME TO THE SHEEP YEAR ROUND.

later, it is a thriving permaculture community that continues to develop creative solutions for better living, through appropriate technology and the observation of nature's patterns. Through permaculture and the growing community at Fuji Eco Park Village, he reports, "I have really started to enjoy life."

CULTURE/EDUCATION

Teaching in a Bilingual Environment: The community at the village is constantly changing, with WWOOFers, students, schoolchildren, and other visitors. Ongoing workshops and events draw young people from all over Japan. Every summer Fuji Eco hosts a six-day Permaculture English Camp, where Japanese schoolchildren learn from a certified permaculture designer in an English immersion environment. Imai has geared the education toward children, and local school groups often visit the site to pick and cook organically grown vegetables, feed the goats and chickens, and take the twenty-five-question on-site Eco-Quiz. The aim is to establish a comprehensive English-language permaculture design course alongside the Japanese courses, which will teach basics of sustainable urban living and self-contained growing systems along with English conversation practice.

TOOLS/TECHNOLOGY

Relying on Renewable Energies: Fuji Eco benefits from Imai's background in electrical engineering and features a design for 100 percent energy self-reliance through harvesting solar and wind energy for heat, light, and electricity. An exhaust fan in the ceiling reroutes hot air rising from the fireplace to heat the floors. There is a wood-fired outdoor pizza oven and solar and wood-fired traditional *rotenburo* (outdoor communal bath), where you can sit and gaze at the beauty of Mt. Fuji. A fleet of electric motorbikes and cars are also available on-site for touring the local countryside, courtesy of Cosmo Wave, Imai's green technology company, which specializes in cutting-edge electric vehicles. "Permaculture is a vehicle in which we can think positively about new technology and actively integrate it into our lifestyles," he says. Fuji Eco also holds workshops where participants can, over a few weekends, convert their own traditional vehicles into electric vehicles.

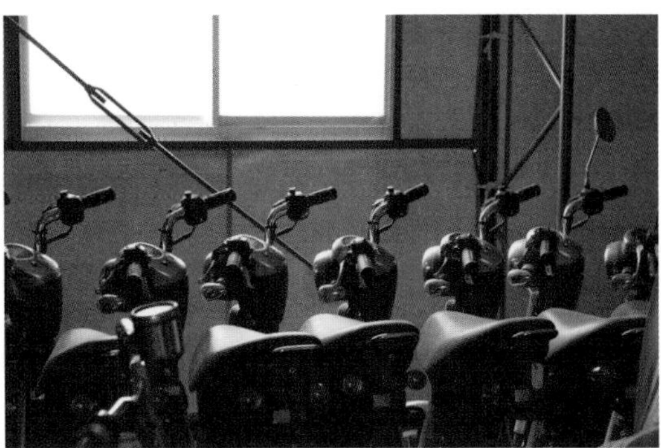

THE SITE'S FLEET OF ELECTRIC VEHICLES ARE CHARGED ON-SITE WITH, CLEAN RENEWABLE ELECTRICITY.

HEALTH/SPIRITUAL WELL-BEING

The Permaculture of Death: Imai sees the opportunity for permaculture ideas to solve some modern problems that are specific to Japan. Traditionally, the Japanese bury the ashes of their dead relatives in stone tombs called *ohaka*. Recent years have seen the traditionally outdoor *ohaka* sites fill up, leaving many Japanese to resort to interring their loved ones' ashes in skyscraper cemeteries. Imai envisions buying abandoned farmland and planting fruit trees to mark where cremated remains are buried. The family of the deceased would pay a fee for the upkeep of the site and would benefit from being able to visit a beautiful outdoor location to pay their respects, while enjoying the fruit of their relative's dedicated tree.

Reporting and photos contributed by Rebecca Williams.

JAPAN'S NATURAL FARMING MOVEMENT

Japanese philosopher, holistic health practitioner, and spiritual leader Mokichi Okada was the first to advocate natural farming in Japan. In 1950 he called his practice the *shizen no hou,* or natural farming method. Around the same time, botanist and philosopher Masanobu Fukuoka was experimenting with natural farming, and in 1975 he published *The One-Straw Revolution: An Introduction to Natural Farming.* Fukuoka's impassioned advocacy of natural farming eventually made him a revolutionary figure in the global movement for sustainable agriculture.

A central hub for the natural farming movement is Akame-juku, a school nestled at the borders of Nara and Mie prefectures. The site was originally an abandoned series of rice paddies and garden terraces surrounded by lush forest. In 1991, Yoshikazu Kawaguchi, a respected practitioner and teacher of natural farming, reclaimed the terraces and founded the school. The school accepts only donations as tuition: each student pays what he or she can afford. Kawaguchi understood that most people attempting natural farming were at a major turning point in their lives and often had no money, whether conventional farmers trying to switch farming methods, office workers looking for a new way to live, or poor students.

Kawaguchi also believes that freedom is essential for learning, so there are no obligatory group tasks, and students are free to spend however much time they can in their rice paddies and gardens. Students choose their plot in February and are encouraged to work in it themselves to cultivate their awareness and experience the depth of the learning that comes from hands-on work.

The principles practiced at Akame-juku are natural: no tilling, no treating weeds or bugs as your enemies, and no using pesticides or fertilizers. Students aid the seedlings they plant only as necessary, experimenting and nurturing life through minimal interference in the natural cycle. Through this practice, they cultivate ecological balance and a meditative state of consciousness.

Akame-juku hosts over 250 students every year; several thousand people have worked on the land since the school opened. Today, dozens of natural-farming schools can be found all over Japan. Kawaguchi says his greatest joy was to see former students starting their own study-groups and learning centers.

The path of natural farming is one of humility, deep observation, and constant flexibility. Kawaguchi has said that he accepts that he cannot fully understand nature but rather can only assist as best he can. Natural farmers realize the futility of imposing control over nature and the unsustainability of standard agriculture's attempts to artificially maximize yields and profits at the expense of the whole system. Instead, through minimal interference in the natural cycle, these farmers are showing the way to a healthy future for the earth and its inhabitants.

Reporting by Kai Sawyer.

Permaculture Center of Japan

Fujino, Kanagawa, Japan

Located on donated abandoned farmland in a narrow and beautiful Japanese valley, the Permaculture Center of Japan (PCCJ) teaches permaculture techniques specifically relevant to Japanese culture and geography. Rice cultivation and working with small, narrow blocks of land are an important factor for densely populated and mountainous Japan, so the PCCJ's location, in the rural mountainous town of Fujino in Kanagawa Prefecture, is the perfect educational venue. The center runs a variety of different programs yearly, including an intensive permaculture design course in the summer, a practical course that meets once a month for one year, and a permaculture course for families with children. Since opening in 1996, the center has trained over five hundred people. Many graduates of the PCCJ courses return to Fujino to live and have created a thriving community centered around sustainable lifestyles and alternative thinking.

"The permaculture movement is growing in Japan because people are looking for connection. For people who don't know what to do, permaculture is a good way for them to take action in their lives,"

PCCJ FOUNDER KIYOKAZU SHIDARA WAS A CONVENTIONAL RICE FARMER WHO TURNED AGAINST THE COMMON USE OF PESTICIDES AND HERBICIDES. "THE TIME FOR TEACHING PERMACULTURE IS OVER. WE HAVE TO CREATE AN ORIGINAL AND EFFICIENT CULTURE NOW."

says Junko Nakazono, cofounder of the Transition movement in Fujino (see p. 252 for more on Transition). Today about 75 percent of the Japanese population lives in cities, with rural areas continuing to suffer socially and economically from urban drift. With Japan importing roughly 60 percent of its food, localization has become one of the hot political issues of the day. In August 2009 the Democratic Party of Japan (DPJ) ended the five-decade, nearly consecutive reign of the Liberal Democratic Party, with food security as one of its main talking points. The DPJ's goal is to increase food self-sufficiency to 50 percent in ten years and to 60 percent in the next twenty. This election saw the mobilization of a usually despondent young Japanese electorate, said to be responsible for the power shift. "Japan relies too much on imports. It's scary! Young people have to learn how to grow their own food," says Taka Yamamoto, a worker at PCCJ. More than 70 percent of Japan's working farmers are over sixty years old, and nearly half are over seventy. The graying of Japan's agricultural sector has caused the area of abandoned or idle agricultural farmland to steadily increase since 1985, standing at the time of this writing at. 1,520 square miles (3,800 square kilometers). In 88 percent of cases, the land was abandoned because the owners said they were too old to work it.

PCCJ founder Kiyokazu Shidara was once a rice farmer but grew disillusioned with the use of pesticides and herbicides. He became interested in organic agriculture and went on to study agricultural anthropology

HYAKUSHO HISTORI CALLY MEANT "ORDINARY PEOPLE" AND THEREFORE "FARMERS"; IT IS NOW BEING RECLAIMED TO EMPHASIZE ITS LITERAL MEANING, "ONE HUNDRED SKILLS" OR, ROUGHLY, "SELF-RELIANCE."

at the University of Georgia. While living with a tribe in Africa, conducting anthropological research, he learned ways of living that were more deeply connected with nature and became determined to practice permaculture in Japan."More than sixty percent of Japan is forest land. Nature is there, but we don't have any relationship with it," says Shidara. Since opening the center at Fujino in 1996, Shidara has continued to expand his permaculture vision with three other branches: Nagano in 2004, Kansai in 2005, and Kyushu in 2008. He is also currently working on establishing an urban permaculture center in Kobe. "I'm not asking people to move from cities, but to change their lifestyles," Shidara explains. "Our grandmothers and grandfathers lived permaculture, but we have abandoned that way of life."

Permaculture in Japan has come on the heels of a general "farming boom" that has seen young people becoming more interested in growing their own food and creating their own lifestyles. "Everyone should be able to support their own lives with their own skills; I ask people to just get one more skill," says Shidara. Passionate about practical change through grassroots action, Shidara and his Permaculture Center of Japan are training the next generation of Japanese farmer/activists to remake the countryside and the country.

Reporting and photos contributed by Rebecca Williams.

Epilogue: David Holmgren on Permaculture and the Future

Photo: Erika Rand

Rebecca Williams: What role do you think permaculture will play in the future of human society?

David Holmgren: You can consider three levels. First, there are permaculture techniques, strategies, and systems that have been developed, such as forms of gardening and natural building, organizational things like LETS systems and community-supported agriculture, all these different bits of sustainable solutions.

Next there is the idea of permaculture as a movement, people having a sense that *"this is my community,"* or *"these are my values, my framework of meaning."*

Then there is the idea of permaculture as an abstract set of design principles, and underpinning them, ethics that provide guidance for how the future emerges. The future impact of these three "permacultures" is not necessarily all tied up together.

I see a lot of the strategies, techniques, and design solutions associated with permaculture spreading rapidly in the future. Whether they grow so fast and spread so wide that they become dominant forms of organization is another question. For example, for community supported agriculture (CSA), farmers' markets and garden agriculture (home production) to become the dominant way of providing food in currently affluent countries with centralized, corporate-dominated food systems, it would be such a massive change that we would not recognize them as the same societies, nations, or even cultures. Even without this revolutionary change, I'm certain that this re-localized food system will grow rapidly in response to the increasing injustice, dysfunction, and instabilities of the centralized systems.

My *Future Scenarios* (2007) work prior to the global financial crisis (GFC) explains how peak oil and climate change are the key drivers generating different energy descent futures. The GFC and its unfolding fallout show how these basic drivers are being expressed through—and are reinforcing—the inherent instabilities of bubble economics and excess debt. The re-localization of our economies and communities through bottom-up, grassroots processes is more likely to be driven by economic necessity than ideology. Economic necessity acts as a savage razor, culling strategies and techniques that do not work in any specific local context, especially if good working models are not in place before the unfolding crisis becomes severe.

Whether the successful strategies and design solutions will be called *permaculture* is highly uncertain. I think that social dynamics in different places are so varied that there is quite a possibility that successful design solutions *won't* be identified as permaculture, and that people may not identify themselves as being part of a permaculture network. It may be that the permaculture movement has a limited life, in that the ideas that are seeded will take different forms as they develop. The influence of permaculture in these indirect ways has been as big as—or larger than—the things directly identified as permaculture.

My greatest hope for the endurance of permaculture is that the underlying ethics and design principles continue to prove useful in stimulating new design methods, strategies, and solutions quite different to the ones we've come up with so far. That they continue, and that people's understanding of them continues to deepen, and that they are adapted and influence the world we're moving into, because they're specifically attuned to a world with less resources. They specifically take that contraction in energy as a driving force, whereas a lot of other sustainability concepts kind of dodge that area and don't really distinguish between, "are we on some kind of amended growth path," "are we on a steady-state stabilization," and "are we in an energy descent mode?"

That determines whether globalization continues to expand. It's not policy choices or personal consumption choices that people make. Those are outcomes based on the fundamental energetic law. If we are moving into a world of less energy, then the world will re-localize in some form or another. Thinking and action for small and slow solutions, diversity, and integration puts you in a stronger position to adapt to the chaos of the future. So that's my great hope. And again, these principles could be called *permaculture* or might not be, but my hope is that this thinking will become the norm. Certainly those that manage to think this way will have an evolutionary advantage as individuals and communities. They will be more capable of adapting to the future.

I am amazed at all of the permaculture activism happening around the world. A lot of things that we struggled to articulate and model decades ago young people just have integrated into their daily lives; it just becomes part of them. That is a success.

From an interview with Rebecca Williams, Melliodora, January 2010.

Notes

Part 1: An Introduction to Sustainable and Regenerative Design through Permaculture

1. Howard Zinn, *A Power Governments Cannot Suppress* (San Francisco: City Lights Books, 2006), 270.
2. Albert Einstein, "Atomic Education Urged by Einstein; Scientists in Plea for $200,000 to Promote New Type of Essential Thinking," *New York Times,* May 25, 1946.
3. Michael Amrine, " 'The Real Problem Is in the Hearts of Men': Professor Einstein Says a New Type of Thinking Is Needed to Meet the Challenge of the Atomic Bomb,' *New York Times,* June 23, 1946.
4. Ker Than, "2012: The Hottest Year on Record for Continental U.S.," *National Geographic News,* January 9, 2013, http://news.nationalgeographic.com/news/2013/01/130109-warmest-year-record-2012-global-warming-science.
5. Toby Hemenway, "What Permaculture Isn't—and Is," *Pattern Literacy,* accessed February 11, 2013, www.pattern literacy.com/668-what-permaculture-isnt-and-is.
6. David Holmgren, *The Essence of Permaculture,* electronic edition (Hepburn Springs, Australia: Melliodora, 2013), 6–7, www.holmgren.com.au.
7. James Davison Hunter, "To Change the World," *The Trinity Forum Briefing* 3, no. 2 (McLean, VA: The Trinity Forum, 2002)
8. James Lovelock, interview by the Creel Commission, August 8, 2005, www.creelcommission.com/interviews .php?action=show&id=3&title=James+Lovelock&date=08-08-2005.
9. Thich Nhat Hanh, "The Next Buddha May Be a Sangha," *Inquiring Mind* 10, no. 2 (1994).
10. Paul Hawken, *Blessed Unrest: How the Largest Social Movement in History is Restoring Grace, Justice, and Beauty to the World* (New York: Viking Penguin, 2007), back cover text.
11. "Our Mission," *Indigenous Permaculture,* 2010, http://indigenous-permaculture.com/index.html.
12. Robyn Francis, "The Dynamics of Culture and Its Relevance to Permaculture," *Permaculture International Journal* (2000).
13. Bill Mollison, *Permaculture: A Designers' Manual* (Tyalgum, Australia: Tagari Publications, 1988), 94.
14. Joanne Tippett, "A Pattern Language of Sustainability: Ecological Design and Permaculture" (BA diss., Lancaster University, 1994). Reprinted with permission of the author.
15. Starhawk, "2012, Climate Change and Permaculture," *Reality Sandwich,* December 3, 2012, www.realitysandwich .com/2012_climate_change_and_permaculture.
16. Tippett, "A Pattern Language of Sustainability: Ecological Design and Permaculture."

Part 2: Tropical/Equatorial Climates: Forest and Savanna Zones

1. Jason Riggio et al., "The Size of Savannah Africa: A Lion's *(Panthera leo)* View," *Biodiversity and Conservation* 22 (2013): 17–35.
2. Cara Goodman and Leandro Ramos, "Brazil: River Turtles Stage a Comeback," *The Nature Conservancy,* last modified September 1, 2011, www.nature.org/ourinitiatives/regions/southamerica/brazil/explore/river-turtles-stage-a-comeback.
3. Juan Pablo Sarmiento Barletti, "*Kametsa Asaiki:* The Pursuit of the 'Good Life' in an Ashaninka Village (Peruvian

Amazonia)," (PhD thesis: University of St. Andrews, 2011), http://hdl.handle.net/10023/2114.
4. Mariela Rosario, "Inspiring Latina: Isabela Coelho Proves That Circus Arts Can Bring About Serious Change," *Latina Magazine*, last modified August 4, 2008, www.latina.com/lifestyle/money-career/inspiring-latina-isabela-coelho-proves-circus-arts-can-bring-about-serious-ch.
5. Isabela Coelho, "Circo Água Viva—Living Water Circus," *Wiser Earth*, 2013. http://wiserearth.org/file/view/e66b167ebc180660a1bda8308370569d.
6. Irene Rodriguez, "Dieta de ticos pierde nutrientes por eliminar frutas autóctonas," *La Nacion*, last modified January 10, 2010, http://www.nacion.com/ln_ee/2010/enero/10/aldea2216591.html.
7. For a detailed discussion, see Spencer Woodard, "Chinampa: Raised-bed Hydrological Agriculture," *Anthropogen*, April 24, 2011, http://anthropogen.com/2011/04/24/chinampa-raised-bed-hydrological-agriculture.
8. Mac Chapin, "The Seduction of Models: Chinampa Agriculture in Mexico," *Grassroots Development* 12, no. 1 (1988), http://native-lands.org/PUBLICATIONS/Pub/SEDUCTION%20OF%20MODELS.pdf.
9. Spencer Woodard, "Chinampa: Raised-bed Hydrological Agriculture," *Anthropogen*, last modified April 24, 2011, http://anthropogen.com/2011/04/24/chinampa-raised-bed-hydrological-agriculture.
10. Anne Prutzman, "The Chinampas of the Valley of Mexico: HBO Studio Productions" (MS thesis, University of California, Berkeley, 1988).
11. M. Coe, "The Chinampas of Mexico," *Scientific American* 211 (1964): 90–98.
12. "HIV/AIDS Health Profile" *USAID*, http://transition.usaid.gov/our_work/global_health/aids/Countries/tanzania.pdf.
13. Dona Willoughby, "Is Hosting Work Exchangers Worth It?" *Communities*, Spring 2007, 41.
14. "Building a Sustainable Future," *Ka'u Landing*, 1999, accessed April 23, 2013, http://permaculture-hawaii.com/about-faqs/articles-testimonials/la'akea-permaculture-gardens-article.
15. Diana Leafe Christian and Patch Adams, *Creating a Life Together: Practical Tools to Grow Ecovillages and Intentional Communities* (Gabriola Island, Canada: New Society Publishers, 2003), 5.
16. Starhawk, "Social Permaculture," Communities, Winter 2011, 14–16.

Part 3: Arid Climates: Desert and Steppe Zones

1. "Tackling Desertification and Food Security Risks in Jordan," *NATO News*, June 15, 2011, www.nato.int/cps/en/natolive/news_75464.htm.
2. "Ancient Fertile Crescent Almost Gone, Satellite Images Show," *National Geographic News*, May 18, 2001, http://news.nationalgeographic.com/news/2001/05/0518_crescent.html.
3. Robert F. Worth, "Earth Is Parched Where Syrian Farms Thrived," *The New York Times*, October 13, 2010, www.nytimes.com/2010/10/14/world/middleeast/14syria.html?_r=0.
4. "Mission Statement," Lotan Center for Creative Ecology, 2009, www.kibbutzlotan.com/creativeEcology/mission_statement.htm

5. "Michael Reynolds—Inspiring Words from the Maverick Eco Architect," *The Environment Show,* February 28, 2012, http://theenvironmentshow.com/2012/02/michael-reynolds-inspirational-quotes-eco-architect.
6. Peter Nabokov and Robert Easton, *Native American Architecture* (Oxford: Oxford University Press, 1989), 356–57.
7. "Permaculture at Lama Foundation," *The Lama Foundation,* 2005, 2. http://archive.is/9I8F.
8. Clyde E. Goulden and Laura Fox, "Notes from the Field—Climate Change in Mongolia," *Scientist at Work* (blog), *The New York Times,* June 27, 2011, http://scientistatwork.blogs.nytimes.com/2011/06/27/climate-change-in-mongolia.
9.Nick Wilson, "Cold, High and Dry: Traditional Agriculture in Ladakh," *The Permaculture Research Institute,* February 6, 2009, http://permaculturenews.org/2009/02/06/cold-high-and-dry-traditional-agriculture-in-ladakh.
10. Helena Norberg-Hodge, *Ancient Futures: Learning from Ladakh* (San Francisco: Sierra Club Books, 2009), 115.
11. "Passive Solar Housing in Western Himalayas," Ladakh Ecological Development Group, http://ledeg.org//pages/what-we-do/projects/present-projects/passive-solar-housing-in-western-himalayas.php.

Part 4: Temperate/Subtropical Climates: Humid and Highland Zones

1. Catherine Brahic, "Drought Warning as the Tropics Expand," *New Scientist,* February 1, 2009.
2. "Ten Basic Human Needs," *Sarvodaya,* www.sarvodayausa.org/learn/10-basic-human-needs.
3. "Bija Vidyapeeth—Earth University," *Navdanya,* accessed April 2013, www.navdanya.org/earth-university.
4. Quoted in Jen Swanson, "Pleasantville," *Motherland,* September 2011.
5. There are numerous drafts of this essay and of essays thematically related to it. The first draft is from 1927, the second was published as "Man: A Transitional Being" in August 1951. See Sri Aurobindo, *Major Works,* vol. 10 *Essays Divine and Human* (Pondicherry, India: Sri Aurobindo Ashram, 1997).
6. Satprem Maini, interview by Juliana Birnbaum, February 2012.
7. Mary Hui, "In Organic-Hungry Hong Kong, Corn as High as an Elevator's Climb," *New York Times,* www.nytimes.com/2012/10/04/world/asia/fearing-tainted-imports-hong-kong-squeezes-in-farms.html?_r=0.
8. "Benjamin Gottlieb, "Crops Out of Concrete: Farming Hong Kong's Urban Island," *CNN,* last modified June 29, 2011, http://edition.cnn.com/2011/WORLD/asiapcf/06/28/hongkong.urban.farming/index.html.
9. J. Todd, E. Browna, and Erik Wells, "Ecological Design Applied," *Ecological Engineering* 20 (2003): 421–40, accessed April 2013, www.uvm.edu/giee/pubpdfs/Todd_2003_Ecological_Engineering.pdf.
10. "The Plowboy Interview: Stephen Gaskin and The Farm," *Mother Earth News,* May/June 1977. www.motherearthnews.com/nature-and-environment/stephen-gaskin-zmaz77mjzbon.aspx#axzz2Yr30wKc6.
11. Elin Lindhagen, "Chikukwa: A Lesson in Self Reliance," *Permaculture,* Summer 2010, 29.
12. Roy A. Rappaport, "The Flow of Energy in an Agricultural Society," *Scientific American* 224, no. 3 (1971): 117–21.
13. Joanne Tippett, "A Pattern Language of Sustainability: Ecological Design and Permaculture." BA diss., Lancaster University, 1994.

Part 5: Temperate/Subtropical Climates: Mediterranean and Maritime Zones

1. Kirk Klausmeyer and M. Rebecca Shaw, "Climate Change, Habitat Loss, Protected Areas and the Climate Adaptation Potential of Species in Mediterranean Ecosystems Worldwide," PLoS ONE, June 29, 2009, www.plosone.org/article/info:doi/10.1371/journal.pone.0006392.
2. Lucilla Borio, "The Passages of Time," *Permaculture,* Autumn 2004, 27.

3. Borio, "The Passages of Time," 27.
4. "Curriculum Eco Israel," *Eco Israel*, accessed March 2013, www.eco-israel.org/curriculum.html.
5. "Building a Food System for Healthy Economics," *Mo' Better Food*, accessed 2012, www.mobetterfood.com.
6. Charles Siebert, "Food Ark," *National Geographic*, July 2011.
7. *Transition Norwich*, accessed March 2012, www.transitionnorwichnews.blogspot.com.
8. Rob Hopkins and Peter Lipman, "Who We Are and What We Do," Transition Network Structure Document, 2009.
9. Low Carbon Communities Challenge Baseline Research, "Mini-Report: Totnes," *GfK NOP Social Research*, 2012.
10. Rebecca Laughton, *Surviving and Thriving on the Land* (Foxhole, United Kingdom: Green Books, 2008), 145.
11. Stephen Tinsley and Heather George, *Ecological Footprint of the Findhorn Foundation and Community* (Moray, United Kingdom: Sustainable Development Research Centre, 2006).
12. Brian Burns, et al., "CIFAL Findhorn" (Moray, United Kingdom: Findhorn Foundation, 2006).
13. David Holmgren, *Melliodora: Ten Years of Sustainable Living* (Hepburn Springs, Australia: Melliodora, 1995), 2012 ebook edition.

Part 6: Snow Climates: Continental and Taiga Zones

1. "What Climate Change Means for Wisconsin and the Upper Midwest," University of Wisconsin Sea Grant Institute, 2012, accessed March 2013, www.seagrant.wisc.edu/Home/Topics/ClimateChange/Details.aspx?PostID=832.
2. Douglas Fischer and Daily Climate, "Shift in Northern Forests Could Increase Global Warming," *Scientific American*, March 28, 2011, www.scientificamerican.com/article.cfm?id=shift-northern-forests-increase-global-warming.
3. *Ecovillage at Ithaca*, accessed February 2013, http://ecovillageithaca.org/evi.
4. Liz Walker, *Ecovillage at Ithaca: Pioneering A Sustainable Culture* (Gabriola Island, Canada: New Society Publishers, 2005).
5. Vladimir Megre, *Anastasia Book 6: The Book of Kin* (Kahului, HI: Ringing Cedars Press, 2008), 254.
6. Leonid Sharashkin, *Family Gardens: Russia's Primary Agriculture* (Kahului, HI: Ringing Cedars Press, 2008), available at www.PrimaryAgriculture.com/dissertation.pdf.
7. Leonid Sharashkin and Michael Gold, "Thirty Million Agroforesters: Russia's Family Gardens," proceedings of the 11th North American Agroforestry Conference, Columbia, MO, June 1, 2009, deepsnowpress.com/downloads/afta09.pdf
8. *The Iceland Journal*, May 16, 2012, http://theicelandjournal.wordpress.com.

Resources

Worldwide Permaculture Network

A rapidly growing interactive database that's showcasing the exciting, solutions-based work being implemented by permaculture projects and practitioners worldwide. Members can register and upload profiles, add project(s), and network with others to share inspiration, resources, and support. www.permacultureglobal.com

Permaculture Principles

Explore the ethics and design principles behind the diversity and creativity of permaculture with practical examples of permaculture in action, featuring David Holmgren's iteration of the framework. www.permacultureprinciples.com

Permaculture Research Institute

The umbrella organization for a number of regional permaculture networks, and a website that is a hub for related news and information, "collaborating to spread permaculture design systems internationally." It also features a number of forums for community participation. www.permaculturenews.org

Permaculture Magazine

Permaculture Magazine is a U.K.-based quarterly featuring practical news and articles on permaculture, self-sufficiency, farming, gardening, smallholding, and sustainable living. www.permaculture.co.uk

Permaculture Activist Magazine

North American permaculture periodical, providing a current listing of upcoming courses and offering articles on permaculture design. www.permacultureactivist.net

Global Ecovillage Network

The Global Ecovillage Network (GEN) is a growing network of sustainable communities and initiatives that bridge different cultures, countries, and continents. GEN serves as umbrella organization for ecovillages, Transition Town initiatives, intentional communities, and ecologically minded individuals worldwide. www.gen.ecovillage.org

Fellowship for Intentional Community

Includes comprehensive directory of intentional communities around the world. www.ic.org

Index

Acknowledgments

We are extremely grateful to each of our contributors, who offered their time and energy to visit sites, take photographs, conduct interviews, and write articles for this book (read more about them on the following pages). This small army of researchers acted as ethnographers of the culture of permaculture, traveling the world in the spirit of inquiry, looking for case studies of sustainable solutions.

We would also especially like to thank Muneezay Jaffery, our London-based assistant editor, who assembled a number of site profiles; Leslie Jonath, our publishing adviser who constantly encouraged and informed us; and Sarah Bell, whose belief in the project from its infancy helped us to obtain a seed research grant from the 11th Hour Project (11thhourproject.org). We are grateful to 11th Hour founder Wendy Schmidt and for the support of Craig Mackintosh, Geoff Lawton, and the Permaculture Research Institute, our fiscal sponsor. We are thankful to David Ulansey, who connected us with Richard Grossinger and Doug Reil at North Atlantic Books and inspired our thinking about cultural transformation. We are extremely blessed to have had the opportunity to learn hands-on about permaculture and communal living through our involvement in Tacotal Ecovillage in Costa Rica, and we're thankful for our incredible fellow-community members and the magical Machuca River there.

We offer this book with gratitude for the movement's co-originators, David Holmgren and Bill Mollison, and in profound recognition of the indigenous science and ethics from the sustainable societies that inform permaculture. Special thanks to Rosemary Fox, Meghan Walla-Murphy, Kevin Bayuk, Ayşe Gürsöz, Jason Taylor, Jonah Sachs, Eric Smith, Alex Cicelsky, Jolana and Shereef Bishay, Jerry Mander, Leslie Dutcher, Tsur Mishal, Josiah Raison Cain, Scott Traffas, Jessica Tully, Sieta Beckwith, Rick Tanaka, and Sarah Lang. We also remember and thank Randall Goffin, who offered generous help in setting up our blog and died suddenly, too young, before this book went to press. May she rest in peace. We thank our daughters, Līla and Serenne, for putting up with their parents' constant attention to this project, our "third baby," during both of their entire lifetimes thus far!

Louis remembers with loving gratitude his father, Joel, who died halfway through the creation of this book, and whose inspired ability to create unique, functional, beautiful homes gave his son the empowering knowledge that we can design the world around us.

Juliana would like to recognize her revolutionary/evolutionary graduate professors from the California Institute of Integral Studies, especially Angana Chatterji, Richard Shapiro, and Mutombo Mpanya, whose teaching shaped her perspective on postcolonial anthropology and her critique of globalization and mainstream development. She is also particularly grateful to have met and been inspired by Benki Piyãko, an Ashaninka tribal leader in the Brazilian Amazon who, along with his family, is leading the charge to increase the capacity of indigenous groups to defend their land from exploitation through spreading ecological design principles. She extends special thanks to her parents, Susan Bietau and Steve Birnbaum, and to Erika Rand, Hisae Matsuda, Jennifer Eastman, and Paula Morrison, whose hard work editing and designing made this book possible.

We write this from own "edge"—the San Francisco Bay Area on the California coast—a nexus for cultural pioneers, dreamers, and poets. We are profoundly grateful as we recognize the labors of those change-makers at the margins, both throughout history and right now, all around us—tending bees, planting spiral gardens, and rebuilding community through ritual and story.

Contributors

Melina Angel is a Colombian biomimicry researcher and permacultural practitioner who has been inspired to apply patterns from nature to solve human problems, especially social and organizational challenges. She has used biomimicry to help businesses and cooperatives to find system innovations to increase efficiency in teamwork, resources, and information flows and is part of a project called "How Does Nature Store Energy," examining life-friendly batteries technology.

Erik Assadourian is a senior fellow at the Washington DC–based Worldwatch Institute, where he has studied cultural change, consumerism, economic degrowth, ecological ethics, corporate responsibility, and sustainable communities over the past eleven years. Erik has directed two editions of *Vital Signs* and three editions of *State of the World,* including *State of the World 2013: Is Sustainability Still Possible?* Erik also directs the Transforming Cultures project (www.transformingcultures.org), which explores innovative ways to transform cultural norms toward sustainability.

Albert Bates is cofounder of Global Village Institute for Appropriate Technology, the Ecovillage Network of the Americas, and the Global Ecovillage Network. Author of thirteen books on the environment, health, and history, Bates has been a resident of The Farm since 1972. A former attorney, he has argued environmental and civil rights cases before the U.S. Supreme Court and drafted a number of legislative acts during a twenty-six-year legal career. He also holds design patents and invented the concentrating photovoltaic arrays and solar-powered automobile displayed at the 1982 World's Fair. He served on the steering committee of Plenty International for eighteen years, focusing on relief and development work with indigenous peoples. An emergency medical technician, he was a founding member of The Farm Ambulance Service.

Kevin Bayuk works at the intersection of ecology and economy, where permaculture design meets cooperative organizations intent on meeting human needs while enhancing the conditions conducive to all life. He is a partner at LIFT, a business design firm, where he provides strategy and guidance for social enterprises. He also frequently teaches classes, facilitates meetings, plans events, and provides one-on-one mentoring as a founding partner of the Urban Permaculture Institute San Francisco. He is as fluent with information technology as with perennial polyculture agroforestry.

Ron Berezan is an urban permaculturist, teacher, designer and consultant based in Powell River, British Columbia, Canada (see www.theurbanfarmer.ca). He has collaborated on numerous community food projects, urban agriculture initiatives, and experiential learning programs across Canada and beyond. Over the past six years, Ron has worked closely with FANJ in Cuba and has taken many groups of Canadians to Cuba for permaculture and agroecology tours and internship programs.

Rosa Elena Blanco is a pioneering member of the Tacotal intentional community in Costa Rica. She has been a co-organizer of the national ecovillage annual gatherings since 2009 and is a founding member of the regional sustainability network CASA (Consejo de Asentamientos Sustentables de las Americas). She leads women's gatherings and Dances of Universal Peace, Sufi lineage, and is a believer in experiential learning by living and doing.

Roger Bybee is a Milwaukee-based freelance writer and a visiting professor in labor education at the University of Illinois. His work has appeared in numerous national publications, including *Zmagazine, Dollars & Sense, The Progressive, Progressive Populist, Huffington Post, The American Prospect, Yes!* and *Foreign Policy in Focus*. (More writing can be found at www.zcommunications.org/zspace/rogerdbybee).

The Común Tierra Project, founded in 2009, is a mobile project in Latin America that teaches sustainability. It documents innovative solutions, sustainable communities, and permaculture projects through short films and a multimedia website to promote sustainable living (www.comuntierra.org). Ryan Luckey, from Oakland, California, and Leticia Rigatti, from Porto Alegre, Brazil, live and travel full-time in Minhoca ("earthworm" in Portuguese), a mobile demonstration center for sustainable technologies, including solar power, bicycle-powered machines, a dry composting toilet, recycling, and composting. The project hosts solar-powered film screenings, local seed exchanges, and workshops for kids and adults on regenerative living techniques.

Nicollette Constante is a student and researcher interested in topics such as poverty, development, and agriculture. She is from the Philippines but considers herself a world citizen and currently resides in California.

Robert Cork first became involved in agricultural and community development after volunteering in Cambodia for a year. The threads of his background (he grew up in agricultural setting in Australia and worked professionally as an environmental engineer) came together when he completed a permaculture design certificate in Tanzania in 2007. Since then, Robert has remained the permaculture lead for FoodWaterShelter and continues to assist with improving the sustainability of projects in Tanzania and Uganda.

Briana Dickinson is a performing artist, writer, and trained permaculturist. She has spent the last seven years exploring and living in intentional communities based on the principles of social transformation and sustainable agriculture in the United States, Indonesia, and Australia. She holds a bachelor's degree in cultural anthropology from the University of California at Santa Cruz and a master's degree in transformative inquiry from the California Institute of Integral Studies, and she is a graduate of Tamalpa Institute. Her focus is on using the mind, body, soul, and spirit to craft artful and viable solutions to the existential challenges of everyday life, and on learning within community what it means to respond creatively to the mystery of life, in light of the individual and greater soul of humanity.

Leila Dregger is originally from Germany and is currently a resident of the Tamera Ecovillage in Portugal. An activist, editor, and author, lately she is working on establishing a school for peace journalism. Since 2008 she has been collaborating with Sepp Holzer to publish his work related to permaculture and the development of water landscapes to stop the desertification.

Kelly Jean Egan is a poet and scriptwriter for comedic educational films in San Francisco. She has also taught poetry in translation to elementary school students with Poetry Inside Out. She enjoys exploring the landscape of the Bay Area and drawing inspiration for an alternative lifestyle of the future.

Charles Eisenstein is a teacher, speaker, and writer focusing on themes of civilization, consciousness, money, and the cultural evolution of humanity. His writings on the web magazine *Reality Sandwich* have generated a vast online following. He speaks frequently at conferences and other events and gives numerous interviews on radio and podcasts. Eisenstein graduated from Yale University in 1989 with a degree in mathematics and philosophy and spent the next ten years as a Chinese-English translator. He currently lives in Harrisburg, Pennsylvania, and serves on the faculty of Goddard College.

Chuck Estin uses his varied background (as a research scientist, an educator, and a consultant in school restructuring) to apply the principles of natural systems in his work as a permaculture designer and teacher. Chuck has been designing perennial, polyculture food systems and ecosystems of native plant for ten years. He has recently focused on economic permaculture, designing permaculture-based strategies for localizing community economies. Writing his current book, on Transition economics, led him to spend three months living and learning as a New Life participant in the Federation of Damanhur in northern Italy.

Eliane Fernandes Ferreira was born and raised in Brazil and is currently a lecturer at the Institute of Cultural Anthropology and Cultural Research of the University of Bremen in Germany. She studies the perception of environment and nature among indigenous and nonindigenous citizens of the Upper Juruá River of the Amazon basin.

Robyn Francis is an award-winning permaculture designer, educator, presenter, pioneer, and writer. She has trained thousands of people from around the world, designed ecovillages, consulted on hundreds of projects internationally, played a key role in accrediting vocational permaculture courses in Australia, and was the founding director of Permaculture International Ltd. A pragmatic idealist, practical dreamer, and visionary, Robyn is also a poet, musician, singer/songwriter, artist, gardener, and philosopher.

Susanna Frohman is an award-winning freelance photojournalist based in Marin County, California. During her career as a staff photographer at several Bay Area newspapers, she received awards for her work from international, national, and regional organizations. Susanna has also mentored students in photography nationwide. A student of permaculture, she is currently earning a permaculture design certificate from the Regenerative Design Institute (RDI) in Bolinas, California. Susanna was born and raised in The Farm community. Her website is www.susannafrohman.com.

Monika Goforth did postgraduate work in development studies at the University of Newcastle, Australia, in 2010 and 2011, and assisted Terry Leahy (another contributor to this book) with interviews and field notes for his African research. She wrote her research report on the original data coming out of the Chikukwa project in Zimbabwe. She is now working in sustainable development in South America.

Benjamin Gottlieb is an award-winning multimedia journalist from Los Angeles, California. His work has been featured in a variety of news outlets, including the *Washington Post*, the *Los Angeles Times*, *CNN International*, *NPR*, *Global Post*, and *DAWN* (Pakistan's largest English-language publication). A seasoned backpacker and self-proclaimed troubadour, Benjamin is constantly seeking new ways to tell stories. Samples of his work can be found online at gottliebmedia.com.

Alice Gray is a permaculture teacher and consultant who has lived and worked in the Palestinian West Bank for seven years. She specializes in water management and dryland agroforestry and has years of experience working in grassroots environmental activism and environmental development projects. She is the coordinating teacher in the Bustan PermaNegev Program, a six-week intensive Permaculture Design Certificate course that is held in the Bedouin village of Qasr-a-Sir in the Negev desert of Israel.

Shelini Harris is a scholar in the field of peace and conflict studies, focusing on the relationship between spirituality, values, and sustainable lifestyles. She is currently completing doctoral work at the Australian National University in Canberra and practicing permaculture and other organic and sustainable methods of living. She is especially interested in the significance of moral and cultural change for addressing the current environmental crisis.

Maryellen Hearn earned her BA in Environmental Studies and Music from Bowdoin College and has contributed to environmental projects including building graywater systems with Women in Action in Managua, Nicaragua; encouraging bike transportation with Biciaccion in Quito, Ecuador; and increasing energy efficiency and indoor air quality of Seattle homes with the City's Community Power Works program. Since fall of 2011, Maryellen has supported climate and energy projects at Cascadia Consulting Group in Seattle, Washington.

Lori Henry is a travel and culture writer, author, and dancer based in Vancouver, Canada. Her work focuses on traditional cultures, self-propelled outdoor activities, sustainability, and an anthropological exploration of dance. Her latest book is *Dancing through History: In Search of the Stories that Define Canada.*

Amelia Heron is a passionate student of permaculture who loves the simple pleasures of gardening. She calls northern California home, when not traveling and studying the planet's diverse and arresting landscapes, cultures, and people. She enjoys dancing in fields, is a self-appointed inspector of storms, and hopes to fly with migrating birds.

David Holmgren is best known as the co-originator, with Bill Mollison, of the permaculture concept, following the publication of *Permaculture One* in 1978. Since then, he has written several more books, developed three properties using permaculture principles, and conducted workshops and courses in Australia, New Zealand, Europe, and Japan. David is respected for his commitment to presenting permaculture ideas through practical projects and for teaching by personal example that a sustainable lifestyle is a realistic, attractive, and powerful alternative to dependent consumerism.

Muneezay Jaffery is the assistant editor of this book and works as an independent consultant in the field of international development and environmental sustainability. At the moment, she is designing projects and writing grant applications for various nonprofits based in the United Kingdom (she currently makes her home in London) and Pakistan (where she grew up). In 2010 she gained a master of science in environmental sociology, with a postgraduate thesis on permaculture and the relationship humans form with nature when pursuing sustainable growing techniques.

Rachel Kaplan is a somatic psychotherapist and the founder of EcoSomatic Action, an education project with a mission of teaching people to effectively engage their sensing, feeling, and action in the work of culture repair.

She works as a writer, educator, permaculture designer, activist, and mother. Her theater work has toured internationally, and she is the author and editor of numerous books, including *Urban Homesteading: Heirloom Skills for Sustainable Living*. She lives in Petaluma, California with her partner and their daughter on a little homestead they call Tiny Town Farm.

Sarah Lang is currently a graduate student in sustainable development at the University of Edinburgh, and she assisted in preparing the manuscript of this book for publication. She plans to write her dissertation on permaculture and is particularly interested in how permaculture can be applied to development work, economic systems, and formal education. She also works for the university's Sustainability Office and is heavily involved in Hearty Squirrel, the university's student-run food cooperative. Always trying to catch an elusive ray of the Scottish sun, she loves singing, dancing, and cooking experimentally with whole foods.

Geoff Lawton is a permaculture consultant, designer, and teacher who emigrated from England to Australia and later studied permaculture with Bill Mollison in Tasmania. He established the Permaculture Research Institute at Mollison's Tagari Farm in New South Wales, Australia, which was later moved to Zaytuna Farm, in The Channon, where it continues today. Since 1985, Lawton has undertaken many jobs teaching permaculture and consulting for, designing, and implementing permaculture projects in over thirty countries around the world. Clients have included private individuals, groups, communities, governments, aid organizations, nongovernmental organizations, and multinational companies. He has currently educated over six thousand students in permaculture worldwide.

Dr. Terry Leahy is a professor at the University of Newcastle in Australia and leads the master's degree program in social change and development. He began his research in Africa and rural food-security issues after ten students came to study in Australia from the departments of agriculture in South Africa. He followed this up with fieldwork in a number of African countries, looking at what makes food-security projects work and what makes them fail.

Lorna Li is web geek, social entrepreneur, and Amazon rainforest crusader. When she is not consulting with sustainable brands and innovative technology startups on Internet marketing, she spends extended periods of time with indigenous tribes deep in the Amazon Basin. To connect with Lorna visit her website at LornaLi.com.

Matthew Lynch is a reformed capitalist exploring regenerative resign at the forefront of human innovation. Since stumbling into a permaculture design course, his work in restorative agriculture, regenerative enterprise, and sustainable economic development has taken him to Australia, New Zealand, Mongolia, Germany, Vanuatu, and back to Hawaii. He believes strongly in the power of human relationships and community and is a self-described "Apocaloptimist"—someone who knows it's all falling apart, but thinks it's all going to work out in the end.

Scott MacDonald received his master of landscape architecture degree from the Rhode Island School of Design in 2011. He is an aspiring landscape architect in Seattle, Washington, where he works on projects in urban planning, art, and design. He has lived at the Bullock Permaculture Homestead for various intervals since 2003, when he first took the Bullock permaculture design course.

Craig Mackintosh is a professional photographer, writer, editor, and information technology manager. Having studied organic biological agriculture and having lived and worked in many countries and cultures, Craig works to help promote and fast-track the uptake of the sensible solutions found in permaculture design systems. You can find Craig's work on the Permaculture Research Institute website (www.permaculturenews.org) and in 2011 he launched the Worldwide Permaculture Network (www.permacultureglobal.com).

Erin Marteal is the executive director of the Ithaca Children's Garden, a 3-acre public garden in Ithaca, NY, where she is actively integrating permaculture principles into the site and educational programming. Marteal interned with Durban Botanic Gardens in 2009, assisting in the development of the school permaculture program, and studied permaculture in public gardens in Australia, New Zealand, and Trinidad in 2010–2011. Marteal holds a master's degree in public garden leadership from Cornell University.

Phil Moore is a student of permaculture, a writer, a filmmaker, and a bicycle enthusiast. He toured the Americas, visiting a number of permaculture projects, and is currently dreaming about and designing his own home.

Jenny Pickerill is a reader in environmental geography at University of Leicester in the United Kingdom. Her research focuses on how we understand, value, and (ab)use the environment. She is particularly interested in inspiring grassroots solutions to environmental problems and in inspiring hopeful and positive ways to change social practices. She has a particular interest in innovative eco-housing, having worked with ecovillages and self-built eco-communities in Wales, England, Spain, Argentina, Australia, Thailand, and the United States.

Erika Rand is a creative director, filmmaker, and photographer. Her clients include Dreamworks Pictures, Metropolitan Museum of Art, and Elie Wiesel. She cofounded Evolver and designed *Evolver* magazine, directed a short climate change film with Free Range Studios, so far seen by over 1.5 million US high students, and served as a film curator for TED.com's Pangea Day, broadcast live on over 60 million screens around the world. She recently produced a feature film on Tibet, and organized a Times Square action for Tibet, which was featured in articles by the *New York Times*, Huffington Post, AFP, and broke past the Chinese firewall. Her website is www.erikarand.com.

Kai Sawyer is a permaculture activist, facilitator, and blogger. He currently lives in Tokyo, conducting research on Transition Towns as part of the graduate program in sustainability sciences at the University of Tokyo. He is involved in natural farming, urban permaculture, the Fukushima nuclear crisis, and youth empowerment. His blog, Living Permaculture, covers a wide range of topics, starting with his two seasons as an intern at the Bullock's Permaculture Homestead and his work with the City Repair movement in Portland, Oregon, and more recently with the post-nuclear democracy movement in Japan.

Colette Schmitt is a permaculture nomad. After graduating from American University with a degree in international development and relations, she was drawn to permaculture and its revolutionary paradigm. Since then she has thrown herself into the permaculture world and has studied, worked, and taught about the framework and related issues in over thirty countries.

Dr. Leonid Sharashkin holds a doctorate in forestry from the University of Missouri for his research on Russia's permaculture gardening movement. He is editor of the Ringing Cedars and Gardening with a Smile book series.

As a cofounder of one Russia's first ecovillages, he has given talks and presentations on organic gardening and sustainable living around the world.

Dr. Vandana Shiva is a world-renowned environmental thinker, activist, physicist, feminist, philosopher of science, and author. She serves as an ecology advisor to several organizations, including the Third World Network and the Asia Pacific People's Environment Network. In 1993 she was the recipient of the Right Livelihood Award, commonly known as the Alternative Nobel Prize. Director of the Research Foundation on Science, Technology, and Ecology, she is the author of many books, including *Staying Alive: Women, Ecology, and Development*, *Soil Not Oil: Environmental Justice in an Age of Climate Crisis*, and *Earth Democracy: Justice, Sustainability, and Peace*.

André Jaeger Soares has been a permaculture designer and teacher since 1992. After establishing the Permaculture Institute of Central Queensland in Australia, André returned to his native Brazil and cofounded Ecocentro IPEC with his partner, Lucy Legan. Together they have designed ecovillages, sustainable homes, and published several books on education and design for a sustainable future.

Starhawk is the author of twelve books on Goddess religion, earth-based spirituality, and activism, including *The Spiral Dance*. Her latest book, *The Empowerment Manual: A Guide for Collaborative Groups* was published in the fall of 2011. She also directs Earth Activist Trainings, offering permaculture design courses with a grounding in spirit and a focus on organizing, and collaborates with community organizations to bring permaculture to the inner city. Together with director Donna Read Cooper, she created the documentary Permaculture: The Growing Edge, released in the fall of 2010. She is currently working with Yerba Buena Films to produce a feature film based on her novel, *The Fifth Sacred Thing*. She is working on building earth-centered ethics and permaculture principles into the film production itself. Her website is www.starhawksblog.org.

Victoria Tauli-Corpuz is a social-development consultant, indigenous activist, civic leader, human rights expert, public servant, and an advocate of women's rights in the Philippines. She is the founder and executive director of Tebtebba Foundation (Indigenous Peoples' International Center for Policy Research and Education). At present, she is the chairperson of United Nations Permanent Form on Indigenous Issues. She belongs to the Kankan-ey Igorot peoples of the Philippines' Cordillera region.

Dr. Joanne Tippett is a lecturer in spatial planning at the University of Manchester, where she conducts research on sustainability skills (see more at www.roundview.org). Joanne invented Ketso, a hands-on kit for creative engagement that provides a way of including everyone's ideas in permaculture designs for villages in southern Africa. It has since been used on every continent except Antarctica, in contexts ranging from health and well-being to planning for environmental change and enterprise development. She still works as the managing director of Ketso (www.ketso.com).

Rebecca Williams is a designer, photographer, and cultural documentarian interested in sustainable design, permaculture, and eco-localism. Passionate about the idea that craft is a reflection of place and community, she works to document and revitalize indigenous craft traditions. Rebecca has traveled extensively for cultural research related to textiles and the use of natural dyes and has worked with artisans to design modern marketplace applications for their craft.

About the Authors

Photo: Louis Fox

Trained as a cultural anthropologist and skilled in four languages, **Juliana Birnbaum** has lived and worked in the U.S., Europe, Japan, Nepal, Costa Rica, and Brazil. In 2005 she founded Voices in Solidarity, an initiative that partnered with Ashaninka indigenous tribal leaders from the Brazilian Amazon to support the development of the Yorenka Ãtame community-led environmental educational center featured in this book. She has written about ecovillages, native rights, and social justice issues in a variety of newspapers, indigenous journals, and anthologies including *E-The Environmental Magazine, Bridges, The Rising Nepal, El Reportero, World Rainforest Movement Bulletin, Quechua Network,* and *Cultural Survival Quarterly.* She holds a masters degree from the California Institute of Integral Studies and was the first graduate of the Cornerstone Doula School, one of the most rigorous programs in the country, focusing on natural birth and a holistic model of care.

She is engaged variously as writer, editor, teacher, midwife assistant, and mother when not attempting yoga postures or learning how to garden.

Photo: Erica Priggen

Louis Fox is a storyteller, strategist, photographer, puppeteer, and filmmaker dedicated to looking at the world as it truly is, while also envisioning it as it could be. Since cofounding Free Range Studios in 1999, he's created some of the most successful online cause-marketing campaigns of all time. His work for clients like Amnesty International, the Organic Trade Association, Patagonia, and Greenpeace has been featured in the *New York Times, USA Today, The Washington Post, CNN, FOX News, NPR, Smithsonian Cooper-Hewitt Design Museum, The Colbert Report,* and *Fast Company* magazine, which named him one of the fifty most influential social innovators of 2007.

As a filmmaker, he has directed and cowritten over a hundred short live action and animated films. His projects The Meatrix, Grocery Store Wars, and the Story of Stuff series have been viewed by more than 60 million people and have garnered top honors at dozens of international film and media festivals.

Juliana Birnbaum, **Louis Fox**, and their daughters Lîla and Serenne live in California's San Geronimo Valley and are founding members of a collective permaculture farm in Costa Rica.